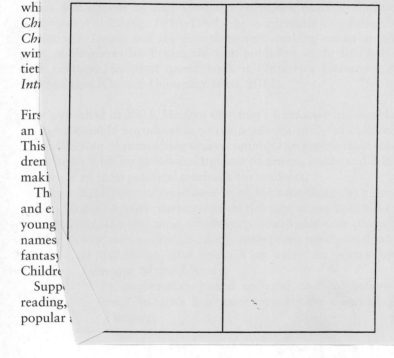
Cat... ... lling ... ... Professor of ... ... at the University
of t... ... ... ren's
liter... ... ... *hing*
Chi... ... ... *ooks*
(wi... ... ... vels
for ... ... atest
is *T*... ... 2011).

Kim ... ... l of
Eng... ... ... UK.
Re... ... ... ning,
whi... ... ... *itish*
Chi... ... *ing, 19*... ... ... *ives:*
Chi... ... ... left-
win... ... ... wen-
tiet... ... ... *hort*
Int... ... (Cambridge University ... 2011).

Firs... ... ... in 2011, *Modern Children's Literature* ... ... lf as
an i... ... ... luable introduction to the academic study of children's ... ature.
This ... ... chil-
dren... ... ... exts,
maki... ... ...

The ... ... ated
and e... ... ... and
young... ... ... ding
names ... ... ches,
fantasy ... ... rmer
Childre... ... ...

Supp... ... ... rther
reading, ... this
popular ... ...

Also by Catherine Butler

Reading History in Children's Books (with Hallie O'Donovan) (Palgrave Macmillan, 2012)
Roald Dahl: A New Casebook (ed. with Ann Alston) (Palgrave Macmillan, 2012)
Twisted Winter (A&C Black, 2013)
Philip Pullman: A New Casebook (ed. with Tommy Halsdorf) (Palgrave Macmillan, 2014)

Also by Kimberley Reynolds

Children's Literature in the New Millennium (rev. 2nd edn of *Children's Literature in the 1890s and 1990s*) (Northcote House, 2012)
Children's Literature Between the Covers (Modern Scholar, 2011; audio book)
Children's Literature: A Very Short Introduction (Oxford University Press, 2011)
Children's Literature Studies: A Research Handbook (ed. with M. O. Grenby) (Palgrave Macmillan, 2010)
Radical Children's Literature: Future Visions and Aesthetic Transformations (Palgrave Macmillan, 2007)

Modern Children's Literature
An Introduction

Second Edition

Edited by Catherine Butler and Kimberley Reynolds

macmillan
education

palgrave

First edition published 2005
Second edition published 2014 by
PALGRAVE

Palgrave in the UK is an imprint of Macmillan Publishers Limited,
registered in England, company number 785998, 4 Crinan Street, London N1 9XW.

Palgrave Macmillan in the US is a division of St Martin's Press LLC,
175 Fifth Avenue, New York, NY 10010.

Palgrave is a global imprint of the above companies and is represented
throughout the world.

Palgrave® and Macmillan® are registered trademarks in the United States,
the United Kingdom, Europe and other countries

ISBN: 978–1–137–36471–5 hardback
ISBN: 978–1–137–35745–8 paperback

This book is printed on paper suitable for recycling and made from fully
managed and sustained forest sources. Logging, pulping and manufacturing
processes are expected to conform to the environmental regulations of the
country of origin.

A catalogue record for this book is available from the British Library.

A catalog record for this book is available from the Library of Congress.

Printed in China

To Jessie, for the distraction. (CB)

Contents

List of Figures

List of Boxes

Acknowledgements

The editors and publisher wish to thank the following for permission to use copyright material:

Random House Group, for the cover from *Child of the May* by Theresa Tomlinson (Random House); the illustration from *Beegu* by Alexis Deacon (Hutchinson Children's Books); both reproduced courtesy of the Random House Group Ltd.

Bloomsbury Publishing plc for two illustrations by Dave McKean from *The Wolves in the Walls* by Neil Gaiman and Dave McKean (Bloomsbury).

Every effort has been made to trace the copyright holders but if any have been inadvertently overlooked, the publisher will be pleased to make the necessary arrangement at the first opportunity.

Notes on Contributors

Peter Bramwell lectures on the Open University's Children's Literature course, for which he was also a consultant during its development.

Catherine Butler is Associate Professor in English Literature at the University of the West of England. She has also published six novels for children and teenagers.

Judith Graham taught in London schools, at the University of London, Institute of Education, the University of Greenwich, the University of Roehampton and in the Faculty of Education, University of Cambridge.

Peter Hunt is Professor Emeritus in Children's Literature at Cardiff University. He has lectured on Children's Literature at over 150 universities in 23 countries, and has written or edited 29 books and nearly 500 papers, reference-book entries and reviews.

Gillian Lathey is Reader in Children's Literature at Roehampton University, London. She is both co-founder and a member of the judging panel of the Marsh Award for Children's Literature in Translation.

Farah Mendlesohn is Professor of Literary History at Anglia Ruskin, Cambridge.

Maria Nikolajeva is a Professor of Education at the University of Cambridge, previously a Professor of Comparative Literature at Stockholm University, Sweden.

Lucy Pearson is Lecturer in Children's Literature at Newcastle University.

Pat Pinsent is a Senior Research Fellow at Roehampton University, specializing in Children's Literature, the subject matter of most of her 15 books.

Kimberley Reynolds is Professor of Children's Literature in the School of English Literature, Language and Linguistics at Newcastle University, United Kingdom.

Michael Rosen is a poet and former Children's Laureate, and Professor of Children's Literature in the Educational Studies Department at Goldsmiths, University of London.

David Rudd is Professor of Children's Literature at the University of Bolton, where he runs an MA in Children's Literature and Culture.

Lisa Sainsbury is Director of the National Centre for Research in Children's Literature at the University of Roehampton.

Richard Shakeshaft is a PhD student at the University of Cambridge's Centre for Children's Literature; his current research is into the representation of the posthuman and technology in contemporary Young Adult titles.

Introduction

Catherine Butler

Background

The first edition of *Modern Children's Literature* appeared in 2005. In the years since then, the study of children's literature as an academic discipline has proliferated, while children's literature itself has moved into a complex, 'post-Harry Potter' phase of development in which no single genre or style can truly claim dominance. Meanwhile, the position of children, who are both the primary readership of this literature and represented so centrally in its pages, continues to be subject to redefinition and negotiation by parents, teachers, policy makers and children themselves, and these are processes in which the writing and reading of children's literature play a significant part. The present volume is intended to serve as an introduction to the study of this fascinating and diverse world.

Many of the issues involved in studying texts published for children are the same as those involved in studying literature of any genre or period, written for any audience. Questions of form, theme, cultural contexts, influence and style apply in this area, just as they do in the study of Shakespeare or Virginia Woolf. Nevertheless, there are some unique features in Children's Literature Studies that deserve to be highlighted. One is the comprehensiveness and range of the expertise it demands. As Kimberley Reynolds noted in the Introduction to the first edition of this book:

> Those who have not ventured into the field of children's literature may assume that it is in some ways easier than the study of 'adult' literature. Nothing could be further from the truth. A key reason for this can be seen in the fact that no academic, teacher or researcher would be described as an expert in 'adult literature'. There are specialists in periods, movements, individual authors, categories, genres and forms. Some academics are primarily interested in the tools of literary scholarship, such as literary criticism and research methodologies; others concentrate on bodies of work such as postcolonial writing. Although academics and students are often interested in more than one of these areas, to say that someone specialised in adult literature would mean that they were expected to know about everything that has ever been published for adults to read. This, in fact, is the situation for those working in the field of Children's Literature Studies, creating both unique opportunities and significant demands.

As Reynolds notes, Children's Literature Studies is a potentially huge field, and the story of the last two decades has been one in which scholars have been exploring and mapping this vast territory. The community of children's litera-ture critics is now sufficiently large, and its corpus of published work suffi-ciently voluminous, that a critical mass may have been reached at which the generalist approach described above has begun to be superseded, with scholars and academic courses focusing on one or more specialisms – in fantasy, picture-books, young adult literature, the history of children's books, and so on.

Whereas those writing about children's literature once typically migrated from other fields of research and practice (adult literature, education, cultural studies etc.), there are now many scholars who have specialized in children's literature at an early stage in their careers. This is a welcome development insofar as it marks children's literature's maturity as an academic discipline, although the diversity of experience, skills and insights previously derived from its mixed origins are a valuable heritage worth trying to preserve. However, we should not let the newly capacious nature of Children's Literature Studies blind us to the extent to which it remains underrepresented within literary studies as a whole. Children's literature continues to be taught at only a minority of United Kingdom universities, for example, where it is frequently based within Education rather than Literature departments. The relative marginal-ization of children's books as literature, and of children as readers, represents a continuing challenge to academics working in the field.

That challenge is in fact symptomatic of the equivocal position of children and childhood within Western culture. The sense of children's literature as semi-detached from 'literature' in general is not anomalous, but typifies a wide-spread habit, worthy of study in its own right, of insisting upon (perhaps even fetishizing) the differences between childhood and adulthood. This insistence takes numerous and sometimes even contradictory forms: hence, childhood is portrayed both as a valuable state of innocence needing to be shielded from the corruption of the adult world, and also as an inferior or at best incom-plete condition, a waymark on the road to full personhood from which adults have a duty to extricate the young. A *New Yorker* cartoon by Robert Weber from 18 November 1991 neatly sums up these conflicting attitudes. It depicts some prospective parents being shown around a nursery class by a teacher, who informs them of the school's ethos: 'We teach them that the world can be an unpredictable, dangerous, and sometimes frightening place, while being careful to protect their lovely innocence. It's tricky.' As this suggests, the unre-solved status of childhood results in incoherent demands being made on those adults who have anything to do with children, whether as teachers, parents, children's writers, or as scholars of children's literature.

Probably the most abiding debates within children's literature studies over the last three decades have centred on definitional questions about children and childhood, and on the relationships between children and adults. How can we best discuss adult writers' representations of children, either directly as characters on the page or indirectly as the implied readers of children's texts? How far can adult appropriations of childhood experience be justified, especially when they serve – as they invariably do to some extent – ideological and didactic ends? These questions are central to many critical works on chil-dren's literature, from Jacqueline Rose's *The Case of Peter Pan* (1984) to Perry

Nodelman's *The Hidden Adult* (2008) and David Rudd's *Reading the Child in Children's Literature* (2013). Even when they are not its explicit subject, however, such concerns are inevitably involved in writing children's literature criticism. This is because scholars of that literature cannot simply conflate their own position as critics with that of the implied readership of the texts they discuss. Critics working in other branches of modern literature frequently elide the distinction between themselves and lay readers, presenting their readings both as exemplary performances carried out with expert knowledge and insight, and also as representative of what any reader might expect to find in, or make of, a text. Where the critic is an adult and the implied reader a child, however, this is a more obviously problematic procedure. For this reason children's literature critics have a particular incentive to take into account both their rhetorical positioning as 'experts' and the power relations involved in writing about a literature produced for an audience of which they are not a part. Even most practical, text-based criticism of children's books is typically informed by some consideration of these issues.

The organization of this book

The first edition of *Modern Children's Literature* grew out of the MA course taught at Roehampton University. Its origins were reflected in its selection of texts and its interweaving of critical approaches, and also in its authorship, which consisted of Roehampton staff and alumni. This gave the volume a coherence and interconnectedness that has proved one of its most valuable features, and in this new edition we have been keen to preserve this quality as far as possible. Accordingly, most of the chapters from the original edition have been retained, although all have been revised and thoroughly updated to take account of developments within the field and the appearance of important new texts for children during the intervening years. However, we have also aimed to broaden the volume's scope by increasing both the range of texts considered and the variety of critical approaches, and new chapters have been contributed by a number of prominent scholars: Peter Hunt, Farah Mendlesohn, Maria Nikolajeva, Lucy Pearson, Michael Rosen, David Rudd and Richard Shakeshaft.

A volume such as this necessarily involves reaching compromises between desirable goals. As the title *Modern Children's Literature* suggests, the emphasis here is on children's literature of fairly recent date, and we have attempted to reflect contemporary developments in our coverage. However, we also acknowledge contemporary children's literature's rootedness in older traditions, and 'modern' for our purposes is a flexible term that may on occasion encompass much of the last century. Similarly, while we have attempted to be wide-ranging in our coverage of texts, genres and critical approaches, and to give an accurate impression of current debates, this volume is not to be regarded as a textbook in the sense of providing a methodical, comprehensive survey of its field. The voices here are those of individuals, and the arguments they make – in some cases surprising and even provocative – are their own.

Modern Children's Literature is divided into three sections. The chapters in 'Mapping the Territory' take a relatively panoramic view of their chosen areas, discussing numerous texts in order to gain an overview of a general issue, genre or critical approach. In the opening essay, Peter Hunt uses an analysis of the publishing phenomenon of 'classic' series to question the nature of canonicity and classic status as applied to children's literature. Farah Mendlesohn's account of twentieth-century children's fantasy draws on her own fourfold taxonomy of fantasy types – the portal quest, the immersive, the intrusive and the liminal – in order to provide a structure for our understanding of this central genre. In David Rudd's chapter on psychoanalytic approaches we are given an insight into some of the ways that psychoanalysis, which has traditionally drawn so heavily on the desires, fantasies and frustrations of childhood, can be deployed in discussing works written for that age group. Judith Graham's discussion of picturebooks considers the complex relationship of text, picture, graphic design and physical artefact in this unique genre. In the final chapter of this section, the poet and former Children's Laureate Michael Rosen offers both an overview of the many forms of writing that may be considered 'poetry for children' and a personal retrospective on his own induction into poetry.

The chapters in the other two sections differ from those in 'Mapping the Territory' in that they draw on a limited selection of texts in order to examine children's literature through close textual engagement. The 'Texts and Genres' section, as its title implies, highlights some of the genres that have been influential in recent decades. In the case of the first two chapters, this is a matter of relatively venerable genres reinventing themselves in the face of changing historical and social circumstance. In tracking some of the many changes that have taken place within the family story from 1930 to 2000 Lucy Pearson inevitably reflects on developments in homes and families beyond the page, a process complemented by Pat Pinsent's account of the changed setting and *mores* of the school story. While the family and school story genres come with relatively well-defined narrative conventions, novels about war and social justice – the subjects of the succeeding chapters by Gillian Lathey and Pat Pinsent – appear to be more loosely defined genres, united thematically and through their didactic intent rather than by shared formal features, although this distinction may be less clear cut than first appears. The 'Texts and Genres' section ends with chapters (by Peter Bramwell and Pat Pinsent respectively) concerning two sub-genres of the historical novel, which in their distance from each other indicate something of the breadth of this category of fiction. Bramwell interrogates a number of feminist revisionings of the medieval past, examining the extent to which their concern with historical accuracy is inevitably eclipsed by their involvement with current gender politics; while Pinsent considers several contemporary historical novels in terms of their engagement with postcolonial and postmodern attempts to achieve a more equitable reframing of the historical narrative.

In the 'Approaches and Issues' section each chapter tackles a current topic within children's literature. Some deal with recent developments in form or subject matter, while others chart contemporary approaches to perennial issues. In her chapter 'Chronotopes and Heritage', Lisa Sainsbury draws on the ideas developed by Mikhail Bakhtin and Pierre Nora to consider the relationship between the representation of time and place in children's literature, in texts ranging from Mitsumasa Anno's picturebook *All in a Day* (1986) to Hugh Scott's challenging novel, *Why Weeps the Brogan?* (1989). In the following chapter Sainsbury takes the notion of the 'uncanny', first applied to literary texts by Sigmund Freud, and uses it to probe some of the apparently secure oppositions (between night and day, familiar and unfamiliar, and so on) on which the fundamental narratives of children's literature appear to be founded. Peter Bramwell's essay, 'Magic and Maturation', also encourages readers to revisit familiar landscapes of metaphor and association, teasing out the connection commonly implicit in fantasy fiction between emotional or sexual maturity and the acquisition of magical power. Richard Shakeshaft takes as his starting point the extent to which modern technology pervades the lives of young people, which is both a source of adult anxiety and has philosophical implications for where and how we draw the boundaries between human and machine, and considers how these questions play out in a number of twenty-first-century young adult novels. In the volume's final chapter, Maria Nikolajeva also considers recent young adult fiction, this time from a narratalogical point of view. In analysing a number of first-person narratives Nikolajeva brings us round once again to the questions with which we began: who speaks, and on whose behalf, in fiction for young people?

While this edition of *Modern Children's Literature* follows its predecessor in drawing predominantly on texts published in the United Kingdom, other parts of the anglophone world (and some texts in other languages) are also represented. Most of the issues and ideas with which the book is concerned are applicable across national boundaries, and we hope and intend that this volume will be of use to students and scholars of children's literature worldwide.

Several chapters contain information boxes, separate from the main text, which have been used to develop key concepts, critical approaches and other background information. You may find it helpful to look at these boxes before, as well as during, the reading of a chapter. A complete list of the information boxes provided appears after the Notes on Contributors.

Further reading

At the end of each chapter there is a list of books and resources for taking topics further. These provide selected primary texts and critical reading, including material mentioned in the chapters. The general Further Reading section at the end of the book has been thoroughly updated, and provides plentiful avenues for those wishing to pursue the topics raised within the chapters. The essays in this volume provide a good indication of current debates and views, and our hope is that they will equip its readers to read on, argue back, and take the conversation forward.

Part I

Mapping the Territory

The Classic and the Canon in Children's Literature

Peter Hunt

Something nasty in the classic woodshed

Once upon a time (and a very good time it was), critical life was relatively simple. In 1986, Margery Fisher, a critic with an encyclopaedic knowledge of British children's books, wrote in her *Classics for Children and Young People*:

> A classic is a book with two lives. One life depends on the response of a child for whom story and atmosphere are likely to be paramount; the other comes with re-reading, when other elements – of style, of side-issues and subplots, of theme and character – are bought into consideration. A classic must, therefore, be layered and expandable ... (1)

To a literary critic of that era this would have been slightly radical, tuned as it is (if in a fairly rudimentary fashion) to the actions of a specific audience: it tacitly acknowledges that child readers are different from adult readers, and judgements about children's classics are likely to be different from those about adults' classics. More than that, Fisher's canon, which runs from Beatrix Potter's *The Tale of Peter Rabbit* (1902) to Alan Garner's *The Stone Book Quartet* (1976–8), demonstrates how awkward these differences are: childhood is not static, synchronically or diachronically; children's books differ according to when they were written and for whom they were written; they can slide up and down putative age ranges and sometimes disappear altogether. There are books – classics – that *are* for children, and that *were* for children. Children are not, and cannot realistically be considered to be, a homogeneous group (as adults often are by critics who write casually about response or peer understanding). Their canon is fluid, idiosyncratic, personal and contentious.

However, Fisher soon lapses into a more conventional stance that raises even more questions: 'A classic may date in superficial details but it must offer universal truths, universal values, to one generation after another, impermeable to the erosion of Time' (1986: 1). The appeal to universal truths and values is close to the fundamentalist definition of 'classic' in the tradition of T. S. Eliot and F. R Leavis, which is essentially that classics (and the canons into which they coalesce or congeal) are books that are agreed over time to be excellent. The first difficulty with this is the implied (or in the case of Leavis, explicit) elitism and authoritarianism – the 'agreement' is really only between those who are the elect, an attitude which is anathema to the curiously egalitarian world of children's literature. As Terry Eagleton put it: 'The canon represents the meeting point between (1) judgements of the ... value of a text and (2) the presupposition and interests ... of those who make those judgements and have the power to enforce them' (1983: 54–5). In other words, 'the power of the canon lies in the fact that *it creates the criteria by which texts are judged*' (Eaglestone, 2000: 55). Unfortunately, or fortunately, the children's book canon, whatever it is, and its makers, whoever they are, do not have that power.

It is probably true to say that children's book criticism has more thoroughly absorbed the practical implications of poststructuralist and postmodernist theory than any other form of criticism. 'Adult' literary discussion, inside and outside the academy, is riddled with value judgements and appeals to canonicity, as if it were quite natural.

In an article in the *Guardian Review*, for example, David Nichols, discussing film adaptations of *Great Expectations*, wrote, almost casually: '*Great Expectations* is not *Persuasion* or *The Portrait of a Lady*, but neither is it *A Christmas Carol* or *Pickwick*, fine though those stories are' (2012: 3). A contemporary children's literature critic might gaze in simple disbelief (or envy) at a critical world populated with such confidently uncritical judgements. Children's literature (paradoxically) does not occupy an authoritarian world where a literary league table can be applied with any confidence, or even to much purpose. To an orthodox critic, Philip Pullman may be self-evidently a 'better', more 'classic', more potentially 'canonical' a writer than Enid Blyton, and even more so than a manufactured author such as Carolyn Keene (of Nancy Drew fame) or Daisy Meadows, but the relevance of such a judgement to child readers is unclear. Canonical 'standards' or 'values' that are glibly adopted by adult critics continually have to be tested against a 'real' audience. Of course, the fascination with (and reliance on) the idea of absolute values remains strong in day-to-day discourse about children's books, but as Perry Nodelman (1985) famously observed, when he moved from studying Victorian poetry to studying children's books, the children's literature critics that he encountered,

> all made judgements of excellence in terms of the effects of books on their audience – and that astonished me, for in the ivory tower of literary study I had hitherto inhabited, one certainly did not judge books by how they affected audiences; in fact one often judged audiences by the extent to which they were affected by books, so that, for instance, anyone who wasn't overwhelmed by Shakespeare was simply assumed to be an intransigent dummy. (4)

In short, any uninformed, immature reader could choose what, for them, was a classic: and if that is so, what is the place of an adult arbiter – what is the place of a generalized canon?

The second difficulty with Fisher's formulation is the exceedingly variable concept of excellence: Henry James's oft-quoted dismissal of child readers (along with women) as members of the multitude 'for whom taste is but an obscure, confused, immediate instinct' (James, 1956: 32), which clearly implies that a canon of children's books would be a literary nonsense, has, in effect, been taken up by the latest generation of children's-book critics as a flag of honour. The best, the most quintessential, the most *classic* children's books are precisely those that are *not* accessible to adults and adult sensibilities and adult value judgements. Enid Blyton claimed never to listen to any critic over the age of 12 (Rudd, 2000: 190); and William Mayne grumbled that 'adults can read my books if they like, it doesn't matter. I'm not interested in what they think' (Nettell, 1994: 207). Consequently, if by these arguments there could be such a thing as a children's classic canon, it would bear no resemblance to anything concocted by adults. It would, in fact, disqualify itself from being a canon because it would be individualistic, and have no authority or universal application.

Of course, it would also be a hybrid, because there will always be a 'hidden adult' in children's books – there are (or were, until the electronic revolution) very few children's books written by children for children, and even those that are seem likely to be heavily adulterated by the adult-dominated literary culture. But somewhere on the adult–child literary continuum lies a line that the experienced reader only re-crosses in very private or nostalgic moments. (The exceptions are the members of specialist societies devoted to individual authors, whose relationship with childhood and children's books is very complex.)

And now that the electronic revolution has finally compromised the stability of narrative texts, the idea of a value-driven intervention, naming classics and a canon in a world where texts – and especially children's texts – are becoming sites of interactive, democratic play, seems to be increasingly unsustainable.

In short, the idea of the classic and the canon seems to be at first sight – like the term 'literature' – at odds with the nature of texts for children and (quite probably) the responses of a majority of child readers. When adults impose a canon on child readers they are responding to an adult impulse of organization and validation which has little to do with the interaction of the child and the book. It is no coincidence that attempts to create a canon, as we shall see, have coincided with the staking out of children's literature as a separate territory, first by librarians, and latterly by academics.

However, it can hardly be denied that children's classics do exist, theory or no, in huge numbers, and are hugely influential culturally and commercially; they are an embedded part of the commodification of childhood – even if they are rooted in these paradoxes.

There are four definitions of, or reasons for the existence of, children's classics: that they are the 'best'; that they are no more than a cultural habit, books that are famous for being famous; that they are simply part of the commercialization of childhood and texts for children; and that they are a necessary academic evil, tolerated in order to persuade the arbiters of culture to treat the subject seriously.

The best for the children

Perhaps the most common definition (or assumption) is that children's classics are the best books written for children over the centuries, which pass down the values and continuities of a culture to new generations. This approach leads to a good deal of romantic terminological inexactitude: Geoff Fenwick, for example, 'claimed that classics are a body of fiction that is enduring, at the heart of literature and represent the *best* in children's writing' (quoted in Gamble and Yates, 2008: 186). This approach (which, of course, also applies to classics for adults) leads to the twin follies of trying to specify and to search for common qualities in texts, and, worse, to try to find content items that 'classics' share.

However, there are more pragmatic strategies: Victor Watson's group of ten-year-olds suggested that classics were 'books written by dead people', and Watson carefully defined a classic as 'a book whose popularity has survived the age in which it was written ... The great children's classics are those books our national consciousness cannot leave alone. We keep re-making them and reading them afresh' (Watson, 1994: 32, 36).

Equally, if classics – in the broader sense of classics for adults and for children – are *the best* then they should be passed down, forcibly if necessary, through the education system. Michael Gove, then the British Education Secretary, famously (and for some, notoriously) saw, in April 2011, the classics as thoroughly life-enhancing: he was against the ethos of '"the poor dears can't manage it", "the idea of a canon is outmoded", "it's all on the internet anyway" culture which is anti-knowledge, anti-aspiration and antithetical to human flourishing' (quoted in Paton).

But faith in the value of the classics is far from being exclusively politically driven. Liz Waterland, a teacher whose *Read With Me: An Apprenticeship Approach to Reading* (1988) was highly influential in the 1980s, read unabridged classics – including *Alice's Adventures in Wonderland*, *The Hobbit* and *The Secret Garden* – to her class of six-year-olds in order to test whether 'with all their length and complexity, their unfamiliar culture and phraseology, [the classics could] be made accessible to a modern six- or seven-year-old, not in the "retold for young children" version but read aloud as they were written generations before'. Needless to say, she found that the books were entirely successful, both practically – they enriched the children's experience and their language abilities – and culturally: Waterland came to 'value the links the children have begun to forge with their literary roots'. (She does, however, caution that her children had a good deal of experience of being read to: whether this success would have been achieved 'if the children's only experience of the written word had been gained on Ladybird Key Words or Ginn 360, with their emphasis on minimalising both the content and form of language, is another matter' [Waterland, 1989: 188, 193–4, 190].)

Famous for being famous

A somewhat more sceptical view of classics in general is that they are books that are famous because they are famous and not because they have any particular merit (and are not even read any more). More specifically, in the case of children's classics they are books that are bought for (helpless) children by well-meaning, rather than well-informed, grandparents and parents. As Nicholas Tucker observed:

> The concept of a ... classic children's book has often been something of a false friend to many young readers over the years. Adults are good at stocking libraries or buying as gifts books they remember as once having liked, but which, later, have little to say to contemporary children (and, who knows, may also have bored the adult as a child too, before nostalgia started setting in). (1976: 155)

There may have been some truth in this, especially in the 1920s and 1930s when a substantial slice of the children's publishing market in the UK was provided by 'rewards' – books designed as school prizes or as Christmas or birthday presents. A large number of publishers generated series, usually in uniform bindings, and their popularity may have had something to do with not having to pay royalties on older books. J. M. Dent's 'Everyman's Library', first begun in 1906, was planned to contain 1000 classic volumes, a target thwarted by the 1911 Copyright Act, which awarded an author's estate royalties for up to 50 years after the author's death. 'Everyman's Library' was duly followed by Dent's 'Children's Illustrated Classics' and by 1972 the series included 80 titles, of which just seven (*The Wonderful Wizard of Oz*, 1900; *The Riddle of the Sands*, 1903; *The Marvellous Land of Oz*, 1904; *The Wonderful Adventures of Nils*, 1906; *The Further Adventures of Nils*, 1907; *Daddy-Long-Legs*, 1912; and *The Thirty-Nine Steps*, 1915) were published in the twentieth century.

One way to at least partially avoid the royalties problem was to elevate books that the publishers had originated to the status of 'classic'. (Although this has happened with adults' classics, it seems to be more prevalent with children's books.) In the USA in 1922 Louise Seaman Bechtel, the first children's book editor at Macmillan, issued two series – 'Children's Classics' and the 'Little Library' – and in a paper in 1955, 'Thinking about Children's Classics', made a candid contribution to the debate. Sets of classics, she noted 'begin, naturally, with material whose copyrights and plates of early editions belong to each publisher. They continue (or new ones originate) with out-of-copyright material, thus creating many rival editions of older books.' But as for children and classics: 'Children themselves, of course, do not like the word, and today it is fading in importance' (1969: 167–8). In the UK, in 1924, E. V. Rieu began to develop 'Methuen's Modern Classics': 'The idea was to sell at one shilling and sixpence a volume which would be an abridged version of 160 or 192 pages. The aim was to capture the market primarily as class readers for the elementary schools, and the texts were to be drawn from Methuen's own lists' (Duffy, 1989: 89–90). The first five volumes were Jack London's *White Fang* (1906), *The Wind in the Willows* (1908) (Grahame refused to countenance any abridgement), Maeterlinck's *The Blue Bird* (1908), George Burningham's *Spanish Gold* (1908) and a volume of stories by W. W. Jacobs (1924). (The same process occurred in the USA – see Leonard S. Marcus, in *Minders of Make-Believe* [2008: 116–17].) The 'modern classic' was born – but this was only a first step to a long-term saturation of the market, and a long-term shift in the meaning of the word 'classic'.

Classics in today's market

What – in the mind of contemporary British publishers, at least – constitutes the classic canon for children? What does it tell us about the image that publishers have, or seek to create, of children, and of what the general public is encouraged to think of as 'classic'?

The Oxford University Press markets a series – 'Oxford Children's Classics' – in uniform hardback and paperback bindings: 'If you love a good story,' reads the back cover, 'then look no further. Oxford Children's Classics bring together the most unforgettable stories ever told. They're books to treasure and return to again and again.' The 2013 list could constitute a basic canon of children's classics – and yet a close examination of it produces some very curious and revealing oddities. The oddest might be that only seven of the 24 titles satisfy the criteria of being well known and apparently well loved for a long time, and of having been unequivocally intended for a child audience from the outset. Five of these are British, one American, and one Swiss: *Alice's Adventures in Wonderland* (1865), *Treasure Island* (1883), *The Jungle Book* (1894), *The Secret Garden* (1911), *A Little Princess* (1905), *The Wizard of Oz* and *Heidi* (1880). To these we might add four that have always hovered in the Tom Tiddler's ground between books for adults and books for children – all from North America: *Little Women* (1868), *Tom Sawyer* (1876), *Anne of Green Gables* (1908) and *Pollyanna* (1913).

A second group consists of books that were – and generally still are – for adults, and classic though they may be, it is not entirely obvious why they have been co-opted for children: *Oliver Twist* (1838), *Pride and Prejudice* (1813), *A Christmas Carol* (1843), *A Study in Scarlet* (1887), *Huckleberry Finn* (1884), *The Hound of the Baskervilles* (1901), *The Call of the Wild* (1903), and that most intractable of philosophical adventures, *Frankenstein* (1818). There is also a more arguable sub-group – two books that, although intended as adult propaganda of different kinds, soon became adopted by children: *Black Beauty* (1877) and *The Wind in the Willows* (of which more later).

The remaining three are what might be called 'modern' classics, and as such the reasons for their selection are even less clear. K. M. Peyton's *Flambards* (1967), commended (but not highly) for the Carnegie Medal, was the first of a successful trilogy (later a quartet) that was made into a television series, broadcast at peak viewing hours. Whether it now needs or deserves the artificial life support of the canon when it is in print in trade paperback might be debated, as might whether it is any more worthy than its peers – Alan Garner's *The Owl Service* (1967) won the Carnegie that year, and the other commended books were Henry Treece's *The Dream Time* (1967) (highly), Helen Cresswell's *The Piemakers* (1967) and Leon Garfield's *Smith* (1967). The fact that *Flambards* was published by Oxford University Press may start a certain train of thought, but the other two relatively recent books in the list, Leon Garfield's *Jack Holborn* (1964) and Noel Streatfeild's *Party Shoes* (originally *Party Frock*, 1946) were first published by Constable and Collins respectively. In any case, neither would generally be considered by critics to be the best of their author's output.

At this point, it becomes rather easy to overdose on series of 'classics', to the point at which the question of why certain books feature in the lists ceases to be of any great interest, beyond the fact that they are part of a strategy to prolong the shelf life of books whose sales are fading. Penguin's 'Young Puffin Modern Classic' series features successful books of their day such as *Milly-Molly-Mandy* (1928), *The Worst Witch* (1974) and *Mr Majeika* (1984); however, whether the inclusion of two more recent successful (but otherwise undistinguished) Puffin originals, Anne Fine's *Diary of a Killer Cat* (1994) and Jeremy Strong's *The Hundred-Mile-an-Hour Dog* (1996), can be justified on anything but commercial grounds is questionable.

And so it goes: 'Puffin Modern Classics' includes *Charlotte's Web* (1952), *Stig of the Dump* (1963), *Charlie and the Chocolate Factory* (1964), *Carrie's War* (1973) and *Roll of Thunder Hear My Cry* (1976) – all notable in their own ways – but are they canonical? Are they the standards by which other books are judged, or were they merely good in their historical moment?

Constructing the canon

Until the 1960s, the administration, as it were, of children's books was in the hands of librarians, and they were in the front line of establishing children's books as an important part of the culture. In the USA, Caroline Hewins, who wrote the first guide to selecting children's books, *Books for the Young, a Guide for Parents and Children* (1882), also 'established the "Adultist" standard of selection ... children's books must be evaluated in a similar manner as adult literature and must be appreciated by adults as much as by children'. Hewins's spiritual successor, Anne Carroll Moore, was even more influential in 'producing and reproducing ... the foremothers' canon', which was essentially backward looking (Lundin, 2004: 23, 33, 36). A 'definitive' list of classics was published by Alice M. Jordan in the *Horn Book Magazine* in 1947, the result of work by the New England Round Table of Children's Literature (and see Clark, 2003). However, as Kenneth Kidd has pointed out, in the USA from the 1920s, the 'culture of children's book promotion and elevation ... took place alongside a devaluation of children's literature within the academy'

(2011: 56). Consequently, the children's book canon seemed at once to be a necessity for the cultural respectability of children's literature, but at the same time a liability: on a literary continuum it was inevitably inferior to its adult counterparts. Not for nothing did Francelia Butler, the founder of the first academic journal on children's books in 1972, *Children's Literature*, add the subtitle *The Great Excluded.*

But things were about to change: the cultural revolution of the 1960s, with semi-anarchic literary theory close on its heels, shook the certainties of the canons. As Anne Lundin observed, 'If librarians were losing their grip on a canon, who would assert authority? Who would inherit the power to define cultural form and value? The classics began to shift their pride of place uneasily from the library shelf to the academy ...' (see Lundin, 2004: 55; Zipes, 2001: 66–76).

The canon and the academics

And uneasy the shift has remained. It is ironic that the first high-profile academic attempt to produce a children's book canon occurred just as the critical theory which (at least temporarily) swept away the usefulness of the literary canon was rolling over the world of criticism. The Children's Literature Association set up a 'Canon Committee' – and, as Perry Nodelman noted, 'the most arrogant thing about it was its name'. The idea of producing a canon was rapidly abandoned in favour of naming a list of 'Touchstones' – following Matthew Arnold's formulation in 'The Study of Poetry' (1880): 'there can be no more useful help for discovering what poetry belongs to the class of the truly excellent ... than to have always in one's mind lines and expressions of the great masters, and to apply them as a touchstone to other poetry'. Nodelman's introduction to the three-volume collection of essays that resulted is worth seeking out (Nodelman, 1985), for it is a ruthlessly honest account of the struggle, in the 1980s, of the broad church of people concerned with children's literature to agree on what the core of their subject actually was. Much of it harks back to vague, evaluative terminology:

> A list that might actually help to define excellence had to separate the good from the likeable, and the great from the good; we found ourselves eliminating three particular kinds of books. The first were undeniably worthwhile; in other words we realised that we were looking for books that combined distinctiveness with popularity, and that neither alone would do. The third category was the largest and least easy to deal with: those books that were undeniably excellent, and were also widely read, but that were not, for want of a better word, important – books that had elicited admiration but not discussion. (Nodelman, 1985: 7)

The key point here, in the academic world, is that the books 'had elicited admiration *but not discussion*'. From now on, one qualification of a 'classic' would be that it *had been written about*. *Alice's Adventures in Wonderland* has accumulated a whole library of criticism, biography and speculation. Even a book that was, and is, unashamedly popularist, Frances Hodgson Burnett's *The Secret Garden*, has accumulated more than 35 respectable academic papers (and many hundreds of thousands of student essays). A sceptic might say that an academic's children's literature canon is, despite postmodernist claims to the contrary, a godsend to academics who have written the conventional canonical wells dry. Equally, it might remain, at least residually, as a weapon of respectability: the syllabus of the first British university courses in Children's Literature relied heavily on 'canonical' texts – all by men – that were unlikely to be challenged. And canonical works are likely to be perpetuated because, as every conference goer knows, it is far safer to write about a book that everyone has read: as Emer O'Sullivan notes, 'the need for a canon is now ... becoming evident in children's literature studies for the purposes of writing the history of the literature and for university teaching' (O'Sullivan, 2005: 131).

This trend not only limits the number of books that are read, but can affect (and has affected) readings of the history of children's books. If 'classics' are (sometimes) exceptional works, then they are likely to be unrepresentative; worse, if they have been chosen (in the English-speaking world) by a caucus of white, middle-class, conservative and nostalgic males, then they are likely to positively distort what has actually happened.

In pursuit of common factors

The lists of classics above demonstrate that it is futile to look for common factors, either of quality or content, in books nominated as classics. Thus Patricia Beer's judgement that, 'Like nearly every other classic, *Kidnapped* is a thoroughly professional work written for money by a full-time author' (Beer, 1995: 190), excludes *Black Beauty* and *Alice's Adventures in Wonderland*. Victor Watson nominates *Tom's Midnight Garden* (1958) as a classic because 'it exemplifies exactly what I believe the great classics have in common. There is no hint of authorial distress, or sadness, but it is a story about old and young, and how their mutual – but different – needs come together in the form of a story' (Watson, 1994: 37). So much for *Seven Little Australians* (1894), where the narrator is so upset at the end that 'she' brings the story to an abrupt halt, or *Treasure Island*, which is about adults and children and their mutual needs, but not quite, I suspect, in the way that Watson intended.

Equally, there is no commonality about how books become classics: the most common factor seems to be chance. 'Most of the classic tales,' Watson goes on, 'started as stories for real children.' Well, some did: *Alice's Adventures in Wonderland*, *Treasure Island*, *Peter Rabbit*, *Peter Pan* (1904), *The Wind in the Willows*, *Winnie-the-Pooh* (1926), *The Hobbit* (1937), *Swallows and Amazons* (1930) ... But even if that were entirely true – and Stevenson, Carroll and Mrs Grahame, to name but three, have contributed a certain creative myth making to the origins of their stories, and Ransome denied his original impulse – what happened to the stories as their authors 'processed' them into texts makes them very different from each other.

The Wind in the Willows was not intended by its author or publisher to be a children's book at all. Arnold Bennett, reviewing it in 1908, recognized this: 'the book is fairly certain to be misunderstood of the people ... [It is] an urbane exercise in irony at the expense of the English character and of mankind' (Bennett, 1917: 57–8). Frances Hodgson Burnett had to point out to her English publisher that *The Secret Garden* (which was not mentioned in her obituaries) was a book for children, despite its first appearance in an American journal for adults. But for the intervention of W. E. Henley, *Treasure Island* (originally *The Sea Cook*) might never have made it from the pages of *Young Folks* into hardback. Often it is difficult to see why books came to stand out from the crowd: children's bookshelves of the 1890s were littered with books beginning with a rich little girl in her solicitor's office being told of the loss of her fortune; *When We Were Very Young* (1924) and *Now We Are Six* (1927) are indistinguishable from dozens of ideal-child books of verse of the 1920s by, for example, Rose Fyleman, and illustrated by E. H. Shepard or his many imitators; *Swallows and Amazons* was part of a fashion for 'camping and tramping' books, and there is no quantifiable reason why Ransome is still famous while his equally popular contemporaries, Garry Hogg, M. E. Atkinson or David Severn, are not.

Some books owe at least part of their canonical status to retrospectively perceived 'historically important' reasons. *Masterman Ready, or, the Wreck of the Pacific* (1841–2) is a classic because it founded the genre of the boys' sea story: Captain Marryat was provoked to write it after reading *The Swiss Family Robinson* (1812), which, he fulminated, is 'neither "probable nor possible ... Fiction, when written for young people should, at all events, be *based* on truth."' *Alice's Adventures in Wonderland* has been routinely seen as marking a turning point in children's book history. The first serious historian of children's books, F. J. Harvey Darton, described it as 'the first unapologetic ... appearance in print, for readers who sorely needed it, of liberty of thought in children's books' (1982: 260). *Treasure Island* turned a whole genre on its head, undercutting the empire-building heroics of Ballantyne and his followers; *Swallows and Amazons* invented the summer holidays; Joanna Cannan's *A Pony for Jean* effectively invented the pony story in 1937. On the other hand, Thomas Hughes's *Tom Brown's Schooldays* (1857) has survived as the canonical ur-school story, despite that fact that Harriet Martineau's *The Crofton Boys* (1841), which brought together all the 'classic' features, predates it by 16 years.

International classics

The situation is even more mystifying when the children's classic is considered in an international context. What has qualified Johanna Spyri's *Heidis Lehr- und Wanderjahre* (1880), Carlo Collodi's *Le Avventure di Pinocchio: Storia di un Burattino* (1883), Laura Ingalls Wilder's *Little House in the Big Woods* (1932) or Astrid Lindgren's *Pippi Longstocking* (1945) to join the canon? Is Heidi quintessentially Swiss? Is Pinocchio the image of the impulsive, passionate Italian? Is Laura the true image of the stoical American pioneer and Pippi the archetypal Swedish girl? Or has there been a symbiosis here – the national image being derived from the classic? Emer O'Sullivan doubts the very concept of a truly international classic, given the changes that are inevitably made in translation, the influence of globalization (or localization) and the huge silences and gaps that open up as books enter different cultures. As J. D. Stahl put it, 'Transfer classics exist in a more superficial, less conclusive relationship to their society of adoption than to their society of origin' (1985: 27; quoted by O'Sullivan, 2005: 163, n18; and see O'Sullivan, 2005: 81–4 and 130–51). 'International classics' often undergo striking transformations – the tortuous history of the translation and adaptation of Johann David Wyss's *Der Schweizerische Robinson* (1812–13), or Disney's portrayal of *Pinocchio* in a cute Tyrolean outfit (given that Collodi spent much of his life fighting Austria) are classic cases.

And so, do English natives speakers misunderstand *Struwwelpeter* as a comedy, while German readers might see it as representing *Kinderfeindlichkeit* – cultural hostility to childhood? What of *Heidi*, the inspiration for so many sentimental sickness-to-health novels, and the interest in female health – the decade after its publication seeing 'the rise of the German *Reformkleidung* movement, with its rejection of bustles and corsetry, and of the *Wandervogel* movement, which encouraged country rambles and mountain hiking and denounced the corrupting influences of city life' (Skrine, 1994: 162). Wilder's account of Laura's travels is historically, geographically and politically highly partial; Pippi's profound critique of society has been softened into comedy in translation – just as Tove Jansson's 'Moomin' books (1945–70) are read in English as whimsical eccentricities rather than as serious discussions of personal and family identity.

The fact that the English-language canon contains so few books originating from languages other than English reflects both the very small number of children's books translated into English (until recently, barely 2 per cent), and has resulted in some staggering Anglophone arrogance. Alison Lurie, in *Boys and Girls Forever: Reflections on Children's Classics* (2003) (a volume perhaps rather incautiously described by John Bayley in the *New York Review of Books* as 'The best book on the classics of the genre that I have ever read'), observed:

> It is interesting to note that ... so many of the best-loved children's books are British or American. Other nations have produced a single brilliant classic or series: Denmark, for instance, has Andersen's tales; Italy has Pinocchio, France has Babar, Finland has Moomintroll. A list of famous children's books in English, however, could easily take up a page in this volume. (x)

It may be true that English-speaking countries tend to have a longer tradition of books for children than other countries, and have had a massive international influence – but it is far from universal: in Brazil, the pioneering 'Children's Library', edited in São Paulo by Arnaldode Oliveira Barreto, began with *O Patinho Feio* [The Ugly Ducking] (1915). In some parts of the world, for example, China, writing for children and adolescents is 'still in the experimentation stage' (Ho: 2006: II, 1035), but elsewhere there is no shortage of classics: German-language classics could easily take up several pages of this volume. Portuguese has, among many, classics such as Sophia de Mello Breyner Andresen's *A Menina do Mar* [The Girl from the Sea] (1958) and *O Cavaleiro da Dinamarca* [The Knight from Denmark] (1964); the Swiss possibly wonder why *Heidi* is remembered rather than more recent classics such as *Die Kinder aus Nummer 67* [The Children from Number 67] (1933–49) by Lisa Tetzner and Kurt Held; Austrians might feel surprised that Lurie doesn't list Mira Lobe's *Die Omama im Apfelbaum* [The Grandma in the Apple Tree] (1965) among her classics; and Italians ask why she doesn't mention the fact that Italian children's literature 'encompasses a long tradition of ... fantasy texts' (Myers, 2012: 5). And what of Branko Čopić's Bosnian classics, such as *Pričispod zmajevih krila* [Stories Under Dragon's Wing] (1953); the classic work of Bang Chong-hwan (1899–1931) in Korea; or Sazanami Iwaya's *Koganemaru* [Koganemaru, the Dog Who Avenged His Parents] (1891), which marks the beginning of modern Japanese children's literature?

Loose cannons and futures

John Sutherland has suggested that, 'overused and abused as the term is, literature still needs it. Properly applied, the idea of a "classic" points towards something that is centrally important' (2010: 18). But what does 'properly applied' mean in the case of children's classics and the children's canon? Is what is 'centrally important' to adult culture of any interest to children's culture?

The whole question of children's classics and canonicity therefore raises some intractable issues. The days are gone when Fred Inglis could confidently begin a liberal-humanist defence of children's fiction with a direct imitation of F. R. Leavis's *The Great Tradition*: 'The great children's novelists are Lewis Carroll, Rudyard Kipling, Frances Hodgson Burnett, Arthur Ransome, William Mayne, and Philippa Pearce – to stop for the moment at that comparatively safe point on an uncertain list.' Nor is his literary credo likely to find many supporters today: '*Tom's Midnight Garden* and *Puck of Pook's Hill* are wonderful books whoever you are, and that judgement stands whether or not your child can make head or tail of them' (1981: 3, 7).

As we have seen, judgements are now more democratic (or anarchic) – but it is not only judgement that is unstable. What is the 'text' of a 'classic'? A reader may well come to, say, *The Secret Garden*, first through a Ladybird abridgement, or a graded literacy adaptation, through a film, a television series, a computer game, a comic or an interactive website; through a prequel or a sequel. Where does this leave the canon or the canonical text (see Box 1.1)? There must have been many cases of severe culture shock when children moved from Disney's *The Jungle Book* (1967) or *Mary Poppins* (1964) or *Bambi* (1942) to the originals (1894, 1934 and 1923). And as Christine Hall and Martin Coles noted in *Children's Reading Choices*, 'the divisions between high and popular culture in notions of the classic do not bear much investigation' (1999: 29).

BOX 1.1   ADAPTATIONS OF A CLASSIC: THE CASE OF BURNETT'S *THE SECRET GARDEN* (1911)

Children's classics are often adapted more savagely than others, on the grounds that children cannot read the originals 'historically' (O'Sullivan, 2005: 145; and see 130–49). In *The Secret Garden* – a 'classic' by popular acclamation – Burnett expertly handles highly coloured, melodramatic effects, but also reacts to the issues of her time. In the opening paragraphs it is easy to detect a lurking criticism of the British Empire:

> When Mary Lennox was sent to Misselthwaite Manor to live with her uncle, everybody said she was the most disagreeable-looking child ever seen. It was true, too. She had a little thin face and a little thin body, thin light hair and a sour expression. Her hair was yellow, and her face was yellow because she had been born in India and had always been ill one way or another. Her father had held a position under the English Government and had always been busy and ill himself, and her mother had been a great beauty who cared only to go to parties and amuse herself with gay people. She had not wanted a little girl at all, and when Mary was born she handed her over to the care of an Ayah, who was made to understand that if she wished to please the Memsahib she must keep the child out of sight as much as possible. So when she was a sickly, fretful, ugly little baby she was kept out of the way, and when she became a sickly, fretful, toddling thing she was kept out of the way also. She never remembered seeing familiarly anything but the dark faces of her Ayah and the other native servants, and as they always obeyed her and gave her her own way in everything, because the Memsahib would be angry if she was disturbed by her crying, by the time she was six years old she was as tyrannical and selfish a little pig as ever lived.

The 'Ladybird Books' version reduced the text from 75,000 words to 6000, and removed some of the subtleties:

> Mary Lennox was a spoilt, rude and bad-tempered child. She was never really well, and she was thin, miserable and sour-faced. No one liked her at all.
>
> None of this was really Mary's own fault. She was born in India, where her father worked. He was always busy with his work, and paid no attention to his daughter. Her mother was very pretty, and cared only for parties and pleasure. She left Mary in the care of an Indian nursemaid, who gave the little girl everything she wanted so that she would not cry and upset her mother. Mary grew up into a spoilt and most unpleasant girl. (Retold [in simple language] by Joyce Faraday, Loughborough: Ladybird Books, 1994, 5.)

In other versions, the final sentence becomes even blander:

> So, at the age of six, Mary was not a nice child. Nobody loved Mary and Mary loved nobody. ('Penguin Active Reading' series, level 2 [600 headwords: elementary], Harlow: Pearson Education, 2009.)

> Mary quickly became a very difficult and selfish child. ('Macmillan Readers', pre-intermediate level [about 1400 basic words], Oxford: Macmillan Heinemann ELT, 2008, 7.)

> In fact, she was a very selfish, disagreeable, bad-tempered little girl. ('Oxford Bookworms Library', human interest section, stage 3 [1000 headwords], Oxford: Oxford University Press 2008, 7.)

> The question immediately arises: what relation does this text have to the original book? Is its 'classicness' compromised, not least because the more that is left out, the more the reader has to supply – and the inexperienced reader may not be able to supply very much? Equally, the fact that a child reader might begin with the last of these examples, and end with the first, calls into question the whole nature of the experience of the classic children's text.

And where do fairy and folk tales fit into this? In the introduction to her *The Annotated Classic Fairy Tales*, Maria Tatar uses the word only once, claiming that in presenting 'classic' versions of the stories (by which she means, generally, the oldest printed versions), she is offering 'foundational texts ... and ... seeks to reclaim a powerful cultural legacy, creating a storytelling archive for children and adults' (2002: xvii–xviii). This implies that there is an authoritative version of each tale and at the same time that it is *not necessarily* the most valuable version.

In an age when 'classic' is routinely applied to soft drinks, cars and virtually any other consumer product, and 'canon' is associated with prescriptive, authoritarian attitudes, it is obvious that the words should be approached circumspectly. Probably the question most frequently asked of the children's book 'expert' is: 'What will be canonical in 50 years? Harry Potter? Philip Pullman?' This certainly demonstrates the enduring attraction of the idea of the classic, but whether that ensures, as an optimist might say, that 'the future seems to promise a chorus of canons' (Stevenson, 2009: 122), or whether it merely confirms that the term is 'too readily used as a substitute for criticism, and to endorse received judgements' (Hyde, 1973: 30), is a matter for debate.

WORKS CITED AND FURTHER READING

Critical Texts

Bechtel, Louise Seaman. *Books in Search of Children*. London: Hamish Hamilton, 1969.

Beer, Patricia. 'Kidnapped'. In Geoff Fox (ed.), *Celebrating Children's Literature in Education* (pp. 182–90). London: Hodder & Stoughton, 1995.

Bennett, Arnold. *Books and Persons: Being Comments on a Past Epoch, 1908–1911*. London: Chatto & Windus, 1917.

Clark, Beverly Lyon. *Kiddie Lit: The Cultural Construction of Children's Literature in America*. Baltimore, MD: Johns Hopkins University Press, 2003.

Darton, F. J. Harvey. *Children's Books in England: Five Centuries of Social Life*, rev. B. Alderson. Cambridge: Cambridge University Press, 1982.

Duffy, Maureen. *A Thousand Capricious Chances: A History of the Methuen List, 1889–1989*. London: Methuen, 1989.

Eaglestone, Robert. *Doing English: A Guide for Literature Students*. London and New York: Routledge, 2000.

Eagleton, Terry. *Literary Theory: An Introduction*. Oxford: Blackwell, 1983.

Fisher, Margery. *Classics for Children and Young People*. Woodchester, UK: Thimble Press, 1986.

Gamble, Nikki, and Sally Yates. *Exploring Children's Literature*, 2nd edn. London: Sage, 2008.

Hall, Christine, and Martin Coles. *Children's Reading Choices*. London: Routledge, 1999.

Ho, Laina. 'China'. In Peter Hunt (ed.), *International Companion Encyclopedia of Children's Literature*, 2nd edn (pp. II, 1029–38). London: Routledge, 2006.

Hyde, G. M. 'Classic'. In Roger Fowler (ed.), *A Dictionary of Modern Critical Terms*. London: Routledge & Kegan Paul, 1973.

Inglis, Fred. *The Promise of Happiness: Value and Meaning in Children's Fiction*. Cambridge: Cambridge University Press, 1981.

James, Henry. *The Future of the Novel: Essay on the Art of Fiction*, ed. Leon Edel. New York: Vintage Books, 1956.

Kidd, Kenneth. 'Classic'. In Philip Nel and Lissa Paul (eds), *Keywords for Children's Literature* (pp. 52–8). New York: New York University Press, 2011.

Lundin, Anne. *Constructing the Canon of Children's Literature: Beyond Library Walls and Ivory Towers*. London and New York: Routledge, 2004.

Lurie, Alison. *Boys and Girls Forever: Reflections on Children's Classics*. London: Chatto & Windus, 2003.

Marcus, Leonard S. *Minders of Make-Believe: Idealists, Entrepreneurs, and the Shaping of American Children's Literature*. Boston, MA: Houghton Mifflin, 2008.

Myers, Lindsay. *Inventing the Italians: Poetics and Politics of Italian Children's Fantasy*. Bern: Peter Lang, 2012.

Nettell, Stephanie. 'Authorgraph: William Mayne'. In Chris Powling (ed.), *The Best of 'Books for Keeps'* (pp. 201–7). London: Bodley Head, 1994.

Nichols, David. 'Adapting *Great Expectations* for the Screen'. *Guardian Review* (17 September 2012), pp. 2–3.

Nodelman, Perry. 'Introduction: Matthew Arnold, a Teddy Bear, and a List of Touchstones'. In Perry Nodelman (ed.), *Touchstones: Reflections on the Best in Children's Literature* (pp. I, 1–12). West Lafayette, IN: Children's Literature Association, 1985).

O'Sullivan, Emer. *Comparative Children's Literature*. London; Routledge, 2005.

Paton, Graeme. 'Michael Gove: Schools Failing to Promote the Classics'. *Daily Telegraph*, 1 April 2011. http://www.telegraph.co.uk/education/educationnews/8419770/Michael-Gove-schools-failing-to-promote-the-classics.html (accessed 22 January 2014).

Rudd, David. *Enid Blyton and the Mystery of Children's Literature*. Basingstoke: Palgrave Macmillan, 2000.

Skrine, Peter. 'Johanna Spyri's *Heidi*'. *Bulletin of the John Rylands University Library of Manchester*, 76.3 (1994), 145–64.

Stahl, J. D. 'Cross-cultural Perceptions: Images of Germany in America and of America in Germany Conveyed by Children's and Youth Literature'. *Phaedrus*, 11 (1985), 22–37.

Stevenson, Deborah. 'Classics and Canons'. In M. O. Grenby and Andrea Immel (eds), *The Cambridge Companion to Children's Literature* (pp. 108–23). Cambridge: Cambridge University Press, 2009.

Sutherland, John. *50 Literature Ideas You Really Need to Know*. London: Quercus, 2010.

Tatar, Maria. (ed.). *The Annotated Classic Fairy Tales*. New York: W. W. Norton, 2002.

Tucker, Nicholas. (ed.). *Suitable for Children? Controversies in Children's Literature*. London: Sussex University Press, 1976.

Waterland, Liz. *Read With Me: An Apprenticeship Approach to Reading*, 2nd edn. Woodchester: Thimble Press, 1988.

Waterland, Liz. 'Reading Classics with Young Children'. *Signal*, 60 (1989), 187–94.

Watson, Victor. 'What Makes a Children's Classic?' In Chris Powling (ed.), *The Best of 'Books for Keeps'* (pp. 32–8). London: Bodley Head, 1994.

Zipes, Jack. *Sticks and Stones: The Troublesome Success of Children's Literature from Slovenly Peter to Harry Potter*. New York and London: Routledge, 2001.

Fantasy in Children's Fiction

Farah Mendlesohn

Making general statements about English-language children's fiction is difficult because there are two clear markets, in which only certain very well-known texts are shared. These two markets remained relatively distinct until the mid-1990s, when they began to merge, partly as a consequence of the success of Harry Potter, and partly due to the cheap shipping provided by Amazon. One market was the United States, with growing overlap – co-publication – with Canada from the 1970s (the Canadian publisher Groundwood Books, for example, was founded in 1979 and has a strong presence in the USA). The second market was that of the British Empire, later the British Commonwealth and Ireland: for almost a century children growing up in this geopolitical region read the same books, predominantly published and shipped from Britain. Canada saw an indigenous publishing industry emerge from the 1950s, but it was very regional, and it was not until the 1980s in Canada, and perhaps the 1990s in Australia, that indigenous publishing really began to thrive and to export.

Fantasy was particularly affected by these differences, for the 'settler' countries appear to have had some prejudice against the fantastic. Protestant 'realism' and popular objections to magic among some reading communities have been a feature in the USA for at least a century, if not longer; the Australian market has prized realism as most supportive of its children's needs, and much early Australian fantasy (1970s through the 1980s) was intimately connected to attempts to raise awareness of Aboriginal culture, as in the work of Patricia Wrightson. In contrast, in Canada the folklore traditions of England, Scotland and Ireland were transplanted very quickly, and local indigenous folklore co-opted and assimilated (see *Unknown Fairies of Canada*, by 'Maxine', 1926, or H. A. Kennedy's *The Red Man's Wonderbook*, 1934). Until the international marketing of the 1990s, relatively few books crossed over: from the USA, *The Wonderful Wizard of Oz* (1900) (but rarely its sequels), but not the works of E. B. White; from the UK, *The Lion, the Witch and the Wardrobe* (1950); while the works of folklorist writers such as Susan Cooper, Alan Garner and Lloyd Alexander (one transatlantic, one British, one American) have proved marketable in both regions; New Zealander Margaret Mahy was, until recently, the most successful Antipodean author.

The position of children's literature within fantasy, and of fantasy within children's literature, is challenging. Primed by the writings of J. R. R. Tolkien ('On Fairy-stories', 1939) and C. S. Lewis ('On Stories', 1947) and more recent critics such as Michael Moorcock (*Wizardry and Wild Romance*, 1987), along with other critics who have demonstrated the characteristic defensiveness of the genre, we are used to assuming that the Victorians were wedded to mimetic literature and relegated 'fairies' and the fanciful to the realm of infants. This is, as more considered assessments have proved, very far from true. Whether we are talking about the fantasy paintings and writings of the pre-Raphaelite Brotherhood, the overtly sexual imagery of Christina Rossetti's 'Goblin Market' (1862), the elegiac parables of Charles Kingsley or the controlled anarchy of Lewis Carroll, these are works that are aimed firmly at adults, and which also should properly be understood as radically experimental fictions which played with style and rhetoric to create something utterly new. In the 1920s, the radical work of David Lindsay (*A Voyage to Arcturus*, 1920) and Hope Mirrlees (*Lud-in-the-Mist*, 1926) was acknowledged by modernists as part of contemporary literary radicalism. That fantasy became, at the end of the nineteenth century and the beginning of the twentieth, a fiction for children is due to a number of social and literary factors.

The end of the century saw a growing protectionism around children – nicely encapsulated by Lewis Carroll's call, in the introduction to the second edition of *Bruno and Sylvie* (1889), to protect teenage girls from the decadence of Shakespeare. In this context mimetic literature, once prized as a way to teach children the realities of life and render them submissive and chastened Christians, became regarded as corrupting. Fairies, folk tales and fancy could, to those who did not read them carefully, be a means to protect the child from the world.

Simultaneously, in the literary world, Henry James led the charge for a 'grown up' literature which eschewed both adventure and the fantastic and fundamentally changed the trajectory of 'literary' fiction from an outward movement – away from home, into the world and into risk taking – to an inwards one which understood adulthood as a process of settling for home and family. We still see this difference in modern classifications: 'genre' fiction, whether crime fiction, historical, science fiction or even romance, is fundamentally about leaving home and finding risk; 'literary' fiction is overwhelmingly focused on staying put and making the best of a situation. In this context, children's and 'family' fiction became a repository for the outward bound and risk-taking adventure, which may be one reason why fantasies that end with a return home sometimes feel anti-climactic. (Here I include *The Lord of the Rings* [1954–5]: fans may bemoan the loss of 'The Scouring of the Shire' from Peter Jackson's film version, but it was probably the correct decision for a mass audience, attuned to modern quests as narratives of success rather than tragedy.)

The growing interest in children as malleable beings who were themselves worthy subjects of educational experiment also changed the nature of the market. Caroline Sumpter, in *The Victorian Press and the Fairy Tale* (2008), looks at early radicals' attempts to change the nature of literature for children, and mostly records their failure, but in doing so she points to the difference between the conservatism of *fairy*, which – with its twin messages of acceptance of the social order, and the chance of securing a place higher up – proved problematic for those who wanted to overturn the whole thing, and *fantasy*, which, in creating whole new worlds, as William Morris, Lord Dunsany and Hope Mirrlees did, could revision the entire nature of human relations (even while it mostly didn't). In the early twentieth century, for those radicals working outside the mainstream and rather conservative pulp book market, fantasy offered a radical and challenging form in which non-conformist ideas could be expressed.

The period from the late nineteenth century through to the end of the 1950s could fairly be considered a period of literary experimentation in which the major forms of fantasy emerged. There are a number of ways of classifying fantasy – this chapter takes for granted a broad definition of the form as *things that are not possible* – but not all of them work well for this period. Brian Attebery's (1992) division of the genre into indigenous versus other-world fantasy is hampered by the relative paucity of other-world fantasy prior to the 1950s; the popular term 'High Fantasy' is similarly of limited utility because its concern with queens, kings and courts is primarily applicable to the 1970s (although the popularity of the television version of George R. R. Martin's *Game of Thrones* may change that). It could be extended to modern epic fantasy such as the Percy Jackson series, but it rarely is, as that is often connected to the primary world. Furthermore, these are descriptions of settings, and it is too easy to subvert a setting to produce a crossover text: *The Hobbit* is an other-world fantasy, but it is not a 'high' fantasy, being the tale of relatively ordinary folk – hobbits and burghers – proving to king, dwarves and dragons that their time may be past.

Fantasy for adults and fantasy purposely written for children tend in the first half of the twentieth century to occupy different points on the spectrum of this world or other world. Most pre-1950s adult fantasy in the UK centres around either ghost stories (M. R. James) or the gothic (William Hope Hodgson, Arthur Machen), and in the USA around the 'slick' tempter stories in which the devil or an imp makes an appearance and creates chaos, with some orientalist adventure fantasy which comes to be known (rather inaccurately) as 'sword and sorcery'. In contrast, fantasy for children in this period often focuses on disrupted or estranged domesticity (Edith Nesbit, P. L. Travers, John Masefield) with a certain amount of adventure fiction added in (Alison Uttley, Hilda Lewis, Patricia Lynch – all three also deploying time slip), and while adult fantasy temporarily abandoned folklore as its matter, children's fantasy remained enthused in the work of Patricia Lynch, Charles Finger and, of course, J. R. R. Tolkien.

Categories of fantasy

One way to categorize fantasy, and one which helps reposition this period in children's fantasy as highly experimental, is through the linked fuzzy sets[1] offered in my *Rhetorics of Fantasy* (2008). There are essentially four categories within the fantastic: the portal quest, the intrusive, the liminal and the immersive. These categories are distinguished by the means by which the fantastic enters the narrated world. In the portal quest we are invited into the fantastic (Baum's *The Wonderful Wizard of Oz*, 1900 and C. S. Lewis's *The Lion, the Witch and the Wardrobe*, 1950, are the classic examples); in the intrusion fantasy the fantastic enters the fictional world (Susan Cooper's *The Dark Is Rising*, 1973; Stephenie Meyer's *Twilight*, 2005); in the liminal fantasy the magic hovers in the corner of our eye (Louis Sachar's *Holes*, 2000 or Steve Cockayne's *The Good People*, 2006); while the immersive fantasy allows us no escape (Frances Hardinge's *Gullstruck Island*, 2009). Each category has a profound influence on the rhetorical structures of the fantastic: it affects the way in which such texts are written and rhetorical choices for the content of the book. Portal fantasies tend to be restricted to the naiveties of the tourists' eye view (or at best the critical but restricted eye of the journalist). The immersive fantasy can be more questioning, but is very easily broken by over-description and needs to be rooted in an indigenous character; in this respect it is the form most engaged with the cognitive estrangement of science fiction. The intrusion fantasy relies on shock and surprise and must therefore up the stakes at every stage of the adventure; while the liminal fantasy must resolutely refuse the resolution (in the sense of coming into focus) of magic and is very rare in children's fiction. Louis Sachar's *Holes* (2000) may be a liminal fantasy, as may Lemony Snicket's *A Series of Unfortunate Events* (1995–2006), particularly towards the end of the series, and Steve Cockayne's *The Good People* (2006) is either a liminal fantasy or a mimetic story of a child with schizophrenia.

In the UK, intrusion fantasy dominates before the Second World War (Nesbit's *Five Children and It*, 1902; P. L. Travers's *Mary Poppins*, 1934–88). There is a difference, however, between the intrusion stories of the adult market, in which the intrusion is often conclusive – it ends the tale – and those of the children's market of this period, in which the intruder(s) contribute to a child's growth. In the late nineteenth and early twentieth centuries, it is quite striking how little children leave the confines of house and garden (see Mrs Molesworth's *The Cuckoo Clock*, 1877, or Edith Nesbit's *The Phoenix and the Carpet*, 1904, or *The Magic City*, 1910). Children in this period cannot go to magic; magic must come to them, as it does quite clearly in Kipling's *Puck of Pook's Hill* (1906). The intrusion of magic, like the intrusion of a governess or tutor, is the arrival of education; it shifts the protagonist-child's perception of the world. This is clearest in Nesbit's work, where the children are almost continually wrong-footed by the wish-granting Psammead, and, in a particularly clever tactic, are themselves later placed in the ironic position of tutor to the Phoenix; and perhaps less clear in Hilda Lewis's *The Ship That Flew*

(1939), where the acquisition of Odin's ship is an intrusion that will lead to a portal fantasy.

Sometimes the structure of the intrusion fantasy is masked: in John Masefield's *The Midnight Folk* (1927), the intruders are the oppressive governess and guardian who disrupt Kay's world, and the animals who help to disrupt it further that it may be mended. In T. H. White's *Mistress Masham's Repose* (1946), it is an interesting question who is the disruption, the Lilliputians or Maria, for each change the other's life. This book draws attention to the form's politics. Nalo Hopkinson has pointed out (Mendlesohn, 2008: 149), talking chiefly of horror, that there is an assumption that the intruder will be fascinated by us, and that our response to the intruder takes the form of regarding ourselves (our world, our person) as either especially under threat or especially attractive, as in, for example, the sexualization of the vampire's victims, which has recently been depicted most vividly in the Jacob–Bella–Edward triangle of Stephenie Meyer's *Twilight* series.

Traditionally, however, much children's fantasy has taken a slightly different position: the Psammead is grumpy about his intrusion into the children's lives (and rather sees them as intruding on his peace and quiet); he is very much *not* fascinated by them. Similarly, T. H. White's Lilliputians regard Maria as the intruder and she does fit Hopkinson's insight in that she disrupts their lives – and is told by the Professor she consults both this, and that she has no right to do so, that she should keep her fascination to herself. Mary Poppins as intruder does fascinate the children, but although they are the focus of her work she seems rather less than interested in *them*. In Mary Norton's *The Magic Bedknob* (1943), again, the children intrude on the privacy of the life of the local witch, and their adventures are her attempt to buy their silence. E. B. White's *Stuart Little* (1945), in which a New York family gives birth to a mouse, may be the closest to the classic intrusion fantasy in the first half of the twentieth century, as we watch the world and Stuart come to terms with each other, but even here the rhetorical position is firmly with Stuart.

The reversal described here may be a clear reflection of the different experiences of children and adults in a pre- 'child-centred' world, in which adult time and space is sacrosanct and children are continually told to go away. Children before 1970 knew they were intrusions on the peace of adults/fairy. Certainly, it is in the 1970s when children's fantasy begins to use widely the classic construction of the intrusion fantasy, in which it is children's ordered lives that are disrupted by an intrusion and they themselves who tame it and return the world to a *preferred* normality. One of the best of the more recent works is Frances Hardinge's *Verdigris Deep* (2007; USA: *Well Wished*), in which an ill-advised plundering of a wishing well leaves the children obligated to the spirit of the well; one becomes its eyes, another its voice and the third its hands. The chaos it wreaks has to be repelled and the spirit appeased. But even here, there is a sense that the spirit is not attracted so much as dragged into the real world, resentful and hurting from the weight of wishes that have been inflicted on it.

There are some portal fantasies in this early period: *The Wonderful Wizard of Oz* (1900) from the USA, and from the UK *The Box of Delights* (1935) by John Masefield or *The Ship that Flew* (1939) by Hilda Lewis, but the true immersive fantasy did not emerge in children's fantasy until well into the 1970s post-Tolkien boom. Even *The Hobbit* (1937), though set fully in a secondary world, tells the story of a young man (hobbits come of age at 33 and live into their hundreds, so at 50 Bilbo is relatively young) taking a tour to strange places that he can barely understand. However, the full immersive fantasy only came into its own from the 1950s onwards.

In 1950, the publication of *The Lion, the Witch and the Wardrobe* began a shift in children's fantasy from the intrusion to the portal fantasy. The portal fantasy was not new: *Alice in Wonderland* and *Through the Looking-Glass* are clearly portal fantasies, but these are books where the other side of the portal is essentially incomprehensible. The decisive rhetorical move in the portal fantasy, and the one which set up its current structure, is the idea that on the other side of the portal (in a new country, a new state, a new job, a new school) is a world that can be learnt, negotiated and, significantly for the politics of the form, conquered. The American classic *The Wonderful Wizard of Oz* fits this description perfectly. Baum himself was fascinated by the child transportations of the late nineteenth century (Dorothy's aunt and uncle might be interpreted as courtesy relations in a world where 'Aunt' and 'Uncle' were common terms of respect). Oz is a representation of the promised land of opportunity that had tempted many 'orphans' to accept the placement in the disappointing lands of Kansas and Ohio.

In the years after the publication of the first Oz book, the US saw many sequels, while the British Empire market saw a number of individual titles that repurposed the portal fantasy from the explore-and-rule meme that runs through the Oz books, to an explore-and-treasure-hunt theme. We can see this in the Canadian Grant Balfour's *On Golden Wings through Wonderland* (1927), Catherine Clark's in *The Golden Pine Cone* (1950) (also Canadian), in Hampden Gordon's *The Golden Keys: being some further account of adventures with Paradoc the gnome among modern fairies* (1932) and in E. A. Wyke Smith's *The Marvellous Land of Snergs* (1927). Each of these titles uses the treasure hunt as structure and positions the children as helpers to the inhabitants of Faery. *The Lion, the Witch and the Wardrobe* was to combine the 'help' meme with the explore-and-conquer meme and so shift the role of the child protagonist from 'helper' to 'rescuer' in ways which affected the depiction of children in a range of different fantasies.

The rhetorical strategy of the portal quest fantasy is a backhand trick. In the portal fantasy the protagonists must learn everything from the start and can take nothing for granted; but the portal fantasy was constructed in a period in which children were expected to respect and trust their elders. (This shifts dramatically to a position of mistrust in the 1970s, manifested in the *minotaur* style of stories, a form which shows adults sacrificing their own children to a greater good, and which has culminated most recently in *The Hunger Games*.) Thus portal fantasies are constructivist rather than behaviourist, associating learning with active teaching rather than exploratory learning. In both *The Wonderful Wizard of Oz* and *The Lion, the Witch and the Wardrobe*, as well as the inter-war adventure portal fantasies, there is always an active teacher, a

Mage or Wizard whose role is to corral exploration and to shape interpretation, whether this be a humble figure such as a beaver, an indeterminate semi-human companion like Gurgi in Lloyd Alexander's *Prydain* series (in one sense an immersive fantasy but with the rhetorical structure of the portal quest), or else a great one, such as Aslan or the mages and wizards of every writer from Alan Garner's *The Weirdstone of Brisingamen* (1960) to Maurice Gee's *The Halfmen of O* (1982), or indeed Dumbledore in the Harry Potter novels. (In the final book, *Harry Potter and the Deathly Hallows*, even Hermione feels that Dumbledore has shaped the quest.)

The closed political and educative framework of the portal fantasy means that the worlds on the other sides of portals are tourist destinations for the traveller: it is rare for the protagonist to learn, for example, how the kitchens work or to freely explore the streets. It is unfortunate that the portal fantasy came of age in the 1950s at the very end of Empire, for the attitudes of the British and other colonists to their empires, combined with this tourist position, embedded in the portal fantasy the meme of 'rescue' and paternalism which I referred to above. Over and over again children in portal fantasies are, literally, the great white hope. Even self-consciously postcolonial writers such as Hiromi Goto (*The Kappa Child*, 2001) and Nnedi Okorafor (*Zarah the Windseeker*, 2005) have been unable entirely to escape this. The Marxist writer China Miéville sought, in *Un Lun Dun* (2007), to subvert the trope by abandoning the 'chosen one' as the protagonist and opting for her side-kick, but even though she was Indian and the salvation of the underworld was subversive, the paradigm of external rescue and native subservience remained untouched. Two authors who do seem to have broken the structure are Rhiannon Lassiter (UK) and K. A. Applegate (USA). In *Borderland* (2003) Lassiter's children arrive without a guide and, imbued with the lessons from the portal fantasies they have read, they set out to save the world. The result is not unlike the West's attempts to 'save' Iraq, and this reality might explain why the classic portal fantasy is relatively uncommon in modern children's fantasy. In a post-imperial world, it has become harder to believe in the rhetoric of the form and it has yet to be fully renewed. Sadly, the series was never finished and we cannot know if the subversion was sustained. K. A. Applegate's *Everworld* (1999–2001) sends five children into a pocket universe full of gods, without a guide and without a purpose: they simply go slowly but inevitably insane and make very little difference to the world in which they are stuck.

Sometimes the portal crossed is not a place but a way of being: Darren Shan's *Cirque du Freak* (2000), for example, sees a boy turned into a vampire. The subsequent adventures are focused on growing into the role with or without a guide, following advice or not following it. In this form of the portal the metaphor for crossing the boundary into adulthood is obvious, although no less effective for that.

From the 1920s through to the 1970s social realism dominated: authors such as Diana Wynne Jones did well, but she was known primarily to the cognoscenti – both adults and children – emerging only as a hugely respected author in the 1990s, when her child readers had turned into adult children's literature critics (Mendlesohn, 2005: 196). Other authors such as Lloyd

Alexander, Susan Cooper, Alan Garner, Margaret Mahy and Ursula Le Guin achieved critical acclaim, but fantasy was regarded as a minority taste. This changed in the 1990s as a direct consequence of the success of J. K. Rowling and Philip Pullman. It is frequently mentioned that Rowling was rejected by many publishing houses, but this is typically used to deride their taste: it is more helpful to consider that, at the time, fantasy was seen as a very poor seller, and the publishers were acceding to conventional wisdom. Evidence of this can be seen in the original cover of *Harry Potter and the Philosopher's Stone* (1997). It depicts a schoolboy with school scarf, in front of a steam train, and is more reminiscent of 1930s school stories than of fantasy: only the eagle-eyed and analytical might notice that the boy's shirt is undone, that he carries a backpack, and that there is a very modern-looking London bus in the background. Bloomsbury deliberately sent the book into the marketplace 'undercover', with as many 'this is a realistic book for boys' signals as they could manage. The ruse succeeded in that the book became a word-of-mouth success among children and eventually among adults who would not consider themselves fantasy readers. But the changing market had been there for the perceptive for some time.

Terry Pratchett had been selling increasing numbers of his *Discworld* series from 1983 onwards. By 1997 there were 21 in print and it had become normal for a new Discworld to top the best-seller lists in the UK every winter. Assuming that people started reading Pratchett in their late teens (librarians loved the books for their ability to keep 15-year-old boys in the library) or early twenties, by 1997 many of his readers had children of their own, or taught in schools, or ran libraries, or were in the publishing industry: and people who like fantasy buy fantasy for their children and certainly do not regard fantasy as illegitimate reading. Pratchett himself took advantage of this by writing fantasies specifically for children, first with his *Bromeliad* series (1989–90) and then, more successfully, with the Johnny Maxwell trilogy (1992–6). By 1995, when Philip Pullman's *Northern Lights* was published, there was a clear, if not yet fully visible, market among both children and adults.

Both *Northern Lights* and *Harry Potter* are portal quest fantasies, and as such, although both felt radical to a market only just emerging from the dominance of social realism, both are structurally rather conservative texts. Pullman's series, although ending with a radical sense of loss, returns Lyra to her own world of Oxford at the end, completing the classic circle. In contrast, the Harry Potter sequence becomes less 'portal' with each book, and by the end has effectively reversed the trajectory so that it is 'our' world that seems to be the portal into which Harry occasionally enters/takes shelter and the world of the wizards which has emerged as the primary world, and which like many a primary world fantasy is dealing with a series of intrusions (the incursions and threats of Lord Voldemort).

In the wake of Pullman's and Rowling's success, many of the writers of the previous 30 years were brought back into print and many new writers such as Darren Shan, Garth Nix and Eoin Colfer launched very successful careers. However, two lessons came out of the boom for book publishers: that series fiction in particular could work for fantasy (previously most fantasy came as standalone books), and that fantasy in which there was an external threat was rather powerful.

Among the series fiction writers, the most successful has been K. A. Applegate, who began as a writer of (very good) romances. In 1993 she published the first of a science fiction series named *Animorphs* (1996), which ran to 54 titles: in these, children were given the gift (by an alien) of being able to turn into a single animal. Unusually, one of the children chooses his animal life over his life with abusive parents (in most other fantasies there is a reconciliation to the self, if not to the parents). For teens, as noted above, there was *Everworld* (1999–2001), a particularly dark portal fantasy in which the world the five teens enter is a complex pocket universe inhabited by the retired gods of various times and planets. The general nastiness and unpredictability is enhanced because when the teens sleep each night they find themselves back in the primary world negotiating high school life. They all gradually go mad.

The immersive fantasy is the fully closed fantasy; there is no 'other world' and the trajectory of the story needs to stay within that world. This latter point is problematic and is why quests are associated with portal fantasies, because the moment the protagonist leaves the place with which they are familiar, often the rhetorics of the quest fantasy intrude, and the protagonist becomes dependent once again on the guide. As a result, the quest fantasy has trouble staying immersive. The immersive fantasy creates its own bible (a word used to describe the set of givens handed to writers who work on established series, television and text), and the protagonists operate within it. The immersive fantasy relies on the protagonists living within the bible, and taking its contents as the physics of the world. In this structure, therefore, neither Philip Pullman's *His Dark Materials* trilogy (1995–2000) nor J. K. Rowling's Harry Potter novels (1997–2007) are immersive fantasies because the protagonists of both constantly need to have the salient realities of their worlds explained to them.

In Pullman's *His Dark Materials* trilogy, the wrenching of Lyra out of her home environment renders her dependent upon and accepting of the explanations she receives of the world around her (made most vivid in the episode with Mary Malone in *The Subtle Knife*, 1997). It renders her a peculiarly passive protagonist in the face of the many direct statements of her importance and character. For all of the detail of this fantasy, Lyra is not immersed in the world we see. Rowling's Harry Potter series begins as a portal fantasy and by the end of the seven books has turned Harry (and Hermione) into a native of the world, but Harry continues to rely entirely on the explanations of others, disguised somewhat because some of those explanations come from Hermione. The frequent speculations about the consequences for the books if Hermione had been the protagonist tend to focus on gender, but there is a more interesting question as to what these books might have felt like if Ron, a native of the world, had been their focalizer. Harry seems to remain in a perpetual position of surprise as to what is possible in the magical world. Hermione, on the other hand, accepts its rubrics and its possibilities rapidly, and this gives her a facility and creative antagonism to the world around her. In her immersive fantasy *Year of the Griffin* (2000) Diana Wynne Jones shows a group of students working on an assignment. One of the students takes a spell and shows how new spells might be developed from it. This is what Hermione is capable of doing, because she works with the world, while Harry sits upon its surface. These two positions encapsulate the difference between the protagonists of the two forms of immersive and portal fantasy.

The immersive fantasy is relatively rare in children's fantasy, in part because of the rhetorical and socio-biological position of children as discoverers of the world, and because the cultural trajectory of youth in the modern West is outward, to work and family (this has not always been the case): effectively through the portal. However, a character left within a world long enough acquires immersion. Tamora Pierce's *In the Hand of the Goddess* (1986), while beginning with the classic portal structure as Alanna enters the new world of a knight's training, rapidly embeds both Alanna and the reader in the world as the series extends. For a fully immersive fantasy we can look to Diana Wynne Jones: several of her *Chrestomanci* stories fit the bill: *Witch Week* (1982), for example, is set in a world where witchcraft is a given and the existence of witches is taken for granted. It is only the peeling back of the taken-for-grantedness of the immersive world that can provide the solution to that world's problems. More political is *Drowned Ammet* (1977), part of the Dalemark quartet: Mitt's movement outwards is, for much of the book, a series of realizations about his world. Instead of Mitt seeing more, he sees deeper and the world becomes more immersive as he moves out of the childish rhetoric of heroes and revolutions and into the quagmires of class, civil war and familial dysfunction.

I have classified Frances Hardinge's *Gullstruck Island* (2009) as immersive fantasy because the main character is knowing, but it is worth pointing out that the protagonist's trajectory, in which she moves out of her world when her village and people are destroyed, would usually lead this to be categorized here as a portal fantasy. But Hathin does not enter the larger world as an innocent. Hathin is the 'translator' for her sister, one of the Lost, children who can communicate telepathically, but who, in this case, appears mentally subnormal. In order to maintain the pretence of her sister's role Hathin has kept her ears and eyes open. Hathin may be marginal to her society but she is absolutely of it. In *Gullstruck Island* we can feel the difference when Hathin travels among the Cavalcaste – the ruling peoples – whom she knows even if she doesn't understand them, and when she and her sister take refuge among Sours whom she barely knows of at all and must learn about as if she has passed through a portal. The effect of the latter encounter is stronger because it turns out that Hathin's sister is not mentally damaged but has merely been skipping 'school' and hanging out telepathically with the Sours. Almost all of these immersive fantasies host an intrusion fantasy which disrupts the world and creates the plot, leading the characters on a trajectory to *find out*, but for the immersion to remain intact that which is found out needs to be consistent and congruous with the world as understood, so that the protagonists can engage critically (dark lords, evil wizards and demons are common).

Although by the 1990s the portal quest fantasy had become, for a while, the default position of children's fantasy (see authors such as Tamora Pierce,

Garth Nix, J. K. Rowling, Philip Pullman etc.), the intrusion fantasy remained a key element of young people's fantasy. It had remained particularly strong in the form of supernatural fiction throughout the 1970s and into the 1980s. In the UK this tended to involve the intrusion of folklore into the landscape. Authors such as Penelope Lively (*The Wild Hunt of Hagworthy*, 1971; *The Ghost of Thomas Kempe*, 1973) demonstrated that the veneer we call civilization was thin and porous. In *The Dark Is Rising* sequence (1965–77) Susan Cooper had the fantastic breach the boundaries of our world (and interestingly, succeeded in setting a quest fantasy in the primary world). Margaret Mahy's *The Changeover* (1984) decisively linked the teenage years to internal intrusions as supernatural possibilities become available to a young girl as she reaches physical maturity. By the 1990s, intrusion fantasy had mutated in the children's market away from classic horror to two approaches, crime novels such as Derek Landry's *Skullduggery Pleasant* (2007) and the 'paranormal romance': the first sign of this last had been Anne Rice's *Interview with the Vampire* (1976), written for adults but hugely popular with teens. When those teens began writing this meme spread, with writers such as Laurell K. Hamilton and Charmaine Harris achieving considerable success in the 2000s.

What almost all post-1950 fantasies have in common is that they are *aspirational* – directed to the delights of adulthood and very different from their predecessors, which tended to celebrate childhood and encouraged staying there (see *Peter Pan,* or 'the Lamb' in *Five Children and It*). From the 1950s, fantasy had frequently ascribed adult roles to children in the position of kings, queens, prophets, warriors and just generally Important People. Fantasy – like its sister science fiction – was notable for spending little time on social or romantic relationships. It is perhaps not coincidental, therefore, that when the Young Adult turn came to fantasy in the 1990s it came in the form of the intrusion fantasy, for adolescence and romance are a genuine intrusion into the life of a young person, however welcome.

Prior to the mid-1980s, 'children's fantasy' meant, roughly, a target audience of 8 to 15 years old (the age range at which children's fiction has been targeted maps efficiently to the rising school age). The market assumption was that many would continue to read the form but would gradually transfer to the adult market through 'writers whom teens like' such as Stephen King, Anne Rice, Terry Brooks, Stephen Donaldson, Piers Anthony, Laurell K. Hamilton and many others; there was no market *for teens* as such (Levy and Mendelsohn, forthcoming: chapter 6). Unlike the children's science fiction market, which in the 1980s and 1990s had relatively little overlap with that for adults, fantasy for children had traditionally inspired a great deal of interest among adult readers, regularly appearing on awards lists and being retained as part of the common canon among fans. In the 1990s a new phenomenon appeared, the Young Adult fantasy.

The Young Adult (YA) novel had appeared in the 1970s in socialist realist publishing. It was defined by many as being concerned with adult issues and more realistic than the previous 'Juvenile' category, but it would be more accurate to say that it reflected a different definition of a teen which emerged as the school leaving age in the USA and UK rose, away from a person concerned with entering the world of work (where sober responsibility was a premium) to one concerned with acceptance in social circles, emotional development, and the risks and temptations of the increasingly responsibility-free life of the middle-class teen. The 'adult' issues of YA are often sex, pregnancy, abortion and drugs, but they are rarely work.

The first really successful repurposing of the intrusion fantasy was in the TV show *Buffy the Vampire Slayer* (1997–2003). Until season five, when the death of Buffy's mother forces her into a genuinely adult role of bread earner and parent, Buffy's young adult concerns are popularity at school, dating (school work barely gets a look in) and vampires: sometimes, the two even cross over. Stephenie Meyer's *Twilight* sequence (2005–8) took the same approach, although Bella does actually have to have a job to support her lifestyle and takes on the role of housewife for her father; the result is that this accords with the classic romance trope in that her vampire promises to take her away from all her troubles, even if this does require rather more dependency than many feminist scholars have been comfortable with.

The paranormal romances practised by writers such as Meyer and Cassandra Clare are distinctive in that they run two trajectories simultaneously: although the old approach of repelling the intrusion frequently structures the adventure, the main story is of *taming* the intrusion. In sharp contrast to the portal quest fantasies, adulthood is achieved not by entering into the strange world, but by pulling the strange world into one's own, and absorbing it. Catherine Jinks's *The Reformed Vampire Support Group* (2009) shows the desperate attempt of a group of very depressed vampires to fit in.

Not all YA fantasies, however, are as romantic as Meyer's. Although Meyer has been described as 'dark', the work of Margo Lanagan has provoked genuine shock from readers and critics. Lanagan began as a writer of non-fantasy YA but entered the fantasy market first with short story collections *White Time* (2000) and *Black Juice* (2005). Her 2009 novel *Tender Morsels* can be described in very conventional terms as a YA fantasy about a young girl who takes refuge from horror in a pocket universe and is based on the old fairy tale 'Snow White and Rose Red', but the execution is brutal and the ending far from consolatory or aspirational.

Conclusion

Modern children's and YA fantasy is both diverse and speciated. From its beginnings as a radically experimental fiction, it is currently locked into sub-genres not dissimilar to those of fantasy aimed at adults: it both leads children and teens to the wider market and retains its readers into adulthood. It has proven astonishingly versatile as a market, adapting to changing ideas of the child – both in terms of what age the child reader might be, and to new social contexts and constructions – and absorbing new myth traditions and new environments into its 'stuff'.

WORKS CITED AND FURTHER READING

Children's Books

Applegate, K. A. *Animorphs*. 54 vols. New York: Scholastic, 1996–2001.
Applegate, K. A. *Everworld*. 12 vols. New York: Scholastic, 1999–2001.
Baum, L. Frank. *The Wonderful Wizard of Oz*. Chicago and New York: G. M. Hill, 1900.
Carroll, Lewis. *Bruno and Sylvie*. London: Macmillan, 1889.
Cockayne, Steve. *The Good People*. London: Atom, 2006.
Cooper, Susan. *The Dark Is Rising*. London: Chatto & Windus, 1973.
Hardinge, Frances. *Gullstruck Island*. London: Macmillan Children's, 2009.
Hardinge, Frances. *Verdigris Deep*. London: Macmillan Children's, 2007.
Jones, Diana Wynne. *Drowned Ammet*. London: Macmillan, 1977.
Jones, Diana Wynne. *Witch Week*. London: Macmillan Children's, 1982.
Jones, Diana Wynne. *Year of the Griffin*. London: Gollancz, 2000.
Lanagan, Margo *Tender Morsels*. Oxford: David Fickling, 2009.
Lassiter, Rhiannon. *Borderland*. Oxford: Oxford University Press, 2003.
Lewis, C. S. *The Lion, the Witch and the Wardrobe*. London: Geoffrey Bles, 1950.
Lewis, Hilda. *The Ship That Flew*. London: Oxford University Press, 1939.
Mahy, Margaret. *The Changeover*. London: Dent, 198).
Masefield, John. *The Midnight Folk*. London: Heinemann, 1927.
Meyer, Stephenie. *Twilight*. New York: Little, Brown, 2005.
Miéville, China. *Un Lun Dun*. London: Macmillan Children's, 2007.
Nesbit, E. *Five Children and It*. London: T. Fisher Unwin, 1902.
Norton, Mary. *The Magic Bedknob, Or, How to Become a Witch in Ten Easy Lessons*. New York: Hyperion/Putnam's 1943.
Pierce, Tamora. *In the Hand of the Goddess*. Oxford: Oxford University Press, 1986.
Pullman, Philip. *Northern Lights*. London: Scholastic, 1995; *The Subtle Knife*. London: Scholastic, 1997; *The Amber Spyglass*. London: Scholastic, 2000.
Rowling, J. K. *Harry Potter and the Philosopher's Stone*. London: Bloomsbury, 1997.
Shan, Darren. *Cirque du Freak*. London: HarperCollins, 2000.
Snicket, Lemony. *A Series of Unfortunate Events*. 13 vols. New York: HarperCollins, 1995–2006.
Tolkien, J. R. R. *The Hobbit*. London: Allen & Unwin, 1937.
White, E. B. *Stuart Little*. New York: Harper and Brothers, 1945.
White, T. H. *Mistress Masham's Repose*. New York: Putnam's, 1946.

Critical Texts

Attebery, Brian. *Strategies of Fantasy*. Bloomington IN: Indiana University Press, 1992.
Butler, Catherine. 'Modern Children's Fantasy'. In Edward James and Farah Mendlesohn, *The Cambridge Companion to Fantasy Literature* (pp. 224–35). Cambridge: Cambridge University Press, 2012.
Butler, Charles. *Four British Fantasists: Place and Culture in the Children's Fantasies of Penelope Lively, Alan Garner, Diana Wynne Jones and Susan Cooper*. Lanham, MD: Children's Literature Association and Scarecrow Press, 2006.
James, Edward, and Farah Mendlesohn (eds). *The Cambridge Companion to Fantasy Literature*. Cambridge: Cambridge University Press, 2012.
Levy, Michael, and Farah Mendlesohn. *The Cambridge Introduction to Children's Fantasy Literature*. Cambridge: Cambridge University Press, forthcoming 2015.

Lewis, C. S. 'On Stories' (1947). In C. S. Lewis, *Of Other Worlds: Essays and Stories*, ed. Walter Hooper. London: Geoffrey Bles, 1966.

Mendlesohn, Farah. *Diana Wynne Jones: Children's Literature and the Fantastic Tradition*. New York: Routledge, 2005.

Mendlesohn, Farah. *Rhetorics of Fantasy*. Middletown, CT: Wesleyan University Press, 2008.

Mendlesohn, Farah, and Edward James. *A Short History of Fantasy*. London: Middlesex University Press, 2009.

Moorcock, Michael. *Wizardry and Wild Romance*. London: Gollancz, 1987.

Nikolajeva, Maria. 'The Development of Children's Fantasy'. In Edward James and Farah Mendlesohn (eds), *The Cambridge Companion to Fantasy Literature* (pp. 50–61). Cambridge: Cambridge University Press, 2012.

Nikolajeva, Maria. *The Magic Code: The Use of Magical Patterns in Fantasy for Children*. Stockholm: Almqvist & Wiksell, 1988.

Sumpter, Caroline. *The Victorian Press and the Fairy Tale*. Basingstoke: Palgrave Macmillan, 2008.

Tolkien, J. R. R. 'On Fairy-Stories' (1939). Revised in J. R. R. Tolkien, *The Monsters and the Critics and Other Essays*. London: HarperCollins, 1997. Expanded as *Tolkien: On Fairy-stories*, ed. Verlyn Flieger and Douglas A. Anderson. London: HarperCollins, 2008.

Zahorski, Kenneth J., and Robert H. Boyer. 'The Secondary Worlds of High Fantasy'. In Roger C. Schlobin (ed.), *The Aesthetics of Fantasy Literature and Art* (pp. 56–81). Notre Dame, IN and Brighton: University of Notre Dame Press and Harvester, 1982.

NOTE

1. Fuzzy as in not clearly defined, a mode first offered by Brian Attebery, in *Strategies of Fantasy* (1992), where he suggested (pp. 12–13) that there was a single, fuzzy set of fantasy.

Psychoanalytic Approaches to Children's Literature

David Rudd

Introduction

The 'modern child' and psychoanalysis are about the same age, and would seem to have similar concerns. In 1900 Ellen Kay (1909) declared that it was the 'century of the child', just a few years after Sigmund Freud (1856–1939) had launched psychoanalysis, provocatively claiming that we should look to childhood to understand many psychological problems. For Freud, this new science, psychoanalysis – the scientific study (*analysis*) of the mind (*psyche*) – involved probing regions that lay beneath what might seem a sanguine surface; this was the realm of the Unconscious, which Freud regarded as his main discovery. It was seen as an area of the mind radically unknowable since we are barred access to it: it is repressed. So we only know of it indirectly: through such things as slips of the tongue, behavioural 'tics' and dreams, although even the latter material is disguised. Given psychoanalysis's stress on the significance of the early years, when a child must adjust to its parents and the wider culture, it is hardly surprising that popular culture simplified Freud's ideas, such that, as Adam Phillips (2000: 42) notes, the figure of the child became 'the unconscious *live*', where 'you could see it in action'. It was but a short step to see children's books as representing such candid insights, too – and being interpreted in such terms (e.g. Phillips, 1972).

This is one reason why a psychoanalytical approach is not straightforward, because of its appropriation by popular culture, with Freudian terms becoming part of everyday life (e.g. *being anal*, or *tight-arsed*; *repressed*; *narcissistic*). We might add to this the fact that psychoanalysis is primarily a therapy, a way of coming to terms with problems caused by repressed material, not an abstract body of thought. Lastly, Freud himself not only reworked his ideas substantially, but others have relentlessly modified them, often taking them in new and sometimes conflicting directions.

In this chapter I will outline some general psychoanalytical terms, illustrating their applicability to various children's texts, before moving on to show how Freud's insights have been extended: first in popular conceptions of psychoanalysis, amongst which I will include ego psychology and Jungian approaches; then the object–relations school, which opposed the ego psychologists; and finally, in a more radical, poststructuralist reworking associated with Jacques Lacan. This, because of its influence and complexity, will be given most attention.

The Freudian terrain

Freud came to see the mind as comprising three parts, all deriving originally from the first of these, the *id*, which works in terms of the pleasure principle; that is, it demands instant gratification (I want it *now*!). The *id* ('it' in Latin) is driven by *libido*, a basic psychosexual energy that underlies all behaviour. Out of the id arises the *ego* (Latin for 'I'), which, for Freud, is the public face of the personality, and one that recognizes its social obligations, deferring gratification (e.g. going to the toilet) till a suitable place and time arise. However, the ego has only become so law-abiding as a result of the third part of the mind, the *superego*, which is the voice of authority (parents, teachers), acting as a conscience. Had Dr. Seuss's *The Cat in the Hat* (1957) been available, it would have provided Freud with a useful template. The Cat himself is the irrepressible id, carefree and reckless (with his Things, One and Two), while the children exhibit their budding egos as they worry about the consequences, especially as the voice of the superego, the goldfish, is forever telling them to behave responsibly. Many texts for the young explore this conflict, but picture-books are often most stark in its representation, with Mo Willems's *Don't Let the Pigeon Drive the Bus* (2003) being a popular recent example. Here child readers are clearly invited to participate in the story, bolstering their emergent egos by refusing to let the pigeon (the id) have his way, in the absence of the superego, the driver.

Freud saw these three aspects of the mind as part of a developmental framework, with the child beginning life as what he termed 'polymorphously perverse'; that is, seeking to gratify desire in any way possible. At this stage there are no notions of gender-appropriate behaviour, or of pleasure being delimited to particular areas. Such civilized refinements begin only as the child passes through various psychosexual stages of development, starting with the *oral*, initiated by the child's experience of the breast (then, often, with substitutes, like a thumb or dummy). This oral stage is followed by an *anal* one, when the child becomes fascinated with its bowel movements, and particularly by its parents' reactions to them, their joy or disappointment (when a movement is withheld).

Normal development then moves on to a *phallic* stage, followed by a period of *latency* before a fully *genital* sexuality emerges. However, if development is in some ways not successful, a person can become fixated at one of the earlier periods. For example, the orally fixated person will crave food, or something similar, rewriting that hospital bed instruction to '*All* by Mouth'. Mickey, from Maurice Sendak's *In the Night Kitchen* (1970), exhibits oral tendencies, as does Winnie-the-Pooh. It would be too banal to link Pooh with the anal phase, of course, even though his name might afford readers some libidinal satisfaction. This latter phase, the anal, is associated in the public imagination with hoarders, obsessive collectors and misers (the 'tight-arsed'). However, Freud's notion is more complex, for this stage of toilet training usually involves a struggle for control between parent and child. If the process is too strict, Freud argues, it can result in a retentive personality (obsessed with order and cleanliness), but there is an opposite tendency arising from too lax a training: of being 'expulsive', or messy. One of the most popular, recent examples of this is Andy Griffiths's scatological trilogy, beginning with *The Day My Bum Went Psycho* (2001). The premise of these stories is that bums have their own volition, and are in danger of 'revolting' with their capacity for noisy farting and noxious fluids. The crude humour knows no bounds, with lakes of excrement, pus and fart-powered energy producing endless [*sic!*] puns (Arsetralia, Bumbay, etc.).

It is the next stage that is most infamous, though, and that for which Freud is perhaps best known: the *Oedipal* (or phallic). As with so many of his concepts, Freud found insights in literature, in this case from a son who unwittingly kills his father and marries his mother, thereby acting out something that, Freud argues, we all desire. However, most of us accept the superiority of the father (he could otherwise castrate us); we therefore forego the mother and seek a partner elsewhere. This lopsided explanation has long been criticized for ignoring female development (attempts at formulating a parallel 'Elektra complex' are flawed), let alone its heterosexist bias. In literary criticism, though, the Oedipal has been a productive conceit, perhaps most famously applied to Hamlet, initially by Freud, to account for Hamlet's indecision in avenging his father's murder (by his uncle, Claudius, who removed Hamlet's father and possessed his mother). In children's literature, the obvious example might seem to be *Peter Pan* (1904), written during the very period that Freudian ideas were first formulated. However, there are problems interpreting the text this way (Egan, 1982). Although Peter Pan vanquishes the fantasized father figure, Hook (forever doubled with Mr Darling), the boy resolutely refuses to complete the Oedipal journey and take up the paternal role himself. He opts, instead, for eternal childhood (Rudd, 2013).

But while Freudian notions often falter in their specificity, their general appeal deserves attention. Why do sex and sexuality play such a huge role in our cultural negotiations, shaping the very way we think and speak? Thus, in a film like *Stand by Me* (Rob Reiner, 1986), the four boys' journey towards manhood is suffused with notions of 'standing out'. Not to do so is, in their favourite put-down, to be 'a pussy'. When they find themselves in a leech-infested swamp, the 12-year-old protagonist, Gordie, reaches down into his pants and comes up with a bloody, flaccid leech before fainting, as though emasculated – or, even worse perhaps, experiencing his first period. The Oedipal, then, remains a powerful explanatory device, even if misconceived. So the link between notions of castration and losing one's sight (following Oedipus's self-blinding with a brooch pin) has also become culturally embedded. Freud uses this trope in his interpretation of E. T. A. Hoffmann's story 'The Sandman' (1816), the title of which alludes to the mythical being who throws sand in children's eyes. This story is central to Freud's famous essay, 'The "Uncanny"' (1919), which, for him, was fundamentally concerned with Oedipal issues – with, as he more generally describes the uncanny, 'that class of the frightening which leads back to what is known of old and long familiar' (Freud, 1985: 340). In other words, the homely turned unhomely (the literal meaning of *unheimlich*, the German term for 'uncanny'; see also Box 13.1).

Feminists have pushed this Oedipal association of sight with masculinity further. Laura Mulvey (1975) famously wrote about the power of the male gaze, sanctioning men's freedom to look, whereas women could only be looked at, being rendered passive under that active, male stare. In 'Snow White' then, we might note how both Snow White and her wicked stepmother are framed by the patriarchal gaze of the mirror (Disney, notably, gives the mirror a male voice), passing judgement on their looks; and later, Snow White again finds herself framed, this time within a glass coffin, similarly to be gazed upon (Gilbert and Gubar, 1979; Lacan's notion of the gaze is dealt with later).

So, whether or not one agrees with Freud's ideas, their cultural penetration has been extensive – and, of course, contentious, as the competing approaches, below, demonstrate.

Popular psychoanalytic approaches: ego psychology, Bruno Bettelheim and beyond

As noted earlier, popular culture's appropriation of psychoanalytic terms and ideas (e.g. that everything comes down to sex) has proved persuasive, and features extensively in 'psychoanalytic' criticism. Thus, for many people, a psychoanalytical approach involves either exploring authors' lives or having their literary characters recline on the therapeutic couch.

The former – biographical criticism – is particularly prevalent in Children's Literature Studies, where writers are readily seen not to have grown up themselves (hence writing for the immature), with critics trawling their backgrounds in search of developmental problems. Hans Christian Andersen's 'The Little Mermaid', then, might be seen as expressing Andersen's repressed bisexuality, and particularly his love for Edvard Collin, who did, in fact, become engaged at the time Andersen wrote his tale of unrequited love (Wullschläger, 2002). Andersen's passion was also mute because it was a love that dared not speak its name, not only because it was homoerotic, but because of class divisions: it was a world where the unusually tall Andersen would always find himself uncomfortable on his gawky legs.

The psychoanalysis of character has also proven popular, if problematic. Mark West's essay on Toad furnishes a convenient example. West laments that 'Grahame provides little information about Toad's childhood', but what he does provide 'suggests that Toad may not have experienced the mirroring process'; he concludes that 'Toad's mother may not have been available to help build her son's sense of self' (Rollin and West, 1999: 50). But, of course, none of the characters' childhoods is discussed, because, as literary creations, we only have their textual representation; otherwise, they are blank pages.

'Ego psychology' has also proved particularly popular, especially in America, thanks to the work of Freud's daughter, Anna, where it appealed to notions of the American (if un-Freudian) Dream; that is, it presumes that there is a more *conscious* way of achieving self-improvement. In this conceptualization, the child, aligned with the impulsive id, with the 'pleasure principle', is required to repudiate childish impetuosity (arrest that pigeon!) and, in line with the 'reality principle', to defer gratification, subordinating his desires to the control of the ego.

Bruno Bettelheim (1903–90), one of the most influential critics in this area, reads fairy tales (and the Grimm Brothers' versions in particular) in this manner, seeing them as vehicles for helping children come to develop ego control, which, in effect, amounts to parental control. His very title, *The Uses of Enchantment* (1976), reflects this rather utilitarian standpoint. Thus, in his reading of 'Hansel and Gretel', it is the children who are at fault, not the parents. The gingerbread house represents their oral greed, as they 'show how ready they are to eat somebody out of house and home, a fear which they had projected onto their parents as the reason for their desertion' (Bettelheim, 1991: 161). Ultimately, they learn that such desires must be outgrown, and return home with more developed egos.

While psychoanalytic criticism is renowned for taking us out of our comfort zones, articulating contentious and perturbing views, this does not absolve it from critical scrutiny. And there are two, particularly noteworthy things about Bettelheim's reading. One is that, though the child is made central, this is only to highlight his need to see the error of his ways (the generic pronoun, regrettably, is always masculine in Bettelheim). Adults are thereby exonerated. Thus it is Little Red Riding Hood who is guilty of having Oedipal desires, rather than the wolf being guilty of rapaciousness, just as it is Hansel and Gretel who are at fault, above. Second, Bettelheim plays somewhat loose with the Grimms' text, repeatedly referring to the 'mother', not the stepmother; so when he writes that the children 'free themselves of the image of the threatening mother – the witch – and rediscover the good parents' (1991: 162), most readers would question the latter's goodness, especially the stepmother's; hence her twinning with the witch, often made explicit (for example, Anthony Browne's *Hansel and Gretel*, 1981, renders it visually by having the conical gap between two draped curtains form the shape of a witch's hat on the stepmother's head). And, of course, after the witch's death, the stepmother too dies (something, again, that Bettelheim does not mention).[1] The Grimm Brothers, of course, were well aware of the stepmother's shortcomings, hence their replacement of the actual mother (as she is in their original manuscript) with a non-biological carer.

Bettelheim, then, is quite prescriptive (ego-centred, we might say) in his interpretations, as he is in his choice of versions of the tales, declaring the Grimm ones pre-eminent. However, in the more theoretical, first section of his book, he does formally champion individual engagement with these texts, recognizing that they will mean different things at different times, dependent on individual states of mind. In this, he moves away from a notion of the psychoanalyst/critic as the one 'in the know' to a more modern approach, which recognizes the provisional and idiosyncratic nature of textual engagement. It is this stance that will inform the rest of this chapter. That is, rather than seeking to 'explain away' a work, by psychoanalysing either authors or characters (and, thereby, relying on extra-textual knowledge), it explores the relationship between reader and text: the way that the text operates on us as much as we do upon it.

Peter Brooks's (1984) approach to narrative has been one of the most influential in this regard, drawing on Freud's 'Beyond the Pleasure Principle' (1920). It is here that Freud surmises the existence not just of a libidinal energy (*eros*) but of a countervailing 'death drive' (*thanatos*). Freud explored this after noting the way that victims of the First World War would compulsively repeat disturbing, unpleasurable scenarios. He had also witnessed his own grandson, Ernst, repeating a game with a cotton reel and thread, throwing it out of his cot then hauling it back, saying '*fort*' and '*da*' ('gone' and 'here'). Freud surmised that the child was coming to terms with the absence of his mother, the repetition compulsion giving him a sense of mastery over his fate. Brooks claims that novels work similarly, such that we have a 'transferential' relationship with them; that is, by reading about characters and situations, our own concerns are worked through by proxy. More specifically, through the repetitions of various elements – such as thematic concerns and plot complications (obstacles and diversions) – we experience a feeling of satisfaction as the 'sense of an ending' approaches, of having 'mastered' the plot. This doesn't mean that a work has to finish with 'they lived happily ever after' (as children's books, traditionally, have been seen to do); simply that a sense of design is revealed (the plot), which we feel has some justification, whether this involves characters triumphing (e.g. Dahl's *Matilda* and *Danny, the Champion of the World*) or, indeed, expiring (*The Enormous Crocodile* and *The Twits*).

A Jungian approach

Carl Gustav Jung (1875–1961) was one of the first to take issue with his master's teachings. Unlike Freud, he did not see sex as central, preferring to speak of the libido as a more diffuse life force. In general, Jung (1976) is far more optimistic, such that the unconscious and our dreams provide us with clues as to how we might come to realize ourselves through a process he calls 'individuation'. This is represented in countless myths and stories, but perhaps most overtly in quest tales (e.g. *The Wonderful Wizard of Oz*, *The Hobbit*). Thus Jung notes such recurrent patterns as the protagonist's seeming death and subsequent resurrection, or rebirth, as in Jonah and the Whale, or in Pinocchio's journey towards real boyhood (Collodi, 1883/2009). In many stories, this development involves undergoing a 'dark night of the soul'. Such 'katabatic' narratives involve a journey underground before a character's rebirth. Lyra Belacqua, in Philip Pullman's *His Dark Materials* (2008), experiences this when she visits the land of the Dead, being forced to face up to her true story (not her idle fabrications as 'Silvertongue') before she can proceed on her way; likewise, Alice's journey down the rabbit hole (the original manuscript was called *Alice's Adventures Underground*) traces her growth and metaphorical rebirth.

Freud also saw themes repeated in myths and tales, but for Jung their repetition across cultures was a result of our collective unconscious, a trans-individual memory store from which different civilizations retrieve similar 'archetypes', as he called them, which can then take more local form. They are archetypal because they relate to basic things like creation and death, and deal with stock figures; some of these are self-explanatory, like the Wise Woman, the Wise Man and the Trickster; other less so, like the Shadow, the Animus and Anima. The last two, for example, represent the complementary aspects of each gender, as evoked in the phrase about a male 'getting in touch with his female side': his anima, or soul image. This notion is made concrete in Pullman's *His Dark Materials*, where each character in Lyra's alternative world has a dæmon of the opposite gender, which the character needs to come to acknowledge fully. As for the Shadow, this represents one's darker, more primitive side, often repressed, Dr Jekyll's Mr Hyde being a key example. In children's literature, Ursula Le Guin has a character in *A Wizard of Earthsea* (1968) explicitly called The Shadow, which represents the dark side of the wizard, Ged. Again, Jung makes the point that the Shadow is a part of ourselves that we need to come to terms with, if we are, indeed, to become whole, to individuate.

While Jungian insights can be applied to many texts in this piecemeal way, identifying particular features, it is often difficult to see what they add that cannot be derived from a more traditional close reading in terms of character analysis and development. It is of note, then, that Jung's work is often deployed as part of larger critical schemes (e.g. Campbell, 1949; Frye, 1957). Moreover, Jung's tendency to universalize and generalize (implicit in the idea of a 'collective unconscious') has made him less popular in recent criticism, which is often more nuanced, taking the distinct perspective of particular interest groups (women, people of colour – or, indeed, children). Finally, Jung's lack of close attention to language put him out of favour with the 'linguistic turn' in criticism that marked the arrival of poststructuralism in the 1970s. This said, a number of Jungians have produced rewarding readings of cultural works (e.g. Franz, 1996; Rowland, 2008), and Jung's terms, like Freud's, have become part of everyday cultural discourse (e.g. 'synchronicity', 'extrovert' and 'introvert', aside from those above).

Object relations

Melanie Klein (1882–1960) was to found the next major reworking of psychoanalysis in 'object relations' theory. The word 'object' is a stumbling block for many, though it was introduced by Freud, who deliberately talks about the sexual 'object', rather than the person; for, as we know, infants relate to 'part-objects' before they are cognizant of the whole, whether this be the breast, the voice, or other parts (and, of course, for those who hold on to such part-objects, it can result in fetishism – Prince Charmings beware!). That other term, 'relations', is important too, for this approach always stresses the interdependence of people. Thus Winnicott, to whom we will come presently, once declared that there is no such thing as a baby, for it exists only in relationship to its carer (Phillips, 1988: 5).

This approach has proved remarkably productive, especially in feminist circles, for it concentrates on the importance of life prior to the male-inflected Oedipal stage, and, in particular, stresses the significance of the mother in early development. Aside from this, Klein was one of the first psychoanalysts to work with actual children, rather than, as Freud did, rely on adult reports. Klein watched children playing, inferring their internal states from the way they interacted with toys, just as Freud interpreted his grandson manipulating the cotton reel. With toys, Klein believed, children played out their fantasies, their relationship to their world.

The breast was the first object, onto which the child projected two basic emotions, love and hate, in what Klein intimidatingly calls the 'paranoid-schizoid' position. The breast is thereby split into two objects: the good and the bad. The former is that which is proffered on demand, satisfying the child, whereas the latter represents the child's anger at its removal and, therefore, it has an aggressive, destructive potential. This idea of separating one's feelings into distinct parts can be seen in many literary works. As has often been noted of fairy tales, for example, a good fairy, or godmother, is often counterpoised with a malevolent equivalent (as in 'Sleeping Beauty'); and, as noted earlier, in *Peter Pan* we have the good Mr Darling juxtaposed with the more wicked Hook.

Margaret and Michael Rustin (1987) have read a number of children's fictional works in object relations terms, showing how the authors have represented particular emotional states using objects. Sometimes these are actual dolls and toys, as in Lynne Reid Banks's *The Indian in the Cupboard* (1980) or Margery Williams Bianco's *The Velveteen Rabbit* (1922; see Daniels, 1990), but in others the objects are sentient beings that help mediate family relationships by displacing a child's concerns; thus, in E. B. White's *Charlotte's Web* (1952), Fern's relationship with her parents is worked through by having Fern mother her own child, the pig Wilbur, whom we see, in the fantasy, negotiating his own place in the world thanks to his relationship with the spider, Charlotte.

D. W. Winnicott's (1896–1971) more popular and digestible version of object relations theory introduced the phrase 'transitional object' to depict these symbolic containers that are, simultaneously, 'me' and 'not me', hovering between subject and object. The most obvious examples stand in place of the breast, such as thumbs and comfort blankets, which help the child let go of the mother. Like the cotton reel, such objects bridge the gap, making absence tolerable. The child thus feels that she has some control over the world, while also learning how to deal with close relationships. Winnicott argues that it is through such transitional objects that social play later emerges, and, beyond that, artistic activity. As Winnicott once expressed it, 'in considering the place of these phenomena in the life of the child one must recognize the central position of Winnie the Pooh [*sic*]' (1980: xi); that is, the teddy bear who, with his oral fixation, could be seen as a projection of the child's need to feel some connection with the primary caregiver – something that is neatly captured in that capitalized, close homophone of the mother: 'HUNNY' (Milne, 1965: 57).

As others have pointed out, Winnicott is unusual in that his psychoanalytical model finds a place for 'art' other than as a sublimated form of libido (i.e. psychosexual material elevated and transformed into a socially acceptable form). However, his model has also been criticized for having a fairly stable sense of self present from the outset. Also, in common with a Jungian approach, object relations theory pays little attention to the role of language in the process of identity formation. It is these shortcomings that Lacan's model is seen to respond to, in his controversial 'return to Freud'.

The Lacanian, poststructuralist approach

Certainly, since the 1970s Lacan's psychoanalytical approach has proved one of the most popular with literary critics – and with many therapists too. Its attention to language, which Freud was also keenly attuned to, undoubtedly found it favour, but beyond that, Lacan (1977: 20) suggests that we are linguistic beings with the unconscious itself being 'structured like a language'. However, unlike some of the stand-alone insights of others (Jung's archetypes and Winnicott's transitional objects), Lacan's system requires more extensive elaboration.

Jacques Lacan (1901–81) suggests that humans are unique in existing in two realms that stand outside our biological existence in what he terms 'the Real'. The Real is the unnamed stuff of the universe: the realm where animals eat, sleep, reproduce, and so on. For us, in contrast, such activities are always already overlain with language (except, perhaps, for neonates). So sleeping means 'bedtime', a period suffused in ritual (including the bedtime story, and the numerous stories that instruct the child on what bedtime is meant to involve) (e.g. Brown's *Goodnight Moon*, 1947; Fox's *Time for Bed*, 1993; see Chou, 2009). Humans, therefore, only experience the Real indirectly, tangentially. The two other realms emerge sequentially, but are thereafter always with us. First, there is the Imaginary, which famously emerges at the mirror stage, when the child sees itself reflected as a whole, and out of which its ego emerges. However, as Lacan points out, the child at this time is anything but coherent. Its image of wholeness is therefore a misrepresentation and, significantly, something external to the child. Our egos, likewise, are false idealizations.

The move into the last realm, the Symbolic, represents a further externalization, in that language now irrevocably comes to represent our individuality. And language, of course, pre-exists us, so rather than us finding words to express our unique experience, words give us the very terms from which our experience is constructed; in short, as 'subjects' who can say *I*, we are 'subjected'. This latter shift occurs at the Oedipal stage, which Lacan rereads metaphorically: it is not that the male child is threatened with actual castration if he does not temper his desire for the mother; rather, we are all – boys and girls alike – required to move away from this more sensuous realm (the Real) to one where words, instead, formulate our wants. It is a poor substitute (think of the letters, 'Mum', replacing the physical and sensual maternal presence) but one that we must all accept as 'subjects' of society (under patriarchal Law). Castration, then, involves no surgical procedures, but a more metaphorical notion of being 'cut off' from immediate pleasures, being confined to signifiers instead (separate words, slicing and dicing experience). In formulating this psychoanalytic process, Lacan drew on the linguist Ferdinand de Saussure's conceptualization of the verbal sign, which ties together a particular sound (a signifier) with a particular meaning (a signified). Whereas Saussure prioritized the signified (a conceptual representation of the thing itself), Lacan suggests that things themselves are lost, unrealizable, such that all we have are relatively empty signifiers (as seen with 'Mum', above). This is what drives humans, as we strive to overcome the sense of lack we experience, desiring to re-attain the Eden we think we once inhabited.

Images of wholeness therefore beguile us, which is what advertising campaigns trade on ('Buy X and you too could be like this!') and, of course, in language we try to articulate our desires, moving from one signifier to the next, forever trying to repair our sense of incompleteness. This is what literary works temporarily proffer. For example, Anthony Browne's *Willy the Wimp* (1984) 'buys' into just such an imaginary notion of masculinity, demonstrating how we are strung between these three separate realms of existence: Willy's construction in the Symbolic as a 'wimp', as opposed to his imaginary sense of being an alpha-male, a superhero; and then his undoing in the Real as he collides with a lamppost.

To make this more concrete, let us return to Toad in *The Wind in the Willows* (1908). Incarcerated by friends, Toad creates imaginary scenarios (involving bedroom chairs) of driving motor cars, before he then steals one, his ego triumphant: 'he was Toad once more, Toad at his best and highest, Toad the terror, the traffic-queller, the Lord of the lone trail ...' (1925: 85). As with the advertising copy mentioned above, Toad has underwritten his imaginary ideal with apposite phrases. But the narrator then builds on this image (if only ironically) in the Symbolic, characterizing Toad as 'a criminal of deepest guilt and matchless artfulness and resource' (1925: 87), using the mock-medieval language of Victorian romance. The barge woman Toad encounters, though, will have none of this, seeing him only as a 'horrid, nasty, crawly Toad', whom she flings by two of his four legs (not arms) into the river (139). For Toad, this might seem an intrusion of the Real, as he is reduced to bestiality and engulfed by the elements. However, the Real is only experienced momentarily (it stands outside language) and, of course, the irrepressible Toad quickly bounces back. It is also worth noting that the discourses of the Symbolic are at their most invisible for those who stand closest to the establishment and its institutions; thus Toad, for all his bestiality, can pass as 'a very well-known, respected, distinguished' being (138) whereas, for a lower-class female, the Symbolic is more porous, just as it is to the young boy in Andersen's (1974) 'The Emperor's New Clothes'.

The Real, of course, can only be alluded to, for it resists symbolization. But one might argue that Grahame seeks to capture its flavour in 'The Piper at the Gates of Dawn', with its glimpses of the sublime, rendering Rat and Mole virtually speechless: 'it is the real, the unmistakable thing, simple – passionate – perfect –' (99), Rat stutters before forgetfulness supervenes. Generally, though, the Real is felt only in those gaps between signifiers, to which the title itself alludes, which Mole, 'with his ear to the reed-stems', hears early on: 'something of what the wind went whispering so constantly among them' (14). Lacan also maintains that certain areas of the body (part-objects) are more likely to generate a feeling of the Real because they gesture towards the loss of the mother: a rem(a)inder, simultaneously a reminder and a remainder. The mouth is one such part (prioritized in Freud's oral phase), revealing the body's porosity, its lack of wholeness; moreover, it is a place where our dependence on the Real is manifest (as we imbibe sustenance) but also where our distinctiveness as beings in the Symbolic is demonstrated: a disembodied voice utters signifiers, but is itself dependent on the opening and closing of the Real mouth. Grahame seems to be trying to capture this ineffable sense, with the wind blowing through the reed stems evoking the piper, Pan himself, blowing through his reed pipes – the wind being a common trope of Romantic writers seeking to represent the spiritual.

To recap, then, we are creatures on the borders of three orders, which often pull us in different directions. For Lacan, it is precisely our loss of the Real – a result of our status as 'speaking-beings' – that gives us a sense of lack, which in turn mobilizes our desire to attain wholeness once again. In Grahame's text such desires manifest themselves in the characters' perennial attempts to attain a satisfactory sense of home ('*Dulce Domum*', as chapter 5 is called), starting with Mole at the novel's beginning and ending with the recapture of Toad Hall, the account of which itself parodies a hero's return home, with Toad and his friends' exploits in wresting his home from the Wild Wooders mirroring (in this imaginary and second-hand way) Ulysses' return to oust the suitors of his wife, Penelope (the chapter entitled 'The Return of Ulysses').

To take this further, we should recall Freud's interpretation of his grandson's *fort–da* experience, attempting to come to terms with his mother's departure by repeatedly dismissing then re-summoning a cotton reel. In Grahame's novel, we have a similar oscillation between home and away, as the characters strive to locate that perfect home (oneness with the mother, of course, representing our original abode), either in terms of actual residences (in Mole's case) or in what seem more desirable visions of a fulfilled existence, such as we witness with the old Sea Rat (himself a Siren figure) tempting Ratty. The novel, then, displays repeated attempts to regain this sense of wholeness. Notably, the original 1908 text had but one illustration, a frontispiece with a quotation from Genesis: 'And a river went out from Eden'. However, the Eden that Grahame's text seeks to recapture is a rather distorted one – in which Eve, the feminine, has been repressed. It is of note, for example, that there is no Penelope waiting at Toad Hall: it is a bachelor gathering, just as the Sea Rat is a male Siren. In fact, male characters are emblematic of their species throughout the text.

In order to explore this repression, it is necessary to introduce two mechanisms that Lacan took from Freud's theory of how dreams revealed their unconscious content: 'condensation' and 'displacement'. The former process is evident in puns, which tie together several meanings in one word, or in literary creations where signifiers cluster and enrich each other thematically. Thus, Lyra Belacqua's first name suggests both a liar ('Silvertongue') and someone accomplished at storytelling (the instrument, the lyre, originally accompanied recitations, hence the word 'lyrics'); Belacqua, on the other hand, is a denizen of Purgatory in Dante's *The Divine Comedy*, who repeatedly puts off confessing the truth of his life, commenting that the 'bird of God' would not let him through (and, beyond that, Belacqua is thought to have been based by Dante on a Florentine lute player – the lyre being a type of lute). All this, of course, feeds into Pullman's narrative; indeed, these signifiers might themselves have suggested certain narrative possibilities to Pullman. As for displacement, this is in some ways the opposite, where attributes are dispersed rather than concentrated. We have seen examples of this in the way that good and bad qualities are split between different characters. But Lacan's innovation was to see both these processes (condensation and displacement) as equivalent to the workings of metaphor and metonymy. By looking closely at the way these literary figures operate, he thought that we could discern the unconscious workings of a text.

Home, then, stands as a metaphor for that unattainable Eden, for a sense of oneness, for what Rat calls 'the real, the unmistakable thing' (99) – which is also represented in that more amorphous yearning for what the reed stems convey, and in the stories told by the river (running out of Eden, of course). Via nature, we might say that this longing is shown in a more metonymic way; for home, of course, metaphoric of the mother, is as readily metonymic of her (that womb with a view). However, as intimated above, some of these associations the text seeks to repress. It is significant, for example, that even Mother Nature seems to have been downgraded in this book, displaced by Pan, with his 'rippling muscles' and 'shaggy limbs' (94–5), which is also how the river is depicted, as a 'sleek, sinuous, full-bodied animal' beside which Mole trots, as 'by the side of a man' telling stories, as it flows down to the sea (3) – the conventionally female sea, of course, being represented by the male Sea Rat. And, predictably, the 'baby otter', Otter's son, is found 'nestling' with Pan (95).

Mother Nature is reduced to a more inert presence that needs animating by the male, just as Pan blows through its reeds (and, in myth, he fashioned his pan pipes out of reed stems, one of which was the transformed body of the nymph, Syrinx, initially turned into a reed to protect her). This displacement of the feminine is most apparent in the Wild Wood, which is depicted as an unruly realm with its fickle seasonality: 'bare and entirely leafless ... in her annual slumber', having 'kicked the clothes off' and been 'stripped of ... finery' (31–2).

As I've commented elsewhere, the imagery used to depict the Wood is evocative of 'a predatory, feminine sexuality' (Rudd, 2010), almost *vagina dentata*-like, with much talk of '[h]oles, hollows, pools, pitfalls, and other black menaces' (37). These 'holes made ugly mouths at [Mole] on either side', before he sees a 'little evil wedge-shaped face, looking out at him from a hole', to be followed by 'hundreds' more – that is, holes with faces. The imagery is not just sexual, either, but seems to mount in excitement:

> He passed another hole, and another, and another; and then – yes! – no! – yes! certainly a little narrow face, with hard eyes, had flashed up for an instant from a hole, and was gone. ... Then suddenly, and as if it had been so all the time, every hole, far and near, and there were hundreds of them, seemed to possess its face, coming and going rapidly, all fixing on him glances of malice and hatred; all hard-eyed and evil and sharp.   (33)

At the novel's end, of course, it is stressed that this lawless realm has been subjugated: 'the mother-weasels would bring their young ones to the mouths of their holes, and say, pointing, "Look baby! There goes the great Mr Toad!"' (184). For these disturbingly mouth-like holes are also homes, and if they evoke that part-object in the Real, they also evoke our original home, the womb, which Freud would turn to in discussing the Uncanny, along with the female genitals and their transformation into Medusa-like heads, as evoking a particular form of fear, disturbing precisely because of its familiarity, its home-liness (hence *unheimlich*).

Not only is the mouth evoked here, but so too is another thing that Lacan saw as disturbing, gesturing towards the Real; for, just as the mouth produces a disembodied voice, so the eye emits a seemingly disembodied gaze: a look that seems to emanate from no specific place, which thereby upsets our sense of autonomy. Mole certainly experiences this, with the whole Wild Wood seeming to have its look fixed on him (the mole, of course, being almost blind, is a particularly apposite creature). It is the nearest thing to a sense of the uncanny that this text evokes, and once again, makes the female pres-ence itself *unheimlich*, Medusa-like and repressed. And, as other commenta-tors have pointed out, the females that do actually appear in the book are marginal figures.

Before concluding this reading, Julia Kristeva's (1941–) work needs mentioning for, like Klein, she is particularly concerned with the child–mother relationship. Her influential concept, the abject (Kristeva, 1982), is of note here, for she argues that the young child needs to definitively assert her distinctness from the mother by abjecting all that is associated with the maternal; that is, stuff that might get in the way of the child's crystallizing body image: milky, viscous liquids, bodily secretions and the like, which become increasingly distasteful, disturbing. Certainly, in Grahame's work the feminine seems to be abjected, with the Wild Wood and its '[h]oles', 'black menaces' and so on most powerfully revealing the dangers of the unconscious, the disarming gaze of the repressed feminine; hence the Wild Wood's taming at the novel's end.

I have spent some time exploring *The Wind in the Willows* from a Lacanian perspective, but clearly, one could look at it from other psychoanalytical stances, too. Thus an ego psychology interpretation would be more likely to see Toad as, finally, less id-like, his fragile ego reining him in with the help of superegoic 'adults' like Badger and Ratty. A Jungian approach would also, no doubt, find the extrovert Toad interesting, but as more of a trickster archetype like his ancestor, Ulysses. Toads, as amphibious, betwixt-and-between figures, are well suited to this role, hence Toad's facility in morphing and disguising himself. Once again, one can see a journey towards individuation, in which Toad can be fruitfully contrasted with the more introverted Mole. From a Kleinian perspective, the book very interestingly seems to explore the paranoid-schizoid position, with Toad alternately demonstrating his passion for objects and his wish to destroy them; moreover, such recklessness and self-centredness also suggest a profound narcissism. Once again, his eventual return home might then be read in terms of an attempt at making what Klein calls 'reparation'.

Conclusion

As should now be apparent, a psychoanalytic approach is often little different from others: it too attends to character, situation and language. However, its distinctiveness lies in its commitment to a subtext. Whereas Freud sometimes located this subtext within the author, or an author's characters, elsewhere he did try to explain how the text itself operates on us (e.g. in 'The "Uncanny"' – see also Box 13.1). It is this latter notion that other psychoanalytical theorists have taken up, particularly Lacan, arguing that we too are texts. But we are not simply that. The Symbolic, then, as its name avers, will always seek to encompass us in terms that do not quite fit; we have the feeling that a more meaningful existence – allusive, occluded – beckons: where categories and boundaries are not respected, where desires overspill grammatically constrained sentences with their artificially separated words. A psychoanalytic approach is therefore relentless in pursuing the subtext; except that this term is itself inadequate: real meanings are not hidden as though beneath a trapdoor. More profitably, we might speak of an omni-text, whose centre is everywhere and circumference nowhere; where the unsaid and the marginal – hinting at more meaning-full assemblages – free us from our more conventional ways of categorizing the world and offer, instead, an illicit fulfilment of our desires. Books, in short, can deliver a sense of extra-textual perception.

It is not surprising, then, that Lacan saw Descartes' claim, 'I think therefore I am', as misconceived. More correctly, he suggested, it thinks (i.e. the id, the Unconscious) where I am not (i.e. the ego), but where it might be fruitful for me to be. Literary texts, certainly, allow us room to inhabit such spaces.

WORKS CITED AND FURTHER READING

Children's Books

Andersen, Hans Christian. 'The Emperor's New Clothes'; 'The Little Mermaid'. In *The Complete Fairy Tales and Stories*, trans. Erik Christian Haugaard. London: Gollancz, 1974.

Banks, Lynne Reid. *The Indian in the Cupboard*, illus. Robin Jacques. London: Dent, 1980.

Barrie, J. M. *Peter Pan*. Harmondsworth: Penguin, 1986; orig. *Peter and Wendy*, 1911.

Bianco, Margery Williams. *The Velveteen Rabbit, or How Toys Become Real*, illus. William Nicholson. New York: Doubleday, 1922. http://digital.library.upenn.edu/women/williams/rabbit/rabbit.html.

Brown, Margaret Wise. *Goodnight Moon*, illus. Clement Hurd. New York: Harper & Bros., 1947.

Browne, Anthony. *Hansel and Gretel*. London: Julia MacRae, 1981.

Browne, Anthony. *Willy the Wimp*. London: Julia MacRae, 1984.

Collodi, Carlo. *The Adventures of Pinocchio*, trans. Ann Lawson Lucas. Oxford: Oxford University Press, 2009; orig. 1883.

Dahl, Roald. *Danny, the Champion of the World*. Harmondsworth: Penguin, 1977.

Dahl, Roald. *The Enormous Crocodile*. London: Jonathan Cape, 1978.

Dahl, Roald. *Matilda*. London: Penguin, 1989.

Dahl, Roald. *The Twits*. London: Penguin, 1982.

Fox, Mem. *Time for Bed*, illus. Jane Dyer. Boston, MA: Houghton Mifflin Harcourt, 1993.

Grahame, Kenneth. *The Wind in the Willows*. London: Methuen, 1925; orig. 1908.

Griffiths, Andy. *The Day My Bum Went Psycho*, illus. Nicole Arroyo. London: Pan, 2001.

Grimm, Brothers. 'Hansel and Gretel', 'Snow White', 'Little Red Cap', 'Brier Rose [Sleeping Beauty]. In *The Complete Fairy Tales of the Brothers Grimm*, trans. with introduction Jack Zipes, illus. John B. Gruelle. New York and London: Bantam, 1987.

Le Guin, Ursula. *A Wizard of Earthsea*. Berkeley, CA: Parnassus Press, 1968.

Milne, A. A. *Winnie-the-Pooh*, illus. E. H. Shepard. London: Methuen, 1965; orig. 1926.

Pullman, Philip. *His Dark Materials*. London and New York: Scholastic, 2008.

Reiner, Rob (dir.). *Stand by Me*. Culver City, CA: Columbia Pictures, 1986.

Sendak, Maurice. *In the Night Kitchen*. New York: Harper & Row, 1970.

Seuss, Dr. *The Cat in the Hat*. New York: Random House, 1957.

White, E. B. *Charlotte's Web*, illus. Garth Williams. New York: Harper & Bros., 1952.

Willems, Mo. *Don't Let the Pigeon Drive the Bus*. New York: Hyperion Press, 2003.

Critical Texts

Bettelheim, Bruno. *The Uses of Enchantment: The Meaning and Importance of Fairy Tales*. Harmondsworth: Penguin, 1991; orig. 1976.

Brooks, Peter. *Reading for the Plot: Design and Intention in Narrative*. Oxford: Clarendon Press, 1984.

Campbell, Joseph. *The Hero with a Thousand Faces*. New York: Pantheon, 1949.

Chou, Wan-Hsiang. 'Co-sleeping and the Importation of Picture Books about Bedtime'. *Children's Literature in Education*, 40.1 (2009), 19–32.

Daniels, Steven V. 'The Velveteen Rabbit: a Kleinian Perspective'. *Children's Literature*, 18 (1990), 17–30.

Egan, Michael. 'The Neverland of Id: Barrie, Peter Pan, and Freud'. *Children's Literature*, 10 (1982), 37–55.

Franz, Marie-Louise von. *The Interpretation of Fairy Tales*, 2nd edn. Boston, MA: Shambhala, 1970)

Freud, Sigmund. 'Beyond the Pleasure Principle'. In *On Metapyschology*, trans. James Strachey (pp. 269–338). London: Penguin, 1987; orig. 1920.

Freud, Sigmund. 'The "Uncanny"'. In *Art and Literature: Jensen's Gradiva, Leonardo da Vinci and Other Works*, trans. James Strachey (pp. 339–76). London: Penguin, 1985; orig. 1919.

Frye, Northrop. *Anatomy of Criticism: Four Essays*. Princeton, NJ: Princeton University Press, 1957.

Gilbert, Sandra M., and Susan Gubar. *The Madwoman in the Attic: The Woman Writer and the Nineteenth-Century Literary Imagination*. New Haven, CT: Yale University Press, 1979.

Jung, Carl Gustav. *The Portable Jung*, ed. Joseph Campbell. London and New York: Penguin, 1976.

Kay, Ellen. *The Century of the Child*. New York: Putnam's, 1909; orig. 1900.

Kristeva, Julia. *Powers of Horror: An Essay on Abjection*, trans. Leon S. Roudiez. New York: Columbia University Press, 1982.

Lacan, Jacques. *The Four Fundamental Concepts of Psycho-analysis*, trans. Alan Sheridan. London: Hogarth/Institute of Psycho-analysis, 1977.

Mulvey, Laura. 'Visual Pleasure and Narrative Cinema'. *Screen*, 16.3 (1975), 6–18. In *Visual and Other Pleasures*. Bloomington: Indiana University Press, 1989.

Phillips, Adam. *Promises, Promises: Essays on Literature and Psychoanalysis*. London: Faber and Faber, 2000.

Phillips, Adam. *Winnicott*. London: Fontana, 1988.

Phillips, Robert (ed.). *Aspects of Alice: Lewis Carroll's Dreamchild as Seen through the Critics' Looking-glasses, 1865–1971*. London: Gollancz, 1972.

Rollin, Lucy, and Mark I. West. *Psychoanalytic Responses to Children's Literature*. Jefferson, NC and London: McFarland, 1999.

Rowland, Susan (ed.). *Psyche and the Arts: Jungian Approaches to Music, Architecture, Literature, Painting and Film*. London: Routledge, 2008.

Rudd, David. 'Deus ex Natura or Non-Stick Pan?: Competing Discourses in Kenneth Grahame's *The Wind in the Willows*'. In Jackie Horne and Donna R. White (eds), *Kenneth Grahame's* The Wind in the Willows: *Children's Classics at 100* (pp. 3–21). Oxford: Scarecrow Press, 2010.

Rudd, David. *Reading the Child in Children's Literature: An Heretical Approach*. London: Palgrave Macmillan, 2013.

Rustin, Margaret, and Michael Rustin. *Narratives of Love and Loss: Studies in Modern Children's Fiction*. London and New York: Verso, 1987.

Winnicott, D. W. *Playing and Reality*. Harmondsworth: Penguin, 1980; orig. 1971.

Wullschläger, Jackie. *Hans Christian Andersen: The Misunderstood Storyteller*. New York and London: Routledge, 2002.

NOTE

1. Towards the end of his reading, Bettelheim slips in, parenthetically, that '[i]t is females – the stepmother and the witch – who are the inimical forces' (1991: 164), though his interpretation generally presumes a more beneficent maternal figure.

Reading Contemporary Picturebooks

Judith Graham

Illustration is everywhere, not only in children's books but in books for all ages; in comics and magazines; in advertisements; on posters; on food and other packaging; in brochures; and on the television and computer screen. Though many of these outlets for illustration seem utterly contemporary, illustration has been around for a long time, perhaps over 3000 years if we think of Egyptian papyrus rolls. In its purist sense, illustration is a series of pictures connected to a text and 'illuminating' it in every sense of that word. Illustration in children's books may be simply decorative, but more often it aims to interpret or supply narrative meaning that is not present or accessible in written text alone. Two succinct definitions of the picturebook (rather than the illustrated book) are useful to hold in the mind. (I write 'picturebook' as one word; it is frequently written both as 'picture book' and as 'picture-book', although 'picturebook' seems to be more frequently used nowadays.)

> A picturebook is a text, illustrations, total design; an item of manufacture and a commercial product; a social, cultural, historical document; and foremost an experience for a child. As an art form, it hinges on the inter-dependence of pictures and words, on the simultaneous display of two facing pages, and on the drama of the turning page. (Bader, 1976: 1)

> Picturebooks – books intended for young children which communicate information or tell stories through a series of many pictures combined with relatively slight text or no text at all – are unlike any other form of verbal or visual art. (Nodelman, 1988: vii)

Bader and Nodelman define the picturebook; the illustrated book usually has a written text that, while it may be enhanced by the illustrations, can survive without them and indeed may have existed without them for a great many years. Few, if any, picturebooks are republished with a different set of illustrations; illustrated texts frequently reappear with new illustrations, with *Alice's Adventures in Wonderland* perhaps topping the charts as the most frequently re-illustrated children's book. Though both are equally valid art forms and both have contributed significantly to children's literature, this chapter is primarily concerned with the picturebook rather than the illustrated book.

It would be wrong to imagine that reading a picturebook is a simple operation. When John Burningham's *Come Away from the Water, Shirley* was first published in 1977, it was apparent that many adults, expecting pictures to duplicate the written text, were bemused by the apparent mismatch and failed to see the more subtle interaction going on between word and picture. In this book, as in many picturebooks, the words are few and can be read in a short space of time, but the pictures need more time and scrutiny if their detail and meaning are to be perceived. Becoming alert to the way a written text constantly pushes the reader while a picture stops us in our tracks and slows down the reading is the first requirement for students in their appreciation of picturebooks. As Nodelman puts it: '[The] sort of ironic relationship between the sequential storytelling of words and the series of stopped moments we see in a sequence of pictures is, I believe, the essence of picturebook storytelling' (1988: 239).

It is also important to appreciate how very varied the picturebook can be. Pictures in reading schemes may intentionally show what the written text indicates ('here is a dog'; 'here is a ball') but most illustrators are more ambitious than that and will aim for the unusual or unexpected, a secondary story, a running gag, a surreal embroidering, incongruity, ambiguity and irony, even in books aimed at the youngest audience. Writers will also want to focus on what words can do best (what things and people are called, what people say and think, when things happen, what happened earlier or later – off-stage as it were) and eliminate language made superfluous by the illustration. Illustration, for its part, is better suited to creating mood and atmosphere, using colour, tone, light and dark; showing characters' clothes, faces and expressions of feeling; or representing their spatial relationship to one another and what places look like.

A popular picturebook, *Handa's Surprise* (1994) by Eileen Browne, exemplifies some of these points and is a good example of how the picturebook medium can be effectively exploited. As with Pat Hutchins's well-known *Rosie's Walk* (1968), it is a perfect example of the written text and the pictured text being balanced to provide different information. Handa is preparing a present of seven delicious fruits to take to her friend Akeyo in the next village. Off she goes, basket on head, speculating on which fruit Akeyo will like best. Unknown to her, and uncommented on by the narrator but seen by the reader, the pieces of fruit are filched from the basket by seven different animals.

Just as Handa arrives at Akeyo's village with her now empty basket, a goat breaks free from its tether and, after a series of small frames showing his headlong charge, butts a tangerine tree. The tangerines conveniently fall into the basket (the mound breaks through the frame to draw the reader's attention). Akeyo's delight at the gift of tangerines, her favourite fruit, is matched only by Handa's surprise. The delight that young readers experience in realizing what is happening ahead of Handa, and of the narrator, bonds them to the book and makes each rereading an exciting experience. In this book (and this is different from *Rosie's Walk*) the written text does something that it is difficult for pictures to do: it gives us Handa's thoughts. 'Will she like the spiky-leaved pineapple, the creamy green avocado or the tangy purple passion fruit?'

With such a wealth of picture and illustrated books available, it is necessary to try to impose an order if newcomers to the field are to have any chance of finding a way through. I have chosen to divide the field into four categories and within those categories to discuss a few titles in detail. The four categories are: books of pictures, novelty books, wordless books and picture storybooks.

Books of pictures

Into this category come those books with minimal written text, which are designed particularly for the inspection and enjoyment of the pictures. The written text is not only minimal; it is frequently a 'given', with little or no variation possible, as in the case of most alphabet and counting books. Concept books, designed to teach colours, shapes, materials, animals, and much else, also come into this category. While there are obvious restrictions in terms of what may be done with the written text in such books, the very constraint seems to attract and inspire illustrators. There are ABCs dating from the mid-eighteenth century (which is when we can say children's books began), and several of those created in the nineteenth century (Edward Lear's *Nonsense Alphabet* and Kate Greenaway's *Apple Pie ABC*, for instance) are still popular today. Currently, there are thousands of alphabet books and thousands of counting books and probably tens of thousands of concept books. Many of these are extraordinarily inventive and even approach being works of art. Many of the most talented illustrators are drawn to create an alphabet at some point in their careers and the originality on show is impressive.

These books may appear to be produced for the youngest children, but it should not be forgotten how much readers know and need to know if they are to enjoy books. The 'rules', codes and conventions for reading words and pictures have to be learnt (technical terms describing this process, which is unconscious in most readers, are found in Box 4.1). At six months, babies tend to chew their books, which explains why 'rag' books have come into being. Children may hold their books the 'wrong' way round, they may turn the pages from back to front and possibly turn several pages at a time. This is not only a question of manual dexterity; the appreciation that stories have a logical sequence, requiring readers to start at the beginning and look from top to bottom and from left to right (though not in all scripts), is a necessary aspect of a child's learning. Many children's books tell their stories through double-page spreads, which may not obviously be organized on the principles of left and right, so learning how to read these has to be mastered too.

BOX 4.1   VISUAL TERMINOLOGY

Bleed   A picture in a picturebook 'bleeds' or is 'bled' to the very edge of the paper when it has no frame and leaves no margin. The effect is to pull the reader more actively into the picture. See also *frame*.

Closure   Of particular relevance to comic strips, this refers to the way in which readers must make sense of (interpret) the gaps in information left between one frame and the next (McCloud, 1994: 60–93).

Double-page spread   An opening in a picturebook where the image spreads over the two facing pages. See also *page opening*.

Endpapers   The pages (in hardbacks) which are immediately inside the front and back covers. The story in a picturebook often starts or ends here, though the illustrator may use the endpapers decoratively or symbolically. Paperback picturebooks are sometimes, regrettably, published without the original endpapers.

Format   The physical size and shape of the book. 'Portrait' format is taller than it is wide; 'landscape' is wider than it is tall. The choice should be influenced by the nature of the illustration, with portrait more commonly used when a focus on character is required and landscape for when the setting is more important.

Frame   The border around an illustration, which may simply be the white margin of the page or can be a printed line, a drawn free-hand line or a decorated band. Often the separate illustrations on a page are called separate frames. When a picture bursts through a frame ('breaks the frame'), extra momentum and significance are added. 'Frame' is also used occasionally in a very different sense to indicate everything about a book that is not the text; in other words, those elements, such as the author's and illustrator's names, title, blurb, typographic aspects, publishing details, etc. which surround the book and package it. See also *peritext*.

Gutter   The grooved space at the centre of a book, created by the binding, where pages abut; the space between frames in a comic strip or between different frames on one page of a picturebook.

Page opening   Where the picture on the left is distinct from the picture on the right.

Page turn   Turning the page in a picturebook is a different experience from turning over the page in an unillustrated text; it requires the reader to pause and peruse the picture. At the same time, the written text (if there is one) – especially if the turn comes in the middle of a sentence – impels the reader to turn over. The text may sometimes foreshadow the next picture so that the reader is in a state of high anticipation as the page is turned. Turning the page may also reveal surprising information or effects. All of this creates a typical picturebook rhythm for the reader, whether reading aloud or silently.

Peritext   All the material that is not the text itself (see *frame* above). In a picturebook where the illustrations and written text together count as text, the peritext does not include the illustrations, though a case could be made for the peritext to include the cover illustration. Typically, the peritext is not in the author's nor in the illustrator's control and is the domain of designers, typographers, publishers, publicity and marketing people.

Pictorial/iconic sequence   Of particular relevance to comic strips, this refers to pictorial or iconic frames placed in a narrative sequence (as opposed to the self-contained frames you might find in illustrations).

Recto   The right-hand page of a book.

Speech bubble   Typically found in comic strips and graphic texts, this refers to dialogue which is contained within a stylized 'bubble' and which is usually superimposed onto pictorial images. Speech bubbles frequently break frames (see *frames*) and can be used to indicate who is speaking, or to convey sound.

Tone   The level of brightness, lightness or darkness used in coloured images.

Verso   The left-hand page of a book.

Viewpoint   The position from which the reader views the illustrations. There may be a static viewpoint, where the illustrations are seen from the same point throughout, or the illustrator may change the viewpoint from, perhaps, a high position where the scene is surveyed from above, to a low viewpoint, where the image dominates.

Many other intellectual/perceptual challenges face the young child. If we look out of a window, the view could be considered to make a picture. Yet it is utterly different from a printed image, particularly because everything is moving. How do we come to accept static representations? How do we learn that objects shown in two dimensions, sometimes far too small, occasionally too big, stand for those objects in real life? Why do we accept heavy lines drawn around items, the incompleteness of some items, the fact that backgrounds may be absent so that the characters appear to float in space?

A further challenge is that the child is asked to accept things that are never normally encountered in life. Perhaps more than half the output of children's books features animals or toys as characters, often in clothing, usually speaking, living in recognizable human houses and behaving rather as humans do. And then there is a whole cast of witches, monsters, dragons, goblins and others who are pictured for us but which have parallels, if at all, only in our heads. Even when children are the main characters, they may seem to exist without adults to care for them, and they often do impossible things. Of course, such books appeal to children for a variety of reasons to do with their inner lives and their delight in topsy-turvydom; nevertheless, the taking on board of these facets of picturebooks has to be learnt.

Helen Oxenbury is an author and illustrator who, in the 50-plus years that she has been at work, has created several classic books for babies and several award-winning books for older children. Her *ABC of Things* (1967) encapsulates many of the characteristics of the book of pictures. The organizing principle of the alphabet is probably lost on most of the children who are looking at the book, though naming the pictured items will certainly be a game that develops. The primary interest is the pictures. The left-hand page shows the upper- and lower-case letter 'A', the right-hand page shows a large, exquisitely drawn apple with an ant crawling on it. The words, 'ant' and 'apple' are given at the bottom of the left-hand page. So far, this is a standard ABC approach.

But Helen Oxenbury is a narrative illustrator, and even in that first simple image, which combines the items, there is the germ of a story. 'B' follows, with 'baby', 'badger', 'baker', 'bear' and 'bird'. The image shows the weariest of bakers submitting to the other creatures, who swarm all over him. Oxenbury is guiding the child to see cause (four demanding creatures) and effect (fatigue), a skill that will be necessary in reading texts in the future. 'C' has a cow and a cat waiting in pleasant anticipation, bibs in place, for a crow to bring a cake with candles. And so we go on. Every now and again the image covers the two pages of an opening, changing the rhythm of the book agreeably. There is no connection between pages, so making narrative links between the openings is not required of the young reader. But the book goes beyond the average ABC book in terms of the narrative interest within each picture, in the surprising combinations, the humour and the careful draughtsmanship.

Counting is something children do even before they learn the alphabet, so inviting a child into the world of numbers and counting has always interested illustrators. Mitsumasa Anno is one of Japan's leading illustrators and designers and, as well as an ingenious alphabet book, which has the designated letter apparently but impossibly fashioned from wood, he has produced *Anno's Counting Book* (1977). There is a simplicity to the design of this book, with each double-page spread exemplifying the numerals up to 12. Every picture, neatly framed and drawn and therefore read from a fixed position, shows a landscape bisected by a river but, as the numbers increase, so do the numbers of children, adults, birds, buildings, trees, animals and much else. Child beholders need to bring what they have counted, sorted, classified or grouped from one picture to the next. So, on page one, the reader identifies a single sun, a single house, a single boy and a single girl, but for the number two, the memory of what has happened on the previous page needs to be evoked so that when the picture shows that a church has been built, it is now necessary to talk about two *buildings*. Similarly, the boy and the girl now count as two *children*, and Anno has helpfully grouped them together. Frequently, as the numbers mount, the image shows, for example, two cats facing three cats, so that there is an opportunity not only to count but also to add. As well as one-to-one correspondences, groups and sets, there are the changing seasons, and human activities to observe. Those familiar with Anno's wordless travel books will know that it is worth poring over every picture to detect additional narrative details. For instance, just before the page turns from '7' to '8', readers can spot the builders who will construct building number eight, looking at their plan.

An intriguing concept book, which could also be discussed in the category of wordless picturebooks below since the title is the only written text, is *The Colors* (1991) by the Swiss illustrator Monique Felix. Some readers will already know the small mouse who is the main character in Felix's previous titles. Trapped in the books, he needs to nibble his way to freedom. In *The Colors*, he nibbles his way *into* the book (the hard cover has a tangible hole and teeth marks) and through the page to find he is alongside the art materials of a young girl whom we can see leaving the room. Colours, first of all the three primary colours, are introduced to the reader by the small mouse, who squeezes oils from the tubes of paint and then runs over to the empty left-hand page with his loaded paintbrush. With great effort, he squeezes two tubes together to make green, then orange and then purple. He dunks himself in the jam jar of water and escapes through his hole in the page just before the girl returns – with a cat who looks as if she can smell mouse!

In addition to the understanding about how pictures and books work, which children need to have acquired in order to enter a text, they must also realize that here, although the mouse is shown several times in a single picture, this does not mean that there are several mice in the story. Moreover, there are gaps between the pictures: not every race across the page is shown; children must fill in the unpictured events. The perspective has to be understood: the door through which the girl disappears and reappears is tiny, as the viewpoint is from the nearby table top. Perhaps most challenging is the conceit of the drawn hole that the mouse has nibbled. Child readers cannot poke a finger through it (as in Eric Carle's *The Very Hungry Caterpillar*, 1968) but must read the delicate pencil lines as representing a hole.

The conceit of eating through the very pages (including the cover) that the reader turns; the running mouse leading the eye from paint box on the right and empty page on the left; the playing with perspective; the tension building up as we see the mess the mouse is making; the astonishment, mischief and delight present in the mouse's expression; this interplay between the book's form and design and its narrative content is a great achievement.

Novelty books

Into this category come those books where the reader lifts flaps, pulls tabs, spins discs, reveals three-dimensional panoramas on the turn of the page, removes items from integrated pockets or envelopes, unfolds hinged pages, looks through holes, turns over half-pages and engages with the book in many another active way. 'Movable' is the more accurate term for those books where the reader physically manipulates a device in the book. Such books come closer to toys than other books, though these are often more fragile than toys, and the best of such books are those in which the paper engineering is not merely clever, but closely linked to the story.

Some of the most successful novelty books are designed for very small children and have simple flaps, holes or half-pages. Rod Campbell's *Dear Zoo* (1982), Jan Ormerod's *Peek-a-boo!* (1997) and Lucy Cousins's *Where Does Maisy Live?* (2000) are all small masterpieces, principally because the folded paper flap is integral to the story. So, each animal that is sent to the narrator in *Dear Zoo* arrives in its own crate/box/basket, and the reader must reveal its occupant before sending it back. Jan Ormerod's babies are playing the timeless game of peep-bo and so, to see their faces, the reader must peel back the towel, the dress, the quilt, the teddy, the gloved hands, the bib. Looking for Maisy involves opening up the henhouse, pigsty, kennel and stable before she is found in her house.

Allan and Janet Ahlberg, with *The Jolly Postman* (1986), created a hugely significant, multilayered novelty book which seemed to have everything to engage the reader: rhyming text, fairy-tale characters, extra story to pore over in the illustrations, jokes – both visual and verbal – and, above all, a wonderful series of letters, circulars, little books, postcards, birthday cards, even paper money that can be extracted from the pages, which are folded to resemble envelopes. Knowledge of the textual references increases pleasure in this book, since, then, such details as Baby Bear's repaired chair or Jack's paper plaster can be searched for in the illustrations, but the book and its sequels also create a curiosity about these traditional stories which a parent or teacher can satisfy. The Ahlbergs conceived of this book after noting their daughter Jessica's keen interest in the mail that came through the door every morning; the book nicely builds on this cultural activity. It is a pleasure to see that, since Janet's early death, Jessica has become Allan's illustrator. Their recent *Goldilocks* (2012) begins with the standard Goldilocks story and then launches into ever more absurd alternative versions. It carries on the tradition of intertextual references, inventive layout, parody, books within books, a delight in excess, interactive invitations and much else.

In the same vein as the Ahlbergs' work, though in no sense derivative, is Cressida Cowell's *Little Bo Peep's Library Book* (1999). A replica of a date-stamping page is on the first endpaper, fixed at the top as in all the best library books, and by the end of the book readers have taken down from the shelves several real books: a cookery book, *Basic Little Girl Cookery*, which interests the wolf, who has his eye on Bo Peep; *Who Stole the Tarts?*, which the Queen is sadly studying; and *How to Find Sheep* (by A. Shepherd). Each of these little books is fully developed and by the end, Bo Peep has had her library book stamped, has returned home, read it and found her sheep (observant readers will have seen that the sheep have always been behind Bo Peep). Cultural and literary references and jokes abound, and understatement (the wolf's tail is trailed before we see him) and overstatement (*scores* of sheep follow Bo Peep home) add to the richness of the text. Once again, the novelty book is able to draw on literature, cultural events and activities to engage young readers; perhaps for those who are not library users, this book might even establish the practice.

One problem with novelty books is that a tension can be created between the narrative, which wants to go forward, and the need to lift flaps and explore other effects. Certainly, the Ahlbergs' and Cowell's books require readers to interrupt the narrative to read the letters and the little books that are inserted into the body of the texts. But because (as with all picturebooks, which by their very nature require pausing to inspect images) these books are usually revisited frequently by their readers, the disturbance to the narrative flow may only be a problem on the first reading. In addition, it may be that the very interruptions build a facility in the reader for putting narrative on hold and then picking up the threads again. For these reasons, such books are read rather differently from other books; the insertions may be read later – or even before a straight run-through of the book. Children treasure these books; their 'loose parts' are not usually lost, as was initially feared, indicating both care for the books and a recognition that such parts are integral to the narrative.

Wordless books

Picturebooks with no words other than the title form a small fraction of the sum total of picturebooks, but they are a sub-genre that repays attention. Many illustrators are drawn to the wordless book, perhaps because they rise to the challenge to tell a story using only images, and perhaps because they enjoy the prospect that their books will be bought and read by those who respect and enjoy close examining of pictures. Because there are no words to alert readers to what is significant or absent in the pictures, the reading of wordless books is not as straightforward as is often assumed. Until children are experienced with story structures, they may perceive the task of recounting the story of a wordless book as detailing everything that is taking place, which is both confusing and exhausting. Work that I have done (Graham, 1998) with books such as Quentin Blake's *Clown* (1995) suggests that narrative inexperience rather than visual literacy is the problem for children. The inexperienced reader–viewer cannot always perceive significance and sequence and if they see, for instance, a person doing various chores, they will list them all. An experienced reader will group various pictured activities and say 'the woman is spring-cleaning'. With experience comes the ability to recognize both the general point being made and its place in the narrative.

That said, visual literacy is certainly important; illustrators of wordless books frequently employ a language that owes much to comic strip, film and animated cartoons that use a pictorial sequence (see Box 4.1). Thus a wordless picturebook may use many more frames than one with words in order to close narrative gaps. Use may also be made of a variety of 'shots' – long, medium and close-up – in order to focus the reader on the wider scene, the significant element and then the key emotions or transactions. The viewpoint will also change frequently, according to what needs to be emphasized, and colour may be used more deliberately than in a book with words in order to mark mood and atmosphere.

The wordless book *Sunshine* (1981) by Jan Ormerod contains 70 different pictures. Eighteen small frames alone go to showing a young girl, whose parents are finding it difficult to get up, dressing herself in the morning. That such a sequence enchants the reader is a tribute to Ormerod's accurate observation and shrewd decisions as to how to keep the images lively; for instance, many of the child's garments spill into an adjacent frame. To indicate movement, Ormerod shows her characters *against* a frame rather than *in* one, so that they seem to be forever leaving or entering the stage. In order to keep variety in the text, the illustrator also has several full-page pictures, usually of something relatively static, such as the parents asleep in bed. Other wordless picturebook creators who proceed through the use both of many small frames and intermittent much larger scenes, as if the camera has pulled back, are Peter Collington, Philippe Dupasquier, Shirley Hughes and Raymond Briggs.

Monique Felix's wordless books about mice trapped in books, *The Story of a Little Mouse Trapped in a Book* (1980) and *Another Story of a Little Mouse Trapped in a Book* (1983), use the whole (admittedly small) page, not the frame, to convey the wordless story. The mouse nibbles away at one side and pulls the detached page across to the left to reveal his coveted destination. By folding his detached page into an aeroplane or boat, depending on terrain, the mouse effects his escape. Playing with the book as physical object in order to tell of the mouse's escape makes Felix's titles nicely postmodern.

Australian illustrator Jeannie Baker has a different method again in her wordless book *Window* (1991). Each page turn (until the very last double-page spread) has the reader looking both at and through the same window, but the years are passing and gradual changes are recorded; the cumulative effect is sobering as nature gives way to an urbanized world. Baker's photographed collage constructions use several visual devices to indicate the passage of time – a child growing up (birthday cards on the window ledge, toys deteriorating and changing) as well as the changes beyond the window, where are shown, amongst other environmental destruction, the trees opposite felled and a sign appearing advertising firewood for sale.

David Wiesner is an American illustrator who has come to be associated with the wordless (or practically wordless) picturebook. *Tuesday* (1991) is typical of his work. It is useful to pause for a minute and consider how the reader crosses the threshold into a book such as this. We note the high quality of this production: large, landscape format; loose book jacket and elegant binding; fine quality paper and picture reproduction. Knowledge of the author–illustrator and of his previous wordless books may also be brought into play. Perhaps the starting point comes from the title, *Tuesday*, in its upper-case boldness, and linking it to the clock on the cover showing nine o'clock – what is meaningful about this exact time? At one level the gold 'Caldecott Medal' superimposed on the cover may be registered, alongside the solemn blurb: *The events recorded here are verified by an undisclosed source to have happened somewhere, U.S.A., on Tuesday. All those in doubt are reminded that there is always another Tuesday.* Aspects such as these comprise the peritext – the textual context for the story – and certainly influence entry into the book. *Tuesday* uses a cover illustration that is not one of the illustrations in the story, though once the book has been read, it's clear where it belongs in the narrative and we know how to read it, something impossible before the story has been digested. A cameo illustration on the back cover appears – again before the story is known – to be an innocent frog on a lily pad on a pond. These peritextual elements surround and promote the text and are frequently worth analysing in order to account for the overall impact of a book.

With *Tuesday*, the story begins before the title page (illustrators often need to exploit every one of the 32 pages a standard picturebook allows) as frogs begin to rise from the surface of a lake, each on its own lily pad magic carpet. Through the eyes of a passing turtle (images zoom in on the turtle's astonishment over three horizontal frames), the reader infers that this is indeed a surreal event. The frogs increase in number, become a flying flotilla, and have a wild night on the town. Against a double-page spread of the night, with birds resting on telegraph wires, Wiesner superimposes three horizontal frames of the frogs' increasing relish. Later, he uses three vertical frames against a full double-page spread of a clapboard house to show the frogs (one of whom flies like Superman after an encounter with laundry hung out to dry) entering an open sitting-room window and coming down a chimney. The page turn reveals them settling in (hovering actually) to watch TV around a sleeping granny (and a nonplussed cat). One of the frogs uses his prehensile tongue to change channels on the remote control. An encounter with a dog is also told in three horizontal strips, enabling the incident to keep its momentum and movement. Then, when the magic fades with the dawn, three vertical strips again, against a larger picture of the sun rising and illuminating the landscape, show the frogs falling, diving into their pond and then wondering what on earth all that was about. Two endings are offered. The first shows morning, and the countryside strewn with limp lily pads; the police and the media are out in force to investigate. The second, identified as the following Tuesday, depicts sunset and the shadow of a flying pig on the gable end of a barn. The final image is of pigs cavorting in the sky, visually spelling out that pigs might fly. The book repays study not only in its full range of cinematic techniques, but also in its understated, humorous detail, magical use of night-time colour and witty references to science fiction and super-hero literature.

Picture storybooks

Some children's picture storybooks can engender real tension and be profoundly moving; some can be created principally for humour and pleasure; some picturebooks leave readers reflecting on a sober message; some work well with no message at all. Some picturebooks form a composite text, with words and pictures sharing the telling; others retain a written text that is self-sufficient and use the illustrated text to add extra effects. Some picturebooks include painterly illustrations that could be framed and hung on a wall; some illustrators make skilful use of digital means to add photographic and other textures to the line drawing. In other words, this is a versatile medium capable of conveying narrative at a variety of levels and to different effect. Two titles, *Beegu* by Alexis Deacon (2003) and Lauren Child's *Who's Afraid of the Big, Bad Book?* (2002), illustrate a number of points.

Beegu is the story of a forlorn little yellow three-eyed alien who crash-lands on Earth and finds herself rejected or ignored by all save a playground of children. Ultimately her parents arrive from space to rescue her, and Beegu reports that any hope for Earth creatures lies with the small ones. The themes of this story are not uncommon in children's literature: abandonment, loneliness, rejection and separation. The device of placing a child character (or equivalent) alone in an alien environment enables an author to present the isolation from a viewpoint familiar to young readers who know what vulnerability feels like. In addition, in this story there is the theme of isolation through not being able to communicate – Beegu's language is not understood by the adults on Earth. These factors help the story function on several levels, including as a metaphor for the condition of refugee children.

In a story of fewer than 150 words, and without reverting to sentimentality, Alexis Deacon uses his illustrations to do three (at least) important things. First, he creates interest and concern in his reader for his main character. This starts with a striking cover where the luminous and distinct Beegu appears rather like a sticker applied against a background of dark sky and skyscrapers. Could she be a toy left out on the roof? When seen again on the title page, she is sleeping (or is she dead?) in a bleak and empty landscape, her spacecraft smouldering in the background. The mood is dark. It is a relief when she wakes with the dawn on the next opening; having been beguiled by her three eyes and floppy ears, the reader is prepared to accompany her through the book. She stands out on every page in her glowing yellowness; the mostly dark and sinister backgrounds increase our sympathy.

Deacon indicates the desired mood with a palette of dark turquoise and navy blue, textured backgrounds in grey and brown, line drawing that is also soft and textured, lots of space around the lonely creature, emphasizing her isolation. The pace is calm and measured, with page after page underlining, through repeated incidents, the themes of search and despair.

Finally, the author–illustrator uses his illustrations to extend the minimal written text. Thus the words 'No one seemed to understand her' are followed by three illustrations showing Beegu trying to talk to rabbits (who vaguely resemble her), to a single tree, whose branches perhaps echo her long ears, and to leaves which seem to have life as they whirl around. An uncaptioned full-page illustration ('bled' to the very edges of the page to increase the sense of involvement; see Box 4.1) shows a most dejected Beegu on a city pavement, in a sea of grey-trousered legs.

When at last she finds some friends, her happiness is short-lived. Pictures alone show a supremely sour schoolteacher who has come to remove the alien creature. Where the text says that the children 'want to say goodbye' (Figure 1), the pictures show her playmates squeezing through the school railings and offering her their hoop. Beegu's ears stand up straight, as they do when she is happy. Later, when Beegu is rescued, the donated hoop intrigues her father aboard the rescue spacecraft.

Who's Afraid of the Big, Bad Book? (Lauren Child) constructs the picture-book in an entirely different way. Herb has the misfortune to fall asleep over a book of fairy tales. What's more, they are fairy tales whose illustrations he has previously defaced – a moustache on a princess here, a pair of glasses on a king there. These actions would have made his visit to the stories uncomfortable enough (most of the guests at the royal ball demand restitution), but he also has to cope with a petulant Goldilocks who is furious that he has infiltrated her story.

Later in the story we meet Cinderella who, despite having been deprived of her Prince Charming (excised previously by Herb to serve as a card for his mother), comes to Herb's rescue; and, by clambering up the text, Herb escapes back to his bedroom. The storybook characters have their unsightly extras erased and Prince Charming is prised off the birthday card and sticky-taped back into position, though 'his dancing would never quite be the same again due to severe leg creasing'. Goldilocks, however, is punished for her shrill meanness with a wig of mousy brown hair, and the three bears (who had been very courteous to Herb) have their cottage door protected with a carefully drawn padlock.

'Wait!'

Her friends
wanted to say goodbye.

**Figure 1   Beegu says goodbye to her earth-friends: from
Alexis Deacon's *Beegu***

Those familiar with Lauren Child's work will recognize the characteristic approach she has with words, pictures, layout, fonts and the whole physical object that is the book. The collage effect in her pictures – there is much inspired sticking and pasting and use of photography – complements the cartoon style of her line drawing, and though the pages may strike readers initially as crowded, messy and rather difficult to read, familiarity allows her skill and wit to be appreciated. In any case, child readers probably have the edge on adults here as their reading of such pages is finely honed by contact with screen pages. Kress usefully discusses multimodal texts and the different 'reading paths' that are taken through a text such as this, and the demands made on readers by the screen-organized 'display' genre that he believes is replacing traditional text: 'Reliance on simple linearity is certainly not a useful approach to the reading (of such texts)' (2003: 146).

The use of varied fonts is inspired: the gothic script for Hansel and Gretel's rebuff to Herb ('Get lost!' they shout when he warns them not to eat the gingerbread house); the twirly curlicues applied to the speech of the royals; the uppercase print on a stone tablet reminiscent of tombstones. There's also much else to enjoy – a double pull-out page, a cut-out in the palace floor, spotting the Little Bad Wolf from an earlier Child book.

Child's playful bending and breaking of literary rules and conventions puts her work firmly in the postmodern camp, where effects are achieved by challenge to and parody of traditional forms of storytelling, and by highlighting the very form of the book. Readers move at their own pace through pictured and written text, circling, back-tracking, anticipating in the ways that these multimodal books demand.

With Lauren Child's work, we are firmly in the postmodern picturebook world. A recent title, *Again!* (2011) by Emily Gravett, demonstrates many characteristics of this genre in her tale of Cedric, a small green dragon and the drama of his bedtime story. The story read to him, of a nasty, red, angry dragon, is from a red, clothbound storybook shown inside the cover. As the parent dragon meets the repeated request 'Again!', both the storybook's words and illustrations subtly change and intermingle until eventually we see the parent dragon fall asleep and small, furious Cedric, by now red with rage, breathing such fire that a real, die-cut hole is burnt through the last pages and the back cover. Gravett typically makes the book as physical object as significant as the stories within it. Readers have to be on their toes to construct the multilayered meanings; it is not a straightforward, linear storyline, boundaries between the two stories are much blurred, varying size fonts and pictures take us by surprise, and jokes and self-referential elements are scattered throughout. Of course, this 'work' the reader does makes for a most rewarding experience. Doubtless, there will be many 'again' requests.

In between the very different texts discussed above, there are tens of thousands of picture storybooks. Undoubtedly, age, experience and personal taste guide choice. There are a few titles which appeal to practically everybody – surely Eric Carle's *The Very Hungry Caterpillar* is a universal favourite – but children are as eclectic in their tastes as adults. I watched six-year-old twins spend an hour giggling over *Who's Afraid of the Big, Bad Book?* They long to own all Lauren Child's equally inventive books, but their three-year-old brother is left perplexed. He much prefers the more 'traditional' narrative of *Beegu*. The Emily Gravett titles appeal to a wide range of readers but the youngest need adults with whom to share the many books she has now written so that her distinctive, playful style becomes familiar. The many exciting postmodern picturebooks which are now appearing are creating an enthusiastic audience amongst the young, but many of the books I have used to structure this chapter have very 'modern' qualities, with their authors happily breaking the rules of what is thought appropriate for the young reader. David Lewis's work (2001) persuasively suggests that readers vary and that the safer, predictable text will appeal to some readers while for others the playfulness of postmodern texts will take away some of the tension that often marks the reading experience. The qualities of all picturebooks are revealed by repeated, patient and close looking and analysis, by sharing readings and responses with others and by keeping an open mind.

WORKS CITED AND FURTHER READING

Children's Books

Ahlberg, Allan, and Janet Ahlberg. *The Jolly Postman, or Other People's Letters*. London: William Heinemann, 1986.

Ahlberg, Allan, and Jessica Ahlberg. *Goldilocks*. London: Walker Books, 2012.

Anno, Mitsumasa. *Anno's Counting Book*. London: Bodley Head, 1977.

Baker, Jeannie. *Window*. London: Julia MacCrae, 1991.

Blake, Quentin. *Clown*. London: Jonathan Cape, 1995.

Browne, Eileen. *Handa's Surprise*. London: Walker Books, 1994.

Burningham, John. *Come Away from the Water, Shirley*. London: Jonathan Cape, 1977.

Campbell, Rod. *Dear Zoo*. London: Abelard-Schuman, 1982.

Carle, Eric. *The Very Hungry Caterpillar*. London: Hamish Hamilton, 1970.

Child, Lauren. *Beware of the Storybook Wolves*. London: Hodder Children's Books, 2000.

Child, Lauren. *Who's Afraid of the Big, Bad Book?* London: Hodder Children's Books, 2002.

Cousins, Lucy. *Where Does Maisy Live?* London: Walker Books, 2000.

Cowell, Cressida. *Little Bo Peep's Library Book*. London: Hodder Children's Books, 1999.

Deacon, Alexis. *Beegu*. London: Hutchinson, 2003.

Felix, Monique. *The Story of a Little Mouse Trapped in a Book*. London: Methuen/Moonlight, 1980.

Felix, Monique. *Another Story of a Little Mouse Trapped in a Book*. London: Methuen/Moonlight, 1983.

Felix, Monique. *The Colors*. New York: Stewart, Tabori and Chang, 1991.

Gravett, Emily. *Again!* London: Macmillan Children's Books, 2012.

Hutchins, Pat. *Rosie's Walk*. London: Bodley Head, 1970.

Ormerod, Jan. *Peek-a-boo!* London: Bodley Head, 1997.

Ormerod, Jan. *Sunshine*. London: Kestrel Books, 1981.

Oxenbury, Helen. *ABC of Things*. London: William Heinemann, 1967.

Wiesner, David. *Tuesday*. New York: Clarion Books, 1991.

Critical Texts

Arizpe, Evelyn, and Morag Styles. *Children Reading Pictures*. London: RoutledgeFalmer, 2003.

Bader, Barbara. *American Picturebooks from Noah's Ark to the Beast Within*. New York: Macmillan, 1976.

Bang, Molly. *Picture This: How Pictures Work*. New York: SeaStar Books, 1991.

Doonan, Jane. *Looking at Pictures in Picturebooks*. Stroud: Thimble Press, 1993.

Evans, Janet (ed.). *What's in the Picture? Responding to Illustrations in Picturebooks*. London: Paul Chapman, 1998.

Graham, Judith. *Pictures on the Page*. Sheffield: NATE, 1990.

Graham, Judith. 'Turning the Visual into the Verbal: Children Reading Wordless Books'. In Janet Evans (ed.), *What's in the Picture? Responding to Illustrations in Picturebooks* (pp. 25–43). London: Paul Chapman, 1998.

Kress, Gunther. 'Interpretation or Design: from the World told to the World Shown'. In Morag Styles and Eve Bearne (eds), *Art, Narrative and Childhood* (pp. 137–53). Stoke-on-Trent: Trentham Books, 2003.

Lewis, David. *Reading Contemporary Picturebooks*. London: RoutledgeFalmer, 2001.

Martin, Douglas. *The Telling Line*. London: Julia MacRae, 1989.

McCloud, Scott. *Understanding Comics*. New York: HarperCollins, 1994.

Meek, Margaret. *How Texts Teach What Readers Learn*. Stroud: Thimble Press, 1988.

Nikolajeva, Maria, and Carole Scott. *How Picturebooks Work*. New York: Garland, 2001.

Nodelman, Perry. *Words about Pictures: The Narrative Art of Children's Picturebooks*. Athens, GA and London: University of Georgia Press, 1988.

Schwarcz, Joseph H. *Ways of the Illustrator*. Chicago, IL: American Library Association, 1982.

Sendak, Maurice. *Caldecott & Co*. London: Reinhardt Books, in association with Viking, 1989.

Sipe, Lawrence. 'How Picturebooks Work: a Semiotically Framed Theory of Text–Picture Relationships'. *Children's Literature in Education*, 29 (1998), 97–108.

Sipe, Lawrence R., and Sylvia Pantaleo (eds). *Postmodern Picturebooks: Play, Parody, and Self-Referentiality*. New York: Routledge, 2008.

Stephens, John, and Ken Watson (eds). *From Picturebook to Literary Theory*. Sydney: St Clair Press, 1994.

Styles, Morag, and Eve Bearne (eds). *Art, Narrative and Childhood*. Stoke-on-Trent: Trentham Books, 2003.

Watson, Ken (ed.), *Word and Image – Using Picturebooks*. Sydney: St Clair Press, 1997.

Watson, Victor, and Morag Styles (eds). *Talking Pictures*. London: Hodder & Stoughton, 1996.

Whalley, Joyce Irene, and Tessa Rose Chester. *A History of Children's Book Illustration*. London: John Murray and the Victoria and Albert Museum, 1988.

Poetry for Children

Michael Rosen

The most common approaches to literature for children attempt to define the field in terms of intention, style, content or audience – or all four. Poetry written for and read by children poses at least one extra problem: a good deal of what has been traditionally served to children – particularly in the context of education – only becomes poetry for children by virtue of being in an anthology clearly marked and framed by its intended audience. So, poems which might start out life (or live for many years) circulating between adults may well be found and approved of by a group of adults (anthologizers, editors, education advisers), who put them in, say, a school anthology, a child's Christmas annual or a commercial out-of-school anthology. Where this differs from the rest of children's literature is that this process happens for all ages of children, including the very youngest. Adult books like *Robinson Crusoe* (1719) and *Oliver Twist* (1838) have, of course, been published for children but with these there is a tradition of editing and abridging the texts, while the anthologized adult poems – Shakespeare's songs, for example – have often been offered in their entirety. This means that such poems become a form of children's literature by virtue of their 'framing' and the 'reading situation'.

Within the English-speaking world, poetry for children has tended to develop a distinctive national – sometimes explicitly nationalist – tradition. This has mainly revolved around the choice of poets put before children in their respective countries. The exceptions are what come to be called 'classic' poems, a tiny few of which travel around the English-speaking world, or where a particular effort is made to publish collections by individual poets from other countries, or specifically international collections with the aim of representing poets from many cultures and countries. An essay could be written about how nation and nationalism have been yoked to poetry for young people in a way that is not done with, say, music. The consequence is that the development and progress of poetry for children in anglophone countries tends to unfold in their respective bubbles. I make this point partly to make clear that this essay is in its own way 'national', as it largely charts the development of children's poetry in Britain.

This follows the pattern laid down by the two most important critical books in this field, *From the Garden to the Street: Three Hundred Years of Poetry for Children* by Morag Styles (1998) and *Poetry's Playground: The Culture of Contemporary American Children's Poetry* by Joseph T. Thomas Jr. (2007).

So, given that there is a distinctive quality to the category of 'poetry for children' (in this case within the UK), one approach that may help us corral and examine the species is to ask, 'Where is poetry for children?'

Here is an outline answer to this question.

Where is poetry for children?

1. *In anthologies made up of many poets, often graded or selected in terms of age, kind of school, sex of child, a particular examination, published in ways that clearly mark them out to be 'school books'.*

So long as we consider the reading habits and tastes of all children, and not a highly specific group of children, it cannot be emphasized enough that education plays the pre-eminent role in the history of the reading of poetry by children. No matter how popular individual poems or poets have been – for example, Robert Louis Stevenson, or Shel Silverstein – the means by which most children become acquainted with what we might call 'literary poetry' has been as a direct consequence of what teachers in schools have done with it. That said, we shouldn't forget that the consumption of the school anthology has had to match the extent of mass full-time education: that is, for very few in 1800, say, but for almost everyone under the age of 11 by 1900.

I suspect that anyone reading this chapter will be familiar with at least one anthology from their time at school, though there seems to be some mystery about when these books first started appearing. An argument could be made that from as early as the mid-sixteenth century, middle- and upper-class boys were taught poetry through special editions of Latin and Greek poets (see Mack, 2002: 17–19). It seems as if it was harder for editors to prove to teachers (or teachers to editors?) that poetry in English (unless it was specifically for initial literacy teaching – see below) had a fit place in the school curriculum. Vicesimus Knox (1752–1821), the editor of *Elegant Extracts: or useful and entertaining PIECES OF POETRY, Selected for the Improvement of Young Persons* (1789), sets out his stall in the Preface:

> if I should be asked what are its [the book's] pretensions, I must freely answer, that it professes nothing more than (what is evident at first sight) to be a larger Collection of English Verse, FOR THE USE OF SCHOOLS, than has ever yet been published IN ONE VOLUME. The original intention was to comprise in it a great number and variety of such pieces as were already in use in school, or which seemed proper for the use of them; such a number and variety as might furnish something satisfactory to every taste, and serve as a little Poetical LIbrary for school-boys, precluding the inconvenience and expence [*sic*] of a multitude of volumes. (vi; apart from square brackets, all brackets and upper case as in original)

Interestingly, according to Susan Allen Ford (2007), one of Knox's collections is mentioned in Jane Austen, and, 'when Thomas James, headmaster of Rugby, in 1798 advised Samuel Butler, new headmaster at Shrewsbury, on developing a library of English books, he thriftily emphasized anthologies'.

This collection lays down something of a blueprint for the category of both the school and home anthology (see (2) below). It is arranged into 'Books'. In Book I, 'Sacred and Moral', the editor offers readers a selection of the Psalms; some hymns including some by the then-living 'Mrs Barbauld' (Anna Laetitia Barbauld, 1743–1825; verses from Isaac Watts's (1674–1748) *Divine Songs* (first published 1715), including 'Against Idleness and Mischief', which begins 'How doth the little busy bee ...' (Vol. I, p. 61) and which would be parodied 60 years later by Lewis Carroll; verse fables from 'the late Mr GAY' (John Gay, 1685–1732, best known for *The Beggars' Opera*); 'FABLES for the FEMALE SEX, by Mr. MOORE' (Edward Moore, 1712–57); and several poems by Robert Burns (1759–96) and Alexander Pope (1688–1744). One clear survivor from this part of the anthology is 'An Elegy, written in a Country Church-Yard' (Vol. I, p. 22) by Thomas Gray (1716–71).

Book II is devoted to the 'Didactic, Descriptive, Narrative and Pathetic'. In this section, names familiar to us now are Oliver Goldsmith (1730–74), Alexander Pope, John Dryden (1631–1700), Thomas Gray, William Cowper (1731–1800) and George Crabbe (1754–1832), the selection of the last two poets putting down a clear marker of the editor's sympathies with the rural poor.

Book III is titled 'Dramatic &c.' and includes 35 extracts from Shakespeare, including (from *The Tempest*) Ariel's songs 'Full fathom five' and 'Where the bee sucks ...' and Caliban's anti-colonial speech, 'This island's mine ...'.

In Book IV, 'Sentimental, Lyrical, and Ludicrous', we find Milton's 'L'Allegro', 'Il Penseroso' and 'Lycidas' (staples of upper-school literature courses in British grammar and public schools), a good deal from Edmund Spenser (c.1552–99), Jonathan Swift (1667–1745), Cowper, Dr Johnson (1709–84) and long-serving anthologists' favourites, Robert Burns's 'To a Mouse' and Oliver Goldsmith's 'An Elegy on the Death of a mad Dog'. Indeed, this 'Book' is full of animals and includes anonymous and comical epitaphs and epigrams (including Rochester's subversive epitaph for Charles II), and Cowper's 'The Negro's Complaint' – suggesting that Knox was an abolitionist – followed by a last section, 'Songs, Ballads, &c. &c.' Survivors from this section include Henry Carey's 'Sally in our Alley' (1687–1743) – clearly thought to be not too risqué, Christopher Marlowe's 'Come live with me, and be my love ...' (1564–93), the subversive 'The Vicar of Bray' (Anon.), and some more Shakespeare songs ('Under the green-wood tree', 'Come follow, follow me'). Number 86 (Vol. II, p. 908) seems to be taken from a popular broadside, telling the story of a 'maid in Bedlam' whose love was sent to sea by his cruel parents. Number 101 (p. 912) is 'The Children in the Wood; or, The Norfolk Gentleman's last Will and Testament', probably taken from a chapbook; Number 102 is 'The Hunting in Chevy Chase', and so on through a strong selection of classic folk ballads (the kind classified by Francis Child) and which Knox could have found in Bishop Percy's *Reliques* (1765) or *A Collection of Old Ballads* (1723) or from even earlier: *Wit and Mirth: Or Pills to Purge Melancholy* (edited by Thomas d'Urfey, 1698–1720). There's even room for a comical broadside 'trade' ballad telling how a barber woos and wins a woman who runs a fish stall at the end of Fleet-market. The fee for the wedding is paid for by the barber shaving the parson's chin, while the bride 'entertain'd him with pilchards and gin' (Vol. II, pp. 952–3). The book ends with a selection of prologues and epilogues. (The 1805 edition comes in at 1016 pages in the two volumes.)

Knox espoused some of the 'progressive' or 'liberal' causes of his day, including feminism and pacifism. In contrast to the school anthologies of the Victorian and Edwardian eras, there is hardly any representation in the book of poems celebrating war, and where later anthologies would overlook women completely, Knox gives a presence to the strongly anti-establishment writers Anna Laetitia Barbauld and Charlotte Turner Smith (1749–1806).

The modern school anthology – that's to say published within an educational market, selling books aimed at every single child – bears the marks of having had to take note of many of the cultural streams of thought hovering in and around the educational world. These, like Knox's beliefs, are 'liberal' ideas to do with class, gender, race, environment and social action. This means that general school anthologies of the last 50 years have tried to represent poets from a wide range of social and cultural backgrounds. The breakthrough moment in Britain for the modern school anthology came with the collections *Voices* (1968) and *Junior Voices* (1970), edited by Geoffrey Summerfield (1931–91) and published by Penguin Education. In the teachers' handbook for *Voices*, Summerfield laid out a programme that has served to inform many since:

> I have not attempted in my selection to provide a bird's eye view of English poetry. I wanted to provide a diverse range of voices that can and will speak to pupils and to their condition. Modern and contemporary poetry dominate: this is due to my own pupils' enthusiasms ... Poems serve to sharpen our sense of life and to present others' sense of life. To the poems we bring our own lives; in sharing the poems with our pupils, we also to some degree share our lives. (1968: 7)

This child-centred view of the anthologist's job reverses the note that many anthologists hit when claiming that a poem will of itself uplift and enlighten. In a short chapter, 'Poetry in the Classroom' (9–11), and in some footnotes on the poems, Summerfield outlines what might appear to some as strange: the guidelines on poetry in the classroom offer a 13-point way 'in which poem, pupils and teacher can meet', but these don't involve the usual closed-ended interrogation that has dominated poetry within education for decades. Instead, the emphasis is on developing interest and taste through choice, discussion, imitation, performance and thought. Through these methods (not instruction), Summerfield claims that the pupils will attend to such matters as 'tone, rhythm, intention, emphasis, form and so on'. At the time, this method was revolutionary; it moved to centre stage in the decades following and in the present era has become revolutionary again – or should I say, in exile? To appreciate what a departure from the previous era this was, we should also factor in the wide range of cultures and poetic types that were represented in these seven volumes.

Themed school anthologies have appeared over the last 30 years which have focused on, for example, the environment, the supernatural, women poets, 'scary' poems, 'world' poetry and Caribbean poetry, while another tug on the anthologist has come from specific curriculum requirements. So, for example, when England and Wales laid down what was in effect a graded (by year, and by term within a year) poetry curriculum as part of a National Literacy strategy, some anthologists stepped in to provide the books to suit the strategy.

It is within the school anthology, particularly since the 1960s, that poems from all over the English-speaking world have reached children in the UK. The presence of poems from Seamus Heaney, Ogden Nash, Rabindranath Tagore, Carl Sandburg, Eve Merriam, Dennis Lee, Mary Ann Hoberman, Nikki Giovanni, Shel Silverstein, Jack Prelutsky, John Ciardi, Langston Hughes, William Carlos Williams, Banjo Paterson, Louise Bennett and many others has been as a consequence of anthologists seeking them out and teachers reading them with children. In addition, a sub-canon of translated poems has been established with strong favourites reappearing from, for example, Arthur Waley's translations of ancient Chinese poetry, Basho's haiku, Miroslav Holub and Christian Morgenstern.

2. *Anthologies made up of many poets, clearly marked for an intended child audience at home.*

As Susan Allen Ford has shown, *Elegant Extracts* not only appears in *Emma* but also had a place on the Austen family's shelves, so we may take it that for some middle-class people, the idea of reading poetry at home and as a not specifically religious practice had already taken root by the late eighteenth century. Another early anthology for children was put together by Lucy Aiken with her collection, *Poetry for Children, Consisting of Short Pieces to be Committed to Memory* (1801), which by its title tells us what one of the purposes and practices of reading poetry was. By virtue of its prosody, reading poetry carefully selected by adults for children may well enable the reader to commit it to memory, but bundled up with that came notions about why this is a virtuous or worthwhile or enlightening activity. This may include any of the following: showing children a correct way to follow religious observations; to open the eyes of children to the nature of God's creation and/or of 'Nature'; stirring children to be patriotic; awakening children to the iniquities, absurdities and mysteries of humanity; showing children that they can meditate or reflect on anything from the smallest to the largest phenomena, and/or their incredible diversity; passing on wisdom; revealing the possibilities and beauty of what can be done with words. In Aiken's words:

> By the aid of verse, a store of beautiful imagery and glowing sentiment may be gathered up as the amusement of childhood, which, in riper years, may soothe the heavy hours of languor, solitude, and sorrow, may strengthen feelings of piety, humanity, and tenderness, may soothe the

soul to calmness, rouse it to honourable exertion, or fire it with virtuous indignation. (3)

We may note that this last intention to do with firing up 'virtuous indignation' was a political statement linked to Aiken's selection of such poems as 'The Vanity of Greatness' (Shirley), 'The Orphan Boy' (Thelwall), 'Against Slavery' (Cowper) and 'The Dying Negro' (Anon.).

In the modern era, sometimes the power of full-colour artwork has been brought to bear on poetry in these home anthologies, while others have produced cheap paperbacks accompanied by black-and-white drawings or cartoons. This divergence expresses a split between, on the one hand, a sense that poetry is, or should be, edifying and uplifting, and, on the other, those who want to revel in its potential for populism – vulgarity, even. At the heart of this discussion is the question of the 'classic' poem and its sub-category, the classic poem for children. A canon is culturally constructed but the exact instruments of the construction are not always visible. In the case of poetry for children, it has been effected largely through co-operation between those at some level of power within education and those who make school and home anthologies. It's a kind of double-sieving process involving recommendations, quotations and presentations.

This raises some questions: what ideological outlook is represented by the canon? What ideological outlooks lie outside of the canon? Does the canon change? *The Puffin Book of Classic Verse*, edited by Raymond Wilson (1995), is divided up into sections: 'Come! Come Away!', 'All in a Day', 'Creatures', 'Very Remarkable Beasts', 'Ghosts, Ghouls and Witches', 'The Sea', 'Mystery, Dreams and Enchantments', 'Love's Moods', 'Song and Dance', 'People', 'Figures of Fun', 'School', 'The City', 'War', 'Reflections', 'Seasons' and 'Journey's End'. Most of the poets are English, male and dead. Non-English poets here include the Americans Robert Frost, Walt Whitman, Don Marquis, Bret Harte, Vachel Lindsay, Ogden Nash, Jack Prelutsky; and the Scottish Robert Louis Stevenson, Irish James Stephens and Welsh Dylan Thomas. There are 19 female poets (out of 146 poets in all, excluding a handful by Anon.) including Christina Rossetti, Emily Dickinson, Elizabeth Jennings, Stevie Smith, Dorothy Parker and Amy Lowell. There are 18 poets in the anthology who were living at the time Wilson was editing the book.

To be absolutely clear: I am not pillorying Raymond Wilson. Far from it. I've edited a collection of 'classic' poetry myself with a not dissimilar distribution of poets! The point I'm raising here concerns the composition of the category 'classic' and the question of why we want or need poetry to be packaged in this way. It should be said that Wilson, in a collection as large as this, has diverged from some aspects of the classic children's poetry mould by adding on what I suspect are personal favourites, while laying to rest some of the more tub-thumping poems of the British Empire that were compulsory fare in British schools until the 1960s. However, there is hardly any room in the collection for poems by anyone of colour – the notable exception being the African-American poet, Margaret Walker. It also goes without saying (though perhaps we should question this) that 'classic' poems do not include anything in translation unless it's from the Bible, or from Anglo-Saxon, or Chaucer. So we can say that Wilson and I find ourselves constructed by the category. This raises the question of whether the term 'classic' suggests to people (adult buyers, probably) that it offers young readers all that's worth reading by way of poetry – that it offers a sufficiency. Or, to reverse that: does the term 'classic' suggest that simply by being given that designation the poem will reach and touch all children? In both cases, I would hope not.

Themed anthologies for home consumption have been published in the present era but they find it difficult to make headway in the market unless they come clearly marked as being comic.

3.   *Verse narratives or verse texts in chapbooks, comics, comic annuals; as the verse narratives or verse texts in stand-alone books.*

From at least as early as 1630, a Londoner could buy from a ballad-seller in the street a printed ballad version of the Tom Thumb story, presented as: 'Tom Thumbe, his life and death: wherein is declared many maruailous [*sic*] acts of manhood, full of wonder, and strange merriments …' (reprinted in Ritson, 1884). Earlier still, the printer Wynkyn de Worde – in around 1512, according to M. O. Grenby (2008: 26) – published the verse narrative, 'The Friar and the boy', a tale of a boy who enchants his stepmother to fart in public. This tradition of popular verse flourished as 'street literature' until the mid-nineteenth century, when it became absorbed by comics. In the present era, there are very few rhyming texts to be found in comics, though the style flourishes in the picturebook tradition, most successfully with Julia Donaldson. There is a revival of this genre, with many authors and illustrators telling stories in picturebooks in verse, most often (apart from Donaldson) in the four-line verse ('quatrain') ballad form that 'Tom Thumbe' was told in.

4.   *As a clearly defined and named category, 'nursery rhymes', to be found in collections of a range of literature for the youngest children, or as stand-along books of nursery rhymes.*

The story of the 'nursery rhyme' has to be told with caution, and fortunately we have the stern hands of Iona and Peter Opie to warn us off speculation and fantasy. Their approach in *The Oxford Dictionary of Nursery Rhymes* (1951, 1997) was to chart the first appearance of or reference to each rhyme. In their Introduction (1997: 1–51), they make clear that the rhymes are mostly not composed by children; they were often fragments of folk songs, theatre songs or ballads. The great majority of the rhymes are more than 250 years old, some much older than that.

Though they appear in popular miscellanies earlier, the first known printed collection is the remarkable little two-volume book, *Tommy Thumb's Pretty Song-Book*, published in London in 1744. Survivors from Volume I (as reconstructed by Andrea Immel and Brian Alderson, 2013) include (probably appearing for the first time) 'See-saw Margery Daw', a version of 'Oranges and Lemons', 'Who Killed Cock Robin?', a version of 'Hey Diddle Diddle', part of 'Sing a Song of Sixpence' and 'Mary, Mary, Quite Contrary', alongside 'Little

Jack Horner' (not first appearance), and from Volume II (which survives), the first appearance of 'Ladybird, ladybird', 'Hickory Dickory Dock' and 'Baa Baa Black Sheep' alongside 'London Bridge' (not first appearance), etc.

So, we can see here a clear laying out of a tradition which survives to this day. What doesn't survive are the bawdy, scatological and what we would now describe as racist rhymes. In the present day, nursery rhymes are not as widely shared as they were, say, 50 years ago. They are missing from modern reading schemes where once they were staple fare, for example, *The Merry Readers* (Benny, 1915), which is made up of 38 nursery rhymes. Publishers keep trying to revitalize the tradition with many kinds of illustration. Perhaps advertising jingles, snatches of songs from singers seen on TV or circulating on iTunes fulfil the nursery rhymes' role.

5. *Rhymes that pass between children, mostly orally, mostly without adult intervention, known mostly as 'playground rhymes' or 'street rhymes'.*
In spite of their obituary having been written many times, these continue to flourish in several forms: clap-rhymes, counting-out rhymes, parodies of carols and modern songs, rude rhymes, nicknames, skipping rhymes. What seems to have almost died out are the rhymes chanted with ball games.

Iona and Peter Opie, with their *The Lore and Language of Schoolchildren* (1959), showed how one rhyme started out its printed life as a poem by Henry Carey (see Carey also for 'Sally in our Alley' above in *Elegant Extracts*) from his 'Namby Pamby' of 1725, and was being recreated orally by children in 1954 in York (Opie and Opie, 1959: 10–11). Over and beyond that, we might assume that children created, parodied and shared rhymes long before then.

6. *Poetry produced by children, mostly as encouraged by teachers and poets working with children in schools, libraries and poetry clubs. The ultimate location of this poetry may be the classroom or library in question, or it may be anthologized into locally produced anthologies, websites, blogs or commercial anthologies where it may appear alongside poems by adults or may be clearly marked as collections of poetry written by children.*
In the old 'public' (i.e. private) schools there is a long tradition of pupils composing new verse in Latin, often for a competition of some kind. Interest in the idea that children in state schools could write poetry in English seems to have begun before the First World War. By the 1920s and 1930s it was possible for a local authority like Tottenham in London to publish *Children's Verse, an anthology of poems, written by pupils of elementary schools of Tottenham* (1937). Again, this tradition survives, sometimes cramped by formulaic methods, other times following the Geoffrey Summerfield or Barry Maybury tradition, putting the child at the centre of the poem and the writing. Key exponents of this way of working now in print are such people as Michael Lockwood, James Carter and Jean Sprackland.

7. *Poetry produced by adults in stand-alone collections of single poets, clearly marked by the publishing industry as poetry for children. In the last 50 or so years, these have occasionally been produced by educational publishers*

but mostly they are produced by the commercial publishers of children's books.

This part of the tradition starts most famously – as a name-on-the-frontispiece and stand-alone author – with John Bunyan and his *A Book for Boys and Girls: or, Country Rhimes [sic] for Children* (1686), though Abraham Chear was, in the late 1670s, a known and much-read poet for children and had his poems collected posthumously in 1673 in *A Looking-glass for Children*. These were both 'Puritan' poets who believed that their poetry could take children along a path of righteousness. The idea of adults writing and producing volumes of poetry for children has ebbed and flowed since then, sometimes with a foot in one or other of the Christian churches and Sunday schools; at other times with a clear view to being 'used' in schools; at other times, particularly since the publication of Spike Milligan's (1918–2002) work in the 1960s and 1970s (e.g. *Silly Verse for Kids*, 1968), with a view to being unofficial, subversive even. My own contribution to this aspect of poetry for children was to write poems (*Mind Your Own Business*, 1974) from the child's point of view – indeed as A. A. Milne (1882–1956) and Robert Louis Stevenson (1850–94) had done – but about the world I had known in the 1950s and knew through my own children from the 1970s onwards.

At times, these stand-alone collections by single authors have done very well in the open market; at others, they have all but died out. My own theory is that the fate of this part of the tradition rests largely on how the school curriculum is devised and dictated. When teachers, advisers and publishers are given the scope and freedom to explore the world of poetry for themselves, many flowers bloom. When the content is dictated by central government, the choice narrows and the numbers of books sold and published dwindles. It's an example of how education policy affects the commercial part of book distribution.

That said, there is a wide range of poets in Britain writing for children, trying many different kinds of poetry. One particularly strong strand has been Caribbean (or Caribbean in origin), with poets like John Agard, Grace Nichols, James Berry, Valerie Bloom, Benjamin Zephaniah and others. Poetry for children by women in stand-alone collections has always been strong, and it still is with Carol Ann Duffy, Mandy Coe, Lindsay MacRae, Jackie Kay, Julia Donaldson, Judith Nicholls and many others, while male poets in the modern era who have excited and interested children include Ted Hughes, Spike Milligan, Adrian Henri, Vernon Scannell, Roger McGough, Brian Patten, Charles Causley, Adrian Mitchell, Kit Wright, Roald Dahl, Allan Ahlberg, Gareth Owen, Spike Milligan, Philip Gross, John Hegley, Wes McGee, Brian Moses, Tony Mitton, Colin McNaughton and John Mole. New poets writing for children tend to find it hard to get single stand-alone collections published, which is why I put them together along with more established writers in my book *Michael Rosen's A–Z: The Best Children's Poetry from Agard to Zephaniah* (2009). The two US poets who have travelled best to the UK in single-poet collections are Shel Silverstein and 'Dr. Seuss'. At the heart of most of this writing is a strong commitment to the idea that poems can do something special with language in order to talk about the world in ways that children can enjoy or even imitate. Each of these poets interprets the world and their place in it with a distinct tone and approach, drawing on many different traditions, landscapes and inner worlds. It might have been possible in the past to distinguish clear divisions between the few poets working in this field, but the key characteristic of the present era is the opposite: a diversity which is hard to grasp in a short but wide-ranging chapter like this one.

8. *More informally, there is a variety of verse for children that exists 'below the radar', not often referred to directly as 'poetry'. However, in terms of affecting the 'repertoire' of poetry known by children, parents and carers, it is quite often significant. So, in no particular order, they are:*

   ■ Since at least the early eighteenth century, published and unpublished poets have written occasional verse for a child or children known to the poet. Like 'The Pied Piper of Hamelin' by Robert Browning (1842; originally written for a boy whom Browning knew, the son of Browning's theatre producer), these may eventually end up in commercial circulation as books or anthologized poems, or they may stay within family groups.

   ■ On school walls, bedroom walls, samplers, in books intended for children, from the medieval period onwards, various kinds of instructions, guidance and etiquette for children have been put into verse.

   ■ There is a long tradition of mnemonics (going back at least to the Roman era) such as those to aid the memorizing of the numbers of days in the months, or various kinds of alphabet poems.

   ■ Initial literacy verse found in primers and reading schemes.

   ■ Recreational books – chapbooks, parlour-games books, annuals – various kinds of puzzle poems, rhyming riddles, 'riddle-me-rees', rhyming rebuses and the like.

   ■ Dedication verse written on books when given as presents.

   ■ In family and social gatherings where a recitation tradition has been active.

   ■ In out-of-school youth groups, various kinds of chants and collectively performed rhymes.

   ■ On birthday, Easter and Christmas cards clearly intended for children.

   ■ In 'reciters', elocution books, collections for poetry performance exams, poems (often with speeches, extracts etc.) either selected or written with the express purpose of being recited for public performance.

   ■ In specifically religious contexts like Sunday schools, or other forms of religious instruction.

   ■ In stories, novels and plays intended for children, where characters have spoken newly created verses, parodies, riddles and the like from within the narrative, or occasionally as prologues and epilogues to novels and stories.

According to Shirley Brice Heath (1997: 26), in 1986 a private collection of a 'nursery library' was discovered that had been created by Jane Johnson (1706–59) for her own children as they were growing up and includes many of Johnson's own rhymes:

The Man with his Dogs
went out to kill Game,
His Gun it went off,
and shot the Dogs
lame.   (1997: 26)

Since the eighteenth century, children have received poems written by parents and carers, or jokey verses made up on car journeys, birthday wishes, Easter rhymes to aid the hunting of eggs, parodies of hymns, carols and songs and the like.

In *The Oxford Book of Children's Verse*, Iona and Peter Opie select as their first poem part of Chaucer's 'Manciple's Tale' (1973: 3) where he imitates an etiquette verse beginning (as translated) 'My son, keep well thy tongue ...'. When religious institutions had great control over the nurture and education of young people, verse admonitions and guidances were extremely common – in particular with the dissenting traditions of Christianity, they mark out the duties of a Christian subject. In the present day, though much of this has disappeared, what survives in some quarters are rhyming and alliterative slogans put up in schools full of words like 'believe' and 'achieve', 'know' and 'grow'. Some of this seems to derive from marketing training where new recruits are told such things as 'retail is detail' or 'eye-level is buy level'.

Not all mnemonics rhyme as does 'Thirty days hath September ...', which seems to have started out life in the sixteenth century. Many people remember such things as the order of the colours of the rainbow ('Richard Of York Gave Battle In Vain'), planets revolving round the sun ('My Very Educated Mother Just Served Us Nachos'), the wives of Henry VIII ('Divorced, beheaded, died; divorced, beheaded, survived'), the order of the geological eras ('Pregnant Camels Ordinarily Sit Down Carefully; Perhaps Their Joints Creak') and the like with poetic phrases. These circulate around schools and families and now online too.

One of the first ABC rhymes was 'A was an apple-pie', cited by the Opies (1997: 53) and known, they say, in the mid-seventeenth century. Since then, many alphabet poems have been composed anonymously, and most famously by Edward Lear (1812–88). Of course, teaching to read didn't have to be done with alphabet poems, and from the early eighteenth century onwards authors and educators had the idea that learning to read was aided by rhymes and alliterative sentences. In 1651, *An English Monosyllabary* produced: 'Ah! wee see an ox dy by an ax', 'Oh God! his game is gon, as sure as a gun. He that did ly on his bum, and ban, was his bane' (Michael, 1987: 18). From the 1830s onwards, children were reading:

Go now to bed,
For you are fed.

If Jem can run,
He has a bun.
Now my new pen
is fit for Ben.   (Avery, 1995: 5)

In the modern era, with the rise of systematic synthetic phonics, rhyme has been given a special place in the teaching of reading. From the late 1950s onwards, 'Dr. Seuss' (Theodore Geisel, 1904–91) wrote early 'readers' based on a different system: simple words from a reduced vocabulary, the first being *The Cat in the Hat* (1957). An argument could be made that for most of us, these early rhymes, banal as some of the most elementary might be, lay down in our minds some long-lasting connections between school, rhyme, reading and childhood.

Puzzle poems flourished in particular in the nineteenth century, with books like *Selections from the Masquerade, A collection of enigmas, logogriphs [sic], charades, rebuses, queries and transpositions*, published in London in 1826. Number XL in 'Rebusses, &c.' is 'A CONSONANT add to a dignify'd Jew / A wild little quadruped rises to view.' This kind of verbal, poetic fun is much harder to find these days and yet, in my experience, when you play these kinds of games with children, they enjoy them a great deal.

In the nineteenth and early twentieth centuries, books known as 'Reciters' created a strong tradition of anthologizing, such as Carpenter's *Penny Readings in Prose and Verse* (1866). In the modern era, as an equivalent to music grades, there are verse reading exams and 'by heart' competitions of various kinds, and anthologies are still made up by the examiners or mainstream publishers with a view to satisfying this demand. When governments decide that this is desirable (as at present), there is an increase in the number of 'by heart' anthologies available. The presence of reciters and of popular traditions of recitation, as with 'The Lion and Albert' (1932), the dialect poems of the Lancashire cotton-workers, Burns Nights and the like, makes it hard to know which traditions survive and where. On occasion, writers (e.g. Jackie Kay, 2011) or interviewees on radio and television reveal that their parents used to recite a mix of poems learnt at school, folk rhymes, limericks, made-up ballads about colleagues and so on.

Members of youth groups, particularly those with a camping tradition, are often inducted into chants. The chant I adapted as *We're Going on a Bear Hunt* (1989) seems to have started life as either a chant worked out in American summer camps or in the Brownies, where the Brownies chant, 'We're going on a lion hunt'. Most of these are unauthored and are part of a communal chanting, reciting or singing that is seen as an important part of companionship, or just a fun way of passing an evening.

The key religious text is Isaac Watts's *Divine Songs, Attempted in Easy Language for the Use of Children* (1715). He writes in his Preface: 'There is something so amusing and entertaining in Rhymes and Metre, that will incline Children to make this part of their Business a Diversion. And you may turn their very Duty into a Reward, by giving them the Privilege of learning one of these Songs every Week well, ...' (unnumbered, p. 2 of 'Preface'). Apart from anything else, Watts explains, the learning and knowing of poems will ensure that children will 'not be forced to seek relief for an Emptiness of Mind out of the loose and dangerous Sonnets of the Age'.

The Sunday school tradition lives on, in particular in the Evangelical churches, but it doesn't seem as if poetry has as large a role to play there as it did in the eighteenth, nineteenth and early twentieth centuries.

In one of the first novels written explicitly for children, Sarah Fielding's *The Governess* (1749), there are several examples of verse, from those in popular style: 'I am a Giant, and I can eat thee: / Thou art a Dwarf, and canst not eat me' (p. 52), to a more homiletic verse about 'Patience'. Lewis Carroll and J. R. R. Tolkien were renowned users of verse within fiction, as was Beatrix Potter with her riddling use of nursery rhymes in *The Tale of Squirrel Nutkin* (1903) and *The Tailor of Gloucester* (1902), among others. The folk tale tradition is rich with short verses: the Grimm Brothers either collected or wrote verses for 'Hansel and Gretel', for example, while African and Caribbean stories are full of verse prologues, epilogues, repeated couplets and the like. It is probably in the storytelling tradition that this idea of including verse in fiction has best survived, and it appears in storytellers' performances in schools, libraries and at festivals everywhere.

An autobiographical approach

With your indulgence, I would now like to invert the process of this chapter from what has been a generalized survey to a highly personalized one. This is not purely an exercise in egotism, but I am hazarding a guess that it might be appropriate on account of the fact that (a) my parents, Harold and Connie Rosen, were professionally active in presenting one particular strand of children's poetry in the 1950s and 1960s; (b) I started writing poetry at that time and have been writing it ever since; (c) my own interests in poetry for children have brought me into contact with most of the locations (or written examples taken from those locations) listed above; and (d) at various times in my writing these examples have been part of my writing intertext.

I represent, then, several different protagonists in the field of poetry for children, from the time I was born in 1946 to the present day. These are, of course, highly specific in relation to location (north-west London suburb), social class origins (my parents were teachers of working-class east London origin), education (state schooling at nursery school, two primary schools and two grammar schools), ethnicity (in origin, secular eastern European Jewish), political world-view (socialist), family intellectual outlook (libertarian, 'progressive'), sex (male), family position (youngest; no specifically named disability; two-parent nuclear family throughout my childhood).

The protagonists I represent across 50 years are, variously: boy audience of poetry in state schools; son of progressive, intellectually committed and active parents; post-Second World War child; teenage writer of poems about childhood; observer of the process of anthologizing and broadcasting poetry for children by my parents and their friends; anthologized poet for children; published poet in single collections of my own work; poet performing in schools; poet writing about poetry; poet running teachers' workshops on poetry.

Within this narrow social, educational and political layer, I can ask myself the question, what was poetry like in the locations identified earlier? And what conclusions can we draw?

My first encounters with poetry were at home: in comics, often as the undertext in comic strips; in nursery rhyme and Beatrix Potter books that my mother read to me; in various 'rude rhymes' or colloquial and familiar rhymes that my father either made up or recalled, some of which were partly in Yiddish. Alongside this, both my parents recited the whole or parts of poems and snatches of Shakespeare, many of which appeared in school anthologies of the time. Sometimes these home recitations were in French, German or Latin – memories mostly from my father's own schooling.

At school, we met poetry in school anthologies, never in collections by individual poets. They were in effect a form of the graded reader. My first memory of poetry, aged seven in 'first year juniors', is of the teacher reading us poems. One boy had learnt a poem and recited it to the rest of the class – 'Autumn Fires' by Robert Louis Stevenson. By the age of ten, I had been selected to be in the Choral Speaking group and was learning and reciting poems, like 'Adlestrop' by Edward Thomas, selected for inter-school competitions.

In the playground, I was with a group of boys who shared a good few rude rhymes and parodies, some of which we thought we had made up. I witnessed girls saying, chanting or singing skipping rhymes, ball-game rhymes and clap-game rhymes. A friend and I read the Winnie-the-Pooh books and we enjoyed reciting, 'My nose is cold, tiddly-pom' together.

As we went up through primary school, the poetry focused most heavily on Walter de la Mare, Robert Louis Stevenson and John Masefield. In the second year at secondary school, we 'did' dramatic monologues by Robert Browning. Homework was to write one. In the second year, in French, we had to learn by heart a La Fontaine fable, 'Maître Corbeau sur un arbre perché / Tenait en son bec un fromage ...' When I was 12, I joined a young persons' theatre group and we learnt poems to recite in choral competitions, like Louis MacNeice's 'Prayer Before Birth'.

In my teens, I became aware of the poetry of D. H. Lawrence alongside American poetry either written or selected for children to read, in particular poems by Carl Sandburg. As Geoffrey Summerfield was a friend of my parents, he brought many of the poems he was trying out with *Voices* and *Junior Voices* into our house.

When I first started writing the poems that eventually appeared in collections for children, I thought that I was writing a D. H. Lawrence/Sandburg style of poetry about childhood primarily for an adult audience. In fact, this didn't happen. By adopting the Sandburg voice, I didn't realize at the time I was breaking with an English tradition of poetry for children which was up till then almost entirely formal verse. As my parents were actively involved in encouraging children to write poetry through their teaching, publications and radio work, I have a sense that I imagined that my poems were in a shape that children could adopt and use to write poetry for themselves.

Another discovery for me was performance poetry, and I joined other writers of fiction and poetry in schools, libraries and at festivals performing to children. As a group of poets, we reach hundreds of thousands through our publications, performances and online presence. It's a diverse group of people drawing on a wide variety of cultural traditions: some of it overlapping with rap, storytelling and folk and rock music; some of it more traditional, drawing on the traditions of poets like Edward Lear, Lewis Carroll and Walter de la Mare.

Geoffrey Summerfield, much inspired by Carl Sandburg's own work of assemblages of oral utterances, tried to widen the range of what is entitled to be called poetry, incorporating riddles, free verse translations, modernist poets' fragments and jokes, folk songs, children's playground rhymes, charms, chants, prose poems, poems and written monologues by children, Humpty Dumpty's prose explanation of 'Jabberwocky' from Carroll's *Through the Looking-Glass*, graveyard inscriptions and so on. It's as if he was saying that, on the one hand, 'all this is poetry', and on the other, that formal poetry of the canon (as understood by critics and publishers) is itself made up of this huge miscellany of utterances which carry many of the characteristics of formal poetry – metaphor, poetic prosody, compression and so on.

My view is that he succeeded, but it has to be said that it was part of a split in the small world of children's poetry: some favouring the clear demarca- tion of the genres 'poetry' and 'poetry for children', as exemplified by, say, Robert Louis Stevenson, but also by the layout on the page of the 'poem', by the poetry collection in a book, situated on a shelf; others finding poetry and poetic utterances everywhere – in those same books, but also on bus shelter walls, in everyday speech, in sports commentaries, the comments of three-year- olds, in puns, montages of song titles and so on. At times, central government has intervened in this discussion and expressed a wish or even a directive that a particular kind of poetry should be taught and learnt in schools. My own view is that this is an attempt to tame poetry and confine it to approved shapes, sounds and meanings.

WORKS CITED AND FURTHER READING

Primary Texts

Aiken, Lucy. *Poetry for Children, Consisting of Short Pieces to be Committed to Memory*. London: R. Phillips, 1801.

[Anon. (ed.)]. *Children's Verse, an anthology of poems, written by pupils of elementary schools of Tottenham, written by the elementary schools of Tottenham*. Tottenham, London: The Borough of Tottenham Education Committee, 1937.

[Anon. (ed.)]. *A Collection of Old Ballads &c*. London: J. Roberts, 1723.

[Anon. (ed.)]. *Selections from the Masquerade, A collection of enigmas, logogriphs, [sic] charades, rebuses, queries and transpositions*. London: Baker and Fletcher, 1826.

Benny, Ada H. (ed.). *The Merry Readers, a whole-word method of learning to read*. London and Edinburgh: T. C. & E. C. Jack, 1915.

Bunyan, John. *A Book for Boys and Girls: or, Country Rhimes [sic] for Children*. London: n.p., 1686.

Carpenter, J. E. *Penny Readings in Prose and Verse.* London: Frederick Warne and Co., 1866.

Chear, Abraham. *A Looking-glass for Children.* London: Robert Boulter, 1673.

d'Urfey, Thomas (ed.). *Wit and Mirth: Or Pills to Purge Melancholy.* London: Henry Playford, 1698–1720.

Fielding, Sarah. *The Governess or, Little Female Academy. Being the History of Mrs. Teachum, and her Nine Girls. With their nine Days Amusement. Calculated for the Entertainment and Instruction of Young Ladies in their Education.* London: 'The Author', 1749.

Hall, Donald (ed.). *The Oxford Book of Children's Verse in America.* New York and Oxford: Oxford University Press, 1985.

Immel, Andrea, and Brian Alderson (eds). *Tommy Thumb's Pretty Song-Book, The First Collection of Nursery Rhymes, A Facsimile Edition with a History and Annotations.* Los Angeles: Cotsen Occasional Press, 2013.

Kay, Jackie. *Red Dust Road.* London: Picador, 2011.

Knox, Vicesimus (ed.). *Elegant Extracts: or useful and entertaining PIECES OF POETRY, Selected for the Improvement of Young Persons.* London and Dublin: J. Johnson et al., 1789.

Milligan, Spike. *Silly Verse for Kids.* Harmondsworth: Puffin, Penguin, 1968.

Mitchell, Adrian (ed.). *A Poem a Day: Helps You Stop Work and Play.* London: Orchard Books, 2001.

Opie, Iona, and Peter Opie. *The Lore and Language of Schoolchildren.* Oxford: Oxford University Press, 1959.

Opie, Iona, and Peter Opie (eds). *The Oxford Book of Children's Verse.* Oxford: Oxford University Press, 1973.

Opie, Iona, and Peter Opie (eds). *The Oxford Dictionary of Nursery Rhymes.* Oxford: Oxford University Press, 1951, 1997.

Percy, Thomas. *Reliques of Ancient English Poetry.* London: J. Dodsley, 1765.

Potter, Beatrix. *The Tailor of Gloucester.* London: privately printed, 1902; Frederick Warne and Co., 1903.

Potter, Beatrix. *The Tale of Squirrel Nutkin.* London: Frederick Warne and Co., 1903.

Ritson, Joseph (ed.). *Ancient Popular Poetry from Authentic Manuscripts and Old Printed Copied,* rev. Edmund Goldsmid. Edinburgh: Privately Printed, 1884.

Rosen, Michael (ed.). *Michael Rosen's A–Z: The Best Children's Poetry from Agard to Zephaniah.* London: Puffin, Penguin, 2009.

Rosen, Michael. *Mind Your Own Business.* London: André Deutsch, 1974.

Rosen, Michael. *We're Going on a Bear Hunt,* illus. Helen Oxenbury. London: Walker Books, 1989.

Summerfield, Geoffrey (ed.). *Voices: An Anthology of Poetry and Pictures.* Harmondsworth: Penguin Education for Penguin, 1968.

Summerfield, Geoffrey. *Voices: An Anthology of Poetry and Pictures.* Teachers' Handbook. Harmondsworth: Penguin Education for Penguin, 1968.

Summerfield, Geoffrey (ed.). *Junior Voices: An Anthology of Poetry and Pictures.* Harmondsworth: Penguin Education for Penguin, 1970.

Summerfield, Geoffrey. *Junior Voices: An Anthology of Poetry and Pictures.* Teachers' Handbook. Harmondsworth: Penguin Education for Penguin, 1970.

Wilson, Raymond (ed.). *The Puffin Book of Classic Verse.* London: Penguin, 1995.

Critical Texts

Avery, Gillian. 'The Beginnings of Children's Reading to c. 1700'. In Peter Hunt (ed.), *Children's Literature, an Illustrated History* (pp. 1–25). Oxford and New York: Oxford University Press, 1995.

Ford, Susan Allen. 'Reading *Elegant Extracts* in Emma. Very Entertaining!' *Persuasions On-line*, 28.1 (Winter 2007) (Jane Austen Society of America). http://www.jasna.org/persuasions/on-line/vol28no1/ford.htm (accessed 6 January 2014).

Grenby, M. O. 'Before Children's Literature: Children, Chapbooks and Popular Culture in Early Modern Britain'. In Julia Briggs, Dennis Butts and M. O. Grenby (eds), *Popular Children's Literature in Britain* (pp. 25–46). Aldershot: Ashgate, 2008.

Heath, Shirley Brice. 'Child's Play or Finding the Ephemera of Home'. In Mary Hilton, Morag Styles and Victor Watson (eds), *Opening the Nursery Door: Reading, Writing and Chilhood 1600–1900* (pp. 17–30). Abingdon: Routledge, 1997.

Hilton, Mary, Morag Styles and Victor Watson (eds). *Opening the Nursery Door: Reading, Writing and Childhood 1600–1900*. London and New York: Routledge, 1997)

Hunt, Peter (ed.). *Children's Literature: An Illustrated History*. Oxford: Oxford University Press, 1995.

Mack, Peter. *Elizabethan Rhetoric, Theory and Practice*. Cambridge: Cambridge University Press, 2002.

Michael, Ian. *The Teaching of English, from the Sixteenth Century to 1870*. Cambridge: Cambridge University Press, 1987.

Styles, Morag. *From the Garden to the Street: Three Hundred Years of Poetry for Children*. London: Cassell, 1998.

Styles, Morag, Louise Joy and David Whitley, (eds). *Poetry and Childhood*. Stoke-on-Trent and Sterling, VA: Trentham Books, 2010.

Thomas, Joseph T., Jr. *Poetry's Playground: The Culture of Contemporary American Children's Poetry*. Detroit, MI: Wayne State University Press, 2007.

Watts, Isaac. *Divine Songs, Attempted in Easy Language for the Use of Children*. London: M. Lawrence, 1715.

Part II

Texts and Genres

Family, Identity and Nationhood: Family Stories in Anglo-American Children's Literature, 1930–2000

Lucy Pearson

6

KEY TEXTS

Cynthia Voigt, *Homecoming* (1981)

Laura Ingalls Wilder, *Little House in the Big Woods* (1932); *Little House on the Prairie* (1935)

Jacqueline Wilson, *The Illustrated Mum* (1999)

Jacqueline Woodson, *From the Notebooks of Melanin Sun* (1995)

In 1917, the poster advertising National Baby Week depicted a maternal Britannia beating back the Grim Reaper, two children clutching at her skirts. The picture is captioned 'Save the Babies', and the implicit connection between the health of children and that of the nation is made even more explicit in another slogan for the same event: 'It is more dangerous to be a baby in England than it is to be a soldier in France'. The elision of family and nation evident in the poster usefully illustrates both the practical and ideological importance of the family: Britannia both *is* the family and is charged with protecting it. National Baby Week, which aimed to improve the health and wellbeing of children and to disseminate parenting advice, exemplifies the increasing concern with both the practical aspects of family life and its ideological significance during the twentieth and twenty-first centuries. As the state and other outside agencies have increased their attempts both to support the family and to define it, tensions between the two aims have become more apparent: in the National Baby Week poster, Britannia is a defender of the family, but (as a symbol of the state) has also supplanted the 'natural' family. This image thus encapsulates many of the issues raised in this chapter: as a primary source of narratives about family, children's literature has been actively engaged in defining, shaping and interrogating the idea of family and its relationship to selfhood, society and the state.

Family matters

The term 'family' is so *familiar* (a word that shares the same Latin root, *familia*, which refers to people and things known intimately) that we rarely stop to consider what it means: *of course* we know what a family is. In fact, most of us probably use the term loosely, to signify a number of relationships. Biologically, we use the word 'family' to mean those who are related to us by blood or through marriage, but socially and legally other definitions are also accepted. For instance, someone who is not a blood relative may legally be incorporated into a family through the process of adoption, and titles such as 'aunt' and 'uncle' are often conferred on family friends to acknowledge a special relationship with the children of another household. Similarly, saying someone 'is family', connotes a special, insider relationship with members of a group, whatever their biological relationships. Expectations of family may also vary widely across times and cultures: up until the early twentieth century, servants performed a large proportion of childcare duties in middle-class families, while today such families typically emphasize the importance of parental responsibility for tasks such as feeding and clothing children. Crucially, however, the term 'family' is not simply a descriptor of a given set of people or roles; in the words of sociologist Judith Stacy, it is 'an ideological, symbolic construct that has a history and a politics' (1993: 545). Constructions of the family are inextricably linked with constructions of gender, sexuality, class, and even national identity, and the family is frequently deployed as an ideological symbol. In the debate about marriage equality, for example, conservative commentators have frequently presented same-sex marriage as a threat to the family, despite its tangible benefits to many actual families headed by same-sex partners. Despite the fluidity of families in the real world, the 'traditional' image of family as 'a heterosexual, conjugal, nuclear, domestic unit, ideally one with a male primary breadwinner, a female primary homemaker, and their dependent offspring' remains a powerful ideological construct (Stacy, 1993: 545). In children's literature, this image of family has certainly been frequently reinforced: in J. K. Rowling's Harry Potter series (1997–2007), for example, the conventional family unit of the Weasleys is a key source of warmth, stability and love for the orphaned Harry. Nevertheless, as this chapter will show, children's books have also interrogated the idea of the 'traditional' family and have offered other ways of viewing family life.

The family in the world

For most of us, the family is the first social unit we will encounter, and the one with the most direct and enduring influence over our lives. It is therefore also a primary mechanism for establishing social roles and relationships. In the nineteenth century, the family was integrated into a hierarchical world-view in which, as David Grylls notes, 'In nature, man ruled over animals, and God ruled over man; in society, kings and governors ruled over their subjects, husbands over their wives, parents over children' (in Alston, 2008: 59). In children's stories such as Mary Martha Sherwood's *The History of the Fairchild Family* (1818), accepting the hierarchy of the family unit is presented as a foundation for understanding and accepting the broader hierarchies of state and religion: the good family produces the good citizen.

As the image from National Baby Week indicates, the beginning of the twentieth century saw a new focus on family which was in part spurred by changes to family life. The absence of any male figure in the picture highlights the way in which real mothers were on the 'front line' of the family in 1917, when many families were deprived temporarily or permanently of their male relatives by war. At the same time, the conflation of individual and state in the figure of Britannia indicates the increasing level of intervention in family life. Baby Week focused attention on the plight of poor families and the responsibilities of the state – a *Lancet* report of 1918 quotes one medical practitioner who questioned 'whether any of us could live healthy lives in houses possessing no larder and no sink' (1918: 18) – but it also represented an opportunity to impress upon mothers their responsibilities, and to disseminate modern, scientific ideas about parenting. This advice reflected anxieties about the child-rearing skills of mothers themselves: Trudi Tate quotes Douglas Sladen's conviction that 'maternal instinct does not confer skill' (2013: 210). This view underpinned the theories of the highly influential New Zealand doctor, Truby King, who advocated a highly regimented model of childcare based on strict routines and advised against lavishing too much attention or physical affection on babies and small children. King's methods – which were influential in the UK and USA as well as in his native New Zealand – now seem punishingly strict, but his emphasis on hygiene and his advocacy of breastfeeding did play a significant role in reducing infant mortality (Cunningham, 1996: 175–6).

Shifting understandings of family, and of the intersection between family and state, are clearly evident in children's literature of the early twentieth century. One notable British example is Eve Garnett's *The Family from One End Street* (1937). Although Garnett has attracted criticism for a rather cosy, patronizing depiction of working-class family life (Townsend, 1983: 183), the book was widely greeted as a ground-breaking text when first published, winning out over J. R. R. Tolkien's *The Hobbit* (1937) for the Carnegie Medal of that year. Waifs and orphans had featured heavily in Victorian literature, but in the context of early twentieth-century children's literature the working-class identity of the Ruggles family (Mr Ruggles is a dustman, Mrs Ruggles a laundress) was in itself a challenge to the norm. In other respects, however, the family conforms to a very traditional model; indeed, we are told that the neighbours regard the large family (six children in all) as 'Victorian' (Garnett: 9). The Ruggles' pride in their large family in itself implicitly resists the model of family promoted by contemporary advice on child-rearing, which was producing smaller families. Scepticism about initiatives like National Baby Week is more directly introduced in an episode in which the youngest child, William, is exhibited at a baby show (a type of event which became increasingly popular during this period as a means of disseminating advice about child-rearing). Mrs Ruggles is critical of 'the Welfare', and is outraged by the mystique of the doctor, who offers platitudes about when baby William's teeth will come through, seems to question the authenticity of his birth certificate, 'and then writes no end of things in a little book' which he won't let her see (103). When William wins second prize in the show (narrowly missing first prize because of his lack of teeth) it is a vindication not of scientific child-rearing practices but of Mrs Ruggles' mothering within the context of her 'Victorian' family unit. Despite this ambivalence about state interference in family life, the text shows a more positive approach to state support. When Kate Ruggles wins a scholarship to secondary school, her father is (rightly) confident that 'The government'll do summat towards' the cost of her school uniform (32). Although Mrs Ruggles is hostile to state interference in her mothering, she too welcomes the idea of state help, reflecting after a hard day with the children that 'she would support no Government in future that did not promise immediate erection of Nursery Schools to accommodate under-school-age offspring, and relieve harassed mothers' (100). The text has a nuanced approach to the intersection of state and family, advocating the benefits of practical and financial support for poorer families while recognizing that the concomitant interference in family life could be a source of resentment. While the vindication of Mrs Ruggles' mothering instincts is rendered less challenging by the traditional conformation of the family, the subtle implication that the greatest challenge to working-class families was poverty rather than poor parenting is radical.

Little House series: the 'traditional' family

It is perhaps unsurprising that the 'Victorian' family of *The Family from One End Street* appears secure in its identity; as John R. Gillis has pointed out, 'Families past are presented to us not only as more stable but as more authentic than families present' (1996: 3). One text which has significantly contributed to the ideological construction of the 'traditional' family is Laura Ingalls Wilder's Little House series (1932–43), one of the best loved family stories of the twentieth century. Written in the 1930s, it is a fictionalized account of Wilder's own childhood in 1890s America, and follows the Ingalls family on their journey westwards from the Big Woods of Wisconsin to De Smet, North Dakota. Wilder herself conceived of the series as a national as well as a family history, stating in 1937, 'I understood that in my own life I represented a whole period of American history' (in Jameson, 2002: 75). The construction of family in the series is therefore closely intertwined with a construction of American identity. The series' popularity has given it an enduring influence: Anita Clair Fellman argues that the series is 'fully woven into American culture in a variety of ways' (Fellman, 2008: 5).

Whereas Eve Garnett presents state support of the family as potentially beneficial, Wilder constructs the family as a self-sufficient unit. The first book in the series, *Little House in the Big Woods* (1932), situates the family in the Big Woods of Wisconsin, where 'as far as the little girl could see, there was only the one little house where she lived with her father and mother, her sister Mary and baby sister Carrie' (2). This isolation reinforces the importance of family as a primary socializing force: for much of this book it is literally the only society that Laura experiences (the real Ingalls family interacted much more frequently with extended family during their time in Wisconsin). It is also the primary economic unit: *Little House in the Big Woods* focuses on the day-to-day work of the family, presenting them as almost entirely self-sufficient. Their success rests upon the willingness of every family member to take part in this work: even as a small child 'Laura always wiped carefully her own little cup and plate' (21). Help from outside the family is only reluctantly accepted: Laura's mother comments in *Little House on the Prairie*, 'I don't like to be beholden, not even to the best of neighbours' (87), a tenet which is upheld throughout the series. When the family do receive help from others, it is usually from the 'extended family' of their community: Wilder includes an incident in which a visiting preacher leaves behind money to help pay for her sister Mary's education at a college for the blind, but omits any mention of state support (the real-life Mary Ingalls' education was partially subsidized by the state of Iowa). Ann Romines (1997) and Anita Clair Fellman (2008) argue that both Wilder and her daughter Rose Lane, who collaborated closely on the series, were hostile to the New Deal politics of the 1930s, and concerned about what they perceived as the increasing encroachment of the state on the lives of individuals (Lane was an active proponent of libertarian politics). While Wilder does not engage directly with the contemporary family, then, her emphasis on self-sufficiency and resourcefulness as key family values is a direct response to the shifting relationship between family and state.

Although Wilder was writing in the 1930s, she was representing the family life of the 1890s, and her narrative contains many of the same values found in nineteenth-century family stories. Children's obedience to parents is prized: while one of the most appealing aspects of the books is their portrayal of Laura's struggles with obedience – she is particularly resistant to her mother's attempts to enforce gendered norms of dress and behaviour – the importance of obeying parents without question is reinforced. In one key episode in *Little House on the Prairie*, a creek rises suddenly while the family are making a crossing, and the children are instructed to lie quiet in the back of the wagon while their parents work together to keep the horses under control. They make the crossing successfully, but afterwards Laura reflects, 'if Laura and Mary had been naughty and bothered [their mother], then they would all have been lost' (22). In this context, obedience is literally a matter of life and death. While this is a message which would have been familiar to Mary Martha Sherwood's nineteenth-century readers, Wilder renegotiates some of the hierarchical assumptions inherent in the construction of the 'traditional family' in ways which conform to her construction of American identity. This is most apparent in *Little Town on the Prairie* (1942), in an episode in which Laura attends a Fourth of July celebration, which includes a recitation of the Declaration of Independence:

> [Laura] thought: God is America's king.
>
> She thought: Americans won't obey any king on earth. Americans are free. That means they have to obey their own consciences. No king bosses Pa: he has to boss himself. Why (she thought), when I am a little older, Pa and Ma will stop telling me what to do, and there isn't anyone else who has a right to give me orders. I will have to make myself be good.   (60)

In texts like *The Fairchild Family*, obedience to parents was the foundation for obedience to the monarch in adult life. Significantly, Wilder does not adapt this concept for an American context by substituting a democratic head of state; instead, American independence from the 'parent' monarch is seen as part of the necessary transition to adult life. Whereas Eve Garnett's construction of the family emphasizes the benefits of the incipient Welfare State, then, Wilder constructs an ideal of the family and the American citizen as both self-sufficient and self-regulating.

Changing families

By setting the *Little House* books in her own childhood, Laura Ingalls Wilder was able to construct an idealized picture of the 'traditional' family. As this chapter has shown, however, her series owes much to the rapidity with which ideas about family were *changing* during the period within which the books were written. Theories such as those of Truby King displaced the authority of the parent in favour of a scientific and government-sanctioned method; as psychoanalysis became more familiar to the middle classes, the influence of this model of child-rearing was itself contested by more child-centred models of parenting. One of the most influential was that of Doctor Benjamin Spock, who asserted, 'Your baby is born to be a reasonable, friendly human being', and rejected the need for strict training (Spock, 1946: 19). Spock reassured parents that physical affection and strong bonds between parent and child were a natural part of parenting, and advocated being responsive to the needs of the individual child. This approach to child-rearing, which was widely influential on both sides of the Atlantic, inevitably challenged the hierarchical model of family with its emphasis on obedience. Instead, family life became increasingly child led. In children's literature, this shift is reflected in a greater focus on the internal lives of children and their psychological development. This shift is already apparent in Laura Ingalls Wilder's focus on Laura's interior experiences and conflicts, but whereas in the *Little House* books Laura must learn to suppress her 'naughtiness' and disobedience, books such as Dorothy Edwards's *My Naughty Little Sister* (1952) and Beverly Cleary's *Beezus and Ramona* (1955) seek to explain such impulses. Both narrated by older sisters, these two books offer an insight into the psychological world of the child.

For instance, one day when the family plans an outing to a fair, My Naughty Little Sister refuses breakfast, calls her food 'nasty' and spills her milk. The narrator immediately steps in to explain *why* her sister behaved in this way (and by extension, to the child listening to the story why s/he has done similar things in the past): 'Shall I tell you why my naughty little sister hadn't wanted to eat her breakfast? *She was too excited*. And when my naughty little sister was excited, she was very cross and disobedient' (8). Similarly, when Ramona has been particularly naughty one afternoon, Beezus's aunt (a primary school teacher) explains how best to deal with the behaviour in a way that demonstrates knowledge of child psychology: 'I wouldn't say anything more about it,' said Aunt Beatrice. 'Lots of times little children are naughty because they want to attract attention. I have an idea that saying nothing about her naughtiness will worry Ramona more than a scolding' (98). In both these texts, then, naughtiness is presented as part of the natural development of the child rather than as an impulse which must be controlled.

In the context of this child-centred mode of child-rearing, the role of mothers (and of other supportive female figures like Beezus's aunt) became ever more important. Mother was responsible not only for the child's physical wellbeing, but for its emotional and psychological growth: while the father only rarely appears in *My Naughty Little Sister*, Mother is always there as a supportive and responsive presence. By the end of the 1950s, however, criticisms of this idealized portrayal of motherhood had begun to emerge. Psychologist Donald Winnicott emphasized the importance of the family in child development, but recognized that it might be difficult for women to live up to idealized images of motherhood, and that women could feel ambivalence or even hate for their children. Winnicott's notion of the 'good enough' mother who would meet most, but not all, of her child's needs was aimed at creating a more attainable model of parenting (although it still positioned the mother as a primary influence on the child's wellbeing). The demands placed on women by the idealization of motherhood were to be more fiercely critiqued by later theorists such as Nancy Chodorow (1978), who challenged the construction of mothering as an exclusively female role, arguing that it contributed to problematic gender divisions within society.

Ideals about motherhood were not the only aspects of the 'traditional' family to fall under question. From the 1960s onwards, the idea of the nuclear family itself came under fire. Psychologist R. D. Laing argued that, far from providing stability, the family was a common source of mental problems; and Edmund Leach stated that the family, 'with its narrow privacy and tawdry secrets, is the source of all our discontents' (Dollimore, 1983: 61). At the same time, more liberal divorce laws and access to effective contraception and abortion were making it possible for many more people in the Western world to escape the nuclear family, and children's literature increasingly began to feature stepfamilies and divorced parents. For many writers the focus was on overcoming these 'problems': one typical example is Judy Blume's *Not the End of the World* (1972), which follows 12-year-old Karen's struggle to come to terms with the breakdown of her parents' marriage and her gradual realization that divorce is 'not the end of the world'.

Tillerman series: the new pioneers?

In the 1980s, the changing understanding of family became a central focus for conservative politicians who advocated a return to 'traditional family values'. These values were predicated on the idea of a two-parent family with a male breadwinner and a female homemaker, and were closely associated with the values of self-sufficiency, independence and freedom from government interference that run through the *Little House* books. It is therefore unsurprising to find Ronald Reagan numbered among the fans of the television adaptation of Wilder's series, *Little House on the Prairie* (1974–83). It is also significant that 1981 saw the publication of another story about a 'pioneer' family, Cynthia Voigt's *Homecoming*, which engages with many of the debates about family that had emerged over the previous 20 years. Set not on the American frontier but in the late 1970s, the book follows the four Tillerman children as they travel on foot from Connecticut to Maryland. *Homecoming* shares many themes with the Little House series, but the book and its sequels interrogate both the construction of family established in the Little House books, and the socio-political ideologies it transmits.

Homecoming opens with the abandonment of the four Tillerman children, Dicey, James, Maybeth and Sammy. The family are en route from Provincetown, Massachusetts to Bridgeport, Connecticut, where their single mother hopes to find her Aunt Cilla. Like the Ingalls family, then, the Tillermans are journeying to find a new home, but whereas for Laura the journey west always takes place under the protection of at least one of her parents, the Tillermans' journey is interrupted when their mother leaves them in a car park and walks away, never to return. Single-parent families were a chief target of criticisms by 1980s proponents of 'traditional family values', and Momma's abandonment of her children initially seems to confirm the negative portrayal of single mothers. When the children continue the journey alone, hoping to find 'Momma's Aunt Cilla and her big house in Bridgeport that Momma had never seen, and her rich husband who died' (10), the book appears to hold out the possibility of the reconstitution of the family along more traditional lines (even if the male figure is still absent). In an era when single-parent families were often criticized for being over-reliant on the state, the Tillerman family share the independent spirit celebrated in the *Little House* books. Like the Ingalls family, Dicey is suspicious of interference by the state, fearing that it will result in the splitting up of the family. State support is also rejected: when a police sergeant asks whether her mother had ever sought welfare support, Dicey responds, 'She said charity was not for the Tillermans' (146), a libertarian stance which is reiterated later in the novel by their grandmother. When the children reach Bridgeport, Dicey's suspicion of outside intervention in family life seems to be vindicated: the involvement of church, police and other outside agencies in the children's lives serves to threaten their close bonds, and while they are taken in by a family member (their Cousin Eunice) this is contingent on their good behaviour, and the threat of adoption or fostering remains.

In many respects, then, *Homecoming* appears to reinforce many of the ideas about family and its relationship with the state which had appeared in the

Little House books and which had reappeared in the socio-political discourse of the 1980s. However, as the narrative progresses Cynthia Voigt increasingly problematizes this traditional construction of the family, and the associated ideals of self-sufficiency and limited state involvement. Although their mother has abandoned them, the novel consistently emphasizes the ways in which she has provided her children with a sense of love and support. When Cousin Eunice suggests that her adoption of the children will ensure they 'have a good mother', Dicey mentally insists, 'We already have a good mother' (167), an idea which is reinforced by both the resilience of the children and their unanimous belief in their mother's love for them. If Momma has failed the children, it is implied that this is a result of the pressures on her as a single mother, rather than her own failings, a view consonant with the theories of feminist scholars like Nancy Chodorow.

The book moves further away from traditional ideas of family with the introduction of the children's grandmother, Gram, with whom the children seek refuge after Cousin Eunice's care proves unsatisfactory. The story of Hansel and Gretel is a recurring motif throughout the novel, and on her first meeting with Dicey, Gram explicitly identifies herself with the wicked witch of the fairy tale. She observes: 'I sometimes think people might be good to eat ... Especially babies ... Or children. Do you have brothers and sisters?' (277). As Ann Alston has noted, the witch in Hansel and Gretel signifies the threat of the deviant mother, who consumes rather than nurtures the children (Alston, 2008: 113). However, the food Gram serves to the children does not resemble the alluring gingerbread cottage of the story: despite claiming that she cannot offer the children a home, she serves them potatoes, green beans and steamed crabs, all produced from her farm and the river on which it is situated. She is therefore shown to be capable of playing the role of nourishing mother rather than cannibalistic witch, and by the end of the meal all the children have identified their grandmother's home as a good place for them to stay. By subverting the Hansel and Gretel narrative, Voigt suggests that the single or surrogate mother can form a viable family unit.

Cynthia Voigt's critique of traditional models of family is intensified through Gram's account of her own experiences of the heteronormative nuclear family:

> I was married for thirty-eight years and my husband just died these four years ago. Until then, until he died – when you marry someone you make promises. I kept those promises, love and honour and obey. Even when I didn't want to I kept them. I kept quiet when I had things to say. I always went his way. (330)

This fidelity to her marriage vows is presented as damaging rather than praiseworthy: Gram identifies her husband's assumption of power and her own acquiescence as a source of anger and shame which ultimately resulted in the estrangement of her children, who 'ran as fast and as far as they could' (332). The mental breakdown of the Tillermans' mother is also implicitly linked to the failures of the family, an outcome which seems to confirm R. D. Laing's criticisms of the nuclear family and its effects on its members.

The novel ultimately demonstrates that the creation of a successful family unit for the Tillermans depends on their ability to move beyond the traditional model of family rather than their success at replicating it. Most notably, the children reject the hierarchical power dynamics which characterized their grandparents' family and which Gram initially tries to replicate in her parenting of her grandchildren. Dicey repeatedly comes into conflict with Gram about the best way to parent her siblings, rejecting a punitive approach in favour of addressing 'bad' behaviour through dialogue and reasoning. When Gram asserts that Sammy is 'wilful and needs to learn', Dicey responds, 'He doesn't need to learn to give in and give up' (318), presenting Sammy's 'stubbornness' as more valuable than unquestioning obedience. Ultimately, Gram comes to accept this alternative model of family, which depends on consensus and mutual respect rather than hierarchical power. This more equal distribution of power within the family is married to a distribution of responsibilities: the children 'earn' their place in Gram's house by demonstrating their ability to contribute to the family by maintaining the household and farm, taking on paid work, and supplying ideas for how their grandmother can earn more money (for example, by renting out unused land on her farm). As in the *Little House* books, all members of the family have a responsibility to contribute, but the hierarchical power dynamic is supplanted by a more collaborative and consensual model in which each member has both a role and a voice.

The collaborative model of interactions *within* the family is mirrored by a network of connections *beyond* the family, and the ideal of the completely self-sufficient family is increasingly questioned as the novel progresses. Dicey's fierce determination to preserve her family unit is ultimately achievable only with the help of a variety of different people. At one point in the novel, Dicey reflects: 'A lot of people had little bits of her life now, and they were tied to her now, or she was tied to them … You didn't just let people go … you always did what you could' (267).

The idea of being 'beholden' to someone, as Laura Ingalls Wilder terms it, is here reframed as both inevitable and positive, and the Tillermans' initial emphasis on the independence of the nuclear family is exposed as unsustainable. Significantly, this ethos extends to the family's interactions with the state as well as with the community. Gram's hostility to the idea of claiming financial support from the state is explicitly rejected by her friend Millie, who rebuts Gram's assertion that 'I didn't work to pay it in', saying: 'No more you didn't, Ab Tillerman, raising three children and working on that farm. Your John did, too, every year in his taxes. It's for widows and their children, as much as for people older than we are, and helpless' (346). This advocacy of state support for the family has particular narrative weight because Gram has cited the expense of raising children as one reason the Tillermans cannot stay with her. The reader is therefore primed to welcome Gram's decision to 'see lawyers about adoption and take government money' (349). Although accepting help from outside the family may be difficult, Voigt suggests that it is also necessary for the preservation of the family unit.

In *Homecoming*, then, Voigt rejects the hierarchical nuclear family in favour of a model of family which encompasses links with many people from the wider community and from the state, and which does not require a father in order to be successful. Although the Tillermans' journey across America echoes some of Laura Ingalls Wilder's celebration of the family as a close-knit, independent unit, the book ultimately demonstrates that the family must learn to become more porous, more connected and more able to accept help in order to survive. This message is profoundly antithetical to the construction of family deployed by conservative commentators at the time the book was published.

Jacqueline Wilson: child parents and alternative families

Despite the attempts of conservative commentators in the 1980s to revive notions of the 'traditional' family, the changing understanding of family evident in the Tillerman series has become increasingly prominent in Western life. One British writer who has become well known for her portrayals of many different kinds of family is Jacqueline Wilson, who has explored looked-after children in *The Story of Tracy Beaker* (1991), child carers in *The Illustrated Mum* (1999) and single fatherhood in *Candyfloss* (2006), to name just a few. Many of Wilson's books scrutinize the idea of the 'good' family; while they maintain the idea of family as a crucial foundation for a happy and secure foundation which has been an enduring part of family stories for children, they offer the possibility of finding this foundation in a variety of different family environments. *The Illustrated Mum*, one of Wilson's books for older readers, is characteristic in exploring the conflict between ideals of the 'good' family and the lived experience of real children. At the opening of the book, the protagonist Dolphin draws her mother, Marigold, a birthday card depicting Marigold's favourite things, which include 'the Rainbow Tattoo Studio and the Victoria Arms and the Nightbirds club' (5). Marigold's distressed observation that 'These aren't mumsie things. Dol should have drawn ... a kitten and a pretty frock' epitomizes a central conflict within the narrative: as a young single mother whose colourful tattoos exemplify her unconventional approach to life, Marigold does not conform to societal expectations about the 'good' mother. It quickly becomes apparent that in many respects her mothering is not only unconventional but problematic. Her untreated mental illness contributes to a family dynamic in which the role of parent and child is often reversed: Dolphin observes that Marigold is 'like our big sister' (11), while her real big sister, Star, is responsible for most of the practical support of the family. Marigold's instability frequently results in an inability to provide her children with a stable home life or nutritious food, two key markers of the 'good' family.

Wilson is explicit about the toll this role reversal takes on both children; nevertheless, her narrative does not work to simply condemn the unconventional family. On the contrary, she emphasizes the strength of the bonds between Marigold and her children. Among the first things Dolphin includes on Marigold's birthday card are herself and Star, reflecting her understanding that her mother does view her children as central to her life. Micky, Star's father, is also included in the picture, a presence which symbolizes Marigold's aspiration to form a more conventional nuclear family. This theme is played out through the rest of the novel, during which both Marigold and Star make abortive attempts to form a family relationship with Micky, so it is significant that the book ends with: 'The three of us. Marigold and Star and Dolphin' (223). Although Marigold's mothering is imperfect, the happy ending is not predicated on the successful formation of a more conventional family unit.

One significant theme which runs through much of Wilson's work is the role of the state in relation to the family. In *The Story of Tracy Beaker* the state literally replaces the family, since Tracy lives in a care home. For much of *The Illustrated Mum*, such state intervention is presented as a threat: Marigold perceives mental health treatment as 'torture' (40) and her bad experiences of foster care have led Dol to believe that social workers '*don't* care. They smack you and they tell you off' (187). The successful resolution at the end of the novel, however, depends on more rather than less state intervention in the lives of Marigold and her family: following a crisis, Marigold receives appropriate treatment for her mental illness, while Dol is placed in a supportive foster home. In both cases, institutional support is shown to be valuable rather than punitive, and Dolphin is able to conclude that 'we'd always have our mum, Marigold. It didn't matter if she was mad or bad' (223). While at the start of the novel, the family's neighbour vilifies Marigold for 'let[ting] the state fork out for her and her children' (16), Wilson strongly implies that the state has a responsibility to support families of all kinds, and that such support can supplement the loving family bonds which are often present even in problematic families.

Jacqueline Woodson: families, communities

The shift towards more diverse images of family over the last few decades is strongly evident in the work of Jacqueline Woodson, whose books not only explore different configurations of family (single parents, sibling-parented families, looked-after children) but also interrogate relationships within the family and between family and community. The fact that Woodson's work primarily features African-American and mixed heritage families in itself situates her books within a political discourse: as Vonnie C. McLoyd, Nancy E. Hill and Kenneth A. Dodge argue, 'African American families, especially those at the lower end of the income distribution, often have been at the center of these debates [about family], owing to their differences from "mainstream" American families in terms of family structure, living arrangements, and child-rearing practices' (in McLoyd et al., 2005: 3). Woodson herself highlights how her gender and race contribute to the politicization of her work, stating that 'as a woman who is African American, my whole world is political so of course my writing is' (Woodson, 2001: 48). The intersection of the personal and political is a clear theme in her books. In *From the Notebooks of Melanin*

Sun (1995), 13-year-old Melanin reflects on the way his family conflicts with socially acceptable constructions of the 'good' family: *'[F]ew people were willing to take a single mom and her dark baby son into their building. ... So many landlords said no to Mama. They wanted me to have a daddy. They wanted Mama to have a car. They wanted Mama to be older, to have more money, nicer clothes, better teeth, straighter hair'* (8, italics in the original).

Woodson makes it clear that Melanin's mother is a loving and successful parent; nevertheless, her socio-economic status, the fact that she is a single parent, and the fact that her son has darker skin than her contribute to a perception of their family as a threat. When a landlady asks, 'How come he [Melanin] so dark, anyway? You're brown-skinned', her reaction not only suggests racially motivated mistrust, but also subtly implies that the element of racial difference within the family makes them suspect (8). Woodson thus makes clear that social constructions of the 'good' family do impinge on the experiences of those who do not conform to them.

Like Cynthia Voigt, Jacqueline Woodson presents family as part of a wider network of community. This is particularly evident in *The Dear One* (1991), which depicts friendship groups as an important part of the extended family. The book centres around 12-year-old Afeni's struggle to come to terms with her mother's decision to take in Rebecca, the pregnant daughter of her friend Clair. Despite the fact Clair has become estranged from Afeni's mother and her other friends in the preceding years, they are committed to providing Rebecca with the emotional and material support she needs during her pregnancy. The extended family of choice is thus shown to provide more support than either the nuclear family – Rebecca's father has abandoned his family – or the state. Afeni initially criticizes Rebecca's evident poverty and complains that the family should get some money 'From wherever ...' (53), but is brought to realize, 'We were Rebecca's wherever' (53). In this respect, Woodson continues some of the resistance to state interference that was evident in earlier American family narratives like the *Little House* books.

Vonnie C. McLoyd, Nancy E. Hill and Kenneth A. Dodge note that extended families are more common in African-American communities, and Jacqueline Woodson frequently portrays extended families formed around friendships and racial ties. In *The Dear One* Afeni's mother encourages Afeni to attend the Jack and Jill club for African-American children, arguing, 'black kids need a place to meet other black kids' (12). In *Melanin Sun*, the intersection between race and the creation of an extended family is explored in more depth. The major conflict of the book centres on E.C.'s announcement that her new partner is a woman, and Melanin's struggles to come to terms with what this means for his sense of identity and for their family unity. Significantly, Melanin is threatened not only by his mother's lesbian identity, but by the fact that her new partner, Kristin, is white. Before he meets Kristin, he speculates on whether she might be the 'fine sister' he has met with his mother, but, 'Not only was she not the fine sister. This woman wasn't fine *or* a sister. She was white. White white. Like Breck shampoo white but with glasses. And those straight white-people-teeth that you know must have cost her parents a million dollars in dental bills' (31).

Melanin's repeated observation that Kristin is 'not a *sister*' draws attention to the way her relationship with his mother impinges on the construction of family ties along racial grounds. Kristin, with her 'straight white-people-teeth' is both racially and socio-economically Other. As a woman, she is also threatening to Melanin's family ties because she causes him to wonder whether his mother hates men and – by extension – Melanin himself. Kristin therefore poses a challenge both to elements of the traditional family – heteronormative, focused around the bond between mother and child – and the alternative family Melanin has constructed along racial and socio-economic lines.

Although Melanin resists Kristin's intrusion into their family unit, his mother reinterprets her partner's outsider status as beneficial, stating: 'I like the contrast of us, the differences between us – and I like the way we've found our way to each other across color lines' (104). If Cynthia Voigt suggests that the family unit can only exist within a wider network of community ties, Woodson goes further, suggesting that the family itself can be defined by these emotional ties rather than by commonalities of kinship or identity. This idea of the 'family of choice' has become increasingly important in recent decades, as families have gradually tended to have fewer children and limited access to the extended family (because of distance or because of economic factors), which has led to more reliance on friends. Critics such as Jack Zipes (2001) have argued that these 'families of choice' reflect an era of consumer capitalism in which the emphasis on constructing brand loyalties has resulted in young people forming stronger loyalty to consumer culture than to their families. In Woodson's novel, however, Kristin explicitly articulates the benefits of the family of choice, noting that her blood family have rejected her for her sexuality but that she has replaced them with 'The family I made for myself. Close friends' (122). The family of choice is therefore empowering rather than problematic, providing a support network when the nuclear family fails. Like Jacqueline Wilson, Woodson illustrates the value of alternatives to the traditional nuclear family, but a more American ethos is evident in her focus on community rather than state as the source of such support.

Conclusion

Since the beginning of the twentieth century, ideas about family have undergone radical changes, and stories for children have portrayed an ever more diverse image of family. What has remained constant, however, is the idea that family itself is important, whatever form it may take. At the close of *Little House on the Prairie*, the family has been uprooted from its 'little house', but Laura is secure in the knowledge that 'They were all there together' (222). Sixty years later, Jacqueline Woodson resolves *From the Notebooks of Melanin Sun* with Melanin's understanding that he and his mother 'would always have each other' (126). The fact that family is of enduring importance, and yet remains almost infinitely malleable, makes it a powerful ideological construct. As this chapter has shown, depictions of families in children's books have consistently worked not only to help child readers understand the family and their place within it, but also as a forum for understanding and negotiating the relationship between families, communities and the state. As a primary means of shaping the ideas of the next generation, then, the family story also represents an opportunity to shape the society in which they will live.

WORKS CITED AND FURTHER READING

Children's Books

Cleary, Beverly. *Beezus and Ramona*. New York: Avon, 1990; first published 1955.
Edwards, Dorothy. *My Naughty Little Sister*. London: Egmont, 2010; first published 1952.
Garnett, Eve. *The Family from One End Street*. Harmondsworth, Puffin: 1974; first published 1937.
Voigt, Cynthia. *Homecoming*. London: Lions, 1990; first published 1981.
Wilder, Laura Ingalls. *Little House in the Big Woods*. Harmondsworth, Puffin: 1962; first published 1932.
Wilder, Laura Ingalls. *Little House on the Prairie*. Harmondsworth: Puffin, 1988; first published 1935.
Wilder, Laura Ingalls. *Little Town on the Prairie*. Harmondsworth: Puffin, 1969; first published 1942.
Wilson, Jacqueline. *The Illustrated Mum*. London: Corgi Yearling, 2007; first published 1999.
Woodson, Jacqueline. *The Dear One*. London: Penguin, 2004; first published 1991.
Woodson, Jacqueline. *From the Notebooks of Melanin Sun*. London: Puffin, 2010; first published 1995.

Critical Texts

Alston, Ann. *The Family in English Children's Literature*. New York: Routledge, 2008.
Chodorow, Nancy. *Reproduction of Mothering: Psychoanalysis and the Sociology of Gender*. Berkeley: University of California Press, 1978.
Clark, Dorothy G. 'Edging Towards Bethlehem: Rewriting the Myth of Childhood in Voigt's *Homecoming*'. *Children's Literature Association Quarterly*, 25.4 (Winter 2000), 191–202.
Cunningham, Hugh. *Children and Childhood in Western Society since 1500*. London and New York: Longman, 1996.
Dollimore, Jonathan. 'The Challenge of Sexuality'. In Alan Sinfield (ed.), *Society and Literature, 1945–1970* (pp. 51–86). London: Methuen, 1983.
Fellman, Anita Clair. *Little House, Long Shadow: Laura Ingalls Wilder's Impact on American Culture*. Columbia, MO: University of Columbia Press, 2008.
Gillis, John R. *A World of Their Making: Myth, Ritual, and the Quest for Family Values*. Cambridge, MA: Harvard University Press, 1996.
Jameson, Elizabeth. 'Unconscious Inheritance and Conscious Striving'. In Dwight M. Miller (ed.), *Laura Ingalls Wilder and the American Frontier: Five Perspectives* (pp. 69–94). Lanham, MD: University Press of Oxford, 2002.
Jameson, Fredric. *Postmodernism: or, The Cultural Logic of Late Capitalism*. London: Verso, 1991.
'Lessons from Baby Week'. *The Lancet* (6 July 1918), 18–19.
Marwick, Arthur. *British Society since 1945*. London: Penguin, 1996.
McLoyd, Vonnie C., Nancy E. Hill and Kenneth A. Dodge (eds). *African American Family Life: Ecological and Cultural Diversity*. New York: Guilford Press, 2005.

Mowat, C. L. *Britain Between the Wars, 1918–1940*. Cambridge: Cambridge University Press, 1955.

Reynolds, Kimberley. 'Changing Families in Children's Fiction'. In M. O. Grenby and Andrea Immel (eds), *The Cambridge Companion to Children's Literature* (pp. 193–208). Cambridge: Cambridge University Press, 2009.

Romines, Ann. *Constructing the Little House: Gender, Culture, and Laura Ingalls Wilder*. Amherst: University of Massachusetts Press, 1997.

Sinfield, Alan. *Literature, Politics and Culture in Britain*. Oxford: Basil Blackwell, 1989.

Spock, Benjamin. *Baby and Child Care*. New York: Pocket Books, 1946.

Stacy, Judith. 'Good Riddance to "The Family": A Response to David Popenoe'. *Journal of Marriage and Family*, 55.3 (1993), 545–7.

Stevenson, John. *British Society, 1914–45*. London: Penguin, 1984.

Stover, Lois Thomas. *Jacqueline Woodson: 'The Real Thing'*. Lanham, MD: Scarecrow, 2003.

Tate, Trudi. 'King Baby: Infant Care into the Peace'. In Trudi Tate and Kate Kennedy (eds), *The Silent Morning: Culture and Memory after the Armistice* (pp. 104–30). Manchester: Manchester University Press, 2013.

Townsend, J. R. *Written for Children: An Outline of English-language Children's Literature*. Harmondsworth: Kestrel, 1983; first published 1965.

Winnicott, D. W. *The Child and the Family*. London: Tavistock, 1957.

Winnicott, D. W. *The Child, the Family and the Outside World*. Harmondsworth: Penguin, 1976; first published 1957.

Winnicott, D. W. *The Family and Individual Development*. Abingdon: Routledge, 2006; first published 1967.

Woodson, Jacqueline. 'Fictions'. *Obsidian III: Literature in the African Diaspora*, 3.1 (2001), 48–50.

Zipes, Jack. 'The Cultural Homogenization of American Children'. *Sticks and Stones: the Troublesome Success of Children's Literature from Slovenly Peter to Harry Potter* (pp. 1–23). London: Routledge, 2001.

Theories of Genre and Gender: Change and Continuity in the School Story

7

Pat Pinsent

More than most varieties of literature, the school story can be described as a *genre* (see Box 7.1); it is not entirely confined to children's literature, though most of its best known exemplars clearly presuppose an audience at least partly made up of young people. The genre of school fiction has certain characteristics, though not every individual novel featuring a school automatically displays these. Some of these characteristics appear in the earliest examples of school stories, while others emerge during the course of the school story's long history; this chapter sets out to display these with particular reference to the work of one of the most popular twentieth-century writers of school fiction, Elinor Brent-Dyer.

Critics and historians of the school story genre have often indulged in generalizations about its health, or indeed its continued existence. P. W. Musgrave's forecast in *From Brown to Bunter: The Life and Death of the School Story* (1985) of its impending demise has demonstrably proved to be false, given the fact that literally hundreds of children's novels with a school setting have been published since the mid-1970s. Nevertheless, during the last third of the twentieth century, the genre underwent a paradigm shift. As a result, this chapter has two centres of interest: the school stories characteristic of the first two-thirds of the twentieth century, focusing on the work of four of the most

---

---

notable writers, Elinor Brent-Dyer (1895–1969), Enid Blyton (1897–1968), Antonia Forest (1915–2003) and Anthony Buckeridge (1912–2004); and the developments in the school story genre in the last third of the century.

Any discussion of twentieth-century school fiction needs, however, to be set in perspective by a brief glance at its earlier development, not only to contextualize the books considered, but also to justify the fact that, despite the prestige of boys' fiction, of the novels examined below only Buckeridge's are set in an exclusively male school. Since the majority of these stories are set in girls' schools and written by women authors, another critical stance that inevitably comes to the fore is that of gender studies, particularly with a feminist emphasis.

The history of the school story

The relative merits and respective primacy of boys' and girls' school stories have been much disputed. For some critics only the boys' story is truly canonical. In her introduction to *The Encyclopaedia of Girls' School Stories* (2000), Sue Sims quotes the comments of such otherwise sensitive critics as Elizabeth Bowen and Margery Fisher, revealing their hostility to the girls' stories. Nevertheless, it is generally agreed that the predecessor of the entire school-story genre is the eighteenth-century work by the sister of the better-known author of *Tom Jones*. Sarah Fielding's *The Governess, or The Little Female Academy* (1749) is set in a girls' school which has only nine pupils; as Sims remarks, it was not until the work of the girls' school pioneers had been validated in 1868 that the 'full-blown' girls' school story could emerge (2000: 3). Nevertheless, other early writers, such as Maria Edgeworth (1767–1849), Elizabeth Sandham and Mary Hughes (dates uncertain but both writing in the early 1800s), produced stories which anticipate the much more considerable achievement of L. T. Meade (1844–1914), whose over 200 titles include a number set in schools and other places of education.

However, the school story whose title is likely to be most familiar, even with those who haven't read it, is Thomas Hughes's *Tom Brown's Schooldays* (1857). Like this text, other well-known Victorian examples of the genre, such as F. W. Farrar's *Eric, or Little by Little* (1858), Talbot Baines Reed's *The Fifth Form at St Dominic's* (1887) and Rudyard Kipling's *Stalky & Co* (1899), tend to be set in schools where the only females to be glimpsed are Matron and possibly the Headmaster's wife. It was in boys' texts such as these that many of the conventions of the genre as we see it today were established; their later development determined what we now recognize as the typical school story.

When Angela Brazil (1868–1947) produced the first of her nearly 50 novels about girls' schools, *A Terrible Tomboy* (1904), she was building on the solid achievement of a considerable number of earlier writers in the girls' sub-genre, although she also incorporated features more characteristic of the boys' school story, notably the emphasis on games and the use of distinctive slang. Her books were extremely popular with girls, including many who were not of the social class likely to attend boarding schools themselves. Brazil was followed fairly swiftly by the authors whom Rosemary Auchmuty (in Tucker and Reynolds, 1997: 79) terms the 'Big Three': Elsie Oxenham (1880–1960), best known for the Abbey School novels; Dorita Fairlie Bruce (1885–1970), author of the 'Dimsie' stories; and Elinor Brent-Dyer, whose Chalet School novels are examined in more detail in the next section. During the same period, there were also many writers who set their school stories in boys' schools: two of the best known of these are Charles Hamilton (1876–1961) and Anthony Buckeridge (1912–2004).

Elinor Brent-Dyer and girls' school stories up to 1970: the Chalet School series

According to the *Encyclopaedia of Girls' School Stories*, 'Elinor Brent-Dyer [writing between 1922 and 1970] is probably the best known and the most popular author in the field of the girls' school story, the standard by which all others are judged' (Sims and Clare, 2000: 75). I shall refer most closely to *Exploits of the Chalet Girls* (1933), a relatively early text, and *The Wrong Chalet School* (1952), a novel from the middle of Brent-Dyer's writing career, since these fairly typical Chalet School books are not only representative of Brent-Dyer's *oeuvre*, but also fit very closely into what might be termed the paradigm of the girls' school story. As there are so many books in the various series by Brent-Dyer, Blyton and Forest, each section includes brief plot summaries of the relevant texts.

Exploits of the Chalet Girls

This book is the ninth in the series, its action occurring four and a half years after the foundation of the Chalet School in the Austrian Tyrol by Madge Bettany, later Mrs Russell. Her younger sister, Jo, is now head girl, with seven fellow prefects all of whom have been at the school for several years. There is little over-arching plot; the incidents described build up a sense of the wholesomeness of the life of the girls at the school: speaking English, French and German; enjoying walks up the local mountains; eating home-made food; and staging concerts which both display their musical and dramatic talent and celebrate festivals, notably Christmas. The main discordancy arrives in the form of a new pupil, Thekla von Stift, the daughter of a Prussian *Graf* [Count]. She thinks herself superior to girls whose parents are in trade or manufacturing, and also has no notion of the schoolgirl code of conduct, displaying herself as a 'sneak' when she informs the staff about some pupils who have interfered with the school clock. By the end of the book, however, 'the atmosphere of the School was doing its duty and she was already a nicer girl than the one who had come in September' (136).

The Wrong Chalet School

The 24th volume of the 58 (see Sims and Clare, 2000: 76–81) is largely set in postwar Wales, where the main section of the Chalet School is now located on a small island near the Swansea coast. Katherine Mary Gordon's aunt Luce, a stereotypically vague artist, having arranged for her niece to enrol at a different Chalet School in Pembrokeshire, arrives with her at Paddington from where the pupils of both schools are departing, and is confused by similarities in the colour of the uniforms. Inevitably, to the reader's satisfaction, Katherine joins 'our' Chalet School. This situation is compounded by the unlikely coincidences that both schools have teachers with the surname Wilson, and *the* Chalet School is expecting a pupil called Mary Katherine Gordon. The reader familiar with Brent-Dyer's work is hardly surprised to discover that the incorrect choice turns out to be absolutely right as far as Katherine is concerned, fostering her ability at games and providing the kind of caring environment much needed by a girl whose parents are lost somewhere in Communist China. The contrast between the two schools allows the author to expound her values: 'our' girls have better manners, a nicer uniform and a set curriculum, unlike the flamboyant colours and free choice of subjects allowed to the pupils at the other Chalet School. As usual, the value of speaking three languages, playing sports and being creative is emphasized.

An aspect common to both these Chalet School books and to most of the others is the frequent incidental mention of prayer and trust in God. In *The Wrong Chalet School* this trust is fulfilled when Katherine's parents are ultimately liberated, and at the end she is awaiting reunion with them.

The girls' boarding-school story paradigm

These summaries reveal the recurrence of certain elements, which are also found in the remainder of Brent-Dyer's work and that of the other girls' school story writers named above, together with later school story writers Enid Blyton (1897–1968) and Antonia Forest (1915–2003). Rather than establishing these characteristics of the genre by herself, Brent-Dyer could be said to have been instrumental in creating a product containing features attractive to readers; some of these also occur in boys' school stories. The list below sets out some of these characteristics:

1   Many girls' school novels tend to start with a train journey during which new girls are introduced and friendships between old pupils are renewed. The journey marks the boundary between home and school territory; when parents are allowed to appear at the school, it is clear that they are present by permission of the authorities, in what is virtually an alien country where their daughters and the staff are the inhabitants. Even in a later period when pupils are likely to have been delivered by car, Anne Digby maintains the 'train' tradition in at least some of her Trebizon books. This characteristic use of the train could be described as a *chronotope* (see Box 7.2 and the discussion in Chapter 12).

2   The school itself often becomes a kind of additional character in the book, moulding its pupils almost in spite of themselves, or of the efforts of the staff, into its own ethos. The strong sense of place and ethos embedded in the school-as-character provides writers with an element of continuity, and a setting that they will not need constantly to describe in detail. Most of the best known school writers for both girls and boys tend to use the same school for a number of different books.

BOX 7.2   CHRONOTOPE

The term *chronotope*, defined by Mikhail Bakhtin as 'the intrinsic connectedness of temporal and spatial relationships that are artistically expressed in literature', and more concisely translated by Maria Nikolajeva (1996: 121) as the indivisible 'unity of time and space' in a work of literature, is seen by Nikolajeva as providing 'an appropriate approach to genres', since 'specific forms of chronotope are unique for particular genres'. The use of the train to travel to boarding school is particularly characteristic of the girls' school story of the first two-thirds of the twentieth century, as well as having been adopted by J. K. Rowling in her Harry Potter saga. The train marks the transition between the parental territory (as it exists in time and space) of the home, and the teacher/pupil territory of the school. It is a kind of liminal time–space zone, in which, by the inevitably scattered nature of authority, no one is in total control and associations of characters are provisional. The chronotope of the school story, then, normally encompasses three distinct domains of time and space: home (or family holiday), train journey and school.

3   Many books in the genre begin with the introduction of one or more new pupils, providing a way in for the reader not familiar with the series, while readers who are already knowledgeable can feel a sense of superiority to the character(s) concerned and enjoy a kind of vicarious meeting with old friends.

4   Much of the plot hinges on events internal to the school, such as selection for sports teams, preparations for dramatic or musical productions, and relationships between pupils and staff. The world outside may impinge through mention of past pupils, parents' situations, or even, in general terms related to the school, a war, but because of the boarding-school environment, pupils themselves are not generally directly involved in activities outside the school.

5   Particularly characteristic of the world of the Chalet School, but also found in other girls' school books to a greater extent than in boys' books, is an advocacy of tolerance for others' differences and abilities, together with a fostering not only of sport but also of artistic ability.

6   Teachers in the girls' schools of Brent-Dyer's era and earlier frequently display a high degree of care for their pupils, all of whom they seem to know well. This does not mean that they are perfect, or never become objects of comedy; some indeed, notably the French teachers, might be seen as 'stock characters'. On the whole, however, even in Blyton's work, there is rather less stereotyping than in the boys' stories. The same is not always true of the school fiction from later in the twentieth century.

7   Brent-Dyer's books, like those of the school story genre as a whole, endorse a school 'code of honour', involving the avoidance of 'meanness' or 'sneak-iness' and a hatred of snobbery, whether this arises from social class or academic excellence. The wrongness of taking advantage of being related to those in positions of power, whether in the school or outside, is also emphasized.

8   There is often an ambivalence about gender roles, possibly reflecting something of the situation actually extant within real boarding schools during the period concerned. These single-sex female environments allow girls to excel at both sport and schoolwork, yet the girls are often told that they must prepare for their roles as wives and mothers. The only Brent-Dyer character who seems capable of combining all these qualities is Jo Bettany, who, as Mrs Maynard, manages to have 11 children while being a successful writer and standing as a model to later generations of Chalet School girls. Her first name, possibly recalling that of Louisa May Alcott's heroine in *Little Women*, is androgynous, as indeed is that of another idealized Chalet School character, 'The Robin'. The use of boyish-sounding names is prevalent in many girls' school books, whereas any use of feminized names for characters in boys' stories is invariably derogatory.

9   As with the vast majority of boys' school stories of the period, these books tend to be set in boarding schools, which are not only detached from ordinary society but also by their nature patronized by the upper class and the upper middle class, even though their readership certainly included a good many children from 'lower' classes. Because of the relatively stable class

structure that obtained prior to the Second World War, this element drew little comment at the time; children who did not attend single-sex schools, let alone boarding schools, were nevertheless prepared to take these not only as the norm, but also as an unattainable ideal. Consequently, there is very little social criticism in the majority of school books before the 1950s, beyond the conventional condemnation of snobbery mentioned above.

10   As with those for boys, girls' school stories often focus on friendships within a fairly small sub-group of pupils.

11   A feature particularly evident in Brent-Dyer's work is the *Bildungsroman* aspect; the characters grow up as readers progress through the series, and indeed are succeeded by further generations of schoolgirls. While many novels, notably *Tom Brown's Schooldays*, portray boys as maturing, character development throughout a series seems less characteristic of the boys' series than of the girls' (contrast Buckeridge's Jennings books with the majority of the books by Brent-Dyer, Bruce and Oxenham).

The way such aspects feature in two slightly younger girls' school writers and in the boys' stories of Anthony Buckeridge is discussed below, followed by a consideration of the changes in the paradigm as far as more recent school fiction is concerned.

Enid Blyton

While Blyton's school stories are sometimes unfavourably compared with those of the 'Big Three' and her own adventure stories, they have remained popular even while boarding-school education has declined. They have also served to introduce many of their predominantly female readers to the genre, since Blyton's work is less demanding than that of many other school authors.

Blyton's three school series – The Naughtiest Girl, St Clare's and Malory Towers – were published between 1940 and 1951, a relatively short period during a writing career which stretched from 1922 to the mid-1960s. Auchmuty (in Tucker and Reynolds, 1997: 82–5) puts forward several possible reasons for Blyton's choice of this genre at this time, ranging from commercial factors and her own family situation to the changes in society, particularly with respect to the situation of women.

The second volume of the St Clare's series, *The O'Sullivan Twins* (1942), focuses on Pat and Isabel; in their second school term they learn that their cousin Alison is joining them. The usual scene at the railway station allows Blyton to introduce both old and new characters. Alison is much too concerned with her appearance and slow to accept that she has to wait on the older girls in what can be seen as a continuation of the 'fagging' tradition, so important in *Tom Brown's Schooldays*.

The main plot, however, centres on the character of Erica, who 'sneaks' on the girls having a midnight feast, and later meanly ruins Pat's knitting. She is eventually rescued from a fire by Margery, an irascible girl whom the other pupils have suspected of the misdeeds perpetrated by Erica. Readers have already been given a clue that Margery cannot really be so unpleasant because she is very good at games. In due course, it appears that the less attractive traits of both Erica and Margery have been triggered by their family situations, unexpectedly bringing in an element of social comment fairly rare in Blyton. Margery is able to reform and stays on, but Erica, too weak in character to remain in an environment where her faults have been discovered, has to leave St Clare's, though she is not expelled.

This novel manifestly displays many of the paradigmatic features listed above. A notable scene is that in which the headmistress, Miss Theobald, makes her views about morality clear, addressing the girls who have been discovered feasting in the music room: 'Although you have broken the rule forbidding any girl to leave her dormitory at night, your escapade is not in the same rank as, for instance, meanness, lying, or disloyalty. Those are serious things; ... [yours is] silly mischief' (45).

Blyton frequently creates similarities and contrasts between pairs of girls. Here, the two girls who have been affected by family situations, Margery, who is bad-tempered but basically honest, and Erica, who is underhand, are contrasted. Similarly, Pat and Isabel, ideal schoolgirls, are contrasted with their cousin Alison, who is 'full of airs and graces' (5) and (ultimate depravity) has had her hair permed at the age of 14. (Today's readers are likely to feel that all the girls seem very young for their age – adolescence does not appear to have happened to them!) Sport features very significantly, acting as an indicator of Margery's basic goodness, while art too is given status by the fact that a very popular girl, Lucy, is an excellent artist. Matron voices a stereotypical view of the female role when she advises Alison: 'You hope to be happily married one day, don't you – and run your own home? Well, you must learn to take care of your own linen and mend it, then' (13).

Antonia Forest

Sims and Clare (2000: 140) describe Antonia Forest as 'widely regarded as one of the best – if not the best – writers of girls' school stories', yet she only produced four books in this sub-genre, all dealing with the adventures of the Marlow family (subjects also of another seven books not set in schools). The first of her school books, *Autumn Term* (1948), introduces Nicola (Nicky) and her twin sister Lawrence (apparently so named because her parents hoped that she would be a boy), who are first seen on the train to Kingscote School, travelling with their elder sisters, Karen (head girl), Rowan (in the netball team), Ginty (in the second eleven hockey team) and Ann (a patrol leader in the Guides). As well as employing the train chronotope to identify these and other characters, Forest furthers the action when Nicola pulls the communication cord and stops the train: her new 16-bladed penknife has dropped out of the window. Despite their desire to distinguish themselves at school, the twins are placed in a low-achieving form, and are suspended from the Guides because of a false accusation. However, both do exceptionally well in a play staged by their form, written and produced by a friend (the headmistress's niece, nick-named 'Tim').

This brief account of *Autumn Term* reveals Forest's use of male names for several characters, as well as certain values characteristic of the school story. It is apparent that when Tim capitalizes on her relationship to the head-mistress she is going against the unwritten ethos of the school; in contrast, Lawrie and Nicola resist the temptation to make use of their family connec-tions with more senior forms. A worse crime is to be dishonest and timid, like the girl who lied to get them into trouble. Although her perfidy is ultimately detected, they are not reinstated in the Guides, nor indeed are they promoted to a higher form. Forest seems to be rejecting the possibility of too facile a happy ending, while ensuring that the twins emerge with a due degree of recognition.

It is not difficult to understand the reasons for the high rating given to Forest's novels by those familiar with a large range of school fiction. Sims and Clare comment that 'her ... characters are individualized not only by their actions and their thoughts but also by their extraordinarily vivid dialogue' (2000: 140–1). Two later novels in the Kingscote School series, *The Cricket Term* (1974) and *The Attic Term* (1976), are relatively little known, perhaps because both were written in a period when the boarding-school story, in both its male and female manifestations, was experiencing a temporary decline.

Boys' school fiction: Anthony Buckeridge

During the period considered above, the most prolific author of boys' school fiction was undoubtedly Charles Hamilton, writing under a variety of pseud-onyms[1] in a number of boys' magazines. The work of Anthony Buckeridge is often, however, acknowledged to be of higher literary quality than Hamilton's; David Bathurst in *The Encyclopaedia of Boys' School Stories* (Kirkpatrick, 2000) describes the Jennings stories as having been 'recognised by critics as being among the best school fiction ever written' (65). All the stories focus on a small group of boys who, even in the later books of the series, never seem to mature beyond prep-school age, and whose exploits are at least possible. These stories share some features with the girls' stories discussed above: for instance, the geographical location of the boarding school, Linley Court, is frequently relevant, making it serve a plot function. Again, as in the girls' stories, the emphasis in the stories is on events within the school. There do, however, appear to be significant differences, as will appear below.

Jennings' Diary (1955) is the fifth in a series of 24 volumes (see Kirkpatrick, 2000 for the full list), most of which are excerpted in *A Bookful of Jennings* (1966), an omnibus collection which facilitates a bird's-eye view of the series as a whole. *Jennings' Diary* tells of how the boy protagonist has been prom-ised a small financial reward by his Aunt Angela if he faithfully writes every day in the eponymous diary. Inevitably, problems ensue: initially purloined by his schoolmates, the diary is then confiscated by a teacher, the stereotypi-cally rule-bound Mr Wilkins. Jennings' efforts to regain the diary and to write interestingly in it lead to comic episodes, most notably one involving a visit to the local museum with a potential exhibit, a wheel, the manufacturer's initials BC on the rim having led the boys to deduce that it is prehistoric. Throughout the series, interaction between Jennings, his friend Darbishire, the rest of their group and two of the masters – Mr Wilkins and the more congenial Mr Carter – provides much of the humour. As well as misunderstandings and unlikely situations, the comedy also derives from outrageous invented slang (e.g. 'crystallised cheesecakes', from *A Bookful of Jennings*: 162) and schoolboy jokes. Interestingly, Jennings himself is often the object of amusement, either by failing to understand something that is already obvious to the reader, or, in the case of the diary, because of the boring predictability of his entries: '*January 1ˢᵗ: Got up … Had breakfast … Did some things … Weather quite hot toddy* [*sic*]' (*Diary*: 15, italics in original).

Humour of a kind to appeal to the young male audience (whether as readers or as listeners to the radio series based on the Jennings stories which ran from 1948 to 1963) seems to be have characterized the boys' school sub-genre generally during this period. Though the girls' school stories do possess humour, their authors seem less evidently to be playing for laughs, preferring to concentrate on the role of the school ethos in forming character, together with that of a circle of friends exemplifying its values. This means that in many respects the girls' stories seem to be closer to the nineteenth-century classics of the boys' school tradition such as *Tom Brown*, *Eric* and *St Dominic's*.[2]

The prevalence of humour in the boys' stories, perhaps fostered by the fact that P. G. Wodehouse produced a number of boys' school stories in the early part of the twentieth century,[3] is also germane to the question of the extent to which stories such as those of Buckeridge and Hamilton relate to the paradigm suggested above for the girls' stories. Buckeridge's books tend to have a static time setting, and there is no evidence of the books providing a *Bildungsroman* of the central character. The whole saga is episodic and not developmental, the masters having a plot function rather than one of nurture. The train chronotope, a liminal feature linking school and home, is generally absent, perhaps because it is more 'manly' in a (twentieth-century) boy to appear independent of his parents. Although Jennings' Aunt Angela and Darbishire's father are frequently mentioned as mentors, the ties to home are seldom in evidence after the initial volume, *Jennings Goes to School* (1950).

Gender is intrinsic to all the areas of differences between the girls' and the boys' school stories, though its effects are inevitably complex. As indicated above, the girls' books display their own ambiguities, resulting partly from female characters often being referred to by male-sounding names. In the boys' books, as in boys' schools of the period, the boys are consistently addressed only by their surnames or by nicknames; for the boys to address each other by first names would have been regarded as effeminate. Deeper emotions are seldom in evidence: however distressing any situation, tears would be inappropriate, and the nearest our heroes get to crying is in the homesickness felt by the boys in *Jennings Goes to School* (1950). Darbishire is missing his home but denies having been crying: 'I've just been wishing I was at home, and it's made my glasses go all misty' (*A Bookful of Jennings*: 11). The boys decide to run away, but the adventures in which they get involved while trying to elude Mr Carter, who is on the bus which they take to the station, soon replace the possible pathos with comedy.

Paradoxically, the way in which sport features seems less similar to the antecedents of the boys' tradition than are, for instance, the stories of Brazil, Blyton and Forest. Cricket is a theme in *Jennings' Little Hut* (1951) and football in *Jennings, of Course* (1964), but in both cases the focus is on the exploits of Jennings and Darbishire rather than the team's success; that Linley Court does in fact win the match is almost accidental, resulting from Darbishire's ineptitude. The team spirit and the honour of the school are less in evidence than in many earlier books, though in some respects the Jennings books have something in common with Kipling's *Stalky & Co* in their advocacy of individualism – a quality regarded at the time as more desirable for boys than for girls.

The differing treatment of gender suggests the different demands of male and female readerships. Publishers and authors seem, presumably on the basis of sales, to have considered that girl readers wanted to see themselves in the books they read – their confiding in each other, their desire to do their best for the good of the house. Such qualities are not lacking in the Jennings books, but it appears that many boy readers of the 1950s were more interested in defeating the system, even while acknowledging that it sometimes had a kindly face (as with Mr Carter). If this could be achieved in a comic way, this was more attractive to the readership than too serious a preaching of ideals. The period during which these books were published was also marked by such explicitly comic series as those featuring Molesworth and St Trinian's – an indication of a gradual change in the expectations held concerning the school story.

School fiction since 1970

Changes in society frequently act as the triggers of changes in literature written for children, though children's books may often be relatively slow in their incorporation of such changes. As Jeffrey Richards comments in his study of public schools in English fiction, 'It is generally acknowledged that popular culture holds up a mirror to the mind set of the nation' (1988: 1). If school takes a different form in the real world, the books and indeed the films and television dramas featuring it also tend to change. Even during the period of greatest popularity of boarding-school fiction the majority of British schoolchildren were attending day schools, but because of the social cachet attached to the boarding school, as well as the advantage given to the author by the virtual 'island', remote from urban society, which this kind of school provided, in particular the removal of the young characters from their parents, boarding-school fiction lingered on well past what might have been seen as its 'sell by' date. By the 1970s, in a society made conscious of equality issues in particular, embracing race and gender as well as class, 'issues-led' fiction began to dominate the children's market, to the detriment of the sales of books set in a single-sex environment where, inevitably, working-class and non-white characters had been few. As a result, during this period, day-school fiction, once very much the 'poor relation' of the genre, became supreme. By its nature, such fiction allows, or even demands, the incursion of the outside world, to an extent less appropriate to the boarding-school novel. As a consequence of their departure from the boarding-school genre, most of the authors to be discussed below are not mentioned in either the girls' or the boys' encyclopaedias of school stories.

Realism and 'issues-driven' school fiction

From its beginnings, morality was a very important theme of the school story. The qualities which make for good relationships in a small community, such as leadership, friendliness and concern for others, are inevitably singled out for praise, while those which could lead to the breakdown of relationships, such as dishonesty, telling tales and snobbery, are censured, either implicitly or explicitly. While this standard of values is certainly not abandoned in later fiction, it is set within a larger context. Because school, now almost always co-educational, is less of a closed community, wider values have more impact. The paradigm of school as a microcosm of society becomes more obvious when the school is set in the wider community, an aspect particularly pertinent to Robert Cormier's *The Chocolate War* (1974), which, as well as providing a severe critique of the practices of an American day school run by a fictional Catholic religious order, can be read as something of a satire on Mafia-like organizations within wider society.

Several British novels from the last third of the twentieth century tackle social issues such as racial prejudice, gender roles and bullying, usually within a day-school context. Recent school-based novels are also prepared to take on questions concerning such problems as drugs and teenage pregnancy. While several of these books are clearly governed by a feminist agenda, and the causes they plead are not yet universally won, even in Britain, a weakness of their position is that in the attempt to redress the gender balance, they often portray being female as something of a disadvantage. The rise of mixed-school and day-school books has had a complex effect on the treatment of gender. It has even been suggested that the single-sex environment of the earlier girls' school books allowed the writers to present a more positive aspect of femaleness, though not necessarily of femininity. Auchmuty quotes Gill Frith (1985), who observes that:

> the school story presents a picture of what it is possible for a girl to be and to do which stands in absolute contradistinction to the configuration of 'femininity' which is to be found in other forms of popular fiction addressed specifically to women and girls … in a world of girls, to be female is *normal* and not a *problem*. (Auchmuty in Sims and Clare, 2000: 29, italics Frith's)

It is apparent that within the category of realism, school books from the 1970s onwards can by no means be classified using the kind of paradigm appropriate to the earlier girls' school books, though aspects such as stereotyping and the 'code of honour' are still evident. Fantasy school fiction, a variation on the genre which became more popular during this period, tends, however, to revert much more to the typology of the earlier school novels, often including the setting of a boarding-school environment.

Fantasy school fiction: the Harry Potter phenomenon

School fiction in the past has nearly always been realistic. In talking of F. Anstey's 1882 novel *Vice Versa* (where a father and son find that their bodies, and consequently their roles, have been interchanged), Robert Kirkpatrick claims that, 'The number of school stories which rely for their central premise on magic and the supernatural can even today be counted on the fingers of two hands' (2000: 29). Such texts often tend to be regarded as outside mainstream school fiction: although the first three of the Harry Potter books are discussed by Kirkpatrick, Sims dismisses them, together with Gillian Cross's Demon Headmaster series, as 'outside the scope of this volume' (2000: 18). Neither of these encyclopaedias mentions fantasy novels by Robert Swindells, Jill Murphy or Anthony Horowitz (named in the Further Reading section of this chapter).

It is not difficult to locate within the Harry Potter books many instances in common with the traditional exponents of the school-story tradition. A notable presence is that of the train journey to school, to the extent that the Hogwarts Express features conspicuously on the cover of the first volume, *Harry Potter and the Philosopher's Stone* (1997). While this book does not actually begin with the train chronotope, when that does occur – once Harry has managed to arrive at the magical platform Nine and Three-Quarters – everything becomes very familiar. Fond farewells are being taken from families, trunks are being stowed away, twins are in evidence and the prefects have compartments to themselves. This feature, together with the link it presupposes between home and school, suggests that the Harry Potter saga is closer to the girls' school paradigm than to the boys', and while in no way being humourless, these books rely little on the kind of episodic structure frequent among the boys' stories. There are other similarities: Ron Weasley's family background at Hogwarts is uncannily similar to that of the twins in Antonia Forest's *Autumn Term*. He tells Harry that he has a lot to live up to: 'Bill was Head Boy and Charlie was captain of Quidditch. Now Percy's a Prefect. Fred and George mess around a lot, but they still get really good marks. ... Everyone expects me to do as well as the others, but if I do, it's no big deal, because they did it first' (75).

This introduction of the boy who is to become one of Harry's two best friends immediately launches the reader into an environment in which success at sport and winning for your house are key factors. Like many series about girls' schools but fewer of those set in boys' schools, Rowling's books can be seen as affording an element of *Bildungsroman* in their gradual development of Harry's character. Nevertheless, some aspects of Rowling's boarding-school world have affinities with the boys' school sub-genre. While the headmaster, Dumbledore, is undoubtedly a sympathetic figure, many of the teachers are so stereotyped as virtually to become comic figures, and on the whole they lack the empathy with pupils which is characteristic in the work of some of the best writers for girls. There is little evidence of musical or dramatic entertainment as the climax of an extended period during which the pupils' creativity is being developed.

The major difference between Rowling's work and the traditional 'realist' school story lies in the fact that in each book Harry is presented with situations which pose a threat to his own life and, increasingly, to the future of the world. Such life-and-death issues are far more the province of fantasy than of the stories which have been considered so far in this chapter. While the kind of behaviour that is censured in the traditional story, such as 'sneakiness', meanness and snobbery, is certainly not advocated (Draco Malfoy is constantly presented as an example of someone far too conceited about his distinguished background), the key virtues which in Dumbledore's speech at the end of the first volume are shown as winning Gryffindor House the house cup are those that have helped thwart Voldemort: skill at chess as exhibited by Ron; logical thinking on Hermione's part; and, most important of all, 'pure nerve and outstanding courage' as displayed by Harry himself (221). The other books in the series also suggest that Rowling wants her reader to be aware in particular of the importance of courage and integrity.

Conclusion

It would be rash to come to any overall conclusions after what has had to be a selective treatment of only a small proportion of the very many school story books. However, it is undeniable that, despite its considerable changes, the school story is far from being either dead or in terminal decline. While it has never been as monolithic as the selective treatment here might make it appear, any semblance of uniformity has now vanished. The traditional boarding-school story still attracts twenty-first-century readers, though its popularity is inevitably less than that of Hogwarts, Harry Potter's mixed and magic boarding school. The day school is a pervasive setting in the genres of both realism and fantasy, allowing the writer to incorporate themes from the everyday world while retaining the authorial advantages of an environment free from the presence of parents. And tackling important issues remains within the purview of the school story: as recently as 2011, the prestigious Costa book award was won by Jason Wallace's *Out of Shadows* (2010), which confronts both race and politics in the environment of a boarding school in 1983 Zimbabwe. It is impossible to forecast future developments within this genre, but it is likely that, as in the past, they will continue to both reflect and subvert the wider society, a society which the schools are at the same time both within and outside.

WORKS CITED AND FURTHER READING

Children's Books

Ashley, Bernard. *The Trouble with Donovan Croft*. Oxford: Oxford University Press, 1974.

Blyton, Enid. *Claudine at St Clare's*. London: Atlantic Book Publishing, 1967; first published 1944.

Blyton, Enid. *The O'Sullivan Twins*. London: Atlantic Book Publishing, 1967; first published 1942.

Brent-Dyer, Elinor. *Exploits of the Chalet Girls*. London: Collins, 1972; first published 1933.

Brent-Dyer, Elinor. *A Genius at the Chalet School*. London: May Fair Books, 1969; first published 1956.

Brent-Dyer, Elinor. *The Wrong Chalet School*. London: May Fair Books, 1970; first published 1952.

Buckeridge, Anthony. *A Bookful of Jennings*. London and Glasgow: Collins, 1966.

Buckeridge, Anthony. *Jennings' Diary*. London and Glasgow: Collins, 1955.

Cross, Gillian. *The Demon Headmaster*. Oxford: Oxford University Press, 1982.

Digby, Anne. *Second Term at Trebizon*. London: Penguin, 1988; first published 1979.

Fine, Anne. *Bill's New Frock*. London: Methuen, 1989.

Forest, Antonia. *Autumn Term*. Harmondsworth: Penguin, 1977; first published 1948.

Forest, Antonia. *End of Term*. London: Faber, 1959.

Horowitz, Anthony. *Groosham Grange*. London: Walker Books, 1995; first published 1988.

Kemp, Gene. *The Turbulent Term of Tyke Tiler*. Harmondsworth: Penguin, 1981; first published 1977.

Leeson, Robert. *Grange Hill Rules OK?* London: Collins, 1980.

Murphy, Jill. *The Worst Witch*. London: Penguin, 1988; first published 1974.

Rowling, J. K. *Harry Potter and the Philosopher's Stone*. London: Bloomsbury, 1997.

Swindells, Robert. *Inside the Worm*. London: Doubleday, 1993.

Swindells, Robert. *Room 13*. London: Doubleday, 1989.

Ure, Jean. *Jam Today*. London: Hutchinson, 1992.

Wallace, Jason. *Out of Shadows*. London: Andersen, 2010.

Critical Texts

Auchmuty, Rosemary. *A World of Girls: the Appeal of the Girls' School Story*. London: Women's Press, 1992.

Cadogan, Mary. *Chin Up, Chest Out, Jemima*. Haslemere: Bonnington Books, 1989.

Cadogan, Mary, and Patricia Craig. *You're a Brick, Angela: the Girls' School Story, 1879–1975*. London: Gollancz, 1986.

Hallett, Cynthia J., and Peggy J. Huey (eds). *J. K. Rowling: Harry Potter*. 'New Casebooks' series. Basingstoke: Palgrave Macmillan, 2012.

Kirkpatrick, Robert J. *The Encyclopaedia of Boys' School Stories*. Aldershot: Ashgate, 2000.

Musgrave, P. W. *From Brown to Bunter: the Life and Death of the School Story*. London: Routledge, 1985.

Nikolajeva, Maria. *Children's Literature Comes of Age: Toward a New Aesthetic*. New York and London: Garland publishing, 1996.

Richards, Jeffrey. *Happiest Days: the Public Schools in English Fiction*. Manchester: Manchester University Press, 1988.

Sims, Susan, and Hilary Clare. *The Encyclopaedia of Girls' School Stories*. Aldershot: Ashgate, 2000.

Tucker, Nicholas (ed.). *School Stories: From Bunter to Buckeridge*. London: NCRCL, 1999.

Tucker, Nicholas, and Kimberley Reynolds (eds). *Enid Blyton: A Celebration and Reappraisal*. London: NCRCL, 1997.

Whited, Lana. *The Ivory Tower and Harry Potter: Perspectives on a Literary Phenomenon*. Columbia: University of Missouri Press, 2002.

NOTES

1. The best known of Hamilton's *noms de plume* are: Frank Richards for the Greyfriars series; Martin Clifford for St Jim's; Owen Conquest for Rookwood; as well as Hilda Richards for the Cliff House Girls' school stories.
2. There are, of course, a number of twentieth-century boys' school authors who emphasize the moral and religious development of their characters in a way that would not have disappointed Hughes, Farrar or Reed, but their works have not, on the whole, remained popular. Several 'evangelistic' women writers (see Sims and Clare, 2000: 385–9) also wrote for boys, notably Audrey Dines, Kathleen MacLeod, Grace Pettman and Elizabeth Pritchard. While there were some male writers whose moral didacticism was scarcely concealed, they tend to have written during the first 20 years of the twentieth century.
3. Notably *The Pothunters* (1902) and *Mike* (1909) (see Kirkpatrick, 2000: 342–5).

Literature of War: Comparative and Autobiographical Approaches

8

Gillian Lathey

The last decades of the twentieth and the first years of the twenty-first centuries saw a marked increase in the number of children's books offering a realistic treatment of war. War is now an accepted, even common, subject in children's books – but why should adults choose to write about war for children? Surely we should protect children from the inhumanity of war for as long as possible? Such questions and arguments arise in contemporary Western cultures where a sanitized construct of childhood, one that cocoons children from the realities of the political world, is promoted by sectors of the entertainment industry. Yet throughout history wars have not spared children: they have been both unwilling victims of conflict as well as enthusiastic wartime propagandists and even combatants. It was, for example, the sight of child victims, the war orphans and refugees who roamed across Europe in the wake of the Napoleonic Wars in the early nineteenth century, that drove Swiss educationalist Pestalozzi to create his children's villages. In more recent times, the fates of children displaced by the Third Reich or made homeless by combat in the Second World War are the subject of numerous fictional and autobiographical accounts. These children were also the targets of wartime propaganda that prepared them for adult combat. In Germany, young people who were enthusiastic members of the Hitler Youth in the 1930s went straight into the armed forces (or, for girls, non-combatant war service) as soon as they reached adulthood; translations from the German of Hans Peter Richter's trilogy for young readers, *Friedrich*

(1987, first published in German in 1961), *I Was There* (1987, German edition 1962) and *The Time of the Young Soldiers* (1976, German edition 1967), chart the deadly momentum that began in childhood.

To find further evidence of active participation in wars by children we only have to look to the examples of young British men falsifying their ages to join the army in the First World War, or media images of child soldiers in a number of conflicts in Africa and elsewhere. It is simply not possible keep children entirely protected from war; even those who are sent away from likely danger at home to distant places are deeply affected for the rest of their lives by that experience. Moreover, war frequently acts as a catalyst in accelerating progress to maturity, even though, as some of the texts discussed in this chapter will show, the necessary but premature acceptance of adult responsibilities can exact a high personal cost. Any children's literature that engages with all aspects of children's lives therefore has to address the subject of war.

The Second World War: comparative literature and translations

Given the vast range of experience outlined above, a closer examination of a limited number of texts is essential in order to investigate the conflicting ideological and national perspectives that underpin them. I have chosen to focus on the Third Reich and the Second World War (1933 to 1945 and beyond), firstly because it is the historical period that has generated and continues to generate the most extensive and varied body of children's literature on war, and, secondly because it inspired new directions in at least two genres of children's literature: the picturebook devoted to war themes, and memoirs of wartime childhoods.

A third reason for the focus on the Second World War is that it is a common subject of the limited number of children's books translated into English each year, which makes it possible to adopt a comparative approach to children's books originating from a number of countries – including those on opposing sides of the conflict at the time. Although a common academic discipline in continental European universities, where staff and students are accustomed to reading across cultures and languages, comparative literature has until recently been a neglected area of study in the United States and remains so in the United Kingdom. This is regrettable, since to pursue influences across national and linguistic borders, to trace the manipulation of stories as they travel, and to place texts from different cultures side by side, can be a most illuminating approach to literary studies. Eminent scholar Susan Bassnett, one of the few British comparatists, offers the definition that comparative literature 'is concerned with patterns of connection in literatures across both time and space' (1993: 1) (see Box 8.1). These 'patterns' may be recurring similarities, as in motifs common to folk tales across the world, or may result from direct cross-cultural influences such as the obvious debt owed by Oscar Wilde, particularly in *The Happy Prince* (1888), to the work of Danish children's author Hans Christian Andersen. On the other hand, the identification of contrasting developments may prove to be just as revealing. In the 1930s, for example, at a time when British children's literature was deeply conservative in its subject matter, there was a political polarization in German children's fiction in the period leading to the establishment of the so-called Third Reich. Texts for children reflected the radical politics of the Weimar Republic, from the urban proletarian novel to the fascist sentiments of a novel such as *Hitlerjunge Quex* (1932) by Karl Alois Schenzinger. Such contrasts highlight the ideological content and historical context of the children's literature of both cultures: an examination of the children's books of a particular period in one country or language can throw into relief qualities previously taken for granted in another.

One significant comparative project on war fiction for children organized by three European countries, Belgium (Flanders), Portugal and the UK, has already produced an informative publication, *An Anthology of War and Peace in Children's Books* (Fox, Leysen and Koenders, 2000), which includes references to literature originally written in a number of different

---

BOX 8.1   COMPARATIVE LITERATURE

What scholars and critics who study literature comparatively do:

- They trace cross-cultural influences between national literatures, whether written in the same or different languages. Scholars have, for example, examined the historical influence of the *Household Tales* collected by the German Grimm Brothers on the literatures of a number of countries. More recently, the impact of the Harry Potter series on developments in children's literatures across the globe has been a fruitful area for comparative investigation.
- They examine literature written in the same period in different cultures and countries to expose and contrast the social, political and ideological content of literatures at a given historical moment.
- Comparatists who work in the field of Translation Studies undertake close analysis of source (the original) and target (the translation) texts to discover evidence of the manipulation of stories, poems, plays and novels as they cross cultural and national boundaries. In children's literature, abridgement, censorship and cultural context adaptation (changing foreign food, coinage etc. to their British, American or Australian equivalents) reveal a great deal about differences in constructions of childhood in the source and target cultures.
- They raise awareness of difference and alternative literary forms, genres and thematic content in literatures across the world.
- They also reveal patterns of similarity in world literatures – for example, the motifs common to folk tales internationally.
- In the field of children's literature, comparatists look at the origins and histories of children's literatures, such as whether or when children's literature became an educational tool and how and why it began to develop as a separate literature in any given language or culture.

languages and therefore facilitates comparative insights for those who only read English.

Translated texts, then, yield significant insights into cultural and socio-historical difference. For young English-speaking readers, Anne Holm's allegorical *I Am David* (1965), translated from the Danish, offers a decontextualized account of a young boy as archetypal victim and refugee, while Tatiana Vassilieva, in *A Hostage to War* (1996, translated from Russian via German), has written a diary account of her transportation from Russia to a labour camp in Germany at the age of 13. Hans Peter Richter's trilogy mentioned above, Gudrun Pausewang's *The Final Journey* (1996) and Reinhardt Jung's *Dreaming in Black and White* (2000), all translated from German, are inscribed with the agonized confrontation with Germany's culpability for the Holocaust and associated Third Reich policies, while German-Jewish author Mirjam Pressler's *Malka* (2002), inspired by a meeting with the adult Malka, charts the gruelling journey of a young Jewish girl escaping from German-occupied Poland. A number of novels recently translated from other European languages have addressed these issues too: Jean Molla's *Sobibor* (2005), translated from French, details a young anorexic girl's discovery of her grandparents' collaboration with the Germans at a death camp in Poland, whereas Stig Dalager's *David's Story* (2010), translated from Danish and drawn from diaries of the period, is an unrelenting account of a young boy's fight for survival in the Warsaw ghetto. Such texts present fictional or memoir-based insights into the experiences of children living in occupied countries, the fate of Jewish children across continental Europe and the lives of German children growing up during the Third Reich. It is always important to bear in mind, however, that a translation is a text that reaches the reader through the medium of a translator, who may practise a degree of contextual adaptation to make the narrative more comprehensible to a reader in the target culture.

Translated texts may also enable readers to appreciate some of the national perspectives on the past in any one country or language. Children's literature on the Second World War has become a significant site for the perpetuation and interrogation of perspectives that form over time as collective memory crystallizes into familiar patterns in the national psyche. In Japan, children are introduced from an early age to picturebooks on the terrible loss of life and injuries caused by the atomic bombs dropped on Hiroshima and Nagasaki, so that the national emphasis on the Japanese as victims is replicated in children's literature. One of the very few texts to question the role of the Japanese armed forces is Miyoko Matsutani's *Yaneurabeya no Himitsu* (*The Secrets of the Attic*, 1988), an account of the testing of biological weapons on Chinese captives by 731 Unit of the Japanese army. Germany's reckoning with its past has produced a range of texts that either evade (see Lathey, 1999 for examples) or address (as in the novels of Gudrun Pausewang discussed below) Germany's national guilt and which, when available in translation, constitute a telling source of comparison with the work of British authors.

Autobiographical fiction

The cross-cultural, comparative discussion that follows, firstly of work by a British children's author, Robert Westall, and a German children's author, Gudrun Pausewang, and secondly of two picturebook artists, Michael Foreman and Tomi Ungerer, can only begin to throw light on commonalities and differences that it would take a large-scale study to substantiate. Nevertheless, books by these authors reveal developing national as well as personal perspectives on the past since 1945, particularly since all four authors and illustrators draw on childhood experience which they then recast as fiction for a child audience. Robert Westall grew up on heavily bombed Tyneside during the Second World War, a time he regarded as the most exciting and dangerous of his life, and which became a recurrent subject in his fiction for children. Gudrun Pausewang was an enthusiastic member of the Hitler Youth organization for girls; since that time she has spent much of her adult life campaigning for human rights and writing about the period for young people in a spirit of shame and atonement. Like Westall, Michael Foreman spent his wartime childhood in a strategic location on the coast, as his native Suffolk was a possible route for invasion. Tomi Ungerer's cultural and national allegiance is more complex, since he lived as a child through the German occupation of Alsace, a border area that has both German and French historical and cultural roots. These four disparate Second World War childhoods are the starting point for a series of books by each author or artist that convey personal experience to the young viewer or reader with a range of didactic and self-exploratory purposes.

In autobiographical fiction, questions naturally arise concerning the accuracy of the experiences represented in each text. It is now commonly recognized in literature on autobiography that memory is deceptive, especially when several decades separate an event from its imaginative reconstruction. Whereas George Gusdorf in his influential essay 'Conditions and Limits of Autobiography' (1956) emphasized the affirmation of individualism in autobiography and argued that 'there is a oneness of the self, an integrity or internal harmony that holds together the multiplicity and continual transformations of being' (1956: 6), later studies (Olney, 1980; Anderson, 2001) have taken a radically different approach. Far from considering the self as an essentially stable and unchanging core, there is in the work of these scholars an assertion that the self is a construct that changes according to psychological need, social and historical circumstance and ideological pressures. The image that an author wishes to present to an audience at the time of writing an autobiography is therefore only the most recent in a chain of multiple identities. The point that autobiography is an imaginative recreation of experience governed by personal interest and changing national ideologies is one that should lead readers to guard against accepting personal accounts of wartime childhoods at face value, and is a further justification for a comparative analysis that highlights the differing interests that shape recollection.

Robert Westall: representing the enemy in
The Machine-Gunners

When writing about wartime childhoods, the ideological starting points for British and German authors could hardly be further apart. Although certain experiences were shared by British and German children – air raids, evacuation, absent fathers, the gleaning of political information from adult conversation and radio broadcasts – others, such as the Hitler Youth rallies and persecution of Jews in Germany, were not. Dominant themes in British autobiographical fiction set in the Second World War are the evacuation of city children to the countryside and the readjustment in family life after the departure of the father, as in Nina Bawden's *Carrie's War* (1973) and *Keeping Henry* (1988) respectively, or the fear and disruption of family life caused by air raids that underpin the work of Westall and Foreman.

Robert Westall first decided to write about a childhood threatened by constant aerial bombing for his own son, so that he could communicate the heady sense of danger and excitement. As he expressed it in an interview with a *Guardian* journalist (28 March 1991): 'For a ten-year old to be lightly bombed – we're talking of five bombers a night – is enormous fun. I've never had an adventure like it, which is perhaps why I tend to return to it.' War was to become a major preoccupation in a career of writing for children that began with *The Machine-Gunners* (1975) and its sequel *Fathom Five* (1979), and continued with the disturbing journey of a young air raid victim in *Kingdom by the Sea* (1990) and the imaginary suspense of *Gulf* (1992), set in the Gulf War of 1990–1.

In *The Machine-Gunners* Westall presents children's positive responses to wartime events that introduce a welcome note of danger into their daily lives, incorporating the tiniest details from his own childhood recollections. In both the novel and a collection of childhood wartime experiences including his own (*Children of the Blitz: Memories of Wartime Childhood*, 1985), for example, Westall compares the sound of approaching bombers to the sound of a stick dragged along iron railings, and flattened bullets found on the street to silver mushrooms. By selecting these authentic childhood sensations, writing in realist mode and including elements of the adventure story genre, Westall creates in *The Machine-Gunners* fiction that has pace, suspense and affective power. Moreover, he deliberately adopts the stock figures and attitudes of existing war stories and comics to attract a young audience, only to undermine expectations as the novel progresses.

The prevailing perceptions of the war in British children's stories published during the Second World War and in the early postwar period echoed the patriotic tradition of First World War fiction. Biggles, the doughty First World War pilot created by Captain W. E. Johns in the 1930s, continued his perilous career in the Second World War, and was still popular reading for boys in the 1960s. In postwar boys' comics, the division between Allied troops and 'the enemy', primarily the Germans and Japanese, is apparent in physical appearance, uniforms and in representations of language. As a result, most boys growing up in the 1950s, 1960s and early 1970s acquired a smattering of German: 'Schweinhund', 'Achtung' and the like. It is a knowledge of such patchwork images of German identity that Westall assumes in his young readers as he begins to convey his own childhood outlook in *The Machine-Gunners*. Protagonist Charles yells 'Nazi pigs!' (12) as he cuts his hand on the fuselage of a crashed German plane, while his arch-enemy Boddser has 'round spectacles and cropped hair like a German' (31). Yet when a German pilot, Rudi, is found and given shelter by Charles and his friends, the ambivalence of Westall's purpose becomes apparent and begins to change the direction of the novel.

Westall was well aware of the need to temper the anti-German sentiments and unquestioning patriotism of his own childhood for a young audience reading the book 30 years after the events depicted, and at a time of changed relations with Germany. By introducing the figure of Rudi he adds narrative tension, allows his child protagonists to develop autonomy as they keep Rudi's existence secret and, even more significantly, creates an opportunity for an insight into the German experience. Westall is not alone in offering a more complex picture of the enemy than was apparent in immediate postwar fiction and comic strips. There is a corpus of Second World War novels, dating particularly from the 1970s, in which an opportunity is engineered for children to meet the German enemy. German pilots fall from the skies or sailors are washed up on British shores with unlikely regularity. In Michael Morpurgo's *Friend or Foe* (1977) and, more recently, James Riordan's *The Prisoner* (1999), it is German pilots the children befriend, while young Simon in David Rees's *The Missing German* (1976) tends and hides a German sailor discovered on a Devon beach. The hiding of an enemy alien, as in Westall's novel, is a plot device that adds suspense to a wartime story; it also enables writers to create a dialogue between children and an adult representative of a nation they had been taught to mistrust or even to hate.

Westall's Rudi is a sympathetic German who confounds all expectations of a 'Nazi'. In passages of self-doubt, he expresses his disenchantment with the Third Reich: 'Besides, he realized sadly, he just didn't want to escape. His patriotism towards the Fatherland was dead. He tried to coax it back to life: thought of the Fuehrer; thought of his old father and mother and how ashamed they'd be of his cowardice' (1975: 140). Rudi's indecisiveness in abandoning an attempted escape and his frequent bouts of introspection counteract the standard image of the ruthless German. At the same time, Westall has Rudi utter phrases that echo the popular war comics and stories of the time with their inaccurate German. 'Dumkopf' loses an 'm', for example, and 'Hande hoch' its umlaut, while Rudi sends the verb to the end of the sentence at every opportunity when speaking English – even where this would not be necessary in German. Rudi, conceived as a figure to counteract the stereotypical German, nevertheless bears the linguistic hallmarks of the imagined Germans of Westall's childhood; his language matches readers' preconceptions, even though his sentiments do not. These linguistic inaccuracies may be an oversight, but they are more likely to be a deliberate ploy to adhere to the comic-strip language which Westall knows will attract his audience in the first instance. Indeed, Westall is caught between a desire to tell the truth – however uncomfortable – about the clear-cut value system of wartime Britain where the British were good and the Germans bad, and the adult writer's entirely laudable intention to convey a more complex and nuanced image of humanity. Childhood excitement and sympathies lend the novel its panache and vigour, whereas didactic undertones result in less convincing characters. Westall's sure hand in creating the salt-of-the-earth Geordies drawn from experience – the grandmother who rails against 'Hitler and his Jarmans' (58), for example – falters when he attempts to portray a credible German, so that the pusillani-mous Rudi is merely a cypher of the 'good German'. Nonetheless, children's encounters with 'the enemy' ultimately lead child protagonists, and therefore child readers, to question adult values generally, especially in the anarchic scenes at the close of the novel.

The urge to present children with a range of points of view on any given conflict continues in fiction set in more recent wars. Westall questions the ideological perversions of war by adding political edge and humane insights to his psychic representation of a young Iraqi soldier in *Gulf*, set in the early 1990s. Similarly, Els de Groen's *No Roof in Bosnia* (1997), translated from the Dutch and set in the conflict in the former Yugoslavia in the 1990s, offers young readers insights into the lives of five young people representing all communities participating in the war: two Serbs, a Croat, a Bosnian Muslim girl and a Romany boy. All five teenagers are clearly delineated characters whose wartime experiences constitute a tapestry of encounters with different ethnic and religious groups; the bond they form with each other transcends past allegiances.

German writers and the legacy of the Third Reich

If Robert Westall is at pains in *The Machine-Gunners* to attempt a revision of his childhood allegiances, what might be the position of German writers who were members of the Hitler Youth and gave their support to a regime that was responsible for the Holocaust? How do they look back on the exhilaration of a mass movement that was cleverly orchestrated to appeal to the insecurities of the young? Westall addresses personal and national history by drawing on the comic strip and war story genres, but the option to couch childhood memory in the patriotic sentiment of the time was not open to his near contemporary Hans Peter Richter, who grew up in Germany in the 1930s, became a member of the Hitler Youth, and served as a young soldier in the Wehrmacht. Richter's trilogy based on his own Nazi childhood and youth belongs to a first wave of German novels to address the persecution of German Jews. The narrator of the first volume of the three, *Friedrich* (1987, translated from *Damals war es Friedrich*, 1961), a young German boy, befriends the Jewish Friedrich who lives in the same building. Gradually, as the Nuremberg laws come into force, Friedrich and his family are subject to various forms of persecution. Finally, after his mother's death and the deportation of his father, the destitute Friedrich is left to die outside the air raid shelter in which the narrator's family takes refuge from Allied bombs.

Friedrich was one of the earliest examples of a body of German children's literature set in the Third Reich that was for many decades almost exclusively autobiographical. It is as though the appropriation of such momentous and emotionally charged events to create fiction would represent a travesty of the country's sombre history. Yet there exists a tension concerning the degree and manner of any acknowledgement of collective national guilt for the Holocaust in autobiographical writings. Writing for children enables some authors to suppress any sense of responsibility for the policies and crimes of the Third Reich by adopting the point of view of an uncomprehending younger child or by attributing all blame to Hitler and the Nazis (Lathey, 1999; Shavit, 2005). Others acknowledge complicity: Richter does so obliquely in his spare and elliptical narrative in *Friedrich*. It is against this background that Gudrun Pausewang wrote *The Final Journey* (1996, first published in Germany in 1992), a novel that is in no way autobiographical, yet arises from the same impulse that underpins her earlier novels on childhood in the Third Reich and its aftermath. *The Final Journey* represents a watershed in Pausewang's crusade to inform the young about Germany's history and to write her way towards personal and collective atonement.

Gudrun Pausewang: *The Final Journey*

Gudrun Pausewang's *The Final Journey*, an imaginative recreation of a child's journey to a death camp, is a courageous moment within Pausewang's largely autobiographical series of novels that circles, and finally confronts, a sense of national responsibility for the Holocaust. Pausewang's novel belongs to a tradition of children's literature on the concentration camps that began in the late twentieth century and reflects the ways in which postwar writers have gradually extended the boundaries of what is acceptable in children's books. Whereas Eric Kimmel, writing in 1977, was able to cite only one children's book that addressed the 'ultimate tragedy' of the death camps, the Holocaust has in recent decades been the subject of a large corpus of literature for children. This corpus, reviewed in critical surveys by Bosmajian (2002) and Kokkola (2009), encompasses novels, personal memoirs by Jewish writers and both fictional and non-fictional picturebooks.

Pausewang's Holocaust novel originates in the guilt of her childhood allegiance to the Nazi cause and in her subsequent experience as a refugee. During her childhood in a German-speaking area of what is now the Czech Republic, Pausewang belonged to the generation of young people who idolized Adolf Hitler. At the end of the war, after her father – whose Nazi sympathies she followed – had been killed on the Russian front, Pausewang, her mother and five younger siblings had to flee the family homestead to escape reprisals by local Czechs. With just a handcart on which to transport their belongings, the Pausewang family made their way on foot to Hamburg, some 300 miles away. It was during this journey at the edge of survival that the 17-year-old Pausewang first began to confront the vacuum created by the collapse of the value system that had led to the Holocaust, to reassess the past and reconsider her future. As a result, all of Pausewang's subsequent work as a children's writer has been driven by a desire to warn and politicize the young. Protagonists in Pausewang's novels are frequently one-dimensional figures whose fate is set against the broader, more compelling canvas of human suffering and the collapse of the social order, as is the case in her two dystopian novels based on nuclear catastrophes, *The Last Children* (1989) and *Fall-out* (1994).

In a number of autobiographical texts (as yet only available in German) that address the legacy of the Third Reich directly, Pausewang treads a fine line between the recollection of personal trauma and the didactic impulse to acknowledge collective culpability. These are self-conscious narratives, addressed initially to her son and interrupted by passages of retrospective commentary. A later volume includes an account of the reconciliation with the Czech family living on the smallholding Pausewang's family had left behind in 1945. In *The Final Journey*, written after the completion of her autobiographical odyssey, Pausewang turns to fiction in depicting the last days of a young Jewish girl, Alice, as she travels with her grandfather in a railway wagon to Auschwitz. Any German writer who represents this 'final journey' is of course open to critical attack by survivors or their relatives and descendants, yet Pausewang's own history compelled her to take that risk.

The Final Journey is designed to provoke reflection as well as disgust in the young reader, and Pausewang orchestrates a number of narrative strategies to achieve both of these aims. The intensity of aggressive human interaction and foetid living conditions in the wagon is punctuated by flashbacks to the period when Alice was in hiding, thus offering the reader some respite. By creating a protagonist who has been both over-protected and deceived by adults, Pausewang elicits empathy in her young audience. Alice is almost 12, yet she has only limited knowledge of sexual behaviour and childbirth, of the anti-Semitic policies of the regime that dictates her fate, and even of the likely destination of her missing parents. As she quickly learns about life by witnessing the birth of a baby and the physical intimacy of couples, and from conversations with her peers, Alice begins to reject her family's values. She confronts her grandfather, demanding to know why she is ignorant of information about the concentration camps that is common knowledge to others of her age. In a line that might be taken as a justification for addressing the subject at all in children's fiction, Alice expresses a sense of outrage with which many adolescent readers can sympathize: 'Do you think I can't stand the truth?' (1996: 72). Alice's progress towards adolescence is accelerated; in a few short days she rejects past values, revises her understanding of national identity, gains a degree of political understanding, and experiences her first period as she enters the gas chamber.

Within the confined space of a cattle truck, Pausewang presents a microcosm of society that includes representatives of different age groups, social classes, family constellations and occupations. Although such social engineering seems artificial, it enables Pausewang to achieve a number of objectives. First, hers is not the idealized portrait of Jews of which Zohar Shavit (2005) is critical with respect to *Friedrich* and a number of other German novels for the young with a Third Reich setting. Alice befriends a young mother, Ruth Mandel, and learns that Ruth's husband divorced her because he was only half Jewish and wished to save himself, an act of expediency that was not uncommon at the time. There is even an indication that the persecuted have the potential to become persecutors when the 'trench-coat woman', irritated by the behaviour of the mentally retarded adult Ernstl, suggests that 'that sort should be in a special truck' (1996: 80). Second, different points of view enable Alice, and through her the reader, to interrogate concepts of national and ethnic identity and responsibility. Alice thinks of herself as German rather than Jewish, in line with her grandfather's opinions: he instructs her to clench her teeth to suppress the pain of an upset stomach and reminds her that 'A German girl is not afraid'. Ruth Mandel, on the other hand, responds angrily to such a display of the kind of nationalistic interpretation of all aspects of behaviour that was propagated during the Third Reich. In contrast to Alice, both Ruth's daughter Rebekka and the young boy Aaron express pride in their Jewishness and avoid any mention of their German nationality. Aaron also predicts Germany's future as a pariah nation. Thus Pausewang presents her young audience with a gradation of response that is in contrast to the image of the Jew simply as victim.

When comparing Pausewang's Second World War fiction with that of Robert Westall, it is immediately striking that Westall in the first instance subordinates a didactic or therapeutic purpose to the desire to engage his audience by telling a good story. In doing so he naturally rekindles childhood excitement, and has indeed described reading chapters of The Machine-Gunners aloud to his son as a dialogue of equals: 'Twelve spoke to twelve, without interruption' (1979: 37). Westall's son was the very first young reader he wished to transport to an era when life was permanently spiced with fear: times were hard but never dull. While including a good German to enlighten his young readers, Westall could also convey his childhood exhilaration. Pausewang's autobiographical account of her refugee trek, too, was dedicated to her son, but in both that text and in The Final Journey the dominant intention is to use harrowing stories to educate and to warn. Nostalgia and the representation of positive memories have no place in the writing of those who inherit the legacy of a Nazi childhood, no matter how much authors may have enjoyed Hitler Youth rallies or camping trips. Pausewang's memoirs and novels are part of a long-term national, as well as personal, process of reassessment that places heavy moral and historical expectations on texts for the young.

The historical development towards a reflective, morally responsible approach to war fiction for children is nowhere more apparent than in Germany, where children's literature has played an essential role in the process of personal and national catharsis and continues to do so, even in more recent works by younger writers such as Reinhardt Jung (Dreaming in Black and White, 2000). Educational policy makers have also turned to children's literature; accounts of childhood experience during the Third Reich by both German and Jewish writers have long been required reading in the school curricula of both the Federal Republic of Germany and of the former German Democratic Republic before reunification in 1989 – and indeed since that date. In this instance, and in the work of all writers addressing the legacy of the Holocaust, children's literature becomes a potential channel for national atonement. British children's fiction on the Second World War, although taught in schools, is not part of such a high-profile national programme of reconciliation, so British authors are free to address a range of imaginative purposes ranging from a focus on the distressing consequences of war to the fond backward glance. In the picturebook memoir, too, there are parallel contrasts between culturally and politically determined visions of the past.

Images of wartime childhoods: Michael Foreman's *War Boy* and Tomi Ungerer's *A Childhood Under the Nazis*

Picturebooks for the very youngest children often mediate the harshness of the subject of war by couching a pacifist message in an allegorical tale, as in Elzbieta's gentle animal allegory, *Go Away War* (1994, translated from the French), or through the use of the attractive colours and unrealistic presentation found in the controversial concentration camp setting of *Let the Celebrations Begin!* (1991) by Australians Margaret Wild and Julie Vivas. With a rather older audience in mind, however, picturebook artists give the impact of the image free rein in expressive paintings of burning human flesh in Toshi Maruki's *The Hiroshima Story* (1983), or of concentration camp inmates in Roberto Innocenti's *Rose Blanche* (1985). Artists Michael Foreman and Tomi Ungerer place themselves centre stage in representations of their own childhoods in texts that are not intended for the youngest children, but are ambivalent in their implied audience. Both represent memories of the war years in a hybrid of the picturebook and illustrated information book forms usually associated with a young audience. Yet Foreman's *War Boy* (1989) has been enjoyed by many of his reminiscing contemporaries, and a review of the French version of Ungerer's book in *Le Monde*, after pondering the question of audience, had to conclude that it was a book about childhood for all. Such initial points of contact between the two artists only emphasize the divergence in the narrative and visual stance towards the past adopted in each case.

Foreman's *War Boy* is set on the British east coast in the rural village of Pakenfield near Lowestoft. A vision of early childhood is suffused with the positive memories of a secure domestic setting. In a series of images that delight the eye at the turn of every page, Foreman mixes exact technical drawings copied from original sources with humorous vignettes and glowing watercolours. The reader certainly recognizes the ultimate danger of war as Foreman's mother flees from an incendiary bomb with her son in her arms, and in a core of sadness for the soldiers the young Foreman met who did not return from the battlefields. Nevertheless, the general impression is that of a childhood savoured by the adult who presents the ideology of the period uncritically. The written text closes with a paraphrase of the popular song, 'There'll be bluebirds over the white cliffs of Dover', which was frequently performed by singer Vera Lynn and came to epitomize the British patriotic spirit. Foreman's personal recollections culminate in a reaffirmation of adult belief in a victorious outcome for Britain as expressed in the final lines of the book: 'So it was true, all the things the grown-ups had said during the dark days. Now the war was over everything would be all right, there'll be blue birds over the white cliffs, not barrage balloons. And men with rainbows on their chests would, like my kite, come home' (1989: 95).

Tomi Ungerer's *A Childhood Under the Nazis* is, in contrast, an uncomfortable, self-conscious text set in Alsace and caught between the languages and cultures of France and Germany. Ungerer's conscience is troubled on behalf of those French nationals who collaborated with the German occupying forces, and by his own part-German cultural heritage. In line with a bilingual upbringing and its political connotations, Ungerer first published his autobiography in French (as *À la guerre comme à la guerre*, 1991), then 'reconceived' the book in German (*Die Gedanken sind frei*, 1993) and, finally, wrote an English edition for the US market in 1998 (references are from the American edition unless stated otherwise). This account of a childhood in German-occupied Alsace opens on an apologetic note, as Ungerer regrets that his childhood perception of war as a great spectacle might 'appear to be a trivialization of the great dramas of misery, torture and violence' (1998: vii). Indeed, Ungerer even questions the text's authenticity by claiming to mistrust childhood memories (German edition, 1993: 82). A chronological gap between text and pictures intensifies this vacillation with regard to the past: the images are those drawn at the time by Ungerer between the ages of 9 and 14, but the text was written by the reflecting adult.

Ungerer's view of humanity is marked by wartime experience that compels him to eschew sentimentality and to assume a pragmatic, even cynical attitude to childhood events. In the German edition he reflects on the consequences of his own successful, if subversively critical, adaptation to life under the aegis of the Third Reich. Ungerer's description of being caught up in the nazification process and the necessary development of 'chameleon-like' (German edition, 1993: 57) qualities lead him to acknowledge a degree of moral flexibility. The child who was a French boy at home, a German pupil at school and an Alsace lad with his friends gave expression to the duality that shaped his daily life by making two sets of cards for playing the game Old Maid, one featuring French characters and the other Germans. In drawings indicative of his outstanding graphic talent, Ungerer satirizes both cultural groups: the naive-looking French boy scout is paired with the sweating member of the Hitler Youth banging his drum (1998: 80–1). But Ungerer also used his artistic gifts to conform to a school exercise to draw a Jew (1998: 42), producing on his mother's advice a caricature that met the expectations of his teachers. Later, in 1948, and in what can be read as an artistic act of reconciliation, Ungerer drew a bleeding and despairing concentration camp inmate with the caption 'Dachau Buchenwald Ausschwitz' (1998: 162).

Throughout his childhood memoir Ungerer conducts a process of moral self-examination that seems more appropriate for adults in its sophistication and implied readership, and which is ultimately inconclusive. Readers are left with the impression that Ungerer's ambivalence towards his past can never be fully resolved, and *Fascination*, a television documentary on Ungerer made for the British TV Channel 4 in 1996, confirms this view. On the one hand, Ungerer demonstrates his admiration for the visual acumen of Nazi propagandists by remaining a keen collector of Nazi memorabilia, while, on the other, he is seen weeping during a regular visit to the concentration camp of Struthof in Alsace.

The closing lines of Ungerer's and Foreman's texts provide the most telling point of contrast between the contradictory nature of Ungerer's response to his wartime childhood in an enemy-occupied area, and the national pride evoked by Foreman. Whereas Foreman expresses a retrospective confidence in the words spoken to him in childhood by adults – 'it was all true, all the things the grown-ups had said' (1989: 95) – Ungerer's experience has taught him to rely on no one. Only the immensity and incorruptibility of the sea, first glimpsed on a visit to Normandy for his sister's wedding, is capable of cleansing and reviving him: 'enough water to rinse my despair, wash out the past, drown my rancor' (1998: 174). Changes in cultural heritage from French to German and back again before, during and after the German occupation, together with the accompanying reversals in political ideology, have made this narrator wary, mistrustful and introspective in his review of wartime adventures. Both Foreman's and Ungerer's views of history are inevitably partial, but comparison raises questions about the interpretation of history presented to the young, and indeed to adults, in picturebook form.

Literature of war: the future

Writing on the Second World War will soon cease to be informed by personal experience. Even those who were children at the time have now reached advanced old age, so that an expression of the experiences that marked the childhoods of Westall, Pausewang, Ungerer and Foreman will soon no longer be possible. As the number of eyewitnesses dwindles, writers who wish to include a degree of personal authenticity in their work have to rely on family memories or research; this is already the case, for example, in the Second World War novels *Goodnight Mister Tom* (1981) and *Back Home* (1985) by Michelle Magorian or Marcia Williams's delightful and informative scrapbook *My Secret War Diary by Flossie Albright* (2008). There will doubtless be new developments in children's fiction on the subject, and we can only speculate on how twentieth-century world wars will be regarded across the world in the decades to come. The response by children's writers to recent conflicts continues to be immediate and uncompromising. From Robert Westall's Iraqi boy soldier in *Gulf*, to Els de Groen's mixed group of adolescents in Bosnia in the 1990s, Bernard Ashley's African child soldier in *Little Soldier* (1999), or Deborah Ellis's irrepressible heroine in the *Breadwinner* trilogy (2009) and *My Name is Parvana* (2012) set in the war in Afghanistan, authors introduce young readers to the plight of their contemporaries in ways that demand a reaction to the injustice and suffering of war. Moreover, an allegorical text such as *The Day My Father Became a Bush* (2013) by Dutch author Joke van Leeuwen emphasizes with a light touch the incomprehensibility of war as seen through the eyes of a young child clinging to one sliver of hope: that her soldier father knows how to keep safe using camouflage. Unfortunately the post-Second World War vision of Jella Lepman, founder of the International Board of Books for Young People, that children's books could be the foundation of international understanding and peace has proved to be over-optimistic. Conflict within and between nations persists, but authors do not flinch from its terrible realities. War is no longer merely the stuff of patriotic adventure yarns for the young.

WORKS CITED AND FURTHER READING

Children's Books

Ashley, Bernard. *Little Soldier*. London: Orchard Books, 1999.
Bawden, Nina. *Carrie's War*. Philadelphia: J. B. Lippincott, 1973.
Bawden, Nina. *Keeping Henry*. London: Gollancz, 1988.
Dalager, Stig. *David's Story*, trans. Frances Østerfelt and Cheryl Robson. London: Aurora Metro, 2010.
Ellis, Deborah. *The Breadwinner Trilogy*. Toronto, ON: Groundwood Books, 2009.
Ellis, Deborah. *My Name is Parvana*. Toronto, ON: Groundwood Books, 2012.
Elzbieta. *Go Away War!* Trans. not credited. London: Hamish Hamilton, 1994.
Foreman, Michael. *After the War Was Over*. London: Pavilion, 1995.
Foreman, Michael. *War Boy*. London: Pavilion, 1989.
de Groen, Els. *No Roof in Bosnia*, trans. Patricia Crampton. Barnstaple: Spindlewood, 1997.
Holm, Anne. *I Am David*, trans. L. W. Kingsland. London: Methuen, 1965.
Jung, Reinhardt. *Dreaming in Black and White*, trans. Anthea Bell. London: Egmont, 2000.
van Leeuwen, Joke. *The Day My Father Became a Bush*, trans. Bill Nagelkerke. Wellington, NZ: Gecko Press, 2013.
Magorian, Michelle. *Goodnight Mister Tom*. Harmondsworth: Kestrel, 1981.
Magorian, Michelle. *Back Home*. London: Viking, 1985.
Molla, Jean. *Sobibor*, trans. Polly McLean. London: Aurora Metro, 2005.
Morpurgo, Michael. *Friend or Foe*. London: Macmillan, 1977.
Pausewang, Gudrun. *Dark Hours*, trans. John Brownjohn. New South Wales: Allen & Unwin, 2006.
Pausewang, Gudrun. *The Final Journey*, trans. Patricia Crampton. London: Viking, 1996.
Pausewang, Gudrun. *Traitor*, trans. Rachel Ward. London: Andersen Press, 2004.
Pressler, Mirjam. *Malka*, trans. Brian Murdoch. London: Pan Macmillan, 2002.
Rees, David. *The Missing German*. London: Dobson, 1976.
Richter, Hans Peter. *Friedrich*, trans. Edite Kroll. London: Puffin, 1987; first published in the USA 1970.
Richter, Hans Peter. *I Was There*, trans. Edite Kroll. London: Puffin, 1987.
Richter, Hans Peter. *The Time of the Young Soldiers*, trans. Anthea Bell. Ashland, OH: Kestrel, 1976.
Riordan, James. *The Prisoner*. Oxford: Oxford University Press, 1999.
Ungerer, Tomi. *Die Gedanken sind frei: Meine Kindheit im Elsass*. Zurich: Diogenes, 1993.
Ungerer, Tomi. *Otto*. Paris: L'École des Loisirs, 1999.
Ungerer, Tomi. *Tomi: A Childhood Under the Nazis*. London and Boulder, CO: Roberts Rinehart Publishing, 1998.
Vassilieva, Tatiana. *A Hostage to War*, trans. Anna Trenter. London: Hamish Hamilton, 1996.
Westall, Robert. *Children of the Blitz: Memories of Wartime Childhood*. London: Macmillan, 1985.
Westall, Robert. *Fathom Five*. London: Macmillan, 1979.

Westall, Robert. *Gulf*. London: Methuen, 1992.
Westall, Robert. *The Kingdom by the Sea*. London: Methuen, 1990.
Westall, Robert. *The Machine-Gunners*. London: Macmillan, 1975.
Wild, Margaret, and Julie Vivas. *Let the Celebrations Begin!* London: Bodley Head, 1991.
Williams, Marcia. *My Secret War Diary by Flossie Albright*. London: Walker Books, 2008.

Critical Texts

Agnew, Kate, and Geoff Fox. *Children at War: From the First World War to the Gulf*. London: Continuum, 2001.
Anderson, Linda. *Autobiography: The New Critical Idiom*. London and New York: Routledge, 2001.
Bassnett, Susan. *Comparative Literature: A Critical Introduction*. Oxford: Blackwell, 1993.
Bawden, Nina. *In My Own Time: Almost an Autobiography*. London: Virago, 1994.
Bosmajian, Hamida. *Sparing the Child: Grief and the Unspeakable in Youth Literature about Nazism and the Holocaust*. London and New York: Routledge, 2002.
Fox, Carol, Annemie Leysen and Irene Koenders (eds), *In Times of War: An Anthology of War and Peace in Children's Literature*. London: Pavilion, 2000.
Gusdorf, George. 'Conditions and Limits of Autobiography'. In J. Olney (ed.), *Autobiography: Essays Theoretical and Critical*. Princeton, NJ: Princeton University Press, 1980; first published 1956.
Kimmel, Eric A. 'Confronting the Ovens: the Holocaust and Juvenile Fiction'. *The Horn Book Magazine*, 53.1 (1977), 84–91.
Kokkola, Lydia. *Representing the Holocaust in Children's Literature*. London and New York: Routledge, 2009.
Lathey, Gillian. *The Impossible Legacy: Identity and Purpose in Autobiographical Children's Literature Set in the Third Reich and the Second World War*. Bern: Peter Lang, 1999.
Olney, James (ed.). *Autobiography: Essays Theoretical and Critical*. Princeton, NJ: Princeton University Press, 1980.
Shavit, Zohar. *A Past Without Shadow: Constructing the Past in German Books for Children*. London and New York: Routledge, 2005.
Westall, Robert. 'How Real Do You Want Your Realism?' *Signal*, 28 (1979), 34–46.

Language, Genres and Issues: the Socially Committed Novel

Pat Pinsent

Historical background: children's novels and social didacticism

Since its earliest beginnings, children's literature has been used by authors to influence young readers to adopt those attitudes and that behaviour considered in any period to be desirable. Didacticism has never been confined to helping readers to accumulate factual knowledge; rather, books have commonly also been used in the attempt to inculcate acceptable morals and ethics, as well as, in the past, a suitably charitable attitude towards the poor in the largely middle-class readership.

Whereas the best-known children's books of the earlier twentieth century seldom confronted readers directly with themes related intrinsically to social issues, some of the most influential nineteenth-century children's authors had been very explicit in bringing to the fore those strata of society that would have been unfamiliar to their middle-class readership. There are some significant differences in approach between these stories and the late twentieth-century texts which will be the major focus in the current chapter. Several of the tales in Maria Edgeworth's *The Parent's Assistant* (1796; 1800 and numerous later editions) give a vivid portrayal of the miserable condition of the poor; 'The Orphans', one of the few set in Ireland, makes evident the needs both for those who have the means to be charitable and for the indigent poor to be scrupulously honest. Similarly, during the last third of the century, in the context of a period which saw much social reform, 'Hesba Stretton' (Sarah Smith) wrote many stories, of which the best known are *Jessica's First Prayer* (1867) and *Little Meg's Children* (1868). These highlight how easy it was for women and children in particular to become destitute, and send a strong message that the best way for the poor to survive was by means of a scrupulous honesty which, she implies, would endear them to potential benefactors. These books are indeed equally concerned with the salvation of the adult characters: respectively, Daniel, who befriends Jessica but needs to learn the lesson of putting charity before human respect, and Kitty, a reformed prostitute who is reunited with her mother. Anna Sewell's *Black Beauty* (1877) was intended not only as a polemic against cruelty to horses but also as a disclosure about the sufferings of the poor who were expected to work for a pittance without even being allowed to rest on the Sabbath day. While books like these do indeed display some of the evils of society, the reader is consistently put into a position of sympathizing rather than empathizing with the impoverished children (or horses), respecting them for their honour and integrity but anticipating that even in their improved fortune they will remain in the class of society in which God has, presumably, set them. Any incorporation of equality issues would have been anachronistic in nineteenth-century society.

Most British children's novels of the first half of the twentieth century, if they touch at all on social issues, do so in order to provide background for the characters. The majority of children's writers, whatever their political convictions, were themselves very firmly of middle-class origin (as in the case of the Fabian socialist, Edith Nesbit). This means that however good their intentions, they inevitably either employed middle-class protagonists, sometimes afflicted by genteel poverty, as in Noel Streatfeild's *Ballet Shoes* (1936), or succumbed to the danger of making lower-class characters somewhat comic, as in Eve Garnett's *The Family from One End Street* (1937 – see Chapter 6 of this volume).

It was not until the 1970s and the beginnings of legislation dealing with issues of discrimination in society that significant numbers of children's authors began to address issues of equality. During this period there was an increasing awareness of how literature could affect social attitudes. In its first stages, such awareness tended to concentrate on how children's books from the past portrayed (or in many cases, failed to portray) females, the working classes, and minority ethnic groups. At the same time, the growth of the academic discipline of sociolinguistics during this period led to a greater sensitivity about the way language was often used in books to disempower characters from minority groups or render them invisible. The initial period of detecting bias was followed relatively speedily by the production of fiction designed to ensure that readers' attitudes towards such groups were compatible with contemporary views about equality.

Although most children's authors prior to this period had not overtly used literature as an instrument to disseminate their views about society, their work often reflects their own preconceptions on this subject. In all periods, writers' views will, directly or indirectly, have been conveyed to their young readers by such means as characterization and plot situations as well as by language. British children's fiction advocating social change, however, became more significant during the last quarter of the twentieth century because of two main factors: the increasing attention which society had been forced to give to the voices of women, and the effect of large-scale immigration into Britain from the Commonwealth. Factors such as these led to social changes that could not be ignored, at least in realistic fiction. This situation was recognized by, for instance, the founding in 1975 of the 'Other Award' by the Children's Rights Workshop; its aim was, as Robert Leeson puts it, to 'encourage new writing free from sex, race or class bias' (1985: 136).

Concerns about bias began to be treated explicitly in children's books, though in some cases it is possible to detect that authors' prejudices, possibly unrecognized even by themselves, may run counter to the views that the writers intend to convey. Novels with a powerful message of equality need to be analysed to determine if there is any tension between the explicit ideology proffered by their authors and any aspects of the texts which suggest implicit acceptance of less enlightened values. Peter Hollindale (1988, revised 2011) provides a useful series of questions designed to aid readers in the task of detecting the ideology of writers who may not have been entirely conscious of it themselves. Interrogation of the ending of a book, for instance, may show that it reaffirms values which much of the text has held in question.

In the case of picturebooks, ideological messages conveyed by the text may be reinforced, or in some instances contradicted, by the pictures, which in the context of books for younger children can be even more powerful in their effects. Although it is not possible here to give attention to this area, some relevant books are listed at the end of this chapter.

Critical approaches

In looking at the books to be discussed in this chapter, account will be taken of how narrative stance affects the reader's positioning in relation to the development of plot and character. Stephens (1992: 136) notes how different modes of narration, such as the use of an 'omniscient' narrator, the employment of first-person, possibly 'unreliable', narrative, or the focus provided by the perspective of a single main character, can in different ways be powerful means of conveying ideology. It is interesting, therefore, to observe the modes of narration employed in the novels which will be discussed here.

Another key feature that affects the manner in which a novel can influence social attitudes is its use of intertextuality (see Box 9.1): the insertion into a novel of themes, or references to named or unnamed existing texts, or the use of genres which derive from related or even unrelated fields. For those who are familiar with these earlier texts, references to them may cause a kind of resonance which has a significant effect on their responses to the books which make these intertextual references.

BOX 9.1   INTERTEXTUALITY

While this term was coined by Julia Kristeva only in 1966, as a way of describing the interactions and interdependences of texts (her examples typically deal only with works for an implied audience of adults), as a phenomenon it has been present in children's literature at least since the eighteenth century, with children's books consciously assuming knowledge of other texts in their readers (a famous nineteenth-century example is Louisa May Alcott's use of *Pilgrim's Progress* in *Little Women*). Intertextuality refers not simply to the use of quotation, allusion and reference, but to the whole network of ways in which one text is read in relation to all the others that reader and writer have read and will read.

Whereas earlier ways of describing relationships between texts assumed a hierarchy in which newer texts were seen as making use of, and so subservient to, works from earlier epochs, Kristeva argued that intertextuality was based on a relationship between equals. All texts depend on other texts for their meanings – and indeed, for their readers' abilities to decode them. This dynamic is particularly relevant to the use and function of intertextuality in children's literature since young readers are necessarily at the start of their literary histories and so have less of a reservoir of literary texts on which to draw – though they are likely to have a greater knowledge of non-literary texts such as television programmes, commercials, popular music, illustrations, films and cartoons, together with a range of material from the Internet and social media. Moreover, with the increasing numbers of books available, including those which are deliberately intertextual, the order in which texts are encountered by the reader may not be that assumed by the writer. For instance, children today may well encounter Jon Scieszka's *The True Story of the Three Little Pigs* (1989) before they know the original tale. According to intertextual theory, the order in which the texts are read is unimportant: both will act on and overlay both each other and other texts whenever they are encountered.

Stephens (1992, chapter 3) distinguishes usefully between the *focus* text (the text being read) and seven categories of *intertexts* (texts that are deliberately interpolated, referred to, quoted or otherwise evoked in the focus text). Included in this list are *pretexts*, or specific earlier texts to which the focus text is consciously and significantly related; for example, the fairy tale 'The Three Little Pigs' and Scieszka's retelling of it.

Central to any discussion of literature, but perhaps particularly significant in considering social issues, is an awareness of the ways in which language is used. In many instances, the differences between the dialects and registers employed by characters from different kinds of social backgrounds are foregrounded by the authors, generally in an attempt to influence the attitudes of the young reader. This is certainly the case in several of the novels to be discussed here.

Race, class and the dystopian novel: Robert Swindells' *Daz4Zoe* and Malorie Blackman's *Noughts and Crosses*

Both Blackman and Swindells use a combination of two well-established genres, the romance (see Box 9.2) and dystopia (see Box 9.3), as a way of confronting contemporary social problems. Romance is one of the oldest literary genres, being particularly prevalent during the Middle Ages, but showing its vitality by its continuing appearance in popular films, television, magazines and books. Both Blackman and Swindells adhere to the convention that love conquers all, even when the lovers belong to antagonistic groups. The love in Blackman's novel, between Sephy (a Cross, a member of the dark-skinned, socially dominant class) and Cal (a Nought, one of the low-ranking whites), has developed gradually from their childhood, when the social factors separating them had not yet become fully operative. In Swindells' book, the attraction between Daz and the wealthy Zoe begins at their first sight of each other, and is mutual and all-absorbing.

BOX 9.2   ROMANCE

The term 'romance' is often used to describe two kinds of writing. Its oldest form and meaning date back to the thirteenth century and refer to fictional works, usually concerned with the world of the court and involving quests, heroic deeds, the separation and reuniting of lovers (including parents and children), and often elements of the supernatural. Early romances tended to make up story cycles, and indeed, the individual stories were usually circular in nature, with protagonists ending up where they began and order being restored. From these roots has grown a contemporary genre, often dismissed as slight and escapist, known as romance fiction, written for both adult and teenage (usually female) readers. While preoccupied with the trials, tribulations and thrills arising from romantic relationships rather than with heroic deeds, these works nevertheless retain many of the elements from earlier romances, even to forming cycles of stories – many of the most popular examples of romance fiction belong to series, such as Sweet Valley High, Point Romance and the Boyfriend Club.

BOX 9.3   DYSTOPIAN FICTION

The word 'dystopia' was formed by analogy with the well-established 'Utopia' (literally meaning 'nowhere') from the Greek prefix *dys*, meaning 'bad', and *topos*, meaning 'place'. Dystopian fiction is usually set in an imagined, possible, unpleasant future, which has much to say about the writer's and the reader's present. Interestingly, in the closing decades of the twentieth century and the first decade of the twenty-first, dystopian writing for young people has increased noticeably, with the element of futurity being diminished. In other words, perhaps in response to social changes associated with 'Thatcherism' and 'Reaganism' and particularly their emphasis on market forces and the needs/rights of the individual rather than society, future dystopias began to be set ever closer to the time of writing, and the worlds they portray tend to be little different from the reader's own (see also Chapters 11 and 14 in this volume). What makes them conform to the genre of dystopian fiction is that in these works current problems are taken to their logical conclusion, to the detriment of community, environment and personal happiness. The impact of dystopian fiction for juvenile audiences is often undercut by offering improbably optimistic endings, usually conceived and engineered by young people.

The dystopia is also very evident in both these novels, set in worlds where society is more polarized than it is today. Swindells has taken to extremes the already existing (in 1990) divisions between the suburbs and the inner cities. The use of established genres does not in any way diminish the originality of Blackman and Swindells, nor indeed does the possibility that, in its use of a romance theme to interrogate a divided society, *Noughts and Crosses* may itself have been influenced by the slightly earlier *Daz4Zoe* diminish the quality of Blackman's response to this subject.

The two novels have much in common, touching on areas such as membership of illegal organizations and the possible justification for terrorism in an unjust society; in both books, members of the families of the protagonists are victims of judicial execution. There are also certain similarities between the respective family relationships, those between siblings in particular. But perhaps the most significant resemblance, from the literary point of view, is that both novels divide the narration between the two central characters, drawn from opposing ranks of society. Particularly in *Daz4Zoe*, this approach not only intensifies the contrasts between the two characters concerned, but also throws into question the perceptions of both the narrators, possibly leading the reader towards the realization that an objective account of events is impossible (see also Box 16.2).

In *Daz4Zoe*, the difference between the reader's world and the fictional location created by the polarization of society is more evident within the inner-city environment of Rawhampton than in the affluent suburbs. Daz has relatively little to say about his background, because it is so familiar to him, but the reader sees the surroundings through Zoe's eyes. Of the Blue Moon club, Daz simply says: 'Nite club. Bands and strippers and pool and that' (14), but Zoe's view is more detailed:

> I looked out and saw what looked like a poky old shop in a dilapidated row. Its window was boarded up and somebody had daubed 'Blue Moon' across the boards with blue paint. ... [we went into] a large, crowded room ... the atmosphere was ninety percent smoke and there was a nauseating smell whose cause I didn't want to think about.   (17–19)

Her own perceptions are, however, changed as, under the influence of several 'lobotomisers', she begins to enjoy the atmosphere.

Zoe's sensitivity to smell provides Swindells with a means of guiding the reader's response in the description provided of her view of Daz's home in the tallest block in the town. First she finds herself in a 'dim' lobby outside the flat; it is covered with graffiti, unpleasant puddles bedeck the floor, and she nearly gags on the smell. When she enters the flat, however, her perceptions seem to be influenced by her love for Daz; the flat is significantly cleaner and, though she observes the need for repainting, the smell, 'like toadstools', is less repulsive (124–5). Daz has already stated that his mother is suffering from depression: 'Our Mam been down a longtime ... wiv the dulleye' (3), and Zoe's description of her is scarcely flattering. Although she is no more than 45, she appears elderly, and with her dull and worn clothes, she virtually matches the 'saggy, colourless armchairs'. '[Her] Grey hair hung in greasy rat-rails [*sic*] to her shoulders. White bony fingers gripped the armrests of her chair and she gazed at her son with lustreless eyes' (125–6). The association between the sagging armchair and the woman with her uninspiring garments and physical features, culminating in the 'lustreless' eyes, encourages the reader to share Zoe's low expectations of her. However, there have already been some correctives to this negative view, particularly in the wit which she occasionally displays in her remarks to her son: 'Wear you bin our Daz, sez Mam. no wear Mam, i sez. that's just wear you sed you was going, she sez. she's dry, our mam' (111). Consequently, we are not entirely surprised when, despite the negative image, she is instrumental in Zoe's escape by swapping jumpers, wearing the discarded one to prevent it being discovered in a search.

This interplay between the perceptions of Daz and Zoe enables Swindells to relativize the descriptions, forcing the reader towards judgements not only about the settings but also about the people who live in them. The possible initial assumption that nearly all the Chippies are, by their own choice, unwashed and correspondingly unintelligent, is subverted, replaced by admiration for the resilience of those who maintain human values in such an unfavourable environment. The contrast between the living conditions of Blackman's Noughts and Crosses is by no means so extreme, nor does she individualize the perceptions of her narrators to the same extent as Swindells.

Like most children's writers, Blackman and Swindells are adults writing for a younger audience, and as writers, they almost inevitably espouse middle-class values, a situation of some complexity concerning their positioning as implied authors. While revealing the defects in the education system of the underclass (and, implicitly, because of its bias, also that of the overclass), both novels nevertheless make the humanitarian assumption that the way towards greater equality is through the gradual recognition by members of both groups that their supposed enemies are human beings, a process to which education is essential. Both imply that the actions of illegal organizations with terrorist aims, such as Swindell's DRED and Blackman's Liberation Militia, are likely to be self-defeating, while FAIR, led in Silverdale by Zoe's elderly grandmother, achieves much more positive objectives.

Both writers tend to assume that their teenage readers will share their belief in the essential equality of all humans, while added complexity is supplied by Blackman's deliberate reversal of power roles within Western society. Not only does she make the dark-skinned Crosses the dominant group, but also she attributes to them many of the worst characteristics of rulers throughout the world, whether black or white. As a black writer, she is clearly on dangerous ground; for oppressed groups, it is always more congenial to claim that if 'we' were in power, society would be much more just than it is when 'they' are in power.

Another situation of some complexity is that regarding romantic love, which is experienced as an irresistible force. The young people who feel this emotion are seen as right to keep their confidences from their parents, an assumption that is likely to appeal to the young reader. Readers who are familiar with the genres of romance and dystopia may form certain expectations about closure, but these may not necessarily be met by the endings of the novels, an aspect which again may throw light on the authors' ideologies. Similarly, those who know, for example, Shakespeare's *Romeo and Juliet* and Orwell's *Nineteen Eighty-Four* will be aware that romances, and to an even greater extent dystopias, do not necessarily end happily; in this regard the fortunate implied escape of Daz and Zoe at the end of Swindells' book may in fact challenge credibility, though by affording some hope for the human race the author is acceding to the conventions of literature for young people.

While the language used in Blackman's novel is not significantly differentiated between the two main characters, and her originality lies less in her linguistic usage than in her narrative strategy, the language in Swindells' book demands more direct attention. An unusual aspect is Zoe's use of a joke to introduce herself: 'Hi, I'm Zoe. Zoe May Askew. Or Zoe may not. (Joke)' (4). Stephens suggests that such jokes may reflect 'an attempt to subvert what is perceived as the dominant discourse' (1992: 93). It certainly implies that Zoe is likely to question the values of the 'Subby' (suburban) society in which she has been brought up. Her use of language is, however, relatively conventional by comparison with Daz's. In the quotation below, his first utterance, I have used upper case for phonetically spelt words, and italics for coinings:

> Daz THAY call me. 2 years back WEN I COM 13 Del that's my BROVVER THAY catch IM raiding WIV the Dred. Top IM don't THAY, and IM just GON 15.
>
> 2 *lornorders* COM TEL our mam, 1 WUMIN, 1 man, nor THAY don't come TIL after THAY DUNNIT NEEVER. Our Mam been down a long-time FORE then WIV the *dulleye*, and she just sort of STAIRS don't she, TIL THAY go OF, and its not TIL NITE she CRYS.
>
> She SEZ don't you never go OF WIV no Dred, our Daz. No Mam, I SEZ, but I never CROST my HART. Don't COWNT LESS you CROST YOR HART, RITE?   (3)

It is easy to see that most of the effect is conveyed by the phonetic spelling, though the coined words, often related to contemporary slang, are an attractive feature. Non-standard syntax also figures largely. Another usage, less obvious in the passage above but evident even in the title of the book, is the use of numbers for words: the numeral 2 meaning 'to' and 'too', and 4 representing 'for'. This device, together with some aspects of the spelling, seems somewhat prescient of the text-messaging popular with twenty-first-century teenagers. It makes it less likely that Daz's use of a form of language very far removed from Zoe's standard English will downgrade him for the reader, or render belief in his status as romantic hero more difficult, though the question remains as to whether he is truly so attractive, or just Zoe's 'bit of rough'. It is significant that at the end of the book, in parallel with the final sentence, 'It was impossible to tell where the city ended and the suburb began', his language style has fused with hers. Despite its relatively optimistic ending, *Daz4Zoe* has its quota of gritty realism in the picture of the tower blocks, the depressed mother and the difficulties of family relationships.

Gender and disability: Jean Ure's *Cool Simon*

During the 1970s and early 1980s, the focus of equality legislation, and consequently of socially committed children's fiction, tended to be on class, race and gender, but in subsequent years, other issues, notably those of age, disability and sexuality, have also become significant. Jean Ure's *Cool Simon* integrates an emphasis on gender with a treatment of the subject of disability, to the extent that the disabled title character ultimately becomes instrumental in action against the sexism of some of the other characters – an aspect which in itself reverses the way in which disabled characters seldom have agency and tend to appear largely as objects of pity.

During the 1970s, when authors began to be confronted by issues of racism in British society, the topic of ethnic bias, as distinct from that of slavery, had not received a great deal of attention in earlier children's literature this side of the Atlantic. The issue of gender had, however, inevitably been present earlier. Before about 1960, the omission of black characters from books set in Britain could be justified by the relative rarity of non-indigenous people among the British population, but the omission of female characters from adventure stories, or their casting into secondary roles when they did appear, had always been possible.

Another genre in which gender issues are inevitably raised is the school story (see Chapter 7). By the 1970s, the long tradition of single-sex boarding-school fiction no longer appeared so immediately appealing to children as it had done in the past, though it has subsequently experienced some degree of revival. The mixed day-school environment provided a setting very suitable for dealing with gender bias, as can be seen in Gene Kemp's *The Turbulent Term of Tyke Tiler* (1977) and Anne Fine's *Bill's New Frock* (1989), while Bernard Ashley's *The Trouble with Donovan Croft* (1974) was one of the first books to exploit the potential of the genre for tackling racism.

Writers committed to social change, however, have gradually become aware that other issues also need to be presented to young readers. The *Grange Hill* TV series (1978–2008), including its book spin-offs, confronted themes inescapable in a school setting, such as bullying, but also to a lesser extent disability. Children's literature has had a long history of portraying disabled people as objects of pity, though sometimes they have been demonized, as in the instance of Blind Pew in R. L. Stevenson's *Treasure Island* (1883). At other times, a happy conclusion to the book has demanded a near miraculous cure, as in Susan Coolidge's *What Katy Did* (1872). Gradually, however, the recognition has dawned that to reflect society properly, the position of disabled children needs attention in its own right, particularly as legislation has made them more numerous within mainstream education. Jean Ure, whose output includes a number of books about Woodside School, clearly appreciates the potential of the school setting as a means of confronting prejudice against disabled children. *Cool Simon* (1990) combines the disability theme, in the form of a deaf boy in mainstream education, with that of gender and social isolation, as focalized through a female character, Sam. An incidental added point is that Simon is black; although the race issue is in no way foregrounded in this book, the fact that Simon is an active and attractive character means that anti-racism is indirectly reinforced.

Unlike the two novels discussed above, the narratorial stance in *Cool Simon* is omniscient, though the all-knowing narrator also relies on direct speech from a variety of different voices. The reader is allowed access to places where the children would not be permitted – notably, in chapter 1, the staffroom, where the comments of the teachers establish details about the various pupils, a scene which is followed by the rather differing perceptions vouchsafed by the children themselves, and interspersed by authoritative third-person description. The first of the two central characters to whom the reader is introduced is Samantha Swales, described by the teaching staff as a 'problem' and by her classmates as 'a *pain* [*sic*]' (3). The description which follows displays the alternation of different voices; I have commented alongside the quotation on the source of the judgement:

> 'Look at her!' Alison Webb ... tossed her hair irritably over her shoulder. 'Great butch thing!' [*Child observation*]
> ... Samantha slouched through the gates. She was dressed just the same as everybody else, in a blouse and skirt, but still she managed to look more like a boy than a girl. It was something to do with the way she had her school bag slung over one shoulder [*3rd-person narrator*] – 'Like a cowboy,' as Shirin had once scornfully said, 'without his horse.' [*Child observation*]
> Sam stood, scowling, just inside the playground. [Another pupil] accidentally brushed against Sam as she went past. You would have thought, from the way Sam furiously chopped at the air with the side of her hand, that it had been some kind of deliberate attack. Sam was *aggressive*. You could tell she was aggressive, just by looking at her. Her face was all scrumpled and pursed from being in a state of permanent crossness. ...   (4)

The final section of this quotation, from 'Sam stood' onwards, is all seen from the perspective of the third-person narrator, but the direct address to the reader as 'you' gives the impression of a voice which is no more sympathetic than Alison and Shirin, but rather more sophisticated in use of imagery. The fact that the third-person narrator seems to endorse the negative judgements made by Sam's classmates might be thought to engender dislike of the character, but experienced readers are likely to anticipate that these adverse verdicts will eventually be reversed.

It seems to be Sam's defiance of female stereotypes that most infuriates her classmates; her desire to join the boys' football team rather than playing the gender-approved netball becomes the crux of the plot, and a central image of the resentment she feels against the whole human race, experienced, we learn, ever since her father left home.

Sam's own voice, incidentally, is not heard until her character has been well established by these other voices, and, significantly, when she first speaks it is to point out how useless it is for anyone to shout at Simon. Her friendship with him seems to result from a combination of her implicit realization that, like her, he is an outsider in the class, together with the fact that she has a cousin who is partially deaf. The book, however, reverses the reader's likely initial expectation that it will be Sam who manages to help Simon to achieve his true potential – rather, the disabled character is the means of ensuring that the 'helper' can find her way towards her own goal (literally!). His negotiation of relationships with the other children, largely through his interest in the school rabbit, in fact precedes his own integration into the class and is the means of hers. His success at his previous school has given him enough confidence to rise above the mixture of sympathy ('Poor deaf child, thought Miss Lilly', 8) and hostility ('Eh! You! What d'you say your stupid name was?') with which he is confronted, though he is still less than happy that the sports master seems to assume that the only position in which a deaf boy can play is goal, whereas at his previous school he had played midfield. After he triumphs through his courage in rescuing the school rabbit from a fire, he obtains agency, not only achieving a midfield position in the football team for himself but also being able to insist that Sam too is allowed to play. In the context of narration it is significant that his is the final voice we hear in the text: 'I goo Dimon an' you my fred ...' (154); by now, readers, like his classmates, are able to understand his use of language. It is clear that despite Simon's being the eponymous hero of the book, it is Sam's isolation that has been the real issue; paradoxically, Simon, despite deafness being a notoriously isolating condition, has never been as alone as Sam.

Ure's technique of using a diversity of voices tends to undercut any authority given to the omniscient narrator and is likely to leave the reader uncertain about the 'correct' attitude to take towards Sam (though it is generally clear that Simon's character should be seen positively). This has the effect of communicating Sam's feeling of uncertainty, even exclusion, and making the final reversal, when Simon insists on her being included in the team, all the more powerful. It also means that it would be difficult to state categorically which is the strongest theme of the book – gender, race, disability or, indeed, the effect on a child of emotional distress and the way that this may isolate her from her classmates.

Asylum seekers and Beverley Naidoo's *The Other Side of Truth*

Another area that has received a good deal of attention is the plight of people excluded from everyday society, a theme which in various ways has always preoccupied Beverley Naidoo. Her fiction is more strongly politicized than that of many children's writers, perhaps because her identity as a white South African did not allow her to shirk the issue of inequality. In a personal account (in Pinsent, 2001), Naidoo describes the evolution of her novels. Her best-known earlier novels, *Journey to Jo'burg* (1985) and *Chain of Fire* (1989), are set in South Africa before apartheid finished, while *No Turning Back* (1995) reveals that its end did not immediately bring a good life to street children in Johannesburg (see Chapter 11 of this volume).

Naidoo's *The Other Side of Truth* is mostly located in Britain, and is one of the most hard-hitting children's novels dealing with the plight of asylum seekers.

Like the other socially committed fiction discussed here, the narratorial stance and the use of intertextuality in Naidoo's novel reward attention. When Sade and Femi, escaping from Nigeria where their mother has been assassinated, are abandoned at Victoria Station by Mrs Bankole, who should have taken them to their uncle, their plight has an inescapable similarity to that of the 'Babes in the Wood' or 'Hansel and Gretel'. Since she was standing in for their own dead mother, Mrs Bankole is something of a wicked stepmother, and the resemblance is reinforced by a reference to the way in which the huge buildings nearby 'loomed over the narrow pavements like a thick forest of brick, concrete and glass' (48).

The urban environment has other threats, also presented intertextually; in the sequence where the children are lost, they encounter a figure who robs them, whom Sade sees as 'Darth Vader of the alley looming up above them, his arm sweeping away their holdall' (58), thus referring to a *Star Wars* character who is the 'dark lord' of an 'evil empire' (Carpenter and Prichard, 1984: 495). The reader nurtured on fairy tale and space fiction will certainly have been expecting monsters and ogres to loom out of the darkness and cold, yet here again the intertextual reference serves to remind us that in such tales, good almost always ultimately triumphs.

A rather different variety of intertextuality is supplied by the tortoise story (191–3) which their father tells Sade and Femi in a letter he writes to them. As he points out, this story, derived from African folklore, represents the tortoise as being artful, cunning, sensible, wise, courageous and daring. Threatened by Leopard and allowed only five minutes before he is devoured, Tortoise marks the earth deeply, so that the struggle between them will be remembered. As well as being a very appropriate story to be told by a journalist who wants the world to know about evils in his country, the story suggests survival (will the leopard in fact be able to penetrate the tortoise's shell?); it also serves to remind the child characters, and thus the reader, of the richness and complexity of the African folk tale tradition, in which the tortoise is often portrayed as a lovable trickster. The tortoise is again referred to near the end of the novel, as an image for the forced mobility of the family: 'Wherever they went, they would have to become like tortoises who carry their homes on their backs. [Sade] thought of Papa's brave tortoise and hoped that at least they would not have to meet any more leopards' (222).

The narrative approach of *The Other Side of Truth* differs from that of the other books which have been discussed, yet it too bears a close connection with the way in which Naidoo conveys her message. The focal character is Sade, and access to the thoughts of other characters is generally only available if mediated through what they say to her. The narrative is generally conveyed to the reader through Sade's consciousness; this is often signalled by the use of expressions that only she would use, as in the words I have italicized here: 'The *Brass Button* officers at the airport would be on alert for *Papa* himself' (75). Frequently, Sade's perceptions are presented conditionally, as if the third-person narrator is speaking ventriloquially: 'She [Mrs King] seemed quite tall but that might have been because her thick grey hair was piled up high' (99); certitude is no more available to the narrator than to Sade, who has presumably made this judgement. Naidoo frequently uses images to elucidate thoughts and situations; such images may be attributed directly to Sade's thought processes: 'Sade imagined a string pulling up her head like a puppet' (99). Quite often, however, there is a degree of uncertainty as to whether or not Sade has actually made the comparison: 'Sade watched in horror, her own silent tears trapped within her, like in a stone. Grief burst around them like a pierced boil' (3). The effect of this technique is that there is a centrality to Sade's perceptions, together with the impression that a more knowledgeable adult is both approving them and working outwards through them.

Additional insights are offered in two main ways, both signalled by changes of typographical font. Sade's father's letters, like Sade's to him and her grandmother, and her class teacher's to her, are printed to resemble typewriting, which inevitably singles them out as carrying a different kind of authority from the rest of the text. They reveal thoughts and events that are not accessible to Sade, unlike other passages, which are italicized to give a kind of dream-like effect, often harking back to earlier scenes thus recalled to Sade's consciousness. The murder scene (chapter 1) is not only repeated almost verbatim (chapter 11), but it is also distorted by a dream (117) where Sade's fear of the school bullies is conflated with her anguish at her mother's death and her feelings of guilt that her tardiness in getting ready for school had delayed their departure and made the family more vulnerable.

Another variant on the nearly exclusive use of Sade's consciousness is the story of her friend Mariam, which is recounted without any access to Sade's response being interspersed (140). This technique gives this chapter a greater impression of objective reportage than is carried by the rest of the book.

Looking at Naidoo's approaches to narrative reveals that this book, which may appear to be a relatively artless production, is in fact a complex tissue of different modes. These enable the reader to take different subject positions and to be encouraged towards forming what feels like an 'objective' judgement, while still remaining close to the perceptions of the focal character.

Since the publication of *The Other Side of Truth*, the topic of asylum seekers has become more frequent in novels for teenagers. Notable instances are Michael Morpurgo's portrayal in *Shadow* (2010) of the notorious Yarl's Wood centre where Aman and his mother, from Afghanistan, are detained, and the much-acclaimed *In the Sea there are Crocodiles* (2012) by Fabio Geda (Italian original, translated).

Conclusion

The extent to which literature can influence attitudes remains debatable, though children's authors from time immemorial have accepted without question that it does so, something which advertisers and writers of newspaper leader columns also continue to assume. Beverley Naidoo herself has

done some important research into the extent to which children's literature can influence attitudes; this is presented in *Through Whose Eyes?
Exploring Racism: Reader, Text and Context* (1992). More recently, in a
talk at Roehampton University, Naidoo spoke explicitly about her intentions in writing her books, all of which, as she says, 'deal with – and reveal –
the impact of the political world on the lives of young people' (in Pinsent,
2001: 14). She described how her books were an attempt to 'win the heart',
to make her own and other fortunate children aware of human suffering,
adding:

> I have always believed in the power of fiction and story. ... Whether
> readers' responses emerge from imaginative empathy or a sense of identi-
> fication with one or other of my characters, what is most important to me
> is that their imaginations have been fired, emotions and intellects stirred.
> That knowledge is surely one of the best rewards that a writer can receive.
> (Pinsent, 2001: 15, 20)

Authors such as Swindells, Blackman, Ure, Naidoo, Morpurgo and many
others have made their social commitment explicit, both within and outside
their work. The ways that they seek to fire the imagination of their readers are
undoubtedly more subtle than is the case with earlier children's writers, but
they are all the more likely therefore to appeal to young readers, who would
probably be resistant to over-explicit ideology.

WORKS CITED AND FURTHER READING

Children's Books

Ashley, Bernard. *The Trouble with Donovan Croft*. Oxford: Oxford University Press, 1974.
Blackman, Malorie. *Noughts and Crosses*. London: Transworld, 2001.
Burgess, Melvin. *Junk*. London: Andersen Press, 1996.
Burningham, John. *Granpa*. London: Cape, 1984.
Burningham, John. *Oi! Get Off Our Train*. London: Random House, 1991.
Cann, Kate. *In the Deep End*. London: Livewire, 1997.
Dickinson, Peter. *Eva*. London: Gollancz, 1988.
Doherty, Berlie. *Dear Nobody*. London: Hamish Hamilton, 1991.
Edgeworth, Maria. *Lazy Lawrence and Other Stories*. London: Watergate Classics, 1948; orig.
    1796 and 1800.
Fine, Anne. *Bill's New Frock*. London: Methuen, 1989.
Garnett, Eve. *The Family from One End Street*. (First published 1937; Harmondsworth:
    Penguin, 1967).
Geda, Fabio. *In the Sea there are Crocodiles*, trans. Howard Curtis. London: Vintage Books,
    2012.
Gleitzman, Maurice. *Sticky Beak*. London: Macmillan, 1994.
Glen, M. *Maggie*. London: Random House, 1990.
Guy, Rosa. *Billy the Great*, illus. Caroline Binch. London: Gollancz, 1991.
Hathorn, Libby. *Way Home*, illus. Gregory Rogers. London: Andersen Press, 1994.
Hoban, Russell. *Mole*, illus. Jan Pienkowski. London: Jonathan Cape, 1993.

Hoffmann, Mary. *Amazing Grace*, illus. Caroline Binch. London: Frances Lincoln, 1991.

Hoffmann, Mary. *Grace and Family*. London: Frances Lincoln, 1995.

Hoffmann, Mary. *An Angel Just Like Me*, illus. Cornelius van Wright and Ying-Hwa Hu. London: Frances Lincoln, 1997.

Howarth, Lesley. *Ultraviolet*. Harmondsworth: Puffin, 2001.

Jung, Reinhardt. *Dreaming in Black and White*, trans. from the German by Anthea Bell. London: Mammoth, 2000.

Kemp, Gene. *The Turbulent Term of Tyke Tiler*. London: Faber, 1977.

Lawrence, Louise. *Children of the Dust*. London: Bodley Head, 1985.

Lowry, Lois. *A Summer to Die*. London: Granada, 1977.

Morpurgo, Michael. *Shadow*. London: HarperCollins, 2010.

Morpurgo, Michael. *The Kites are Flying*, illus. Laura Carlin. London: Walker Books 2009.

Naidoo, Beverley. *No Turning Back*. London: Viking, 1995.

Naidoo, Beverley. *The Other Side of Truth*. London: Puffin, 2000.

Naidoo, Beverley. *Out of Bounds*. London: Puffin, 2001.

O'Brien, Robert. *Z for Zachariah*. London: Collins, 1974.

Rosen, Michael. *This is Our House*, illus. Bob Graham. London: Walker Books, 1996.

Schermbrucker, Reeva. *Charlie's House*, illus. Niki Daly. London: Walker Books, 1989.

Sendak, Maurice. *We are All in the Dumps with Jack and Guy*. New York: Michael DI Capua Books and HarperCollins, 1993.

Sewell, Anna. *Black Beauty*. First published 1877.

Stewart, Maureen. *Out of It*. Harmondsworth: Puffin, 1995.

Stretton, Hesba, *Jessica's First Prayer*. London: Religious Tract Society, 1867.

Stretton, Hesba. *Little Meg's Children*. London: Religious Tract Society, 1868.

Swindells, Robert. *Brother in the Land*. Oxford: Oxford University Press, 1984.

Swindells, Robert. *Daz4Zoe*. London: Puffin, 1992; first published 1990.

Ure, Jean. *Becky Bananas: This Is Your Life*. London: Collins, 1997.

Ure, Jean. *Cool Simon*. London: Orchard Books, 1990.

Welford, Sue. *Nowhere to Run*. Oxford: Oxford University Press, 1999.

Westall, Robert. *Future Track 5*. Harmondsworth: Kestrel, 1983.

Wheatley, Nadia. *My Place*, illus. Donna Rawlins. Sydney: Collins Dove, 1988.

Wilkins, Verna. *Boots for a Bridesmaid*, illus. Pamela Venus. Camberley: Tamarind, 1995.

Wilson, Jacqueline. *The Bed and Breakfast Star*. London: Transworld, 1994.

Wilson, Jacqueline. *The Illustrated Mum*. London: Transworld, 1999.

Wilson, Jacqueline. *The Story of Tracy Beaker*. London: Transworld, 1991.

Wilson, Jacqueline. *The Suitcase Kid*. London: Transworld, 1992.

Critical Texts

Booktrusted News, 2 (Autumn 2002) [featuring disability].

Carpenter, Humphrey, and Mari Prichard. *The Oxford Companion to Children's Literature*. Oxford: Oxford University Press, 1984.

Hollindale, Peter. *The Hidden Teacher: Ideology and Children's Reading*. Stroud: Thimble Press, 2011.

Hollindale, Peter. *Ideology and the Children's Book*. Stroud: Thimble Press, 1994; first published 1988.

Keith, Lois. *Take up thy Bed and Walk*. London: The Women's Press, 2001.

Leeson, Robert. *Reading and Righting*. London: Collins, 1985.

Naidoo, Beverley. *Through Whose Eyes? Exploring Racism: Reader, Text, Context*. Stoke-on-Trent: Trentham Books, 1992.

Pinsent, Pat (ed.). *The Big Issues: Representations of Socially Marginalized Groups and Individuals in Children's Literature, Past and Present.* London: NCRCL, 2001.

Pinsent, Pat. *Children's Literature and the Politics of Equality.* London: David Fulton, 1997.

Saunders, Kathy. *Happy Ever Afters: A Storybook Guide to Teaching Children about Disability.* Stoke-on-Trent: Trentham Books, 2000.

Stephens, John. *Language and Ideology in Children's Fiction.* London and New York: Longman, 1992.

Past Settings, Contemporary Concerns: Feminist Historical Fiction in the Late Twentieth Century

Peter Bramwell

History is 'an unending dialogue between the present and the past' (Carr, 1986: 30), and so is historical fiction. The aspect of this dialogue that will be the focus of this chapter is how the concerns of the time of writing are retrojected into past settings. Children's historical fiction invariably and inevitably addresses present-day issues: even when contrasts are made between the past and the present, this is done with the modern sensibility of exploring and embracing difference. What is accepted as historically accurate and convincing changes over time, so that what is realistic to one generation of writers and readers seems incredible to another. Sometimes a change in the conventions of genre can be revolutionary: a good example is the work of Geoffrey Trease, whose historical and adventure novels from the 1930s onwards reacted against the conventions established in the jingoistic and hierarchical days of the expanding British Empire by using a modern style and a democratic point of view (Agnew, Rahn and Thomas, 2001: 335). Yet *Bows Against the Barons* (Trease, 1934) is just as much a book of its time and ideological context as the kind of historical novels that it reacts against: 'today it is hard not to read [it] as a book drenched in the politics of interwar socialism' (Butler and O'Donovan, 2012: 10). Thus there are three layers of history to any work of historical fiction: the time when it is set, the time when it is written, and any time since then when it is read. All of these interact, but the second and third are the focus here, for my contention is that after only a short passage of time the ideological context of writing becomes readily apparent. Historical fiction for children can be peculiarly ephemeral, a product of its time with a short shelf life.

The texts I have chosen to examine make it particularly evident that children's historical fiction is more about the time when it is written than the era in which it is set. *The Forestwife Trilogy* (Tomlinson, 1993, 1998, 2000; collected 2003), *Wise Child* (Furlong, 1987), *A Year and a Day* (Furlong, 1990) and *The Raging Quiet* (Jordan, 2000) all have overt agendas to do with equality and diversity. This was evident at the time of publication, and has become all the more obvious in the few years since, because while inclusivity continues to be a current concern, its forms and expressions change rapidly. This chapter will focus on the ways in which historical novels by Theresa Tomlinson, Monica Furlong and Sherryl Jordan consciously question and redefine constructions of gender. The focalized young women in these stories gain independence within the context of friendships and collaboration, and are nurtured by mentors from an older generation. In *The Forestwife Trilogy*, *Wise Child* and *A Year and a Day*, the friends and mentors are female, but in *The Raging Quiet* they are male. Indeed, redefining women's roles in these novels has an inevitable impact on men, whether by implication or more directly – either by parodying rigid masculinities, or by presenting 'feminized' male characters. As Christine Wilkie-Stibbs (2002) stresses, *the feminine* cannot be reduced to the sex of authors, characters or readers, but is an order of discourse, a socially embedded system of signification, which is more fluid, plural and egalitarian than the historically dominant patriarchal social order. Questions of gender identity in the work of Tomlinson, Furlong and Jordan are far-reaching, extending to religious difference, and the construction of narratives of history and story, which will be analysed in terms of female chronotope (Nikolajeva, 1996) and Pagan chronotope (Bramwell, 2009) (for more on chronotopes, see Box 7.2). The gender politics of these novels has a distinctly late twentieth-century inflection, notably in the controversial figuration of woman as 'superwoman': tireless worker by day, domestic goddess at night, boundlessly competent and confident. In addition, the cyclic time schemes of these narratives disrupt the distinction between past and present upon which definitions of historical fiction as a genre depend.

Living on the edge

The Forestwife Trilogy, *Wise Child* and *The Raging Quiet* all focus on characters who are displaced to the margins of society. Their crossing of social borders is made concrete by locating their living spaces physically on the edge of communities. These novels thus partake of the 'generic characteristics and plot structures ... symptomatic of cases of *the feminine* in children's literature' that Christine Wilkie-Stibbs finds in works by Margaret Mahy and Gillian Cross:

> all the texts feature a central, focalizing character, either male or female, who, though central to the narrative, is always positioned at the margins of their particular social milieu. S/he is, in some way, either physically and/or mentally displaced from 'home' into another elsewhere ... which becomes their transformational space. (Wilkie-Stibbs, 2002: xiii)

Tomlinson's *The Forestwife* is based on the Robin Hood ballads and legends, but focuses on Marian and the community that gathers around her in a clearing in Sherwood Forest. The story stays with her, while the exploits of Robert (Robin Hood), in his misguided loyalty to King Richard, are reported to her. It is Marian, rather than Robert, who takes up the cause of the sick and poor, and who acts against injustice. And it is Marian who confers the green hood upon Robert. Marian starts out as Mary de Holt (Mary 'of the wood': her surname prefigures her destiny), of noble birth and subject to an arranged marriage. She escapes to the forest, where her nurse Agnes joins her. Mary has to adapt to an environment and people previously alien to her. The forest, and the Forestwife in her hidden clearing, are strange to outsiders, including Mary herself at first, who depends on received prejudices, regarding the forest as 'a place of evil' and the Forestwife as 'a witch of the worst kind' (Tomlinson, 1993: 19). After Agnes becomes Forestwife, she renames Mary as Marian. With her new name, Marian develops a new identity: she becomes physically stronger, and intimately familiar with the forest. She also adopts the dialect of her new community. Marian eventually succeeds Agnes as Forestwife, and so moves from the question, 'But who am I? What part am I to play?' (35) to the knowledge, 'I am Marian. I am the Forestwife' (161).

In Monica Furlong's *Wise Child*, which is set in seventh-century Dalriada (Scotland), the character Wise Child is abandoned by her parents and adopted by Juniper, who trains Wise Child to become a *doran* like herself. A *doran* is a wise person, male or female, Christian or Pagan, who has 'found a way of seeing and perceiving' (Furlong, 1987: 85), and lives 'in the rhythm'. Though a *doran* may be male, what is actually presented in both novels is wisdom being passed from older women to younger ones, making Furlong's *doran* comparable with Tomlinson's Forestwife. Juniper is both needed and feared for her skills, and lives apart from her community. From the outset, the presentation of otherness in *Wise Child* is multilayered and shifting. 'Juniper was different from us' (9) implies identity between the reader and the narrator, but then it becomes clear that not only Juniper, but also the narrator, live in a world different from the reader's: 'In the first place she [Juniper] came from another country – Cornwall' (9). In fact, much of what makes Juniper different from Wise Child's community – and causes her to be both needed and feared as a 'witch' – makes her more like the present-day implied reader, in knowledge, beliefs and artefacts. Juniper is less superstitious and more knowledgeable than Wise Child. She has books and other technologies (a kaleidoscope, a magic mirror which may be a camera obscura) which open new ways of seeing; as she explains, 'What is difficult about learning ... is that you have to give up what you know already to make room for the new ideas' (44).

Marnie in Sherryl Jordan's *The Raging Quiet* is an incomer, and Father Brannan, a man of vibrant and humane faith, warns her that the villagers 'feel threatened by newcomers, especially people they know nothing about' (Jordan, 2000: 61). What is more, she lives independently in a remote cottage with an evil reputation: its former inhabitant was executed as a witch. Marnie herself is suspected of witchcraft after her wealthy and loathsome husband dies in an accident within two days of their moving into the cottage, and she enters into a relationship with a wild, deaf young man whom the villagers regard as demon-possessed.

The strangeness of transitions into new environments in these novels may be regarded as mirroring the experience of the reader of historical fiction, of crossing from the present into an imagined past. Furthermore, the sensibilities of the adolescent protagonists and, often more so, their mentors (notably Juniper and Father Brannan) which make them different from their contemporaries often have a lot of the present about them and so solicit the reader's sympathy and identification. There is always a tension in children's historical fiction between historical credibility (changeable as this notion is, as I indicated at the outset) and the need for children's fiction, whatever the genre and historical setting, to have characters that readers can relate to.

Daring to be different

Sherryl Jordan's 'Author's Note' to *The Raging Quiet* reveals that she is consciously writing a story for our time about difference: 'This tale belongs to any time, even our own; it is about prejudice and ignorance, and a young woman wrongly accused, who is guilty of only one thing – the unforgivable crime of being different' (319). This is very much what is happening in the novels by Tomlinson and Furlong as well: all three authors use historical settings to address current concerns about negotiating gender roles, improving attitudes to disfigurement and disability, and celebrating difference.

Theresa Tomlinson has created in the Forestwife a wise-woman figure whose antiquity, continuity and femininity are signified by the girdle passed on from one Forestwife to the next. The role of the Forestwife is defined by Agnes thus: 'It is an ancient and sacred pact, an agreement, between the forest folk. It will bring us safety, for none will know or even ask our names. The Forestwife may keep her mysteries' (Tomlinson, 1993: 34). The Forestwife's skills and responsibilities include healing, midwifery, and offering food and shelter to the starving and homeless. The righting of wrongs associated with Robin Hood in more traditional retellings is, in Tomlinson's version, ascribed to Marian as Forestwife. The accent is on righting the wrongs of history, retrojecting present-day concerns by redressing injustices to women and by overcoming prejudices about people with disabilities.

In *The Forestwife*, a woman is rescued from the scold's bridle, and the unorthodox Sisters of Mary Magdalen, stockaded for holding their own services, are liberated. Thereafter, the Sisters frequently work together with the Forestwife's enclave, and accept the forest people's nature religion, Mother Veronica affirming Marian's vocation as Forestwife. One of the Sisters, Margaret, was consigned to the nunnery as an unmarriageable daughter because of her harelip. She has her difference accepted and celebrated when the outlaw Much urges her not to cover her face as they dance together to honour the deer slain to feed the forest people through the winter.

There is a shift in emphasis in *Child of the May*, the second book of the trilogy, to the lives of aristocratic women, though the story of the plight of the noble Ladies of Langden is counterpointed by the development of Magda, born and raised in the forest. An aspect of Magda's growth is to overcome her aversion to disfigurement – Robert's facial scar, and the sores which lepers have. She learns from Mother Veronica, who was not harmed by the years she spent caring for people with leprosy. Furthermore, the historical Knights of Saint Lazarus, lepers who 'live in the wilderness as outcast as we' (Tomlinson, 1998: 89), play a significant part in the action of *Child of the May*. The Epilogue to this book enacts Magda's acceptance of physical difference: she and Tom, whose leg was permanently damaged by a mantrap (the anachronism of which might perturb some readers), dance together as May Queen and Green Man: goddess and god.

Magda and Tom's roles at the end of *Child of the May* echo Marian and Robert as green lady and green man in *The Forestwife*. Through Marian and Robert, gender polarities are not so much broken down as reprioritized: while Robert roams wildly in the wider world, Marian is for the most part confined within the compass of the forest, but her role is privileged and focalized, and shown to be more effectual than his. The effect of presenting these characters in divine guises is to sanctify and universalize a reappraisal of gender and other individual differences. However, this universalizing tendency is constrained by the functions of disguise in the trilogy, and by the growing questioning and redefining of the Forestwife's role.

For Magda to go to Nottingham in *Child of the May*, she has to be disguised as a potter's lad. The implication is a feminist critique of the perceived necessity not to appear female to be an actor in the world, and accords with Lissa Paul's (1987) observation that women and children in literature tend to escape entrapment through trickery and deceit. At climactic moments in the third Forestwife story, *The Path of the She-Wolf*, Marian masquerades as the Hooded One. Marian's disguise enables her to act, but its form is also significant: by donning the hood she enters the male side of the binary opposition previously established between Marian/Green Lady/Forestwife and Robert/Green Man/

Hooded One. There is little movement in the other direction, though – Robert still lacks Marian's competence and flexibility.

In her 'Author's Note' to *The Path of the She-Wolf*, Tomlinson highlights the importance of disguise in the Robin Hood legends. She uses this element with increasing self-consciousness and ingenuity, to give agency to the outlaws, and with transformational power in ritual celebrations of May Queen and Green Man. I find that Nigel Pennick's observations about the European guising tradition are closely applicable to the social and spiritual functions of disguise in Tomlinson's Forestwife novels: 'collective solidarity supersedes individual awareness. Guising ... passes through borders across gender ... and into the otherworld ... When this happens, there is a break in the normal social order' (Pennick, 1998: 1).

Marian comes to doubt her assumption that as Forestwife she could not be 'tied to a man', but she continues as before, having an intermittent intimate relationship with Robert but refusing to marry him. By contrast, Marian's successor Magda does combine marriage and motherhood with the role of Forestwife, though Magda finds the forest confining, whereas for Marian it represents freedom. The alternative ways in which these characters balance personal freedom with commitments to vocation and partner may well resonate with readers' potential choices.

The concepts of both the Hooded One and the Forestwife are extended at the end of the trilogy. Robert's ageing is honoured and the Hooded One becomes, like the Forestwife, a role indefinitely passed on, as Tom, Magda's husband, takes over the hood. Marian's ageing is likewise hallowed, as she is identified with the Corn Goddess. The Forestwife's girdle splits in three, so that Gerta, Magda and Brigit are respectively 'The Old One, the Mother and the Maid' (Tomlinson, 2000: 128). This overt, capitalized reference to the three aspects of the Pagan Triple Goddess deifies one model of the ages of woman.

In Monica Furlong's *Wise Child*, the title character adopts new ideas and a new way of life under Juniper's tutelage. Like Marian in *The Forestwife*, Wise Child becomes physically stronger and more skilled; she learns to work with her hands and her mind, when she has been spoiled before. She loathes spinning and sewing, but Juniper insists on their value – thereby privileging what is disdained as 'women's work'. Juniper makes Wise Child confront and overcome her prejudice against people with leprosy, as Veronica does with Magda in *Child of the May*, and with the same generalized lesson for readers in the present about not rejecting but understanding people with illnesses and disabilities. Though Wise Child grows more used to Juniper, Juniper's difference is maintained so that she can still surprise Wise Child, as she does at the Feast of Beltane (May Day): 'I felt separate, in awe of her, as if I didn't know her at all, she was so splendid' (Furlong, 1987: 156).

Similarly, in *A Year and a Day*, the 'prequel' to *Wise Child*, the young Juniper at first dislikes her mentor Euny and is 'afraid of her rags and poverty' (Furlong, 1990: 26), but she comes to understand and respect her, while maintaining a 'familiar sense of being surprised by Euny – of always being on the wrong foot yet of rather enjoying it' (128). Two months of Juniper's apprenticeship are spent at Angharad's, which is more colourful and comfortable than Euny's.

Teaching Juniper to dye wool, Angharad subtly defends Euny: 'the vinegar ... is the biting acid that makes the colour fast' (73). When Juniper returns home after a year and a day, she feels 'as if nothing could console me for the loss of those hard days which, I now realized, had taught me a great deal' (109).

Furlong explores different models of women's power in *Wise Child* through the characters of Juniper and Maeve the Sorceress. Juniper is drawn from but also challenges stereotypes. She is witch as healer, and in adopting Wise Child she is a kind of Virgin Mother. She makes drudgery divine, giving value to women's work in the home, but she is not a stereotyped 'angel in the house', because she is not beholden to any man, and she comes and goes as she pleases. Juniper's spells of absence also make Wise Child more autonomous. Juniper is very much idealized, as a mature role model for Wise Child and the implied reader. She is still, silent and watchful; she is full of laughter and she is slow to chide – she will not get angry or beat Wise Child; she is a marvellous story-teller; she has a house of her own, and she owns land and is kind to her tenants. Wise Child thinks of 'Juniper who did not think in terms of luxury and hand-some husbands, but who lived as if everything in life ... was a joyful and wonderful treat, a source of amusement, of pleasure, of fascination' (Furlong, 1987: 176).

By contrast, Maeve, Wise Child's absent mother, is portrayed as the beau-tiful, seductive and cruel witch. Her hatred of Juniper derives from an old jealousy over a man. She too has independent means, but is cruel to her tenants and servants. Maeve is Wise Child's tempter, offering to spoil her and make her attractive to men. The stereotype which Maeve represents is not interrogated or redefined; it is simply there for Wise Child to reject.

Maeve's magic is evil, according to Juniper, because it is selfish and control-ling – 'forcing you to do something cannot be right' (190). However, Wise Child is coerced into surrendering herself to others' control during the ordeals of her training. Juniper asks Wise Child, 'Would you trust me if I told you to do something you really hated? That scared you? ... Because you would be glad afterwards. It would be very good for you' (73). Juniper and Euny (who trained Juniper) proceed to make Wise Child fast, bathe and strip, and cover her with psychotropic ointment. 'Broken with faintness and nausea, [Wise Child was] too ill now to wonder or do anything but helplessly surrender' (79). What follows is the mystical revelatory experience of 'flying'. Later, Juniper remorselessly drills Wise Child in a magic language until tiredness sends her beside herself, or ecstatic. There is a tension between the value of Wise Child's experiences and the intimidating ways in which they are induced.

Furlong took the opportunity presented by the later book, *A Year and a Day*, to revisit and reappraise the issues of control that arise in *Wise Child*. This process is comparable with Tomlinson's redefinition of the Forestwife's role as the trilogy progresses, and Susan Price's questioning in later Ghost World novels of the disempowering aspects of the shamanism presented in *The Ghost Drum* (compare Chapter 14 in this volume). Unlike Wise Child, young Juniper manifests signs of her gift before she is apprenticed: her birth is accompanied by portents, she is a natural dowser, she sees visions and dreams, and she has a healing gift. It is vocation that compels her: 'I knew that life was pushing me towards the peculiar sort of wisdom that Euny and Angharad had. I felt I had no real choice' (Furlong, 1990: 91). Juniper is forewarned more than Wise Child, and her trust of her mentors is repeatedly spelt out. Ordeals such as being locked in a smoke-filled hut are also somewhat mitigated by the companionship of Juniper's friend Trewyn.

It is also indicated that Juniper's apprenticeship to Euny is less oppressive than the life she has left behind as a marriageable princess, 'having no control over my life, ... being a mere pawn, indeed a lost pawn, in the game being played between Meroot [her aunt] and my father' (135). Becoming a wise woman represents a better alternative to patriarchy than Meroot's malevolent magic, as Angharad explains: 'Among the *dorans* we speak of people having power, you know. We don't mean power like kings or popes have power, of course, but power to bring things back into a sort of harmony' (72). Both *Wise Child* and *A Year and a Day* advocate a social order in which power is not about subjecting and marginalizing others but collaborating with them; not subduing nature, but living 'in the rhythm'.

In Sherryl Jordan's *The Raging Quiet*, Marnie is accused of witchcraft because the villagers of Torcurra distrust her autonomy and her companionship with Raven, a deaf young man with whom Marnie invents a system of sign language. Modern sensibilities enter into a medieval setting, both in the assumed wholesale intolerance of a small community of the time (for the most part presented as an undifferentiated, unnamed mass), and conversely in the very 'modern' traits of the main characters.

Marnie is supported in her independence by Father Brannan, who is 'like her father ... in his gentle manner and easy way of talking' (Jordan, 2000: 61). Marnie credits her biological father Michael with equipping her to gain the skills to be self-sufficient: 'You'd be so proud if you saw me! All those times you let me try things that were different, that women weren't supposed to do – I'm grateful for them, now' (183). Michael has been unable to talk since having a stroke, and Marnie perceives his similarity with Raven, who has 'the eyes of a caged animal, full of intelligence and pleading and pain. It was the same look her father had, since his affliction' (86).

Raven is portrayed as a wise fool – the significance of this theme is signalled by the name of Torcurra's inn, 'The Sage and Fool', mentioned at the beginning and end of the novel. Marnie sees that there is 'something ageless and unworldly about Raven, something akin to innocence ... as if he were empty, pure, unspoiled by the world's guile and complexity' (85). This is the positive stereotype, but stereotype nevertheless, of the disabled person having extraordinary compensating abilities. Raven's inability to talk mirrors the way women are deprived of a voice in patriarchal society. It is Marnie who gives him a voice, by inventing signs. The dramatic physicality of this form of communication writes large the feminist idea of gaining a voice through 'writing the body' (Cixous, 1976). Appropriately, the sign for 'different' is the one that is most elaborately described (131–2).

The villagers of Torcurra fear and persecute Marnie and Raven, regarding their signs as sorcery, and are pruriently suspicious of Marnie taking homeless Raven under her roof, not long after her husband Isake's sudden death.

Isake's brother, like Isake before him, refers to Marnie's physical beauty as 'bewitching', invoking the witch-as-seductress stereotype. Marnie is brought to trial as a witch, despite the accusations against her being unfounded. Father Brannan cannot stop the excruciating trial by ordeal, but he takes control and limits the damage as far as he can. Raven knows 'well the voiceless pain, the raging quiet within' which Marnie endures (268). Father Brannan is convinced of her innocence, which is indeed proved, though the villagers' intolerance is unassuaged.

There are limits even to Father Brannan's tolerance: he thinks Raven and Marnie should marry, as 'you're flying in the face of custom, and you'll be spurned for it' (282). Although Marnie responds by asserting, 'I'll not marry to please you, or to stop people's tongues wagging' (282), she does marry Raven, after they have made love for the first time. Marnie consents with Raven in a way she never did with Isake, but she is passive in bed: 'spellbound, power-less ... she gave herself to him' (289). Such submission reverts to romantic convention and fundamentally undermines the active subjectivity Marnie has gained in the rest of her life.

Clearly, all the texts under discussion promote tolerant, inclusive attitudes and include wise woman figures. In the case of *The Forestwife Trilogy*, and *Wise Child* and *A Year and a Day*, young women are apprenticed to be trained as wise women in an unending female line, whereas Marnie in *The Raging Quiet* is mentored by a male Christian priest. John Stephens includes *Wise Child* in an article about witch figures in children's fiction, seeing it as an instance of the wise woman schema displacing the crone and sorceress sche-mata. He characterizes the wise woman figuration as privileging 'the other over the self, ... emotion over reason, intuition over knowledge, ... nature over culture' (Stephens, 2003: 197). This does seem to fit the characters of Wise Child and Juniper, as well as the Forestwives and Marnie, but the problem is that this is a limiting, biologically essentialist idealization of the feminine. Diane Purkiss argues that 'the midwife-herbalist-healer-witch [who] seems a spectacular collage of everything which feminist historians and others see as the opposite of medieval patriarchy' (Purkiss, 1996: 19) is far from empow-ering, as this figure is not only marginalized and persecuted, but also too super-competent to be a realistic role model. The wise woman figure thus resembles 'the fantasy superwoman heroine of the 1980s and 90s' (20), a professional and domestic goddess with an idyllic country retreat. This is very much what we have seen in children's historical fiction from this era, so that these novels say much more about the time when they were written than about their histor-ical settings.

Chronotopes: female and Pagan

It is possible to see the narrative structure, time scheme and setting of *The Forestwife Trilogy* as an instance of Nikolajeva's female chronotope, such that the feminine operates at a whole-narrative level. Nikolajeva (1996) defines the female chronotope as narrative time-space which is cyclic, recurrent, continuous and closed, whereas the male chronotope is linear, goal-oriented, discontinuous and open. The structure and focus of *The Forestwife* challenge the paradigms of historiography and historical fiction. The trilogy's episodic nature denies the teleology of historical narrative – that is, the goal-oriented, linear structure that is a characteristic of the male chronotope. The central characters of *The Forestwife* are liminal, living on the margins: legendary figures of contended historicity; women and working people largely written out of history until recently. The historian E. H. Carr claims: 'History begins when men [*sic*] begin to think of the passage of time in terms not of natural processes – the cycle of the seasons, the human life-span – but of a series of specific events in which men are constantly involved and which they can consciously influence' (Carr, 1986: 134). By contrast, in *The Forestwife*, such 'his-story' is sidelined and subverted by 'her-story'. Men's actions are not purposive: kings act arbitrarily, and Robin signally fails to influence events, whereas Marian does intervene successfully to redress injustice.

In *The Path of the She-Wolf*, the cyclic narrative embodies Magda's pregnancy, instantiating the generalization made by Roberta Trites (1997: 113) that 'nested narratives can themselves become a child-of-the-mother image … The very structure of a nested narrative places a metaphorical value on birth [and] evokes the awareness of interpersonal connections'. Magda's initial wish for a child has a proleptic and hermeneutic function in the narrative – that is to say, it engages the reader in anticipating and guessing. It is also part of a wider pattern in the last two Forestwife books of visions, forebodings and prophecies, which self-consciously disrupt linear narrative. The process of storytelling itself is foregrounded in a way that shows how present concerns are mirrored in the past: 'Sarah held them enthralled. Her stories [about Merlin and Arthur] told them of a time long ago, a time when hopes of justice had prevailed' (Tomlinson, 1993: 105). In these ways, *The Forestwife Trilogy* contradicts Stephens's (1992: 236) assertion that 'Historical novels generally employ a realistic mode, and avoid any self-conscious reflections on their own narrative strategies' – or rather, it hybridizes historical and fantastic modes into a kind of magical realism with a historical setting.

Stephens and McCallum (1998) find in Robin Hood retellings a predominance of male initiation and bonding. *The Forestwife*, despite being first published five years before their study, is apparently not known to them since they announce that 'we are still waiting for a *Robin Hood* in which Marian is principal focalizer' (181). They do pay attention to Robin McKinley's *The Outlaws of Sherwood* (1988), and I would observe that much of what they find there is echoed by the later Forestwife trilogy: Sherwood is a refuge for oppressed women; female characters are focalizers; 'the patterns of male bonding [are] displaced by an emphasized social concern and conscience' (Stephens and McCallum, 1998: 189); and Robin is 'a transformed and somewhat decentered character' (190). *The Forestwife Trilogy* can be counted among the few exceptions to Stephens and McCallum's observation that the tendency of Robin Hood retellings 'towards socially conservative ideologies […] is unrelieved and systematically programmatic' (198). What particularly distinguishes *The Forestwife Trilogy* is the resonance of its sustained exploration of gender roles, achieved through its female chronotope and through the figure of the Forestwife. Tomlinson's trilogy may be seen as resisting the culturally conservative 'Western metaethic' Stephens and McCallum regard as pervasive in retellings of traditional stories.

Yet *The Forestwife Trilogy* privileges the female side of the female–male binary opposition, rather than questioning the terms of the opposition; gender polarities are not so much broken down as reprioritized. That the female chronotope is eminently applicable is in itself problematic, as the contrast between the cyclic female chronotope and the linear male chronotope could be criticized for being founded on biological determinism, while individuals may find their gender identity considerably at variance with Nikolajeva's scheme.

I would like to propose that my formulation of the Pagan chronotope (Bramwell, 2009) provides a better fit than the female chronotope for *The Forestwife Trilogy*, and indeed also applies to *Wise Child*, *A Year and a Day* and *The Raging Quiet*. Space in the Pagan chronotope includes sacred place and/or landscape, such as henge monuments or wooded groves; spiritual journeys on a physical plane, usually in a northwards direction; and spatial distortions, such as projection or bilocation, caused by the magical abilities of protagonists. Time in the Pagan chronotope is seasonal and cyclic, with stories hinging around Pagan festivals in the annually recurring solar calendar, such as Beltane/May Day, Samhain/Hallowe'en, summer or winter solstice. In all, fictional realizations of the Pagan chronotope are complex and holistic, in that sacred space and non-linear time are intricately interdependent.

The Forestwife foregrounds natural processes, and its sequels are structured around the cycle of the seasons. *Child of the May* begins and ends with the festival of May Day, and is more precise than *The Forestwife* about how the practices of nature religion celebrate the cycle of the seasons (see Figure 2). This is developed further in *The Path of the She-Wolf*, in which festivals are settings for rites of passage – girl to woman on May Day, marriages at Lammas. The novel opens and closes with Brig's Night, encompassing Magda's wish for a child and its multiple fulfilment. Magda's prayer, accompanied by ritually making a bower and a Biddy doll, is answered by 12-year-old Brigit's arrival, by Magda's adoption of six homeless children, and by her having her own baby. Magda's choice to have a child means that the second 'Brig's Night can be my little Eleanor's name feast' (Tomlinson, 2000: 108). Thus, through incidents and at a whole-narrative level, *The Path of the She-Wolf* retrojects current interest in nature religion, and the desire, credible or not, for it to have a history.

The Pagan chronotope is most obvious in *Wise Child*, in a pivotal episode that takes place at the sacred time of Beltane (May Day) in the sacred space of a stone circle (Furlong, 1987: chapter 15). However, something apparently Pagan is Christianized: there are echoes of the biblical story of Abraham and Isaac when Wise Child surrenders herself to be sacrificed, only for a deer (rather than a ram) to replace her. Then, in a ceremony like the Mass, everyone sips from a silver chalice and partakes of the sacrificial deer's flesh. Indeed, in both *A Year and a Day* and *Wise Child*, Monica Furlong experiments with

Figure 2   The cover for Theresa Tomlinson's *Child of the May* shows clearly the centrality of the independent females featured in this historical novel

mixing Christianity and nature religion. In *A Year and a Day*, Euny and young Juniper honour the Mother in the form of a black Madonna by a well, and the trainee *dorans*, Juniper and Trewyn, share bread and wine with their mentors at a stone circle. As in *The Forestwife*, some of the novel's concerns are epitomized in a brief reference to Arthur, whom Juniper's mother Erlain sees as a syncretizing figure who combined Christian with Pagan: 'The Christians say that there is no magic – that the world is ruled by love. I cannot decide whether they are right. Our forebear Arthur was a Christian yet believed in magic' (Furlong, 1990: 27).

In *Wise Child* a rather schematic gendered opposition is set up between the wise woman Juniper, who is tolerant and in touch with nature, and the priest Fillan, who represents a persecuting, punitive, patriarchal version of Christianity that represses the material, natural feminine. Wise Child herself wants 'to be both a Christian and a *doran*' (Furlong, 1987: 170). Furlong's use of children's fiction to challenge and modulate patriarchal Christianity with nature religion accords with her campaign for the ordination of women and her feminist theology; as she observes in *A Dangerous Delight*: 'supposed witches [...] were reminders of a religion much older than Christianity, and were thus regarded as a source of potential subversion. The witches, with their herbal remedies and their interest in the rhythms of nature, hark back to earth religion, to a faith not of domination of nature but of harmony with it' (Furlong, 1991: 26). This was a popular idea at the time Furlong was writing and it certainly persists, but it should be noted that it has been challenged by historians: the idealistic figuration of the wise woman has been questioned by Diane Purkiss (1996, as discussed above), while Ronald Hutton (1999) maintains that the roots of modern Paganism can be traced back no further than the eighteenth century.

Like Wise Child, Marnie in *The Raging Quiet* keeps her Christian faith throughout her experiences. Though she can accommodate the tradition of Midsummer Eve, 'dancing in the fields by huge bonfires, celebrating the summer and the sun' (Jordan, 2000: 174), Raven's instinctive Paganism is at first strange to her:

Like ancient sentinels, the stones leaned dark and overpowering against the wheeling stars. The air seemed alive, the shining silence still ringing with the songs of bygone worshippers. Marnie shivered, remembering warnings she had heard about these places; warnings of heathen gods, spirit forces, and forbidden rites. But Raven embraced the stones, stroking them, sensing their primal force. (Jordan, 2000: 236)

And yet, again like Wise Child, she filters new experience through Christian perceptions: 'Longing for lost innocence, for that oneness with the perfect earth, she yearned to dance as Raven danced – as surely Adam and Eve had danced – in newborn Eden' (236). She does dance with Raven, and feels 'at one with the moonlight and the night, unaware of self, unaware of everything but this freedom, this cleansing unity with the earth and sky and God' (237). Raven's deafness and homelessness have removed him from socializing processes, so that his nature religion appears innate, though Father Brannan and Marnie think it is intuitive Christianity.

Thus the presence of the Pagan chronotope need not entail a Pagan world-view. Of course, C. S. Lewis's Narnia books include Pagan mythological figures, used allegorically for the Christian message which is presented as the summation and fulfilment of Pagan narratives. Tomlinson, Furlong and Jordan allow a more dynamic relationship between Christianity and Paganism, but with a view not so much to embrace Paganism on its own terms as to modify Christianity and make it more palatable to present-day sensibilities by being less patriarchal and more in touch with the natural world.

Conclusion

If indeed '[i]n the last decade ... children's historical fiction has gained some-thing of the popularity enjoyed by fantasy at the turn of the millennium' (Butler and O'Donovan, 2012: 185), then in the run up to the millennium the texts I have been discussing paved the way for this trend, particularly for historical fiction with a spiritual or supernatural dimension. The Harry Potter and Twilight phenomena have created market conditions for children's fiction with a magical twist; whether the setting is historical or contemporary, realist or fantastic, seems immaterial. The Pagan chronotope defines a kind of magical realism that crosses the boundaries of traditional notions of genre, for its cyclic, seasonal time operates regardless of whether the setting is in the past, the present or the future.

This chapter has advocated a relativist approach to children's historical fiction. I have argued that perceptions of historical accuracy and authenticity are contingent, subject to their own times and cultural contexts. The sensibili-ties of the times in which historical novels are written are retrojected into the imagined past, and these values become more evident with the passage of time. My chosen texts, all published less than three decades ago, have agendas that may be agreeable – to do with tolerance, inclusivity and equality – but that now seem all too blatant. Likewise, the ideology of today's children's historical fiction can be uncovered, and will come to be seen as of its time.

WORKS CITED AND FURTHER READING

Children's Books

Furlong, Monica. *Wise Child*. London: Gollancz, 1987.
Furlong, Monica. *A Year and a Day*. London: Gollancz, 1990. (Published in paperback as *Juniper*.)
Jordan, Sherryl. *The Raging Quiet*. London: Simon and Schuster, 2000. (Published in 1999 in the USA by Simon and Schuster.)
McKinley, Robin. *The Outlaws of Sherwood*. New York: William Morrow, 1988.
Tomlinson, Theresa. *The Forestwife*. London: Random House, 1993.
Tomlinson, Theresa. *Child of the May*. London: Random House, 1998.

Tomlinson, Theresa. *The Path of the She-Wolf.* London: Random House, 2000.
Tomlinson, Theresa. *The Forestwife Trilogy.* London: Random House, 2003. Note: page references for *The Forestwife Trilogy* are to the individual volumes rather than the collected edition.
Trease, Geoffrey. *Bows Against the Barons.* London: Martin Lawrence, 1934.

Critical Texts

Agnew, Kate, Suzanne Rahn and Roie Thomas. 'Historical Fiction'. In Victor Watson (ed.), *The Cambridge Guide to Children's Books in English* (pp. 335–8). Cambridge: Cambridge University Press, 2001.
Bramwell, Peter. *Pagan Themes in Modern Children's Fiction.* Basingstoke: Palgrave Macmillan, 2009.
Butler, Catherine, and Hallie O'Donovan. *Reading History in Children's Books.* Basingstoke: Palgrave Macmillan, 2012.
Carr, E. H. *What Is History?* Harmondsworth: Penguin, 1986; first published 1961.
Cixous, Hélène. 'The Laugh of the Medusa'. *Signs*, 1.4 (1976), 875–93.
Furlong, Monica. *A Dangerous Delight: Women and Power in the Church.* London: SPCK, 1991.
Hutton, Ronald. *The Triumph of the Moon: A History of Modern Pagan Witchcraft.* Oxford: Oxford University Press, 1999.
Nikolajeva, Maria. *Children's Literature Comes of Age: Toward a New Aesthetic.* New York and London: Garland, 1996.
Paul, Lissa. 'Enigma Variations: What Feminist Theory Knows about Children's Literature'. *Signal*, 54 (Sept. 1997), 186–201.
Pennick, Nigel. *Crossing the Borderlines: Guising, Masking and Ritual Animal Disguises in the European Tradition.* Chieveley: Capall Bann, 1998.
Purkiss, Diane. *The Witch in History.* London and New York: Routledge, 1996.
Stephens, John. *Language and Ideology in Children's Fiction.* London: Longman, 1992.
Stephens, John. 'Witch-Figures in Recent Children's Fiction: The Subaltern and the Subversive'. In Ann Lawson Lucas (ed.), *The Presence of the Past in Children's Literature* (pp. 195–202). Westport, CT: Greenwood, 2003.
Stephens, John, and Robyn McCallum. *Retelling Stories, Framing Culture: Traditional Stories and Metanarratives in Children's Literature.* New York and London: Garland, 1998.
Trites, Roberta Seelinger. *Waking Sleeping Beauty: Feminist Voices in Children's Novels.* Iowa City: University of Iowa Press, 1997.
Wilkie-Stibbs, Christine. *The Feminine Subject in Children's Literature.* New York and London: Routledge, 2002.

Postmodernism, New Historicism and Postcolonialism: Some Recent Historical Novels

Pat Pinsent

KEY TEXTS

Gary Crew, *Strange Objects* (1990)
Linda Crew, *Children of the River* (1989)
Paula Fox, *The Slave Dancer* (1973)
Jeanne Wakatsuki Houston and James D. Houston, *Farewell to Manzanar* (1973)
An Na, *A Step from Heaven* (2001)
Beverley Naidoo, *Journey to Jo'Burg* (1985)
Gary Paulsen, *Nightjohn* (1993)
Mildred Taylor, *Roll of Thunder, Hear My Cry* (1976)

Written history throughout the ages has generally been created by historians who have viewed events from the perspective of those possessing power, the representatives of the dominant culture. Unsurprisingly, until relatively recently, historians of the British Empire have been likely to display, explicitly or implicitly, completely different attitudes towards those who are exerting dominion over subjugated peoples from those revealed towards the members of the subject peoples themselves. This phenomenon is evidenced also in literature, so that nineteenth-century historical novelists treating the theme of empire for a young audience, such as R. M. Ballantyne (1825–94) and G. A. Henty (1832–1902), were far more likely to present the action through the eyes of the imperialist adventurers than through the 'natives' whom they encounter. Although a few twentieth-century authors, notably Geoffrey

Trease and Rosemary Sutcliff, attempted to portray life from the perspective of a marginalized or suppressed group, this trend remained a minor one in comparison to that material, particularly in comics and boys' magazines, which still adopted a superior attitude towards the majority of the inhabitants of 'the colonies'.

Not until relatively recently have novels set in the past, as well as those depicting present-day situations, virtually taken as a given that marginalized and oppressed groups provide as interesting a focus as characters from the dominant group. This foregrounding of marginalized groups appears to result from a wider understanding of and empathy with the underprivileged; although today's society is no more guiltless of the persecution of minorities than were those of the past, the break-up of empire and the development of mass communications makes it more difficult for writers and readers to be oblivious to the plight of the disempowered.

The texts to be discussed in this chapter represent an attempt on the part of children's authors, whether themselves inside or outside such communities, to foreground the experiences of immigrant or minority groups, or in some cases disempowered indigenous communities, in lands where there are strong, Western-derived, dominant cultures. These books tend to be characterized by the recognition on the part of the authors of the need to give a voice to the voiceless and to relativize the role of those in power by presenting a perspective other than theirs. This contrasts with much of the earlier British children's literature set in outposts of empire, which, however sympathetic the author might be to the underprivileged, automatically presented the perspective of the imperial colonizer. Justice and beneficence were preached in such books, but today such an approach can all too easily appear patronizing. By contrast, in books currently being written on such topics, frequently set in the past, there is a tendency to portray disempowered characters who quite naturally take on such strategies as learning the oppressor's language, or profiting from educational opportunities in order to acquire autonomy, both for themselves individually and for their communities. Such a phenomenon may be recognized in the history of the development of colonial regimes throughout the world, and is increasingly portrayed in the literatures of the United States, Canada and Australia, as well as that of Britain itself.

Associated with this assimilation, both in books and in real life, is the tendency for the powerless to internalize the structures which keep the empowered group in authority, so that these no longer need to be imposed externally. Children may grow up to accept not only the language, but also the culture of the dominant group, rejecting their own. This is the almost inevitable result of liminality; marginalized people who are on the threshold of a more powerful group may strive to be part of such a group. Alternatively, they may seek by subversive means to raise the status of their own community while trying to retain some vestiges of their own identity. The books discussed in this chapter foreground language, education and culture as sites for such processes. In particular, they often emphasize the ways in which religion, song and folk tale serve as means to preserve, or even recreate, a culture potentially subversive to the mainstream.

Critical approaches

All the novels considered here have a strong relationship to history, generally the submerged and almost forgotten history of people regarded as marginal to the main areas of human progress. The approaches to history in these books, although quite varied, all emphasize the personal element, whether that of a first-person narrator or a single focal character, or, in the case of the works of Gary Crew (1947–), that of late twentieth-century characters being exposed to the events of a remote period. In tackling such material, certain critical approaches seem to offer the possibility of most insights: those of New Historicism, Cultural Materialism, and, because of the settings of the novels, Postcolonialism (see Boxes 11.2 and 11.3). As will be seen in the analyses of individual novels, it is not always easy to distinguish between the literary-critical approach employed in looking at the texts, and the historico-critical techniques used by the writers concerned. For instance, in *Strange Objects* (1990), Gary Crew's postmodern (Box 11.1) creation of apparently 'factual' material to be set against the narrative passages involving his protagonist, puts the reader in the position of a New Historicist critic faced with 'real' material. Similarly, the experience of characters learning the majority language and culture tends to encapsulate the development of postcolonial literatures generally: Adopt, Adapt, Adept (Barry, 1995: 195; see also Box 11.3).

In creating a number of what appear to be primary historical sources, Crew is highlighting a dilemma always latently present in the historical novel: the challenge to the reader to be aware of the fictionality of most of the narrative, as opposed to the historicity of the basic situation. As Stephens observes: 'The distinction between what is real and what is fictive is often difficult for young readers to make, so the authority with which fictive events are invested by their

---

BOX 11.1 POSTMODERNISM

Despite a sometimes-expressed fear that the subtleties of postmodern writing might be too demanding for young readers, children's literature has often been foremost in subverting the customary norms of narrative (especially in picturebooks). In *Working with Structuralism* (1981), David Lodge cites a number of characteristics of postmodern texts, all of which function to disorientate the reader, a disconcerting process which is nevertheless a very relevant tool in the hands of any writer who seeks to encourage readers to look at material from a new perspective (as is also the case in the critical approaches of New Historicism, Cultural Materialism and Postcolonialism – see Boxes 11.2 and 11.3). Lodge suggests that in postmodernist works the connections between topics are subverted by such techniques as contradictory items being placed in close proximity, a general avoidance of continuity, and an often apparent randomness in the selection of material. He sees as a characteristic mode of postmodern writing the process of 'combining in the one work the apparently factual and the obviously fictional, introducing the author and the question of authorship into the text, and exposing conventions in the act of using them' (1981: 15).

interaction with actual events will be intensified' (1992: 209). Thus, although the actual events which provide the background of these texts are often only present in a shadowy way, by their factuality they nevertheless invite the young reader to believe in the fictional characters and events within the novels. There is for the reader a delicate balance between, on the one hand, regarding the characters and the specific situations in which they are involved as typical of the experience of members of disempowered communities, and on the other, of being subject to the force of the narrative and actually believing that the novelists' inventions are 'true'. Such a situation invests the author with a high degree of responsibility, lest young readers, once they are disabused of literal belief that the novel itself is history, carry from the experience too high a level of scepticism about what actually happened as well as about the fictional account. The extent of the success of this process in these novels is examined below.

BOX 11.2   NEW HISTORICISM AND CULTURAL MATERIALISM

New Historicism and *Cultural Materialism* share many characteristics, both having been strongly influenced by the ideas of the French philosopher Michel Foucault; his work on discourse and power emphasizes the circulation of power over time and between all social levels, and the resultant fact that the interpretation of events can never be fixed, being subject to shifts of power. The differences between these two influential critical approaches will be considered after a brief résumé of their salient features.

New Historicism is defined by Barry (1995: 172) as 'a method based on the *parallel* reading of literary and non-literary texts'. He suggests that it detaches the literary text from the 'accumulated weight of previous literary scholarship' and focuses attention 'on issues of State power' and its maintenance. Significantly, New Historicism is not a theory and is not theorized; it treats texts from all domains (though particularly archival material and historical documents) as part of culture, which has however been artificially separated into discrete areas. It abhors the separation of history and text, regarding all texts as historical documents and all historical documents as texts. Since the writing of history involves narrative and interpretation, it can be analysed in a similar way to literature. All analysis of the evidence is inevitably subjective, so that historians need to 'reveal the ways in which they know they have been positioned, by their own cultural experience, to interpret history' (Tyson, 2006: 290).

It is easy to see an intersection between the concerns of postmodern writing and New Historicism as a critical approach: when the author sets real or apparent historical sources in parallel with the sections of narrative involving plot and characters, the result is the novelistic creation of what appears to be a New Historicist discourse. Without any label, this practice has been employed frequently in historical fiction, from Sir Walter Scott onwards.

Cultural Materialism developed in Britain as a response to the premises of New Historicism. Jonathan Dollimore and Alan Sinfield, two of the founders of this approach, explain: 'insistence on the process through which a text achieves its current estimation is the key move in cultural materialism' (1994: 28). Lois Tyson summarizes its position thus: 'the ... questions [of cultural critics] ... ask us to make connections between the literary text, the culture in which it emerged, and the cultures in which it is inter-preted' (2006: 297).

Thus while both these approaches are interested in demonstrating that texts and history cannot be separated, New Historicists focus on how the process of combining texts and historical documents helps readers to understand the past, while Cultural Materialists insist that the process is in fact about understanding the present, 'revealing the politics of our own society by what we choose to emphasize or suppress of the past' (Barry, 1995: 184).

BOX 11.3 POSTCOLONIALISM

Postcolonialism foregrounds the way in which European cultural traditions have been taken as the norm, marginalizing the language and *mores* of original inhabitants and minority groups. Edward Said's work (1978, 1993) emphasizes how non-Western cultures have been seen as 'other' or exotic, while another foundational text for this discipline is *The Empire Writes Back* (Ashcroft, Griffiths and Tiffin, 1989), which discusses a broad range of postcolonial texts in the context of relevant cultural issues. Barry (1995: 195) suggests that all postcolonial literatures seem to go through a process of 'Adopt', the unquestioning acceptance of the authority of European models; 'Adapt', when they transmute these to their own subject matter; and 'Adept', a remaking of the forms to their own specifications. He also suggests that '[an] emphasis on identity as doubled, or hybrid, or unstable is a ... characteristic of the postcolonial approach' (195), something which clearly relates to the dual language and culture accessible to people in the postcolonial situation. Another important practitioner in the field of literary postcolonial studies is Clare Bradford, whose theoretical considerations (in Rudd, 2010: 39–50, 229–30) develop out of her own research on Australian Aboriginal texts (2001, 2002, 2003, 2007)

A second edition of Ashcroft et al. includes a substantial review of postcolonialism, which the authors describe as 'one of the most diverse and contentious fields in literary and cultural studies'. They conclude that 'the theoretical issues raised by post-colonial theory: questions of resistance, power, ethnicity, nationality, language and culture, and the transformation of dominant discourses by ordinary people, provide important models for understanding the local in an increasingly globalized world' (2002: 193, 222).

It is evident that New Historicism, Cultural Materialism and Postcolonialism are kindred in their demands for reappraisal of the 'certainties' of the past and for a new positioning of the critic, who needs to acknowledge how personal experience shapes any readings of texts, whether they are derived from past or present, Western or previously colonized, sources.

Equality, anti-racism and multiculturalism

During the 1960s and 1970s, many people in Britain and America began to be increasingly conscious of the importance of children's literature in the process of giving minority groups a more equal role in society. It could help make future citizens aware not only of past oppression, but also of how literature itself had been complicit in this oppression, both in the use of language, characters and situations which took it for granted, and by rendering marginalized groups invisible, together with their experiences. The examination of children's literature was bifocal: first, there was a reappraisal of children's classics of the past in order to determine how characters from minority ethnic groups had been portrayed; and second, and more relevant here, new works of fiction were written with the object of informing white readers about the oppression of other races.

There is no doubt as to the motivation of some of the white authors whose books confronted the issues of racism; however, after a period in which their endeavours were widely welcomed, questions began to be asked about the extent to which, for instance, award-winning novels such as William Armstrong's *Sounder* (1969), Theodore Taylor's *The Cay* (1969) and Paula Fox's *The Slave Dancer* (1973) had too unquestioningly portrayed the slave characters as victims incapable of the same kind of agency as the white characters whose reactions are in general more central to the narrative. The silence and passivity of the slaves in these books may be contrasted with their agency in a later work, also by a white author, Gary Paulsen's *Nightjohn* (1993), which focuses on a young, educated, black man who continually risks mutilation and death in order to bring literacy to groups of slaves. Nightjohn's punishment for illegally teaching the slaves to read is seen from the perspective of a young black woman: 'They hold the foot to the block. John he still not making any sounds, but his face is stiff. Like it's carved out of rock' (50). The force of this image only becomes apparent at the end of the book in an afterword, when Paulsen describes the lives of two slaves owned by Thomas Jefferson (1743–1826), a great exponent of human rights, who seemed unaware of his responsibilities to the slaves in his employ. Of one of these, a carpenter, who built the house where Jefferson lived, Paulsen says, 'His face is not on Mount Rushmore' (171), the mountain on which the faces of US presidents are carved out of stone. For Paulsen, it would appear, those who deserve to be immortalized in this way are people like this carpenter, Isaac, and disseminators of learning such as Nightjohn himself.

During the 1970s critics began to question the legitimacy of writers who did not belong to a minority group 'usurping' the role that properly belonged to members of such groups, and in effect ventriloquizing through the characters as if they were little more than puppets.[1] A black American writer who was eminently successful in communicating the community's values is Mildred Taylor, whose *Roll of Thunder, Hear My Cry* (1976), a Newbery Medal winner, is centred in the consciousness of the young black narrator Cassie, but equally firmly roots her experience within the Mississippi community in which she comes to maturity. Taylor's sureness of touch in depicting the community results from the fact that, as she acknowledges, both the incidents and the characters are based on the experience of her own father, who grew up in the Southern states and benefited by inheriting stories from past generations.

Books such as *Roll of Thunder* show how it is possible to create in young readers a combination of a sense of otherness and an empathy with the characters. On the one hand, this alterity is essential so that readers can appreciate how different the lives and settings portrayed are from their own lives; without this understanding, the plight of people disadvantaged by prejudice cannot be conveyed. Unless this insight is combined with an empathetic sharing in the experience of the characters, however, readers may lack the involvement which creates in them an ownership of such experience; as a consequence they may be too detached from the outcomes to engage with the issues being raised. Taylor achieves both alterity and empathy throughout the book by describing incidents accessible to children of any background, though for most, inconceivable as a part of everyday life. Examples range from the initial description of Cassie, her siblings and other local children walking to school, with her little brother's anger at being splashed by the bus which is taking the privileged white children to their superior school, through the children's resentment at being handed down schoolbooks in poor condition and regarded as fit only for 'nigras', to Cassie's fury at being pushed off the sidewalk by the father of a white girl.

Cassie's mother's presentation of the history of the oppression of black people in America (chapter 6) brilliantly summarizes what readers, like Cassie herself, need to know about this subject for the book to have its maximum effect. The aspect of community is kept to the fore, particularly in a scene set at the church (187), where the 'revival' is much more than simply a religious occasion; it also shows how the church is the centre of the community. This is reinforced by what Cassie's mother has to say about the way in which the slave-owners taught Christianity: 'They didn't teach us Christianity to save our souls, but to teach us obedience. They were afraid of slave revolts and they wanted us to learn the Bible's teaching about slaves being loyal to their masters' (106). Yet the function of the church in maintaining community is apparent, while the role of prayer in Cassie's mother's life is not minimized (107). Members of the oppressed community have transformed and made their own the sacred narratives of the oppressors.

Literature of immigration and postcolonialism

The phenomenon of the displacement of individuals and communities from their native countries is certainly not a new one. The very spread of the human race from its origins in Africa to the whole surface of the globe must have involved this kind of movement. Events such as the creation of empires and the consequent flight of refugees from powerful invaders have happened throughout the ages. The major differences between earlier movements of people and those in today's world are probably the scale and speed of migration, as well as the extent to which modern communications inform virtually everyone in the world about the process. Accompanying this process has been the way in which erstwhile colonial peoples have won their independence and evolved into autonomous nations. Inevitably both processes have formed the subject matter of children's fiction, some of this interest being triggered by the need for newer communities to find their voices, while the acceptability of such narratives for publication for children has been increased by the awareness in privileged Western societies that racism, though officially prohibited, may nevertheless exist below the surface.

It is noticeable that contemporary children's fiction tends to a greater extent than in the past to make readers aware of the migrant community or the emerging, previously disempowered, indigenous group, rather than to represent protagonists either as (often aberrant) individuals or as members of the empowered group. Thus an awareness is created of the lack within such communities of the advantages taken for granted by those who possess power. A consequence is the realization of an ambivalence within the displaced or subordinate groups about the preservation of their culture and language, as well as their subjection to concomitant problems about employment, and resulting failures in self-image, particularly for adult men.

Those children's books which have focused on the plight of migrant communities could be seen as providing something of a bridge between texts (like those discussed in the preceding section) which focus on racial issues or on divisions between long-established minority groups and the hegemonic majority, and texts which can be more accurately described as 'postcolonial', being set in what would once have been termed the outposts of empire, or written by people historically from them. Like the former category, books featuring migrant groups foreground equality issues, while like the latter, they often suggest that the culture of the subordinate group is strange, even exotic, to the majority population. Unlike a great deal of earlier colonial literature, however, they also pinpoint the strangeness of the majority culture as seen by the immigrant group, thus succeeding in relativizing it for the reader. This mutual 'otherness' may simply take the form of differing foods, but quite often it relates to customs, especially those concerned with sex, notably the position of girls faced with a dichotomy between the standards of home and of neighbourhood. Whether or not such books depict the past, a degree of alterity is created by the misunderstandings of the incomers about behaviour in the host community, as well as by a description of their own customs.

A frequently used strategy is to present young characters who find it difficult to understand why they are forbidden participation in the activities of the host community which their schoolmates regard as normal. They also display the need to find a balance between retaining relationships within their communities and attempting to 'get on' in the new society. Another recurring feature in several of these books is what might be termed the emasculation of the father figure. He is shown as all too often incapable of fulfilling the role of bread-winner in the new society, his consequent frustration leading him to resent the much easier integration experienced by his children.

Jeanne Wakatsuki Houston and James Houston's first-person narrative *Farewell to Manzanar* (1973) is presented as an autobiography rather than a novel, being described as 'A true story of Japanese American experience during and after the World War II internment'. The Wakatsuki family and many other Japanese Americans were removed from their homes, which were regarded as too dangerously near a US naval station, and interned in a half-finished and over-crowded camp which all too inadequately provided for their phys-ical and emotional needs, with its 'bare floors, blanket partitions, one bulb in each compartment dangling from a roof beam' (28). The father of the family is arrested on a charge of which he is eventually found innocent, but only released after nine months of imprisonment; during this period his health and self-respect are irremediably damaged. The narrative is prefaced by a fore-word which describes the research for the book, and again stresses that 'this is a true story'. Nevertheless, there is a constant tension between the factual and the fictive, which is most apparent when the authors present, verbatim and at length, conversations which could not possibly have been remembered in such detail. Even more obviously fictional are chapters that recreate scenes that Wakatsuki Houston could not have witnessed, such as the interrogation of her father at his place of imprisonment, Fort Lincoln (chapter 7). There is often a tension between the young child's perceptions and the adult writer's interpretations, as when she first describes how her father continued to use a cane which gave support to an injured leg even when he no longer needed it: 'I see it *now* [my emphasis] as a sad, homemade version of [a] Samurai sword' (47). When after more than three years they are allowed to find their own living accommodation again, the protagonist has internalized the 'shame for being a person guilty of something enormous enough to deserve that kind of treatment' (185).

Linda Crew's *Children of the River* (1989), set in the 1970s, focuses on Sundara, who has escaped with her aunt's family from the Khmer Rouge in Cambodia, leaving her parents behind. She struggles both in adapting to American society in Oregon and in coming to terms with the death of the baby niece for whom she has been a main carer. Crew, while not of Cambodian origin, writes out of her personal acquaintance with Cambodian refugees, so while the events are based on real happenings, this book, narrated in the third person, is more overt in its fictionality than is the case with the other texts discussed in this section. The main emphasis in *Children of the River* is on the clash of cultures, particularly with regard to relationships with the opposite sex. Sundara's struggle to comply with her aunt's prohibition against friend-ship with Jonathan, the son of a doctor, is matched by the boy's total incom-prehension of the impossibility for Sundara even of going to the cinema with him. Finally, Sundara takes control of her own life by spending a day with Jonathan's family, and her aunt comes to understand some of the alien cultural elements.

Both differences in understanding and cultural clashes within the family because of friendships with American classmates also feature strongly as elements in An Na's *A Step from Heaven* (2001), a first-person account of the process towards integration into American society as experienced by a Korean girl, Park Young Ju. One of her first experiences is being introduced in a classroom and hearing the teacher's word 'welcome' as 'Wah ko um'. The school is very different from the more rigid setting to which she is accustomed, but is likely to be more familiar to the majority of readers than would Young's former school. Thus the strangeness experienced by the character, together with the empathy which has probably already been generated in the readers, may enable them to see the problems faced by the characters as if they were their own. While Young is becoming a competent and confident member of American society, she witnesses the disintegration of her family, triggered by her father's violence, a consequence of his low status and dependence on his wife, who works all available hours to support the family. Deprived of his traditional role as provider, he replaces it by the tyranny of forbidding Young to have American friends, even of the same sex. At the same time, she is conscious of the differences between her status in the family and that of her younger brother.

No easy resolution is offered: the father returns to Korea while Young finds some consolation in remembering his role early in her childhood in establishing her confidence by teaching her how to swim. The autobiographical element in *A Step from Heaven* appears to be strong; Na, like her protagonist, was born in Korea and came to America as a child, and met with academic success. An instance of the literary approach of this novel is the way in which the sometimes fragmentary nature of the text, particularly in the early chapters, mirrors the incomplete understandings of the developing child – a technique recalling, for instance, James Joyce's *A Portrait of the Artist as a Young Man* (1916). The book begins:

> Just to the edge, Young Ju. Only your feet. Stay there.
> Cold. Cold water. Oh. My toes are fish. Come here. Fast. Look.
> What is it, Young Ju?
> See my toes. See how they are swimming in the sea? Like fish.
> Yes they are little fat piggy fish.   (9)

The usage is strikingly different from the long paragraphs and more cohesive style at the end of the book.

Despite the different settings and periods of time concerned, these three books have a great deal in common. In all but one instance the authors are drawn from the minority communities depicted, and portray the focal characters as going through the stages that in all probability they themselves as children experienced; first learning the language of the empowered group, then employing it to describe their own culture, and finally becoming so proficient as to appear to be in transition to the majority group. This process is analogous to Barry's summary of the development of postcolonial literature: 'Adopt, Adapt, Adept.'

Wakatsuki Houston and Houston's text could be seen as nearer to the 'adopt' phase; throughout *Farewell to Manzanar*, the protagonist reveals ambivalence about her own culture, almost to the point of rejection, spurred on by her hostility to her father. She is deracinated to the extent of initially being terrified of other Japanese (11) and talking about them as if she were not part of the group, as in: 'There is a phrase the Japanese use in such situations …' (16). Towards the end of the book she discloses, 'I was the first member of our family to finish college and the first to marry out of my race' (186). Her revisiting of the scene of her childhood internment appears to be therapeutic rather than related to any pride in her background or desire to pass it on to her own children.

The situation in the more recent books is more complex. Park Young and Sundara both certainly become 'adept' in the Western language and culture in which they are immersed, and it could be argued that the characters are to some extent rejecting their own cultures. In *A Step from Heaven*, the father's return to Korea, meaning that he virtually loses touch with the family, signifies for the rest of the family a severing of their Korean roots. Nevertheless the strong attachment between mother and daughter suggests some desire to retain the positive elements of the culture. In particular, it evinces Na's wish to 'remake the [literary] form to [her] own specification' (Barry, 1995: 195) rather than simply to 'adapt' it to her own subject matter. In addition to Na's innovative mirroring of her protagonist's mental state throughout the text, she shows her command of symbol by her final image of Young's mother's scarred and work-worn hands. The response to the girl's wistful 'I wish I could erase these scars for you' is:

> Uhmma gently slips her hands from mine. She stares for a moment at her callused skin and then says firmly, These are my hands, Young Ji. Uhmma tucks a wisp of my long, straight black hair behind my ear and then puts her arm around my waist. We continue our walk along the beach. (155–6)

The mother's claim to her total past and her care for the girl's very characteristically Korean hair, together with the setting on the beach, serve as metonyms for the acceptance of both cultures. All these books, in their various ways, indicate how migration stories probably work most effectively when a balance is achieved, both by the characters concerned and in the actual writing, between assimilation into the new culture and an acknowledgement of the influence and value of the old.

Postcolonial literature has much in common with these migration novels, in particular in its response to representations of the non-European as 'other'. Creative writers who are either from minority cultures or have attempted to depict them positively have therefore frequently sought to 'normalize' non-European characters. This process is to be seen in Beverley Naidoo's work; though she herself, as a white South African, would have potentially been a member of the hegemonic group, in her writing and in political action she has allied herself with the oppressed black underclass. In both her early novels, *Journey to Jo'Burg* (1985) and *Chain of Fire* (1989), she presents events entirely from the perspective of the young black children who are sufferers from the government's apartheid policies. In the attempt to render the unfamiliar setting not only comprehensible but also ordinary to the anticipated young audience, Naidoo prefaces the earlier novel with two short annotated newspaper cuttings, dated 1981, which make clear that the hardships portrayed are not from the distant past. Naidoo's later fiction, such as *No Turning Back* (1995), a novel set in Britain, and *Out of Bounds* (2001), short stories set in South Africa, reveal the identity problems of children in conflicted situations (see Box 11.3), epitomizing much of the colonial and postcolonial experience.

The Australian experience

The history of Australia is quite different from that of most of the colonies which made up the British Empire, a fact that has had considerable influence on the many children's books which in one way or another reflect this history. At a considerable distance from the motherland, and in its early years used as what Niall Ferguson (2003: 103) describes as 'a dumping ground for criminals', Australia paradoxically became for much of its history a notably loyal part of the empire. Ferguson suggests that this may have been because the policy of transportation in effect liberated the petty criminals who were sent there, to a much greater extent than would have been possible in England. This sense of liberation, later to be shared by those suffering, for instance, from the 'clearances' in the Scottish Highlands, was fostered by the colonialists' impression of enormous 'empty' spaces, while, less happily, the presence of Aboriginal inhabitants at a lower level of technology meant that the new settlers developed an attitude towards them that had all the hallmarks of racism. Australian children's fiction has consequently been characterized by its exploration of how the land has shaped its people, both the white settlers and the Aboriginals.

Many of the approaches considered above in relation to equality, migrant communities and postcolonialism are also relevant to Australian children's fiction, while the whole issue of fact and fictionality is one of its major themes, as can be seen in the unconventional use of history by one of the most acclaimed recent Australian novelists, Gary Crew. His *Strange Objects* (1990) could be described as a clever collage of different types of (largely narrative) sources. In creating a 'New History', Crew presents readers with the kind of puzzles that an assembly of 'real' historical sources would pose: 'Is this reliable?' 'Did the person who wrote this know from the inside or the outside about the events described?', and, most of all, 'What really happened?' Thus readers are in effect asked to take on some of the disciplines of New Historicist criticism (Box 11.2), in which all kinds of texts are given equal status.

It is surely significant that the question about the reliability or otherwise of traditional approaches to writing history is in fact explicitly asked in the novel; a senior university lecturer who is introducing excerpts from what purports to be the journal of a seventeenth-century shipwrecked mariner, Wouter Loos, blames Columbus's records about meeting cannibals during his New World voyage for subsequent fallacious beliefs: 'for too long, the Western world has been fed his warped interpretation of so-called "History", observed and recorded from his biased point of view' (132–3). Thus, the academic explains, Loos and his younger companion, Jan Pelgrom, did not bring an innocent eye to their encounter with Aboriginals, whom they termed Black Indians; rather they already had a point of view heavily influenced by centuries of distorted presentation of 'native' tribes, to the extent that their fears about cannibalism are always vividly present.

As well as two main fictional narratives – the journals of Loos and of a modern white Australian youth, Steven Messenger, who has discovered the seventeenth-century material – the 'sources' created by Crew include a foreword and afterword by Dr Hope Michaels, from the semi-fictional Western Australian Institute of Maritime Archaeology; she also intervenes in the main story with letters and articles at various points in the text. There are many allusions to existing reference books about the history of Western Australia, interspersed with passages from apparently equally credible sources which only an experienced reader, who observes that no credit is given for copyright to these texts, would realize are part of Crew's invention. Loos's narrative has the closest link with fact, concerning as it does two seamen from the *Batavia*, a ship from Amsterdam bound for the Dutch East Indies, which was wrecked off the Western Australian coast in 1629. The 'Commandeur', Francisco Pelsaert, succeeded in reaching Java in an open boat, but on his return after 14 weeks to rescue the 260 surviving passengers and crew, discovered that over 120 of them had been murdered by a small group of malcontents. Pelsaert ordered seven of these to be hanged, but sentenced two others, a 17-year-old boy, Jan Pelgrom, and a soldier, Wouter Loos, to be cast off in an open boat (41). All this is recorded history, but as Mike Dash (2002) states in his historical account of the wreck, there is little evidence related to their actual survival on the mainland, and none of any contact with Aboriginal inhabitants.

Much of *Strange Objects*, however, consists of the (fictional) journal of Wouter Loos, recording his and Pelgrom's encounter with the 'black Indians', and also describing a white girl, Ela, who, it would appear, has survived from an earlier wreck, that of the *Tryal*, a British ship lost in 1622. Loos's journal, which is made to appear more authentic by its many lists and its use of dates throughout, records the men's attempts to trade with the toys which Pelsaert (really) gave them for this purpose, and the obsessive love which Pelgrom has for Ela, to whom, probably in the hope of sexual favours, he gives a gold ring which he took from a Spaniard (176).

This ring, and Ela's mummified hand, have been buried with Loos's journal, in a cauldron, which is discovered in 1986 by Steven Messenger, whose parallel narrative is entirely fictional. The teenager becomes obsessed with the ring, refusing to give it up despite Dr Michael's pleas. At one stage an almost supernatural impression is created when Steven has a dream about Ela (97–103). The events he dreams of seem to correspond with what later is disclosed as something that 'really' happened. Finally, Steven leaves home, never to be seen again. Questions are raised as to what has happened to him: should readers accept his own interpretation of events, which involves another 'Steven Messenger' character and the possibility of intervention from a mythical figure termed the 'Hitchhiker'; should they see him as suffering from a form of schizophrenia, as Dr Michaels suggests (240); or has his disappearance something to do with the death of his father some months previously, as his mother opines? Readers are not given any answer to this conundrum, a situation consistent with the position in which they have been placed throughout the novel, where no guidance is given as to what is 'true' and what is fictional. Rather, an air of authenticity is conveyed to the fictional material, be it the history of the *Batavia* survivors or the events leading up to the boy's disappearance, by the use of the kind of other material which is normally regarded as factual, such as reference books and newspaper articles. There is also a noticeable inclusion of scarcely relevant details, such as the date of the newspaper in which Steven's journal is covered (3), together with material objects such as the cauldron in which the objects are found, and the ring. This scrupulous care to include everything, even though it may not appear relevant to Dr Michaels' current interpretation of the material, is consonant with a 'New Historicist' cast of mind: it is important to reveal all the detail so that subsequent historians will have the data to form their own interpretations of all the 'objects' concerned, including Steven's writing as well as the seventeenth-century material.

A New Historicist approach is evident in the central enquiry, an attempt to understand the past without imposing on it a unitary and transcendental interpretation. Two pasts are integral to this search, that foregrounded in Dr Michaels' preliminary 'Notes on the disappearance of Steven Messenger, aged 16 years', and the more remote seventeenth-century past of the central enigma: were there really survivors from the *Batavia* and the *Tryal* and how should the 'discoveries' that Steven made be interpreted?

At the same time, Crew's book offers ample scope for the critic who seeks to understand our own culture in the light of what we choose to emphasize or suppress of the past. Particularly significant is the attention given, in different ways, in the narratives of both Loos and Steven to the role and culture of the Aborigines. Loos is portrayed as seeing them in the context of his unquestioning acceptance of Columbus's erroneous belief that the 'Indians' whom he met in the Caribbean were cannibals, together with Loos's ignorance of the fact that the natives whom he has encountered are of an entirely different origin from Columbus's. In the twentieth-century narrative, Steven scorns Charlie Sunrise, an Aboriginal elder highly esteemed by Professor Freudenberg, the translator of Loos's journals, for his 'encyclopaedic knowledge of Aboriginal lore' (211), but despised by Steven because of his 'filthy pants' (199). It would appear that Crew is demanding that his reader apply postcolonial insights in forming any judgement about the events and the behaviour of the characters, both seventeenth century and twentieth.

Crew's deliberate conflating of factual and fictive sources raises the possibility, as suggested by Stephens (1992: 209), that the author's ideology, which underlies the fictional events, achieves a greater effect on the reader because actual historical events are also included. Crew's handling of issues of racism makes heavy demands on the reader's sophistication. A very strong sense of the otherness of the Aboriginal culture is created in the 'historical' sections, where Loos reflects on the childishness of the 'black Indians', displayed by their interest in the tawdry toys he has with him and their superstitious fright at some white stockings; these qualities resonate with both men's totally unfounded fears that they may be cannibals. Twentieth-century Steven Messenger is little better, though because of his greater knowledge he is more reprehensible. The fact that, as noted above, he despises Charlie Sunrise not only causes him discomfort when Charlie sits next to him in the car, but ultimately leads to his being the agent of Charlie's death. While it is clear that Steven is a highly unreliable narrator, and greater authority is given to the high opinion of Charlie held by the local community, it could be difficult for young readers to dissent from the view of a main character whose thought processes are exposed to them.

For *Strange Objects* to be read as a postcolonial text enshrining among other narratives an awareness of the value of Aboriginal culture demands a sophisticated reader, prepared to weigh up the merits of each of the individual 'items' out of which Crew has created his novel.

Conclusion

This discussion has inevitably been selective, concentrating to a greater extent on innovative texts which have raised questions about the portrayal of minority groups from a variety of different types of communities, than on the more traditional novels which have continued to present events from the perspective of imperialist adventurers. In looking at texts of both types, a postcolonialist perspective is often helpful. It is all too easy for readers familiar with, for instance, Marryatt (1792–1848), Ballantyne, Henty and Kipling (1865–1936) to accept rather than to question their imperialist assumptions, at least for the duration of the story. Alternatively, readers may reject this kind of writing altogether, regarding it as too polluted by out-of-date views of empire, and thus expecting writers to be ahead of their time in criticizing such ideas. Looking at earlier writers in the context of non-literary texts, which serve to display the assumptions taken for granted in the period (as in New Historicist approaches), can often provide salutary evidence that authors indeed represented the views of their own time. Cultural Materialism can also provide an invaluable perspective on the 'wisdom' of the present – what we regard as enlightened is likely to be seen as barbarous by later generations!

Reading texts from groups which until recently did not have the kind of literary traditions that in Western culture we take for granted can be particularly informative. In this context, the work of Clare Bradford on Aboriginal picturebooks (2002, 2003) is especially illuminating, showing the ways in which 'Aboriginal textuality engages with Western forms and practices in order to interrogate the assumptions and ideologies of the dominant culture ... [and affirming] the centrality of country to narrative traditions' (2003: 76).

WORKS CITED AND FURTHER READING

Children's Books

Armstrong, William. *Sounder*. London: Gollancz, 1971.
Arrigan, Mary. *Esty's Gold*. London: Frances Lincoln, 2009.
Caswell, Brian, and David Chiem. *Only the Heart*. St Lucia, Queensland: University of Queensland Press, 1997.
Cooney, Caroline B. *Mercy*. Basingstoke: Palgrave Macmillan, 2001.
Creech, Sharon. *Walk Two Moons*. Basingstoke: Palgrave Macmillan, 1994.
Crew, Gary. *Strange Objects*. Sydney: Hodder Headline, 2003; first published 1990.
Crew, Gary, and Peter Gouldthorpe. *The Lost Diamonds of Killiecrankie*. Port Melbourne: Lothian Books, 1999; first published 1995.
Crew, Linda. *Children of the River*. New York: Bantam Doubleday Dell, 1989.

Cross, Gillian. *Where I Belong*. Oxford: Oxford University Press, 2010.
Danalis, John. *Riding the Black Cockatoo*. London: Allen & Unwin, 2009.
Doherty, Berlie. *Abila: The Girl Who Saw Lions*. London: Andersen, 2007.
Fox, Paula. *The Slave Dancer*. London: Macmillan, 1974; first published 1973.
Gavin, Jamila. *The Surya Trilogy*. London: Mammoth, 1995.
Hiçyilmaz, Gaye. *The Frozen Waterfall*. London: Faber and Faber, 1993.
Houston, Jeanne Wakatsuki, and James Houston. *Farewell to Manzanar*. New York: Bantam Doubleday Dell, 1995; first published 1973.
Marsden, John, and Shaun Tan. *The Rabbits*. Melbourne: Lothian Books, 2001.
Marshall, James Vance. *Walkabout*. Harmondsworth: Penguin, 1963; first published as *The Children*, 1959.
Mayne, William. *Drift*. London: Cape, 1985.
Na, An. *A Step from Heaven*. London: Allen & Unwin, 2002; first published 2001.
Naidoo, Beverley. *Chain of Fire*. London: HarperCollins, 1990; first published 1989.
Naidoo, Beverley. *Journey to Jo'Burg*. London: HarperCollins, 1987; first published 1985.
Naidoo, Beverley. *No Turning Back*. Harmondsworth: Penguin, 1996; first published 1995.
Naidoo, Beverley. *Out of Bounds*. Harmondsworth: Penguin, 2001.
Namioka, Lensey. *Yang the Youngest and His Terrible Ear*. New York: Bantam Doubleday Dell, 1992.
O'Neill, Judith. *So Far from Skye*. Harmondsworth: Penguin, 1993; first published 1992.
Paulsen, Gary. *Nightjohn*. Basingstoke: Palgrave Macmillan, 1994; first published 1993.
Smith, Rukhshana. *Sumitra's Story*. London: Bodley Head, 1982.
Taylor, Mildred. *Roll of Thunder, Hear My Cry*. London: Gollancz, 1977; first published 1976.
Taylor, Theodore. *The Cay*. London: Bodley Head, 1970; first published 1969.
Zephaniah, Benjamin. *Refugee Boy*. London: Bloomsbury, 2001.

Critical Texts

Ashcroft, Bill, Gareth Griffiths and Helen Tiffin. *The Empire Writes Back: Theory and Practice in Post-Colonial Literatures*, 2nd edn. London and New York: Routledge, 2002; first published 1989.
Barry, Peter. *Beginning Theory: An Introduction to Literary and Cultural Theory*. Manchester: Manchester University Press, 1995.
Bradford, Clare. 'Aboriginal Visual Narratives for Children: a Politics of Place'. In Morag Styles and Eve Bearne (eds), *Art, Narrative and Childhood*. Stoke-on-Trent: Trentham Books, 2003.
Bradford, Clare. 'The End of Empire? Colonial and Postcolonial Journeys in Children's Books'. *Children's Literature*, 27.4 (2002), 8–25.
Bradford, Clare. *Reading Race: Aboriginality in Australian Children's Literature*. Carlton South: Melbourne University Press, 2001.
Bradford, Clare. *Unsettling Narratives*. Ontario: Wildred Laurier University Press, 2007.
Dash, Mike. *Batavia's Graveyard*. London: Weidenfeld & Nicolson, 2002.
Dollimore, Jonathan, and Alan Sinfield (eds). *Political Shakespeare: New Essays on Cultural Materialism*, 2nd edn. Manchester: Manchester University Press, 1994.
Ferguson, Niall. *How Britain Made the Modern World*. London: Allen Lane, 2003.
Lodge, David. *Working with Structuralism*. London: Routledge, 1981.
McGillis, Rod (ed.). *Voices of the Other: Colonisation and Children's Literature*. London and New York: Garland, 1999.
Pinsent, Pat. '"Bone and Blood a Slave": the Construct of the Slave and Slavery in Historical Novels for Children'. *New Review of Children's Literature and Librarianship*, 8.1 (2002), 189–202.

Pinsent, Pat. *Children's Literature and the Politics of Equality*. London: David Fulton, 1997.
Rudd, David (ed.). *The Routledge Companion to Children's Literature*. Abingdon: Routledge, 2010.
Said, Edward. *Culture and Imperialism*. London: Chatto & Windus, 1993.
Said, Edward. *Orientalism*. New York: Pantheon, 1978.
Stephens, John. *Language and Ideology in Children's Fiction*. London and New York: Longman, 1992.
Tyson, Lois. *Critical Theory Today: A User-Friendly Guide*, 2nd edn. Abingdon: Routledge, 2006.

NOTE

1. Clare Bradford's analysis of some Aboriginal picturebooks (2003: 65–77) makes very explicit some of the pitfalls to which readers from a Western background are liable.

Part III

Approaches and Issues

Chronotopes and Heritage: Time and Memory in Contemporary Children's Literature

12

Lisa Sainsbury

KEY TEXTS

Mitsumasa Anno et al., *All in a Day* (1986)
Anne Provoost, *Falling* (1995)
Hugh Scott, *Why Weeps the Brogan?* (1989)
Marcus Sedgwick, *The Dark Horse* (2002)

Introducing time and memory to young readers

Time is difficult for children to understand, for several reasons. As an abstract concept it can be hard for the youngest of children to comprehend, and a child's relationship with time is complicated by her/his restricted experience of it (particularly of time past). There is often a mismatch between children's knowledge of time and the language available to them to express that knowledge, especially as they encounter new social experiences and move into different environments (e.g. starting school). These observations suggest that our notion of time changes as we grow older, as confirmed by developmental psychologists such as Jean Piaget, and that it has a social function relative to history and culture. While time can be conceived of as a natural phenomenon – the sun rises, seasons change, bodies mature in and through time – with which humans must interact, the acquisition of time sense is part of the socialization process, working alongside the learning of language skills and moral values.

This social dimension points to a fundamental relationship between time and space that undergoes constant flux, as recognized by Stephen Kern who observes that, 'From around 1880 to the outbreak of World War I a series of sweeping changes in technology and culture created distinctive new modes of thinking about and experiencing time and space' (2003: 1). Kern points to 'a transformation of the dimensions of life and thought' wrought by technological innovations including the telephone, cinema and automobile, as well as cultural or scientific developments such as psychoanalysis or the theory of relativity (1–2). Though outside Kern's remit, technological innovations during the late twentieth and early twenty-first centuries, such as the Internet, mobile phone, digital technologies and social media, have had a similarly transformative impact on the human experience of time and space. Add this changeability to the conceptual challenge posed by time and it is clear that children's fiction could have much to offer young readers as they seek (and perhaps struggle) to situate themselves in time.

It seems logical that books for the youngest readers might seek to facilitate a practical understanding of time in the context of everyday experience, and (before moving on to books for older readers) I want to demonstrate some of the complexities underlying the ostensible simplicity of picturebooks for emergent readers. *All in a Day* (1986) by Mitsumasa Anno and a group of international artists introduces children to the 24-hour day and its division into worldwide time zones. A concept book, *All in a Day* is designed to teach children that 'their activities are related to the very different conditions of time and climate that exist in various parts of the earth', as Anno reveals in 'A Note to Parents and Other Older Readers'. Conceptually it is relatively simple, yet its temporal dynamics are sophisticated, allowing consideration of time–space relations in Bakhtin's notion of chronotope, a concept utilized by a range of commentators on children's literature, including Maria Nikolajeva, Margaret Mackey and John Stephens.

Each double-page spread in *All in a Day* depicts eight tableaux of children from around the world, distinguished by place, date and time. New Year, according to Greenwich Mean Time, is the starting point for chronological organization on the first page, so, in the USA, Tom awaits New Year, since the USA (Chicago specifically) is six hours behind Greenwich, England, where James is fast asleep at midnight. Meanwhile, the Kenyan Jomo is also sleeping at 3.00 a.m. Individual tableaux are illustrated by artists from the relevant country, so that the British artist, Raymond Briggs, is responsible for the Greenwich scenes, Nicolai Ye. Popov for the Muscovite images, and so on. Each tableau is stylistically distinctive, adding to the exploration of cultural diversity central to this project.

This stylistic variation highlights the cultural relativism of space and time explored by Kern, though its narrative expression is more usefully considered in relation to Bakhtin's notion of chronotope (see Box 7.2), which describes the literary expression of the unity of space and time. The words labelling a single tableau situate it in time and place, whereas the illustrations are spatial, conveying action within a clearly defined space. As Perry Nodelman suggests in *Words About Pictures*, 'stories, which are about movements and changes, necessarily take place in time, whereas most pictures depict only how things look at one moment separated from the flow of time' (1988: 158). The particular combination of time (verbal) and space (visual) in Anno's picturebook serves to accentuate the unity of time and space suggested by Bakhtin's chronotope. An understanding of chronotope affirms that although these tableaux all represent the same moment in time, the unique relationship between time and space in each one signifies a different chronotope; thus different chronotopes are introduced at the same moment. Anno's text effectively works with a range of chronotopes in dialogue with each other, confirming that chronotope is more than a suggestion of historical period. Chronotope can indicate cultural difference, as in *All in a Day*, or as Nikolajeva suggests, 'specific forms of chronotope are unique for particular genres' (1996: 121) and so the chronotope becomes a way of recognizing and exploring ideology and narrative structure. In this case chronotope serves to celebrate diversity, promoting a humanist rendition of peaceful relations between different societies and cultures.

Closely linked to his notion of chronotope is Bakhtin's concept of dialogism, for utterance and voice always speaks to others in context(s). As Pam Morris explains, for Bakhtin, 'There is no existence, no meaning, no word or thought that does not enter into dialogue or "dialogic" relations with the other, that does not exhibit intertextuality in both time and space' (1994: 247). The contrasting chronotopes in *All in a Day* could be described as dialogic 'voices', each competing for attention. Ensuring that young readers are not bewildered by these disparate voices, Anno draws together the separate tableaux on each page through his representation of 'Uninhabited Island', which is 'in the South Pacific, somewhere near the International Date Line'. Uninhabited Island is situated on the recto (see Box 4.1) of every spread and is placed interstitially on the centre line of the page, occupying a unique space between the surrounding tableaux. It is also the location of Anno's first-person narrator, a shipwrecked child, Sailor Oliver Smith (dubbed SOS), who directly addresses the children depicted in the surrounding tableaux. SOS's narration provides a unifying voice, suggesting that while experience differs in space and time, common humanity might be grounds for experience shared and for the ideological notion of Peace emphasized in Anno's closing note. The island narrative can also be seen as a fantastical element of the text, drawing on the playful capacity of childhood imagination.

In *From Mythic to Linear: Time in Children's Literature* (2000) Nikolajeva maintains that 'contemporary Western children's fiction is written from a philosophical viewpoint based on linear time, which has a beginning and an end, and recognizes every event in history as unique' (2000: 5). *All in a Day* seems to confirm this modern investment in linearity, like other picturebooks that seek to introduce and navigate time through a linear affirmation of chronology and history – such as Jan Mark's *Museum Book* (2007) or Jen Green's *Avoid Joining Shackleton's Polar Expedition!* (2002). Elvira Woodruff's *The Memory Coat* (1999) or Karen Hesse's *The Cats in Krasinski Square* (2004) expose the way in which memory, both personal and public, locates children in linear time. Such texts place an epistemological emphasis on the linear, drawing historical lessons from events that are closed (even if accessible though memory). They also demonstrate the central role narrative plays in making sense of the shared human experience of being in time.

Evidently, even the simplest picturebooks can have a complex relationship with time and such books have a role to play in the cognitive development of children as they master concepts such as time zones and cultural difference. In order to think further about children's books and their relationship with time, however, we need to move from a conceptual notion of time to an understanding of narrative time and its place in children's literature. In *Being and Time* (1927) Heidegger observes that 'Time must be brought to light and genuinely grasped as the horizon of every understanding and interpretation of being' (1996: 15) and he stresses the 'within-time-ness' of momentary experience (311); humans are afloat in a sea of time which is marked through everyday routine. Following Heidegger, in *Time and Narrative* (1983) Paul Ricoeur proposes that grammatical and narrative structures allow for a reckoning with Heidegger's 'within-time-ness', providing expressions – 'take the time to' or 'to lose time' – and signs (words) – now, then, earlier, since, until, during – that permit us to come to terms with and understand our state within time (1990: 62). Ricoeur's notion that narrative helps to shape human experience through time is a useful starting point for any literary exploration of time, though Nikolajeva's distinction between mythic and linear time and its function in children's books is especially useful here.

Nikolajeva proposes that children's fiction can be seen as 'a symbolic depiction of a maturation process (initiation, rite of passage) rather than a strictly mimetic reflection of a concrete "reality"' (2000: 1) and of course this is a temporally marked process. She 'investigates children's narrative fiction in a continuum from texts involving nonlinear time, typical of archaic or mythical thought, toward linearity, typical of contemporary mainstream literature' (1). In Nikolajeva's terms, children's fiction has a peculiar capacity to deal with time in synchronicity with the maturation process (at least as it is perceived and constructed by adult writers), so that fiction associated with younger children (or notions of early childhood) have tended to express notions of everlasting time, or 'once upon a time-ness', such as that expressed in fairy tales or enduring novels such as *Peter and Wendy* (1911), or *Winnie-the-Pooh* (1926). These books invest in circular time (*kairos*) that overcomes death through time everlasting, while the move towards linearity (*chronos*) in contemporary children's and young adult literature subscribes to linear time which 'invokes the problems of growing up, aging, and death' (6). To clarify, Nikolajeva responds to patterns and trends in children's fiction (and beyond) and to changing constructions of childhood; she does not claim that all books for pre-school children make use of mythic time, or that young adult fiction invests solely in linearity. With respect to the young adult texts in this chapter, though, it could be argued that a yearning for *kairos* underscores the struggle to come to terms with *chronos* (and this struggle is presented as an inevitable aspect of human experience), since the linear relationship between past, present and future is configured in terms of loss and suffering (not always without hope) to different degrees.

A brief history of time in children's fiction

Movements back and forth in time have become increasingly popular in children's literature since the early twentieth century, when a number of scientific theories, such as Einstein's 'Special Theory of Relativity' (1905) and J. W. Dunne's *An Experiment with Time* (1927) attracted public attention. H. G. Wells's post-Darwinian fantasy, *The Time Machine* (1895) is one of the earliest examples of the time travel genre, while E. Nesbit's *The Story of the Amulet* (1906) and Kipling's *Puck of Pook's Hill* (1906) were among the earliest children's novels to manipulate time for the purposes of historicized adventure. Moving on through the twentieth century, time travel has been used increasingly by writers to emphasize changes wrought by adolescence; the rupture in time frequently mirrors pre-pubertal or adolescent anxiety, as exemplified in Ruth Park's *Playing Beatie Bow* (1980), or *Charlotte Sometimes* (1969) by Penelope Farmer. In a number of children's novels, such as *Elidor* (1965) by Alan Garner and Marcus Sedgwick's *Midwinterblood* (2011), human relationships resonate deeply and darkly with the past as characters in the present struggle to understand themselves and the world around them. Playing with time also preoccupies innovative and experimental writers such as Diana Wynne Jones in *The Homeward Bounders* (1981), Peter Pohl in *Johnny, My Friend* (1985) or Kate Thompson in *The New Policeman* (2005) as they encourage readers to think about relationships between time, fiction and lived experience.

The popularity of historical fiction endures, though Valerie Krips points to a shift in representations of the past from the literature of 'heritage' which 'is determined to show the past "as it really was"' (1999: 178) – exemplified by such writers as Rosemary Sutcliff or Geoffrey Trease – to books that challenge this authoritative and finite notion of the past. These texts stress the mutable and idiosyncratic nature of time, particularly as it is shaped through memory, and explore the relationship between self-knowledge and the passage of time. This chapter looks at three such books for young people which share an interest in the nature and expression of memory, exploring memory from contrasting perspectives in time and for different purposes. Set in a 'distant past' that might be estimated as the time of the Viking invasion and colonization of Europe circa AD 700, *The Dark Horse* (2002) by Marcus Sedgwick makes interesting use of narrative chronology, emphasizing the way in which memory is manipulated in the telling of stories. Anne Provoost's politically aware novel, *Falling* (1995), is set in contemporary France, exploring the resonance of private and public memory as it shapes perceptions of past, present and future. Finally, Hugh Scott's *Why Weeps the Brogan?* (1989) is a dystopian fable set, ambiguously (Wed, 4 years 81 days from hostilities), sometime in the future, challenging the relevance of authorized versions of history to children's lives in the present. Through their past, present and future settings these novels examine the significance of memory in terms of narrative structure and lived experience, expanding the implied young reader's comprehension of time and memory.

Memories of the past

Sedgwick does not identify a specific historical period or setting in *The Dark Horse*; nonetheless, numerous references to Norse mythology and use of Scandinavian nomenclature indicate that his novel is located at the time of Viking invasions somewhere in north-west Europe. It is not the historicity of the text that is of primary interest, though, rather the complexity of narrative discourse. Dual narration and temporal shifts in the narrators' relative position to the story yield a novel that is embedded in time through its telling, a process which can be elucidated through the categories of narrative structure and diegesis proposed by Gérard Genette in *Narrative Discourse* (1972).

The first chapter opens with a familiar narrating position subsequent to the action described, which Genette confirms is 'the classical position of past tense narrative, undoubtedly ... the most frequent' (Genette, 1980: 217). So commonplace is subsequent narration that although written in the past indefinite tense the narrative relates events that appear to be unfolding in the present (or in the reading moment) at a specific time: 'It was Mouse who found the box ... Looking for sea cabbage washed up in the black sand after last night's storm, because the fishing had been bad again. They were half a day from home' (3). The reader apparently witnesses proceedings as they happen, rather than from the distance suggested by the use of past indefinite and historical setting. Genette accounts for this through the paradoxical stance of subsequent narration, which is possessed of a temporal situation, but is atemporal in essence (1980: 222–3) because the moment in which the narration occurs is not revealed.

The narrative perspective – the children, Mouse and Sigurd, are observed by a detached narrator – also adds to the sense of watching these characters in the present; readers observe the children at the external level of the heterodiegetic narration (i.e. the narrator is absent from the story being related). The chapter closes with the children's removal of the mysterious box and the narrator's pronouncement that 'neither of them noticed the man lying still amongst the rocks ...' (4). This confirms that the narrator is omniscient (functioning on an extradiegetic level, outside of the narrative) and able to access information unavailable to the characters. Thus Sedgwick establishes a diegetic (narrative) level common to storytelling, but a shift that comes in the second chapter makes Sedgwick's text unusual in its temporal stance.

Having established itself as a seemingly conventional narrative, the second chapter disrupts the reader's perspective:

I remember better than anyone.

I remember better than anyone the day we found Mouse ....

I was the only child there, and I was a child then. It was my eleventh or twelfth summer; I can't remember. I was a part of the games Horn and Father played. (5–6)

Any reader expecting a continuation of heterodiegetic narration is likely to be disorientated by this shift into metanarrative (narrative within a narrative).

At first it is unclear who is speaking, until Sigurd identifies himself as the narrator and his status as homodiegetic narrator (a narrator who is also a character – but not the hero/heroine – who observes the protagonist from close proximity) is revealed. The perspective from which Sigurd narrates is also uncertain, though his opening words, 'I remember …', indicate that his narration is an evocation of memory; that he is relating events from his past. Even as the dual narratives converge at the end of the book, it is unclear from which point in time Sigurd is looking back, though it is evidently some years after the events related by the heterodiegetic narrator. Unusually then, this narrative structure has two diegetic levels that proceed from two distinctive chronotopes; it is told from (it is not about) two different moments in space and time (more familiar is the time-slip story, that moves its characters between primary and secondary chronotopes). Although the space (a tribal village by the sea) of Sigurd's experiences with Mouse in the past is geographically the same as the space from which he remembers, it is reshaped through the passage of time and is perceived differently by characters and readers alike. The unity of space and time is particular to each narrative; thus they can be described as distinct chronotopes in dialogue with each other, and so at the level of narrative discourse central themes begin to emerge.

The Dark Horse is essentially Mouse's story. It is the tale of a strangely gifted child, discovered by the Storn (a Norse tribe of fishermen) in a wolf cave. Mouse is adopted into Sigurd's family where it becomes clear that she has an affinity with nature, animals in particular. She and Sigurd discover a strange box on the beach, causing disharmony within the tribe when it cannot be opened. It transpires that Ragnald, the stranger on the beach, had been bringing the box to Mouse, though it is not until the Storn have nearly been destroyed by the powerful 'Dark Horse' tribe that the box's import is revealed. As the tale reaches its climax, Mouse betrays the remaining members of the Storn tribe, including Sigurd, leading them directly to the Dark Horse. Ultimately Sigurd discovers that Mouse is a lost princess of the Dark Horse and that Ragnald had been sent on her trail with a box of her memories. Significantly, then, this is a story about memory, relayed through memory.

The Dark Horse recounts a period in the Storn's history relating to the appearance and eventual departure of a young girl called Mouse. It is told through a dual narrative that switches after each chapter; the pattern of heterodiegetic, homodiegetic, heterodiegetic, homodiegetic is maintained throughout and eventually gives Sigurd the last word. The heterodiegetic narrative is conveyed chronologically, in a linear direction by a distanced narrator, while Sigurd's narrative is retrospective and starts (it transpires) four years prior to Mouse and Sigurd's discovery of the box on the beach. Sigurd's narrative eventually converges with the heterodiegetic narration, moving into the same period and adopting a chronological ordering of events. This suggests a shift from mythic to linear time, perhaps echoing changing belief systems in north-west Europe as an emergent Christian outlook challenged pagan religions (Nikolajeva observes that the Judeo-Christian tradition eschews the circularity of pagan faiths and mythology through its investment in Christ's resurrection as a 'singulative event'; 2000: 8).

Sigurd's retrospective account is a useful tool for introducing suspense, as Sedgwick peppers Sigurd's narrative with ominous observations: 'It was all for nothing' (136); 'As it fell, I was right to worry' (148). The reader is encouraged to anticipate; to move towards the point from which Sigurd tells his tale. As Ricoeur observes, even the simplest stories (moving through a dominant narrative of chronological linearity) escape ordinary notions of linear time, for each new story event involves new contingencies and possibilities to be reckoned with by the reader. Plot cannot evolve in a temporally linear fashion, because the reader is constantly engaged in the process of modification and expectation (Ricoeur, 1981: 170). Sedgwick seems purposely to intervene in this process and uses it to move his reader backwards and forwards in time; to engage in a complex relationship with his central narrative and its status as memory.

At times, Sigurd too withdraws from the past moment of his narrative and reflects from his place in the future: 'I remember, how could I forget? I will remember the words he said next until the day I die' (88), drawing attention to the constructed nature of his narrative and to its status as past event. That he is engaged in the act of reconstructing the past attests to the intrinsic value of that period. This is evidently an episode in Storn history that is worth relating; one that has consequence for future generations.

The Dark Horse addresses time at the deepest level, as it is played out through structure and theme, yet it is not until the closing pages that the thematic significance of memory becomes obvious. Mouse and Sigurd are torn apart by the enmity of their respective tribes, but on parting they heal their sibling bond and Mouse asks Sigurd to 'Keep my memories, for me ... When you find them' (184). When the narrative reaches the moment from which Sigurd has told his story, he reflects on the aftermath of the Storn's decisive battle with the Dark Horse and his own role in it: 'And the years have come and gone, and I think about my own life, and I realise that many of my own memories are memories of blood' (187). Sigurd's observation that his memories are 'of blood' has multiple significance. His memories have included those of bloodshed; even so, they are also the fabric of life (blood), and are central to familial heritage (blood). Mouse was stripped of identity when she lost her memories in the wolf cave, an idea that the box comes to represent. Literally, the box once held her memories, but additionally it serves as a metaphor for Sigurd's engagement with the memory of her story. The box is a route back to the past and Sigurd's act of remembering allows Mouse's tale to be told. The dual structure of the tale also becomes a figure for the working of memory as it fluctuates between past and present, emphasizing the within-time-ness of stories as they help us to make sense of ourselves.

Memories in the present

It is to the aftermath of the Second World War and its implications for contemporary children that Belgian writer Anne Provoost turns in her challenging novel *Falling* (1995). Since I discuss the English translation (by John Nieuwenhuizen, 1997), I do not explore intricate details of narrative structure and language that might have altered in the process of translation. Rather, Provoost's broader treatment of the past and memory forms the basis of discussion (while acknowledging that all elements of narrative are susceptible to the translation process).

Falling is set in the imaginary French town of Montourin, focusing on the experiences of Lucas Beigne during the summer after his grandfather's death. Lucas discovers that incidents from his grandfather's past have been kept from him, and this uncovering of secrets initiates a 'fall' from childhood innocence that implicates him in a tragic incident, on which he reflects early in the novel: 'Going back over it all, I can see that this was the moment everything started to go wrong – but of course that's easy to say with hindsight … I scratch my head and want to reverse time, but it's impossible. I can no longer wake up innocent, as I was that morning' (28). *Falling* is in many ways an exercise in 'going back', of filtering the present through memory in the hope that a new perspective on the past might change the outcome of recent events. Provoost demonstrates that this is impossible under the conditions of linear time, though a new understanding of the past as it is absorbed and altered 'with hindsight' is possible.

To summarize, Lucas and his mother spend the summer in his deceased grandfather's house in the hills of Montourin. Lucas befriends Caitlin, an enigmatic young dancer, who is staying with her mother as the guest of Soeur Béate at the old convent next door. A series of burglaries blamed on immigrant Arabs working in the town leads Lucas to Benoît, a charismatic extremist who involves Lucas in his racist schemes by repeated insinuations about Lucas's grandfather's mysterious reputation. Meanwhile, obscure references are made to the fate of Jewish children once kept at the convent and it transpires that Felix Stockx (Lucas's grandfather) betrayed them to the Nazis after the death of his own daughter through possible malnutrition. It is revealed that Caitlin's mother was one of the children who survived, while several of her friends died at Auschwitz. While his relationships with Caitlin and Benoît progress, Lucas's loyalties are increasingly divided and he is caught in a cycle of guilt and blame. When Caitlin is trapped in a burning car Lucas must make a terrible choice, identifying him as the inheritor of his grandfather's actions. In order to free Caitlin, Lucas cuts off her foot and *Falling* charts his attempts to rationalize and accept this decision through reference to the past.

As Lucas's retrospective narrative suggests, chronology is complex in *Falling*. The novel opens at the chronological end of the story as Lucas waits for Caitlin to return home from hospital, where it seems that her foot has been amputated. The reader can have no understanding of the implications of Caitlin's injury at this point and is engaged immediately in a process of anticipation and retrospective revision, mirroring Lucas's position in the text. In order to understand Lucas's connection to Caitlin the reader must, like Lucas, return to 'the very beginning of it all … back in time … to last winter' (22). It is soon evident that Lucas's attempts to locate 'the beginning' of his story are futile, since events in the present are shaped by the circumstances of his grandfather's life. Linear time reveals itself as tricky, refusing a return to closed events, nonetheless allowing those events to bleed into the present.

Felix Stockx's death is the catalyst for an opening up of the past, giving Lucas access to the unknown events that influence people's perception of him. As Lucas tells Caitlin, 'I'm discovering all sorts of things ... Now that my grandfather is dead, everybody is beginning to talk' (136). It is as if his grandfather's death has catapulted Lucas into William Blake's world of experience whereas he previously enjoyed the innocence made possible by his mother's, indeed the whole town's, silence. His was an uneasy and unnatural innocence, though, embalmed in a desire to suppress and not deal with the past: 'My feet are tangled up in something, but I don't know what. This town feels as if it's preserved in formaldehyde' (96). *Falling* thereby challenges prevailing constructions of childhood, exposing the socio-historical conditions of an innocence that has never been essential to human being.

Lucas becomes almost a *lieu de mémoire* (site of memory), serving as a linchpin for the blame or sympathy of the townsfolk. Valerie Krips adopts the notion of *lieux de mémoire* from Pierre Nora, explaining that 'the sites of memory of which Nora writes, come into being because memory fails. They are the sites at which what remains of collective memory is constellated, where, in other words there is an intention to remember' (2000: 17). This concept usually refers to objects or memorials; artefacts that focus attention on a past moment. In Provoost's hands, Lucas becomes the object of admiration or disdain as people respond to a specific and appalling moment in their history. Their own culpability is distanced from them and Lucas is left to struggle with this unasked-for inheritance. This is not to say that Lucas is innocent himself; his actions in the present may have a bearing on the past, yet Provoost makes it clear that finally he must take responsibility and act without recourse to anyone else. When he struggles to free Caitlin from the car, Lucas recognizes that 'There was nobody to ask for advice ... I felt infinitely alone and knew that, no matter what I did, that feeling would be with me for ever' (235). In this moment a shift from collective to personal responsibility and memory is articulated.

Provoost has observed of *Falling* that 'more important than the question of who is guilty is the problem of inherited versus personal guilt, and the awareness that different kinds of guilt are there, also in other lives and in other situations' (Provoost, n.d.). The nature of guilt, both public and private, in *Falling* is intimately tied to the act of remembering and to the nature of human relationships formed in the present. The only way to deal with such difficult memories is to translate them into the present and move forward; the nostalgia figured in so many representations of the British war experience is not an option when confronted with a barely manageable burden of public and private guilt.

Caitlin's early conviction that events at the convent are unrelated to Lucas and herself in the present – 'It doesn't really upset me, all that. I mean it's a long time ago. It has nothing to do with us and our time' (137) – is gradually unsettled. Caitlin refuses to take part in the process of blame and justification engaged in by Soeur and Felix Stockx, welcoming Lucas as a friend. By the end of the book, however, she is unable to separate the Lucas before her from the boy who destroyed her future career as a dancer: 'When I think of my foot I think of you ... I want to do everything I can to remember you as my rescuer, not the person who mutilated me. That's not easy' (284). Caitlin comes to realize that to be human is to manage the past and the present; to be in time is a constant struggle to make sense of experience. Provoost suggests that the past defines young people as much as the present, though they can confront the past and move forward. In order to move into the future this truth must be accepted. Perhaps less comforting for Provoost's readers is the knowledge that moving forward can be painful, a message implied by Caitlin's loss of her foot and career.

Memories for the future

The museum setting of Hugh Scott's dystopian novella *Why Weeps the Brogan?* is crucial to understanding the ways in which Scott's post-apocalypse story interrogates the status of 'the Museum' (as a cultural concept) and its relationship with the past. *Why Weeps the Brogan?* could be described as an articulation of 'Museum Theory' that recognizes the ways in which adult representations of and attitudes to the past impact on future generations. In his provocative work of museology, *The Representation of the Past* (1992), Kevin Walsh attacks the stasis of museum displays and the heritigization of history as effected by battle re-enactments or 'the cult of the country house' (Walsh, 1992: 75). He argues that the 'powerful gaze' elicited by historical attractions does not empower the individual observer; rather it empowers the authority behind the display, the expert voice which labels the past so neatly. The museum visitor seems to respond to a past inherent within auratic objects – referring to the auras Walter Benjamin ascribed to commanding works of art (see below, and Benjamin, 1969) – yet actually responds to an ideologically bound, contrived representation. The process is mirrored in historical fiction, which seems to connect readers to a moment of 'real' past that is no more than a narrative construction.

Children are particularly vulnerable to displays appearing to convey reliable information about times completely out of their reach for, as Walsh points out in a discussion of open-air historic sites, 'The most dangerous consequence of this type of museum is its effect on those who can not remember. For them, their nostalgia is often second-hand. Their parents or grandparents can pass on their own nostalgia, and before long, a generation will exist whose heritage lies with the heritage industry' (99). Walsh does not suggest that museums must necessarily be detrimental to the child's construction of the past; instead he regrets the distancing of the past from daily life, resulting in a denial of ongoing historical process. He argues for a contextualization of history in which the museum visitor plays an active role and which provides the framework for a 'new museology' that 'must concern itself with involving the public, not just during the visit to the museum through interactive displays, but also in the production of the past' (1992: 161). This museology activates localized environments in which history is recognized as an evolving process created by individuals in the present. That children's literature also has a role to play in this is confirmed by writers such as Provoost, though *Why Weeps the Brogan?* directly takes on the role of the museum in children's response to past and future. *Why Weeps the Brogan?* is postmodern in perspective and structure (see Box 11.1), refusing complete explanations or resolution. Scott's narrative is revealed in an uncannily fragmented fashion, simulating the ruined and collapsing museum in which it is set.

Scott tells the story of Saxon and Gilbert, siblings mysteriously incarcerated in a vast museum; apparently they are the lone survivors of war, destined to an indoor life of perpetual fear. The children's solitary existence is broken only by the sparrows living in the museum's dome, deadly spiders that the children are forced to destroy and, most significantly, the Brogan. The Brogan lives in the museum's shadows and is fed by the children with ritual regularity; they do so out of an ambivalent mixture of fear and pity, stirring memories that linger in Saxon's mind. Snapshots of the children's past existence are provided by tentative allusions to a possible outside world, yet Scott refuses a complete picture of events leading to their incarceration, even after the revelation at the end of the book.

The implied reader of this book is placed in a strange relationship with the protagonists, at once distanced from and involved in narrative developments, and this paradoxical perspective is sustained through received conceptions of museum culture. The reader is alerted to the fact that the children are inside a museum through such ubiquitous signs, appearing in upper case throughout the text, as: ARMS AND ARMOUR, MINEROLOGY, COFFEE SHOP, PRIVATE and JANITOR. The implied reader is expected to recognize these signs and to discern that some refer to exhibits and others to more functional locations within a building, probably located in a town or city, known as a museum. It is precisely this kind of external knowledge that distances the reader from Saxon and Gilbert. The children's regimented existence is founded on their conviction that the museum constitutes a complete universe, or at least that 'outside' consists only of dust and darkness, and the enlightened reader is led to interpret the children's beliefs as false or misconceived. Gradually, the children come to suspect that there is, in fact, a world of light outside the museum, as confirmed by their eventual release when the reader's superior knowledge of 'reality' is seemingly vindicated.

This vindication is destabilized through the narrative disruption of signification and, although the children's reading of signs appears mistaken, it soon becomes clear that their relocation of meaning is a matter of survival. For instance, their ability to differentiate between spears from various lands and times is forged by necessity; as Scott reveals: 'Empty hooks reminded Saxon of their first search for weapons; many weapons were displayed throughout the world, but only African spears were light enough' (47). In Saxon's utilitarian terms, weapons are classified according to portability and destructive capability. In their struggle for survival, the children have little need for the dictates of history and geography; such concepts are rendered useless. Therefore, when Saxon is moved by a display of fossilized tree stumps, it seems unlikely that Scott is responding to Walter Benjamin's notions of auratic beauty:

She wondered at their shape – not measured into straight lines and perfect curves like the world, but – she smiled – like Gilbert, and the sparrows. And the spiders.

How strange that she could divide creation in two: that which is measured, and that which is not. (56)

Saxon is brought to recognize the latent chaos of nature, thus enabling this differentiation between the natural and the fabricated, between reproduction and reality. However, her attraction is enabled less through the inherent aura of the object than through memories of life outside and previous to existence in the museum. Saxon's identification with the artefact is reliant on her own experience; her sense of the thing is activated through reference to herself and the outside environment into which she was actually born. Saxon comes to realize that there is little point in names, labels and classifications unless they have some reference to individual experience. Saxon has to claim a past for herself that bears no relation to the original signification of museum exhibits and the past they evoke; she has no access to the public time described by Kern and so the concept of the Museum as a *lieu de mémoire* is necessarily alien to her.

The children have difficulty remembering their surname because they have lost contact with the people and places that once lent it meaning. Equally, their attempt to learn the names of each museum exhibit is a futile exercise, since their only point of reference is a dictionary; they soon learn that there is no natural affinity between object and label. Their efforts to classify and name are without apparent motivation; still it is implied that they are acting out the earliest lessons of childhood, rendered futile in their social and cultural isolation (a corollary to this is Scott's clear recognition that ideology is the foundation of society; meaning does not simply happen, it is made). Eventually Saxon is forced to reach within herself in order to locate her past; she must face her innermost fears if she is to make sense of the world which once was hers. As the Brogan falls to her death, as the passing (past) of death rushes to meet the present, so Saxon is able to recognize her mother: 'Saxon suddenly knew many things. A great stone falling. A young woman on the steps of the museum' (101–2). Of course the children are not alone in their re-evaluation of signification. At this moment, or perhaps at an earlier moment of realization, the reader is forced to reconsider the title of the book. 'Why Weeps the Brogan?' no longer implicates a terrifying creature as its subject, rather a family destroyed through tragedy. The monster that Gilbert and Saxon have feared for so long is actually their mother; a mother who sacrifices herself in order that her children might have a future.

Like Provoost, having revealed the painful secrets of the past Scott is unwilling to promise his readers a rosy future; such a closure would compromise the complexity of his exploration of identity as constructed through past, present and future (and would undermine the implied political message warning against the consequences of nuclear combat). Both authors confirm that we construct ourselves through time and that this construction is a difficult, often traumatic process. Furthermore, they suggest that while the past should not be privileged over the present (in an exercise of nostalgia), neither should we expect too much from a future overburdened with a troubled past.

Conclusion

This journey through works of children's literature confirms that time is a fundamental aspect of narrative and writers for young adults have increasingly drawn attention to the narrative play of time through metafictive techniques (such as Sedgwick's dual narrative structure, or Provoost's achronological framework) that destabilize and challenge our relationship with time and history. A necessary aspect of lived experience, time is also explored on a thematic level in these books. Authors frequently investigate the resonance of memory and the various ways in which children might come to terms with an unknown past as they attempt to make sense of present experience in preparation for the future.

Marcus Sedgwick and Hugh Scott suggest that the past, and more specifically memory, is accessible through objects. Nonetheless, in line with museum theorists, they suggest that the past cannot be contained within objects such as Mouse's box (as Sigurd's narration of Mouse's tale puts her memories to use they are no longer trapped within the box). *The Dark Horse*, *Falling* and *Why Weeps the Brogan?* each recognize the relationship between individual development and an understanding of time past, present and future. Memories – either the stories we tell ourselves about the past, or those we are told – might be inscribed with the past, yet they have a hand in configuring action, response and identity in the present and for the future. Significantly though, these memories can be shaped and altered by those around us, or by our own variable moods and perceptions; they are not stable and thus we can change, as Lucas does in *Falling*, in response to these retrospective shifts. Linear time might invest in the notion of closed periods marked by history, but each of these authors reveals that closure anticipates a fruitful opening. Recent books for children suggest that children must be taught to 'reckon with time', in Heidegger's terms, and to look to their own place in time if the past is to have any relevance to self-knowledge and growth.

WORKS CITED AND FURTHER READING

Children's Books

Anno, Mitsumasa et al. *All in a Day*, trans. Kuso-Kubo. New York: PaperStar, 1986.
Chambers, Aidan. *Postcards from No Man's Land*. London: Bodley Head, 1999.
Garner, Alan. *Red Shift*. London: HarperCollins, 1975; first published 1973.
L'Engle, Madeleine. *A Wrinkle in Time*. London: Puffin, 2007; first published 1962.
Lively, Penelope. *A Stitch in Time*. London: Mammoth, 1994; first published 1976.
Mark, Jan. *Useful Idiots*. London: Random House, 2005; first published 2004.
Newbery, Linda. *The Shell House*. Oxford: David Fickling, 2002.
Pearce, Philippa. *Tom's Midnight Garden*. Oxford: Oxford University Press, 1958.

Peet, Mal. *Tamar*. London: Walker Books, 2005.
Provoost, Anne. *Falling*, trans. John Nieuwenhuizen. St. Leonard's, NSW: Allen & Unwin, 1997; first published in Dutch, 1995.
Scott, Hugh. *Why Weeps the Brogan?* London: Walker Books, 1991; first published 1989.
Sedgwick, Marcus. *The Dark Horse*. London: Orion Children's Books, 2002.
Sutcliff, Rosemary. *The Eagle of the Ninth*. Oxford: Oxford University Press, 1998; first published 1954.
Wein, Elizabeth. *Codename Verity*. London: Egmont, 2013; first published 2012.
Wiesner, David. *Tuesday*. New York: Clarion Books, 1991.

Critical Texts

Benjamin, Walter. 'The Work of Art in an Age of Mechanical Production'. In *Illuminations*, ed. Hannah Arendt, trans. Harry Zohn. New York: Schocken Books, 1969.
Crossley-Holland, Kevin, and Lawrence Sail (eds). *The New Exeter Book of Riddles*. London: Enitharmon Press, 1999.
Genette, Gérard. *Narrative Discourse*, trans. Jane E. Lewin. Oxford: Basil Blackwell, 1980; first published 1972.
Heidegger, Martin. *Being and Time: A Translation of Sein und Zeit*, trans. Joan Stambaugh. New York: State University of New York Press, 1996.
Kern, Stephen. *The Culture of Time & Space 1880–1918*. Cambridge, MA: Harvard University Press, 2003.
Krips, Valerie. *The Presence of the Past: Memory, Heritage and Childhood in Postwar Britain*. London and New York: Garland, 2000.
Krips, Valerie. 'Presencing the Past'. *Signal*, 90 (September 1999), 176–86.
Morris, Pam (ed.). *The Bakhtin Reader*. London: Edward Arnold, 1994.
Nikolajeva, Maria. *Children's Literature Comes of Age: Toward a New Aesthetic*. New York and London: Garland, 1996.
Nikolajeva, Maria. *From Mythic to Linear: Time in Children's Literature*. Lanham, MD and London: ChLA/Scarecrow, 2000.
Nodelman, Perry. *Words About Pictures: The Narrative Art of Children's Picture Books*. Athens, GA: University of Georgia Press, 1988.
Provoost, Anne. 'If Goblins Don't Exist …'. No date. http://www.anneprovoost.com/English/Essays/EssaysGoblins.htm (accessed 28 September 2013).
Ricoeur, Paul. 'Narrative Time'. In W. J. T. Mitchell (ed.), *On Narrative*. Chicago and London: University of Chicago Press, 1981.
Ricoeur, Paul. *Time and Narrative*, vol. 1, trans. Kathleen McLaughlin and David Pellauer. Chicago and London: University of Chicago Press, 1990; first published 1983.
Walsh, Kevin. *The Representation of the Past*. London: Routledge, 1992.

Childhood, Youth Culture and the Uncanny: Uncanny Nights in Contemporary Fiction for Young People

13

Lisa Sainsbury

KEY TEXTS

Gillian Cross, *Wolf* (1990)
Neil Gaiman, illustrated by Dave McKean, *The Wolves in the Walls* (2003)
Alan Garner, *The Owl Service* (1967)

Legislating the nights

Local Child Curfews in the UK – powers provided by the Crime and Disorder Act 1998 and the Criminal Justice and Police Act 2001 – allow local authorities or police forces to prevent children under 16 from being in a public place between 9.00 p.m. and 6.00 a.m. unaccompanied by adults (Youth Justice Board website). If children under ten contravene curfews they can be made subject to a Child Safety Order (an early intervention measure designed to prevent antisocial behaviour – Youth Justice Board website). While such legislation has only limited relevance to most young people, it reflects enduring and contradictory anxieties about the need to safeguard innocent children, yet also to protect society from the perceived ravages of untamed youth. Configured in legislative terms and in the figurative aspects of fiction for young people from *Tom's Midnight Garden* (1958) by Philippa Pearce to *A Monster Calls* (2011) by Patrick Ness, such anxieties have a chronotopic dimension, played out in terms of space and time, so that the child is endangered or becomes a threat to adult authority and social order if the bounds of domestic space are transgressed at night.

Tracing the manifestation of these anxieties in literature written for young people reveals that they are also linked to the complexities of growing up; specifically, to the transitory phase of human experience that leads from childhood, through adolescence, to adulthood. An important aspect of this journey is the battle – anticipated in Local Child Curfews – between adults and youths who are seeking to negotiate curfews and to establish experience outside of the home. Growing out of childhood and into adolescence is then partly defined by the struggle to move out of sanctioned daytime experience, into night-time experience shared with peers; to take charge of the night-time world of mature adulthood (and its concomitant sexuality).

As well as being an aspect of lived experience for young people, in fiction produced for them the transition between day and night frequently works as a complex metaphor for the psychological domain of young characters, as – in an evocation of the uncanny – the familiar (homely) world of early childhood becomes defamiliarized (unhomely) during the journey to adulthood. Nicholas Royle observes that the uncanny 'comes above all, perhaps, in the uncertainness of silence, solitude and darkness' (2003: 2), and the stealthy approach of such uncanny, nocturnal dread can be traced in the figurative play of this chapter's focal texts: Alan Garner's *The Owl Service* (1967), Gillian Cross's *Wolf* (1990) and *The Wolves in the Walls* (2003) by Neil Gaiman and Dave McKean.

Growing into the uncanny

The uncanny as a concept requires some introduction, given its centrality to my discussion. Freud's essay, 'The Uncanny' (see Box 13.1), is of particular interest given its focus on literary devices that create uncanny effects. Freud is concerned with aspects of the text that produce uncanny dread in the reader and it should be stressed that in Freud's terms the uncanny is a response to literary phenomena rather than a feature of a given text. In 'The Uncanny' Freud uncovers ways in which particular works of art produce certain qualities of feeling that, while related to the feelings of dread and horror aroused by that which is frightening, are not reducible to it (Freud, 1990: 339). During the course of this exploration Freud traces the linguistic development of the term, eventually providing a tentative definition with relevance to prevailing constructions of adolescence (as confirmed in my discussion of *The Owl Service* and *Wolf*). There is a correlation between *heimlich* and *unheimlich*, in which meanings fuse and the familiar becomes unfamiliar as definitions move towards ambivalence (347).

BOX 13.1   THE UNCANNY

The notion of the uncanny is frequently traced to Sigmund Freud's seminal essay, 'The Uncanny' (Das Unheimlich) which was first published in 1919. In 'The Uncanny' Freud attempts to identify and explain the particular type of fear or dread classified as uncanny. He suggests that 'the uncanny' is within the sphere of the frightening, but that 'a special core of feeling is present which justifies the use of a special conceptual term' (Freud, 1990: 339). Freud goes on to trace the etymological relationship between the uncanny/unfamiliar (*unheimlich*) and familiar/homely (*heimlich*), finally concluding that they cannot be understood in oppositional terms, but as ambivalent ideas that coincide; hence 'Unheimlich is in some way or other a subspecies of heimlich' (347). Exploring a range of literature, Freud establishes that certain literary images, such as damage to eyes, the theme of the double or dismembered limbs, elicit uncanny feelings which can be attributed to various psychological anxieties. However, as Nicholas Royle observes in *The Uncanny* (2003), while Freud's essay has influenced a range of contemporary theories from feminism to queer theory, 'The uncanny is inextricably bound up with the history of the Enlightenment' (8) and 'has been the focus of critical, literary, philosophical and political reflection from at least the mid nineteenth century to the present' (3); it is by no means restricted to the domain of Freudian analysis. Several critics writing within the field of children's literature, for example Robyn McCallum and John Stephens (2001), Richard Gooding (2008), Claudia Nelson (2012), Alison Waller (2009) and Lydia Kokkola (2013), have identified uncanny motifs with literature for young people, suggesting that such feelings of dread are common to adolescent experience.

The ambivalence Freud detects in the etymological progress of the uncanny is useful as a way into texts for young people, for, as Perry Nodelman points out in *The Hidden Adult* (2008): 'Children's literature not only expresses ambivalence about childhood, but also, and perhaps most centrally, invites its readers to share it. It is characteristically a literature that addresses a divided child reader' (2008: 185). Of course, not all children's literature elicits uncanny fear as a result of this ambivalence and Nodelman adds that many books work to resolve arising tensions 'by denying one-half [*sic*] of the divided subjects they imply and work to construct' (186). In this chapter, then, I am interested in texts that do not resolve this ambivalence and which use literary landscapes to explore anxieties emanating from this investment in division and uncertainty. Furthermore, I propose that these books are typical of a growing number of children's books that have the potential to generate uncanny fear in the reader and can be seen as artistic expressions of the uncanny. Identifiable attributes of the uncanny take on figurative life and can be identified as features of the text rather than merely a response to it.

Freud's interest in the uncanny is not unique, for the uncanny is central to the thinking of many theorists and philosophers, including Martin Heidegger (in *Being and Time*, 1927) and Jacques Derrida (in *Spectres of Marx*, 1993), while Nicholas Royle conducts an extensive historical, cultural, critical and philosophical exploration of the feeling/concept in *The Uncanny* (2003). Royle's discussion of the uncanny reaches for a series of definitions that bleed into and enrich each other, and his starting point for defining the uncanny offers a useful way into my discussion of uncanny literature for young people:

> The uncanny entails another thinking of beginning: the beginning is already haunted. The uncanny is ghostly. It is concerned with the strange, weird and mysterious, with a flickering sense (but not conviction) of something supernatural. The uncanny involves feelings of uncertainty, in particular regarding the reality of who one is and what is being experienced. Suddenly one's sense of oneself ... seems strangely questionable. (2003: 1)

With this notion of haunted beginnings in mind I look to Gaiman and McKean's picturebook, *The Wolves in the Walls*, as its young protagonist Lucy turns away from and back to childhood (her already-haunted beginning).

Negotiating cavities

The Wolves in the Walls explores visually and verbally Lucy's encounter with wolves in the walls of her home over the course of several nights. Lucy's conviction that the noises she hears are made by wolves is contradicted by her family and when Lucy's wolves do emerge, the family flees to the garden. It is Lucy who engineers their eventual return home and the ejection of the lupine hooligans. This provocative picturebook deals with Lucy's emergent agency as she confronts the possibility of leaving childhood behind (figured in the beloved pig-puppet she forgets and returns to save). *Wolves* also suggests that adult instincts to protect children are rooted in adult fears and specifically in an unwillingness to tackle the unknown or acknowledge uncertainty. In this departure from the homely space of childhood and in the questioning of adult conviction rises the spectre of the uncanny as expressed by Royle when he recognizes in it 'another thinking of beginning' and uncertainty 'regarding the reality of who one is and what is being experienced'.

Lucy's first confrontation is not with wolves; it involves her family who deny the presence of wolves in the walls, each repeating a piece of received knowledge, 'for you know what they say ... If the wolves come out of the walls, then it's all over' (Gaiman, 2003: 9 – numbering commences from the dedication page). When Lucy seeks clarification, asking 'What's all over?', her mother can only respond with, 'It ... Everybody knows that' (9). This exchange questions the conditions of knowledge, suggesting that wisdom embedded in idiom has lost any meaningful relationship to human experience. While Lucy's parents cling to the ostensible certainty of language, Lucy picks at signification and shakes 'her head at this sad display of ignorance' (16). Even though Lucy is disturbed (though she never admits to fear) by the uncanny silence that precedes the wolves' arrival – 'I don't like it,' Lucy told her pig-puppet. 'It's too quiet!' (17) – evidently she accepts the uncanny as a condition of her existence. Lucy's sardonic comment about ignorance points to the book's comic undertow – and Royle argues that the comic is always in close proximity to the uncanny – while Lucy's semantic curiosity in the face of disquieting 'hustling noises' (7) in the walls confirms Royle's related point that 'the uncanny is intimately entwined with language, with how we conceive and represent what is happening within ourselves, to ourselves, to the world' (2003: 2).

Adult authority is undermined and becomes increasingly ridiculous as Lucy's family act on the conditions of spurious knowledge, even when experience contradicts it. Failing to reflect on what the wolves' presence might mean – clearly the family has survived and their house is still standing, so it is hard to see what is 'over' – the rest of Lucy's family consider far-fetched options for finding a new home and they do not attempt to challenge the wolves. Lucy suggests simply that, 'we could go back and live in our house again' (31). Having accepted the existence of the uncanny wolves, Lucy is aware that she can only gain control over her life if she maintains a connection with the familiar; to leave home would be to succumb to uncanny fear. Lucy must claim for herself the nocturnal space rejected by adult denial and resistance (and thereby challenge adult authority) if eventually she is to grow into adulthood.

The wolves can be interpreted variously, though the fact that Lucy identifies them suggests that they relate to her specifically, perhaps to unconscious anxieties about growing up. Royle confirms that 'The uncanny has to do with the sense of a secret encounter ... of something that should have remained secret and hidden but has come to light' (2). This uncanny rising of the once hidden is suggested by McKean's illustrations, amalgamating illustrative techniques with computer-generated or photographic images, so that a realistic wolf's eye peers out at the reader (14), or Lucy's cubist face sprouts real hair on a pillow represented through paintwork and photograph combined (11). The status of the wolves as real, imagined or repressed is questioned by text and illustration. It is clear that Lucy cannot contain or explain the whisperings that refuse to remain within the walls (her unconscious) and that she will have to confront changes without/within herself.

Although Lucy might be unaware of what the wolves represent, hints are provided by figurative play. The visual prevalence of scarlet throughout – flaming lilies (4); red carpets and bedclothes (6, 11); stacks of strawberry jam surrounding Lucy and prepared by her mother (8) – suggests allusions to 'Little Red Riding Hood'. This familiar folk tale (at least in Western culture) is commonly associated with the onset of puberty and sexual awareness, as Jack Zipes suggests when he confirms that 'the oral tale emanates from a region in Europe during the 17th century where ... women told tales representative of their sexual and social initiation' (1993: 6). The behaviour of the wolves when they arrive in the house – throwing a party in the middle of the night (38–9), smearing jam on the walls (42) and playing video games (41) – is also typical of behaviour commonly associated with adolescence and anticipated by the provision of Local Child Curfews. Lucy's eventual banishment of the wolves from her home could imply that she has not yet reached adolescence, or that having reached adolescence she refuses to conform to prevailing notions of young adulthood and is able to control wolfish desire.

If Lucy is not yet adolescent, it is also clear that she is no longer a child, as suggested by enforced separation from her pig-puppet. When the family flees, Lucy is carried downstairs by her father (she is the only family member not actively running away) and her arm reaches back into the house (Figure 3). The ambiguous image depicts Lucy almost touching a shadowy wolf (manifesting the uncanny) leaping on the wall, though her subsequent anxiety about the forgotten toy suggests that simultaneously Lucy is reaching for her childhood companion. When first she hears the wolves, 'Lucy picked up her pig-puppet doll, which she'd had since she was a little, little baby' (10), and speaks to her puppet for comfort, clutching her close in bed when the wolves are about to break through (17). As the wolves/adolescence draws near Lucy relies on the props of early childhood, drawing the familiar world of childhood into the unfamiliar realms of pre-pubescence. However, the dynamics of this relationship change in the aftermath of the wolves' arrival and Lucy's child self retreats as she takes control.

Figure 3   Lucy's family flees the wolves: from Neil Gaiman and Dave McKean's *The Wolves in the Walls*

Visually and verbally this shift is anticipated as Lucy lies at the bottom of the garden, worrying about her puppet, 'She'll be all alone in that house with the wolves ... They could do dreadful things to her' (23). Rising up from the ground behind Lucy is a nightmarish vision of a wolfish demon, sketched in hard, angry lines, dropping a limp and colourless pig-puppet into its open jaws (Figure 4). Although Lucy retreats into the foetal position, assertively she gazes out at the reader, obscuring her sleeping mother. No longer is the pig-puppet a source of comfort, rather she is a focus of concern and during this moment of heightened, nocturnal anxiety Lucy takes responsibility, acting to save her puppet. Entering her home through the walls and finding solace in liminality – as once she did in her pig-puppet – Lucy declares, 'It's kind of nice in the walls', and so confirms that the uncanny (associated with liminal borders and boundaries; in this case the boundary between childhood and adolescence) can offer a way of moving forward and that her return home need not result in an

**Figure 4   A nightmarish wolf: from Neil Gaiman and
Dave McKean's *The Wolves in the Walls***

unhealthy form of regression. Having established this, she is able to cuddle her pig again on different terms and McKean's peaceful illustration (29) – evenly toned and coloured and unusually free of stylistic amalgamation – confirms that Lucy has progressed in her relationship with self and family.

Wolves configures the management of pre-pubescent anxiety in its articulation of the uncanny for younger readers and it also questions a prevalent investment in childhood innocence through its resourceful protagonist. When Lydia Kokkola introduces the conceptual and socio-historical development of adolescence in *Fictions of Adolescent Carnality* (2013) she argues that 'By exaggerating the sturm und drang of adolescence, adults privilege adulthood as a period of balanced maturity and maintain the Romantic myths of childhood long past their "sell by" date' (2013: 6). Gaiman and McKean's picturebook serves to destabilize the boundaries that distinguish childhood innocence and adult maturity, suggesting that each of these categories is socially constructed and historically situated. As the most recent of the focal texts in this chapter, *Wolves* is perhaps the most subversive in its refusal of distinctions categorizing childhood (innocent), adolescence (troubled), adulthood (stable and knowing). Now, I explore two examples of young adult fiction that engage with and play out concepts of adolescence problematized by Kokkola and an adolescence recognized by Alison Waller as 'always "other" to the more mature stage of adulthood' (Waller, 2009: 1).

Constructing adolescence

By the mid-twentieth century, Western cultures had admitted G. Stanley Hall's 1904 psychological portrait of adolescence into the public consciousness. *Sturm und Drang* (storm and stress) was attributed to teenagers by Hall who in 1904 was the first psychologist to identify adolescence as a separate state of human development – recognizing it as a transitional stage between childhood and adulthood during which young people attempt to come to terms with themselves and society. In *Becoming a Reader* (1991), Appleyard explores various psychological accounts of adolescence, each suggesting that associated phenomena are 'manifestations of one central phenomenon: the discovery of the subjective self and of subjective experience as something unique' (Kohlberg and Gilligan, cited in Appleyard, 1994: 96). This discovery frequently leads to a divisive and polarized world-view, in which this new-found and highly prized inner self is valued over the external self that plays out social roles; a polarity that rejects pretence (external self) in favour of authenticity (internal self). In psychological terms there are links to be made between this adolescent preoccupation with division and otherness and Freud's notion of the uncanny. It is also important to consider the social pressures influencing psychological development or disturbance in young people, for Erik Erikson observes that, 'although adolescents undergo a rapid physiological maturation, society (especially a technologically advanced one) postpones their taking genuine adult roles by keeping them in school' (cited in Appleyard, 1994: 97–8). Society forces young people into a liminal space which lies somewhere between childhood and adulthood, but that is essentially distanced from both. It is a period of transition which, given its predisposition to thoughtful introspection (Appleyard, 1994: 97), is obsessively aware of its status as such. Of particular significance here, adolescence is perceived as a time of dislocation, as a phase in which newfound self-consciousness leads to a reassessment of the familiar world, rendering it unfamiliar.

Like many texts dealing in adolescent angst, Alan Garner's *The Owl Service* lends a mythic dimension to its preoccupation with youth. *The Owl Service* is set in a secluded Welsh valley and centres on a triadic relationship between three adolescents – Alison, Roger and Gwyn – as they are drawn into a re-enactment of 'Math vab Mathonwy', a legend from the Welsh *Mabinogion*. Alison and her stepbrother Roger have arrived with their English family to stay in their farmhouse, now used as a holiday home and recently inherited by Alison. Gwyn is the son of Nancy, the Welsh housekeeper who has also been caught up in the cycle along with other adults in Garner's novel. 'Math vab Mathonwy' is a tale of betrayed love in which the enchanter Gwydion makes Blodeuwedd out of flowers as a wife for his nephew (and adopted son) Lleu. Blodeuwedd then falls in love with Gronw Pebyr who is eventually killed by Lleu, while Gwydion transforms Blodeuwedd into an owl as a punishment for betraying his son. In Garner's 'expression'[1] of the narrative, Alison becomes Blodeuwedd to Roger's Gronw and Gwyn's Lleu.

A useful way in to *The Owl Service* is first to consider the *Mabinogion*, the sequence of medieval Welsh tales through which Garner's text expresses itself. In his introduction to the Mabinogion, Jeffrey Gantz explains that:

> Unfortunately, the *meaning* of the word *mabinogi* in the present context is still a problem. Professor Ifor Williams was able to show that *mabinogi* generally designates the story of someone's early years ... Alternatively, Rachael Bromwich has suggested that mabinogi came to signify 'a tale of descendants', and that the Four Branches actually deal with the children of the early Celtic deities ... (1976: 31–2)

Whatever the precise etymology of *mabinogi*, there seems no doubt that it is concerned not only with stories of young people, but with their descent, with the relationship between generations and the tensions which arise as children come into adolescence. Gantz's etymology confirms that the adolescent psychodrama at the core of *The Owl Service* is inevitable if the myth 'Math vab Mathonwy' is to be given any sort of viable expression.

One of the clearest ways in which Garner approaches adolescence *in The Owl Service* is through an evocation of the double. The interweaving of Garner's triple narrative involves a shifting and doubling of identity that permeates the book – for example, gazing from her bedroom window Alison sees 'herself mirrored among haloes that the sun made on the water' (Garner, 1973: 83). The 'phenomenon of the "double"' is often

> marked by the fact that the subject identifies himself with someone else, so that he is in doubt as to which his self is, or substitutes the extraneous

self for his own. In other words, there is a doubling, dividing and inter-changing of the self. And finally there is the constant recurrence of the same thing – the repetition of the same character-traits or vicissitudes, of the same crimes, or even the same names through several consecutive generations. (Freud, 1990: 356)

Freud ponders the source of uncanny terror induced by such doubling, suggesting that the 'double' variously functions as 'an assurance of immortality', while also, in a typically uncanny contradiction of this idea, as 'an uncanny harbinger of death' (357). Freud's doubling echoes Garner's construction of adolescent identity which sees itself reflected in others more clearly than it recognizes itself. Garner's central characters are doubled with their counterparts in previous generations and, in this sense, they are rendered immortal. It is, however, a blighted immortality, structured around death rather than birth. The young people seem to be locked inextricably into past patterns, culminating in death and destruction, in owlish darkness as opposed to flowery sunlight.

If the subject of adolescence is essential to the mythic resonance of *The Owl Service*, so too is it crucial to the reworking of 'Little Red Riding Hood' in Gillian Cross's *Wolf*. *Wolf* tells of Cassy's enforced departure from the home she shares with her grandmother; her journey to the London squat inhabited by her mother, her mother's boyfriend, Lyall, and his son Robert; and her confrontation of the 'wolf' which stalks her from the past and in her dreams (a wolf that seems linked to her absent father). Cassy's trek across London to find her mother is only the latest journey in a familiar, if unwelcome and perplexing, aspect of Cassy's childhood experience: 'Step by step, word by word, they would go through the same pattern as last time – and all the times before' (Cross, 1992: 4). The journey is not in itself remarkable, but the conditions attributed to it are. That Cassy must make this trip alone is significant. Cassy's plea to her Nan, 'But you always take me,' is met with the rejoinder, 'Maybe it's time you were growing up, then' (6). Evidently this is a journey from childhood to adulthood.

It soon becomes apparent that Nan's controlling regime of overprotection, however well meant, has ill equipped Cassy for her adolescent adventure. She must unlearn the rules of childhood in which she sees herself through Nan's eyes: 'Sensible brown eyes. Sensible short brown hair. You only had to look at that face to know she wouldn't do anything wild' (6). Cassy is propelled on a journey of self-discovery, initiated and defined by her grandmother at the outset. Her path leads from the sensible and ordered existence of life with Nan to her mother's emotional and instinctual world, in which Cassy's perception of reality and self are challenged. Throughout this process of defamiliarization, Cassy struggles to maintain links with the conditions of childhood. 'Shocked' and 'frozen' by the distortions of her mother's mirrored room, Cassy 'gripped the handle of her suitcase, standing completely still as she worked out where the boundaries were' (14). Her response to this uncanny environment is to grip the familiar object, the suitcase which she associates with Nan. She reaches for the familiar to make sense of the unfamiliar, but must soon accept that she cannot have one without the other, as Freud's exploration of the uncanny suggests (and *The Wolves in the Walls* appears to confirm). Indeed all three books construct adolescence as a liminal realm in which the unfamiliar forces itself on the familiar, compelling young people to deal with it (successfully or otherwise).

Night into day

In *The Owl Service* and *Wolf* the boundaries between childhood and adulthood are figuratively played out in the passage between night and day. *The Owl Service* opens with Alison in bed during the day, which, while indicating illness, might also suggest that night-time behaviour is bleeding into daytime. With Gwyn's help, Alison attempts to locate the mysterious scratching above her bedroom, and we learn that her nights have been disturbed ever since she arrived in Wales. 'I heard it the first night I came,' said Alison, 'and every night ever since: a few minutes after I'm in bed' (Garner, 1973, 8). Alison's symptoms are connected to these nocturnal disturbances and it seems inevitable that she should see owls (since they are nocturnal hunters) in the pattern on the plates she and Gwyn discover in the loft above her room. One explanation is that Alison has internalized the anxieties brought about by her new familial structure and by the onset of adolescent sexuality. Lucy hears similarly strange sounds in *The Wolves in the Walls*, but the experience does not incapacitate her in the way it does Alison, suggesting divergent attitudes to adolescence in which the twenty-first-century girl confronts the onset of puberty with more confidence.

In contrast to Alison, we first meet Roger among flowers, meadowsweet specifically (11), one of the flowers used to make Blodeuwedd, Alison's mythical counterpart from the *Mabinogion*. Roger is the child of the sun and light and it is logical that it is he who should finally see flowers in Alison at the moment of salvation. Roger is sun ('he felt the sun drag deep in his limbs', 11) to Alison's moon. Metaphorically, Alison is also 'in the dark' when it comes to reading the plates. She does not realize that there is a choice to be made between owls and flowers, while Roger sees the possibility of interpretation. Alison asks:

> 'Don't you see what it is?'
>
> 'An abstract design in green round the edge, touched up with a bit of rough gilding.'
>
> 'Roger! You're being stupid on purpose! Look at that part. It's an owl's head.'
>
> '– Yes? I suppose it is, *if you want it to be.*' (15, my emphasis)

Roger recognizes that choice is possible, that what you see depends on how you look. Alison's approach is instinctive, based on preconceptions that Roger does not share, and his openness to alternative readings allows Roger to save her. This depiction of Alison (like generations of young women before her) as helplessly caught up in a cycle of insanity and violence brought on by puberty and sexual awareness render the night/moon negative figures of an inappropriate female desire that should be hidden and denied; and because hidden it rises through the pathways of the uncanny, which are in turn closed/cured by dominant males. Garner does little to disturb the patriarchal dominance of men over women mapped out in 'Math vab Mathonwy' in his revisiting of the mythic cycle, though *The Owl Service* is not alone in its manifest rejection of female – or childhood/young adult – sexuality. Accordingly Lydia Kokkola protests, 'Carnal desire is as basic a human need as the need for physical shelter. Nevertheless, it has been singled out and reviled as though it were antithetical to all that we value in childhood' (2013: 23). Alison can only progress into womanhood if she denies her sexuality (owls) and turns once more to the perceived/enforced innocence of girlhood (flowers).

In *Wolf* the tension between night and day is manifest primarily through its pervasive dreamscape. The book opens epigraphically with Nan's denial of Cassy's nocturnal consciousness: 'Of course Cassy never dreams, Nan always said. She has more sense, to be sure … There's been no trouble with dreams, not since she was a baby' (2). The fundamental problem with this observation is that Nan cannot know whether Cassy dreams or not. Cross implies that Nan's intervention in Cassy's capacity to dream is related to the effective brainwashing which has led to Cassy's mistrust of her mother and her repression of the past. It is also unclear to whom Nan is addressing this observation. Nan could be talking to herself in an attempt to reinforce her conviction that Cassy's unconscious will not lead to any dangerous or disturbing memories. Alternatively, Nan might be speaking to Cassy's father, reassuring him that his daughter does not pose a threat; that she will not expose him as the Cray Hill bomber. Cross's refusal to identify Nan's addressee is significant, however, for it signals the uncertain nature of Nan's relationship with Cassy from the outset and the level of engagement Cross expects from her readers. *Wolf* is a literary puzzle to be pieced together by Cassy and the reader.

Cassy's father first appears shrouded in mystery and Cassy mistakes him for some bestial creature as 'his feet padded along the balcony', in the middle of the night: 'He came in quickly, in silence, in the dark …' (3). This nocturnal visitor has not yet been identified as Cassy's father, but the strange-yet-familiar figure soon pervades her dreams, lending an uncanny dimension to Cassy's journey of self-discovery at the squat. Cassy's impending access to her dreaming unconscious is signalled by the word 'MOONGAZER' (12), emblazoned across the van belonging to her mother's new boyfriend, and hints at a new source of self-knowledge, free from repression and unhealthy levels of self-control. As moon-gazing suggests, Cassy is to be initiated into a way of life antithetical to Nan's, though it does not come as easily to her as it does to Lyall's son: 'Robert was sure-footed in the dark, but she had to feel her way very carefully' (17). Like Garner's Alison, Cassy is guided by a more enlightened male character, though (unlike Roger) Robert encourages her to see that sometimes absolute conviction can be more destructive than an ambivalence that embraces various ways of being.

Cassy's nightly trips into the unconscious realm of her past disturb her as she confronts her father's predatory sexuality in a recasting of the Oedipal conflict (Reynolds, 1994: 59). She ignores their presence for a time, attempting to return to the dreamlessness of pre-pubescent denial: 'Cassy sat up, wrenching her mind out of the dream. Whatever was the matter with her? She never dreamed. Never, never' (52). Still under Nan's influence, Cassy gropes for logic, aligning the rational routines of daily life with security, wellbeing and familiarity, while her nocturnal dreamscapes represent fear, moral uncertainty and abnormality. Robert encourages Cassy to be more receptive to different levels of consciousness: 'What is this thing you've got about real life?'... 'Real life and real people? That doesn't mean anything. It's just a way of making walls, to shut out what's uncomfortable. And it doesn't work, you know. If things are there, you have to admit it in the end' (81–2). Nan has built walls for Cassy that simplify experience into a dualistic world of good and bad; a fairy-tale world in which justice is clear-cut.[2] If Cassy is to break through these walls (as Lucy does in *The Wolves in the Walls*), she must accept her dreams and confront the knowledge they contain so as to understand her past and embrace the future.

Cassy only gradually comes to discover the positive benefits of integrating experience of night (unfamiliar) and day (familiar), for until she does she will be trapped in an unhealthy obsession with the past (figured in her father's act of terrorism, which Nan has kept from her). *Wolf* underscores the importance of reconciling human experience with the uncanny in a way that *The Owl Service* doesn't quite manage. Notwithstanding the manifest suspicion of dualistic conditions of power (worked out in terms of gender, class, age etc.) in Garner's text, the uncanny remains symptomatic of destruction, exclusion and death. *Wolf* is closer to Gaiman and McKean's rendition of the uncanny's potential to disturb that which should be disturbed; an uncanny that never overwhelms due to its anchoring in familiarity.

Curfew and transgression

The dichotomous boundary between night and day in *The Owl Service* and *Wolf* can be considered usefully in relation to the conflict thrown up between young people and parental authority. Each novel explores the nature of transgression as implied/imposed curfews are breached in a figurative exhibition of adolescence.

The Owl Service is less concerned with direct confrontations between parent and child than with containment as older generations try to control their offspring (and so repress the age-old tragedy underlying relationships in the present). Nancy refuses to explain the significance of the dinner service, while Alison's mother is physically absent. Both attempt to exert authority over their children as, for example, Alison is forbidden from conversing with Gwyn and in turn Gwyn is prevented from speaking to Huw (the 'half-wit' who turns out to be his father). Much of the action centres on the young people's attempts at breaking this silence and uncovering the secrets which they have inherited.

If they are to progress through adolescence and acquire self-knowledge (quite apart from preventing the tragedy engulfing them) these unspoken boundaries must be breached. The mere presence of the young people in the valley seems enough to expose the patterned dinner plates in the attic and the mural of Blodeuwedd long hidden behind plaster. Beyond this, however, it is the disruption of order represented by the various dichotomies (night/day; owls/flowers; self/other; child/parent; Welsh/English; working class/upper class) at work in Garner's text that finally challenges parental authority and lifts the curse of 'Math vab Mathonwy'.

In a pivotal scene, Gwyn and Alison break parental curfew and sneak out of the house at night. Each is forced to confront uncanny dread, reflecting insecurities through troubled, double (or even multiple) identities. They deal with this fear in different ways; nonetheless it draws them together into a violent, pseudo-sexual confrontation that alters their relationship and marks their initiation into (conditional) adult experience. When Gwyn first sees Alison (he thinks), she is half in shadow, dappled in the moonlight (64). This liminal, still and solitary figure ill prepares readers for the discovery of the real Alison. Cooped up in the hen hut, Alison approaches madness – she has lost herself at this moment and become owls: 'All of me's confused the same way. I keep wanting to laugh and cry.' She cannot express herself, 'I haven't the words' (67). This is adolescent trauma at its most extreme, offering a negative and potentially disturbing glimpse of sexuality. Alison is drawn to the darker side of her personality, symbolically represented by Garner's owls, though she is also psychologically disturbed by the night-space in which they hunt. Alison refuses to leave the hut until sunlight, and Gwyn agrees to protect her from the night until morning. Garner's description of their departure from the hen hut suggests a post-sexual euphoria: 'They stepped from the hut into rainbow dew and walked together up to the house through the midsummer dawn' (69). No details of their experience are provided, but Gwyn and Alison have certainly spent the night together.

Whatever the nature of Alison and Gwyn's union, it precipitates the storm closing the book and discharges tensions simmering throughout *The Owl Service*. Although there is a resolution of sorts – the young people survive and the cycle of destructive energy has been dissipated – this involves a retraction of the hen hut coupling that is ambivalent and regressive. Manifest in Gwyn is the impulse to protect and destroy, and these conflicting urges are unresolved as ultimately he is unable to help Alison. Garner implies that Gwyn's problems transcend adolescence; that they are in some way beyond him. Of all the characters he is the most incapacitated by family and social circumstance and does not have the means to challenge the bigotry and class barriers that diminish him. Alison bends to her mother's class prejudice when she abandons Gwyn, while Roger saves Alison through an act of interpretation that reinstates her innocence. This refusal of Alison's sexuality conforms to the patterns of anxiety about adolescence that Kokkola identifies in much writing for young people:

> Since sexuality and desire straddle concerns for and about teenagers, they reveal a society which is ill at ease, a society which is uncomfortable talking

to its young on the same footing as adults, but unclear whether this goal is to protect youngsters from the 'worldliness of the world' (Natov, 2003: 91) or the world from the unruliness of the young. The incompatibility of these desires has resulted in a level of ambivalence that is, at times, hypocritical. (2013: 207)

Garner's novel reveals that a range of different powers compete with sexual passion, resulting in an atmosphere of hypocritical repression. *The Owl Service* richly conveys the inevitable power of carnality and reveals that ambivalence about this power can be destructive – thus it seems that the ambivalence at work in Garner's novel is of a different order to the positive embracing of possibility afforded by ambivalence in *Wolf* and *The Wolves in the Walls*.

In *Wolf* the transgression of authority is complicated by the apparent role reversal of parent and child. This exchange is indicated by Cross's inversion of the traditional sequence of events in which Red Riding Hood travels to her grandmother to deliver a parcel of food on behalf of her mother. In *Wolf*, Cassy is sent by her grandmother to stay with her itinerant mother, Goldie, whom Cassy sees as closer to child than parent. Goldie and Lyall invest in a child-like impetuosity that seems chaotic and irresponsible to Cassy. Goldie actually invites and encourages transgression. She lives in a squat, eschewing social convention, refusing to draw the sorts of boundaries that are the prerequisite of curfew and which Cassy associates with Nan. However, the parental paradigms drawn on by Cassy are not entirely helpful, nor do they result in a successful or complete reversal of roles. Cassy plays at being Nan in order to cover her own discomfort: 'Cassy pulled a face, thinking of food and rubbish side by side. But she knew what Nan would have done so she did it' (Cross, 1992: 20). However, this role is only a short-term refuge from emotional insecurity. If she is to progress, Cassy must accept that her views of Goldie and Lyall are narrow and naive. Cassy must challenge the ideological boundaries set by Nan and find middle ground between two conflicting lifestyles, in which she can come to know herself.

Cassy's rescue of her grandmother is another version of Red Riding Hood's journey, though she is deprived of the traditional basket of goodies. Unable to locate the Semtex demanded by her terrorist father, Cassy arrives empty handed. She is rescued by Goldie, who brings the package herself, demonstrating her capacity for maternal responsibility. This act reinstates the familiar progression of the tale (in which mother gives to daughter gives to grandmother), since this symbolic passing of love from mother to daughter allows an emotionally secure Cassy to care for Nan; as Robert points out, 'When Granny Phelan gets out of hospital, she's sure to need you back' (139).

That Cassy's transgression of Nan's childhood boundaries is a positive experience is confirmed in the final dream sequence. Cassy dreams of herself as a child no longer bound by fear; in her dream, Nan banishes a storybook wolf, but Cassy draws him back, writing to him in her head:

'Dear Wolf, Don't vanish into the dark forest again. I still need to know about you. Perhaps I can come and visit you, or … or …'

Slowly her eyelids drooped. She knew that she wouldn't finish the letter in this dream, but she wasn't worried.

She would write it when she woke up.   (140)

This is no longer an uncanny dreamscape, in which the familiar, everyday world is rendered frightening by its relationship with night-time fears. In letting herself dream, Cassy experiences a merging of night/unconscious and day/conscious, allowing for a more balanced, deep and complete understanding of self.

Differences in the girlhoods framed by Garner and Cross point to a sea change during the 20 years that separate these novels, recasting young women as assertive beings able to challenge authority productively. Although Cassy takes only tentative steps towards embracing the ambivalence that has come to shape her experience, she learns to manage her anxieties and to take control of herself in a manner that is denied to Alison in the more passive version of femininity at work in *The Owl Service*. In Cassy's resilience and desire for knowledge are foreshadowed strong models of female adolescence – such as Lyra Belacqua in *The Amber Spyglass* (2000) or Coraline Jones in Neil Gaiman's *Coraline* (2002) – whose assertive energy stems partly from their transgression of boundaries set for them by hegemonic structures of adult power.

Conclusion

Social life frequently starts within the family and, accordingly, *The Owl Service*, *Wolf* and *The Wolves in the Walls* open with a disruption of family dynamics that instigates a journey away from childhood; a journey played out figuratively on the uncanny border between night and day. Gaiman and McKean's picturebook is not concerned with Hall's adolescent *Sturm und Drang*, yet still it anticipates a disruption to familiar conditions of childhood in its murky, disquieting and witty unleashing of wolfish desecration. In *Wolf* and *The Owl Service* the process of physical and psychological maturation is represented through the figurative boundary of night and day, drawing attention to tensions between adult and child that became a familiar facet of adolescence in the twentieth century.

It is possible to interpret the charting of uncanny territories in these books in terms of Oedipal drama or the stirrings of sexual desire. However, it would be reductive to root the tensions traced in this chapter in the libido, since the socio-political backdrop of these texts plays an important role in the evocation of pre-pubescence and young adulthood. Issues such as class, gender, terrorism and education generate and help to explain the uncanny phenomena arising when owls and wolves dismantle the walls that once cordoned off childhood from the complex world of adulthood.

Literature and legislation alike recognize that tension flares in the liminal byways of human development and experience, throwing up moments of uncanny dread that cannot be avoided. *The Owl Service* warns of the destructive potential of the uncanny and – though Roger's flowers represent a positive reminder that the familiar can always be located in the unfamiliar – Garner's adolescence is an experience to be survived (and not without cost), rather than the journey to autonomy and agency anticipated by Cross, and confirmed by Gaiman and McKean.

WORKS CITED AND FURTHER READING

Children's Books

Cormier, Robert. *In the Middle of the Night*. London: HarperCollins, 2002; first published 1995.
Cross, Gillian. *Pictures in the Dark*. Oxford: Oxford University Press, 2005; first published 1996.
Cross, Gillian. *Wolf*. London: Puffin Books, 1992; first published 1990.
Farmer, Penelope. *Charlotte Sometimes*. London: Puffin, 1972; first published 1969.
Gaiman, Neil. *Coraline*. London: Bloomsbury, 2002.
Gaiman, Neil, and Dave McKean (illus.). *The Wolves in the Walls*. London: Bloomsbury, 2003.
Garner, Alan. *The Owl Service*. London: Lions, 1973; first published 1967.
Mahy, Margaret. *The Changeover*. London: Puffin, 1995; first published 1984.
Ness, Patrick. *A Monster Calls*. London: Walker Books, 2011.
Pearce, Philippa. *Tom's Midnight Garden*. London: Puffin, 1976; first published 1958.
Westall, Robert. *The Scarecrows*. Harmondsworth: Puffin, 1983; first published 1981.

Critical Texts

Appleyard, J. A. *Becoming a Reader: The Experience of Fiction from Childhood to Adulthood*. Cambridge: Cambridge University Press, 1994; first published 1991.
Freud, Sigmund. 'The Uncanny'. *The Penguin Freud Library*: Vol. 14: *Art and Literature* (pp. 335–81). London: Penguin, 1990; first published 1919.
Gantz, Jeffrey (trans.). *The Mabinogion*. Harmondsworth: Penguin, 1976.
Garner, Alan. *The Voice That Thunders*. London: Harvill Press, 1997.
Gooding, Richard. '"Something Very Old and Very Slow": Coraline, Uncanniness, and Narrative Form'. *Children's Literature Association Quarterly*, 33.4 (Winter 2008), 390–407.
Kokkola, Lydia. *Fictions of Adolescent Carnality*. Amsterdam and Philadelphia: John Benjamins, 2013.
McCallum, Robyn, and John Stephens. '"There are Worse Things than Ghosts": Reworking Horror Chronotopes in Australian Children's Fiction'. In Adrienne E. Gavin and Christopher Routledge (eds), *Mystery in Children's Literature: From the Rational to the Supernatural* (pp. 164–83). London: Macmillan, 2001.
Nelson, Claudia. *Precocious Children and Childish Adults: Age Inversion in Victorian Literature*. Baltimore, MD: Johns Hopkins University Press, 2012.
Nodelman, Perry. *The Hidden Adult: Defining Children's Literature*. Baltimore, MD: The Johns Hopkins University Press, 2008.
Reynolds, Kimberley. *Children's Literature in the 1890s and 1990s*. Plymouth: Northcote House, 1994.
Royle, Nicholas. *The Uncanny*. Manchester: Manchester University Press, 2003.
Waller, Alison. *Constructing Adolescence in Fantastic Realism*. New York and London: Routledge, 2009.
Youth Justice Board. 'Child Safety Order'. UK Government Justice website: http://www.justice.gov.uk/youth-justice/courts-and-orders/disposals/child-safety-order (accessed 22 September 2013).

Youth Justice Board. 'Local Child Curfew'. UK Government Justice website: http://www.
    justice.gov.uk/youth-justice/courts-and-orders/disposals/local-child-curfew (accessed
    22 September 2013).
Zipes, Jack. *The Trials and Tribulations of Little Red Riding Hood*. London and New York:
    Routledge, 1993.

NOTES

1. Garner describes *The Owl Service* as 'an expression of the myth found in the Welsh *Math vab Mathonwy*' and an example of his 'present-day activity within myth' (Garner, 1997: 110–1).
2. Cross's postmodern play with signification challenges the typically dualistic structure of fairy tales, for which they are valued by commentators such as Bruno Bettelheim in *The Uses of Enchantment* (1975).

Magic and Maturation: Uses of Magic in Fantasy Fiction

14

Peter Bramwell

Fantasy fiction is set in another world – or a different version of this world – in which magic and the supernatural are treated as realities. My chosen texts come from a specific subset of fantasy: magic realism. Alison Waller defines magic realism with admirable clarity: 'In magic realism ... impossible happenings are incorporated into a worldview that the characters – if not the reader – find natural or acceptable. ... magic realism describes impossible elements as if they were of the same ontological quality as possible events' (Waller, 2009: 21). The hybridity of magic realism means that it partakes of both 'fantasy as a *metaphoric* mode and realism as a *metonymic* mode' (Stephens, 1992: 248) – that is to say, it suggests parallels and resemblances (fantastic metaphor) at the same time as it presents aspects of the real world, 'a slice of life' (realist metonymy).

The framework for the analysis that follows (Box 14.1) is a classification of six uses of magic in fantasy fiction which I proposed in the first edition of this volume, and subsequently developed further (Bramwell, 2009). My approach to literary uses of magic contrasts with Maria Nikolajeva's influential concept of the 'magic code' (1988). Nikolajeva's focus is on delineating a structuralist morphology of the narrative forms of magic in order to define the genre of secondary-world fantasy. My interest lies in identifying functions rather than forms of magic, with the objective of teasing out and interrogating underlying ideology.

BOX 14.1   USES OF MAGIC IN CHILDREN'S FICTION

1   **Maturation**.   Children's fiction uses magic as a metaphor for personal development; the fictional protagonist's maturation offers a model for the reader's own
growth. The magical transitional object (a concept discussed later in this chapter)
becomes dispensable when a maturing character takes ownership of her/his abilities and realizes that a prop is no longer needed.

2   **Imagination**.   Magic is also a metaphor for the child's imagination and capacity
to tell stories. While these abilities are defined and honoured as being characteristic of childhood, they are often presented as being important to preserve and
adapt into adulthood, not least because authors of children's fiction are themselves
imaginative, storytelling adults (which links to self-conscious narration, see number
4 below).

3   **MacGuffin**.   Magic may serve as a plot device, to get into and out of scrapes!
But since magic is never *essential* to driving the plot, its presence upholds a magical
view of reality (see number 6 below). The ambiguities of prophecy and divination
thicken the plot, but they also disrupt its linearity (the cause-and-effect of beginning, middle and end), so they are an aspect of metafiction.

4   **Metafiction**.   Authors of magical fiction may foreground definitions and functions of magic, and 'spell out' analogies between magic and narration, both of which
can play tricks with words and alter perception. Fiction involving magic lends itself
to self-conscious narration, alerting the reader to the artifice of fiction and alternative ways of telling.

5   **Morality**.   Good, evil and false magic are differentiated, though in a more blurred
and complex way in writing for older readers. Good magic tends to be portrayed
as communal, evil as solitary and divisive. Exposing false magic – trickery – lends
credibility to 'true' magic.

6   **World-view**.   Magical thinking need not be outgrown, because magic can be used
in fiction as a vehicle for an outlook on the world, including politics and spirituality.
Magic is defined in terms of this world-view – often magic is used to confound
arbitrary distinctions between natural and supernatural, and to express a sense of
wonder at nature.

The first and second uses of magic correspond to two models of childhood:
respectively, 'childhood as essentially preparatory and developmental, a long
and gradual rehearsal for maturity' and 'childhood as an autonomous part of
life ... enabling the child to be a child' (Hollindale, 1997: 13). The pressures
in favour of a maturational/developmental model and against an imagina-
tive/autonomous construction are strong. A bibliotherapeutic, developmental
imperative often underlies young adult fiction, bolstered by popular understanding of developmental theorists such as Jean Piaget and Erik Erikson. Ever
since J. M. Barrie's *Peter Pan* (1904) exposed the Romantic child as selfish and
lacking in empathy, it has been difficult to resist the rise of developmentalism;
no wonder Peter Hollindale evades the beleaguered term 'Romantic' in favour
of the more neutral 'autonomous'.

In what follows, I apply the six uses of magic when discussing *The Ghost
Drum* (Price, 1987), *Wolf Brother* and *Outcast* (Paver, 2004 and 2007). I do

home in on the first use of magic and the developmental construction of child-hood, but in a critical manner, appraising how limiting or empowering they are for the characters and, by implication, for readers. Jungian individuation offers a particular type of developmental model, and I find *The Ghost Drum* amenable to a Jungian psychoanalytic reading. Ursula Le Guin has argued in her essay, 'The Child and the Shadow' (1974), and shown in her *Earthsea* sequence, that Jungian analytical psychology is relevant to adolescent develop-ment, as presented in fantasy and experienced by its readers. However, there are questions to be asked about the extent to which a therapy developed for middle-aged, middle-class middle Europeans can be applied to fantasy fiction aimed at a different age group and depicting different cultures. When it comes to *Wolf Brother* and *Outcast*, I discern and critique a traditional liberal humanist agenda shaping how character development is portrayed. Finally, I end by reflecting on the appeal of fictional representations of shamanism, and return to constructions of childhood.

The Ghost Drum: Uses of magic

Susan Price's Carnegie medal-winning *The Ghost Drum* (1987) is set in a fantasy Czardom; the protagonist Chingis becomes a witch and shaman, and travels between three worlds: her austere northern home; the Czar's sprawling, opulent palace; and the Ghost World, the world of the dead. An unnamed old witch takes Chingis as a baby and brings her up as her apprentice, training her in herblore and 'the three magics': word magic, the magic of writing and the magic of music. Thus definitions and functions of magic are foregrounded (Uses of Magic 4, in Box 14.1 above).

The way word magic is defined expresses an outlook which has the poten-tial to empower young adults (Uses of Magic 6 and 1). Word magic is potent but mundane, in the literal sense of being of this world rather than supernat-ural. It can be found everywhere and every day, at home and in public places. The sense in which it is 'magical' is that it is tricksy and alters perception. The paradox is that in the process of raising Chingis's (and by implication the reader's) critical language awareness, the old witch subjects her apprentice to the force of rhetoric.

An aspect of the 'word magic' of fantasy is that '"true" or "secret" names command phenomena by expressing essences' (Stephens, 1992: 271). In a way consistent with the definition of word magic in *The Ghost Drum*, *Ghost Song* (1992), the second Ghost World book, bases the magical power of knowing names on their everyday force: 'Others have power over you when they know your name. They call your name, and you are made to look up. And a shaman can use your name for greater magics than that' (Price, 1992: 36).

Born an unnamed slave, Chingis as a young adult (in her twenties, not her teens, in fact) in *The Ghost Drum* spontaneously names herself: *Chingis* is her true name, her name of power. *Chingis* is a variant spelling of *Genghis* (see Magnusson, 1990: 575), indicating Chingis's potential to threaten the Czardom. The name means 'universal' (575), which suggests that Chingis emblematizes a general empowerment of the oppressed. Chingis's mentor, the old witch, is never named. As John Fowles (2000: 33) has said, 'Naming things is always implicitly categorizing and therefore collecting them, attempting to own them.' The unknowability of the old witch's true name means she can never be dominated.

Word magic is also at play in *The Ghost Drum* through self-conscious narration (Uses of Magic 4). The story is told by a cat, which teases the reader about the reliability of its telling, and about what might happen next. Magical prophecy is used in a similar way, disrupting linearity of plot, such as when the old witch proclaims that the new-born slave girl 'will be a Woman of Power, and the son of a Czar will love her' (5). The effects on the reader accord with Stonehill's (1988: 16) observation: 'The most engaging and rewarding self-conscious fictions … are those which manage to combine a story that we care about with reminders that it *is* a story.' *The Ghost Drum*'s self-conscious narration compels readers to be active and reflective in the story's construction. Readers are neither put in their place as spectators, nor do they get lost as participants in the story – that is, subjected – but are attentive and critical co-creators.

As Johnston (1995: 213) points out, since the cat is referred to in the third person ('says the cat'), there is another narrator of *The Ghost Drum*. I would suggest that this overarching narrator, the teller of the story within the story, is in fact Chingis, for the old witch exhorts Chingis to 'remember, it is your duty to write down all you learn, for our sisters and brothers in the future' (62). And so Chingis 'practised her arts and slowly, sentence by sentence, wrote her own book' (63; she continues writing on p. 95). Chingis thereby exercises the power she gains by learning the 'second magic': reading and writing. The old witch explains that there is a 'magic' to reading: 'Every day, people who know nothing more of witchcraft, open books and listen to the talk of the dead. They learn from the dead, and learn to love them, as if they were still alive. That is strong magic' (Price, 1987: 38). Later, when Safa Czarevich is reincarcerated, Chingis's spirit can feel how cramped he is: 'She felt, saw, sensed all this faintly, but clearly – just as we, reading a book, see the scene painted thinly and faintly between our eye and the page' (132–3). The reader is made conscious of the power of reading, while reading.

The third magic that the old witch teaches Chingis, 'the strongest and greatest magic of all', is 'the power of music' (40). Although music magic can be a useful plot device (Uses of Magic 3) – for example, when the old witch sings and drums for a year to make baby Chingis grow to 'a young woman of twenty years' (31) – it is much more than a plot device. The power of music is given the briefest description of the three magics, as it defies and surpasses words. When the old witch chooses to die, she sings 'of every step a spirit must take on the way to the ghost-world' (63).

Music magic is an aspect of the use of magic to convey a world-view (Uses of Magic 6). *The Ghost Drum* offers an outlook on the living world – interconnected, animistic – as well as the afterlife. The interconnectedness of all things is expressed by Chingis thus: 'Nothing can be altered without altering everything that touches it' (97). There are no gods in *The Ghost Drum*, but all people and animals have souls. Chingis can conjure and converse with animal spirits, including a bear-spirit with 'stars of ice – or stars, perhaps – rippling in its fur' (99). The old witch's Baba Yaga-esque hut on chicken legs is a prime example of animism, and it and the ghost drum live on in the Ghost World.

The Ghost Drum celebrates ordinariness and diversity. After Chingis has freed Safa from imprisonment in an onion dome, he discovers that 'the variety and beauty of the world were shocking; and the shock never ended. ... The real, the ordinary, outdid all imagination. ... Difference, difference in everything' (92–3). Thus *The Ghost Drum* evokes a sense of awe and wonder through the perceptions of the characters, without recourse to supernatural explanations. Such a humanist spirituality would fit into a Jungian frame: 'To Jung, religious experience is an authentic psychic event which does not necessarily imply a transcendent reality *external* to the psyche' (Rowland, 1999: 13).

Through following Chingis's training in the three magics, and through the effects of self-conscious narration, adolescent 'readers as thinkers' (Appleyard, 1991) are equipped as critical subjects to decide whether or not to accommodate the ideas encountered in *The Ghost Drum* into their own views of the world.

The Ghost Drum: Shamanism and maturation

Susan Price makes a precise distinction between witches and shamans in *The Ghost Drum*: the former have learned magic and can soul journey, while shamans have gained in addition the ability to travel to the Ghost World, the world of the dead – and to return from it. In this text, shamanism and the shaman's drum function as metaphors for maturation and imagination (Uses of Magic 1 and 2). This section, then, starts by considering the relationship between Chingis's personality and her drum, and then presents a more specifically Jungian analysis of Chingis's shamanism as a metaphor for her development.

The magical object in fantasy can be regarded as a 'transitional object' in two senses of the term. On the one hand, such an object may serve as a developmental prop, which gives comfort at the stage when the child is learning to separate from its parents, but that needs to be outgrown. On the other hand, such magical objects can facilitate transitions in space and time by functioning as a type of portal to other realities; thus the magical object acts as a metaphor for imagination.

The key magical object in Price's novel is the eponymous ghost drum, the defining signifier of the shaman: at the outset, the old witch declares that it is by 'the Ghost-drum at my back [that] you know ... I am a shaman' (Price, 1987: 4). Chingis's drum is a useful, though not essential, means for her to focus her skills. When she does use it for divination, she finds that 'the future [is] not yet set and certain' (65), so that she is not subjected to fatalism, but rather spurred into activity. Later, when she finds that 'The drum tells me nothing' (119), it is because Chingis – and therefore the drum, and not vice versa – cannot anticipate the tricks of her evil antagonist, Kuzma. Chingis is not ruled by her drum; rather, it is a projection of personality, an expression of her will and limitations.

The drum is ultimately dispensable when Chingis's soul achieves its own agency in communion with the other women's souls. Her 'Grandmother', the old witch, commands her, 'Leave the drum, leave the house. We can take nothing from here except courage' (135). Thus it is without the drum that Chingis triumphs in a climactic shape-changing battle with Kuzma. She counters brute force with guile by clinging to him as 'a small, spiked seed-head' and a leech (146). Once more emphasizing her agency, she is 'in her own shape' (147) when she kills him.

The shaman's drum in *The Ghost Drum* is a device to signify the capacities of dream and imagination; its importance is psychological and, as such, the physical object can, indeed must, be put aside. Likewise, in Philip Pullman's *The Amber Spyglass*, Lyra finds, on reaching adolescence and discovering love, that the alethiometer will no longer work for her: in future, truth will be more hard won (Pullman, 2001: 517–20). Xaphania the angel instructs Lyra and Will, and the reader, about travelling between worlds: 'You can learn to do it, as Will's father did. It uses the faculty of what you call imagination. But that does not mean *making things up*. It is a form of seeing' (523). Both novels seem to tell the reader that anyone can travel to other worlds in dream and imagination, and find truth without the interpolation of a magical object.

Imagination – creating images – is essential to personality development in Jungian analytical psychology. Jung's concept of the collective unconscious assumes that all humanity has an instinct for myth making. Universal archetypes from the collective unconscious are imaged in ways modulated by culture and personal experience. Individuals achieve wholeness by integrating into their personalities the 'otherness' of their archetypal images. Susan Price's rendering of shamanism in *The Ghost Drum* offers readers a model for developing subjectivity that is highly amenable to Jungian interpretation.

A Jungian analysis of the fictional shamanism of *The Ghost Drum* seems very apt, for 'Jung ... took a deep interest in shamanism, and his own form of therapy has been likened to shamanic transformation of healer and patient' (Atkinson, 1992: 313). Michele Jamal (1987: 175) describes 'Shamanic awakening' in Jungian terms as 'a time of individuation, when the male and female principles ... come together into an androgynous whole'. Chingis in *The Ghost Drum* achieves personality integration with the old witch, her 'grandmother'; with Safa, her animus; and with Kuzma, her shadow.

According to Jung (1968: 102), the 'grandmother' archetype often 'assumes the attributes of wisdom as well as those of a witch'. This fits Chingis's 'grandmother', who, as we have seen, is a witch who passes on wisdom to her apprentice. Once Chingis's training is complete, the old witch allows herself to die, and so grants Chingis autonomy. Chingis then spends an indeterminate spell alone, an iterative summary telling of her reading, writing and travelling. She observes the great variety of nature, and learns that 'nothing in the world is content to be alone' (Price, 1987: 64).

Chingis is paired with Safa, who could be seen as her animus, a personification of desire who also offers new ways of seeing: Safa is beautiful to Chingis

(69), and from him she 'learn[s] to see anew things which even a witch comes to think of as ordinary' (94). Chingis asserts her independence by taking Safa as 'an apprentice, though ... still so young herself. And ... a male apprentice! And one who was not new-born!' (94). At the same time as affirming her independence, Chingis is entering into a relationship of loving mutual dependence, through which both she and Safa attain their own subjectivity.

A hazard of psychoanalytic criticism is that it becomes, quite literally, egocentric, with all characters being seen as aspects of one. *The Ghost Drum* is resistant to such a solipsistic reading because central to Chingis's character development is her attainment of a role in the community. When she graduates as a shaman, witches from all over the world gather to celebrate (41), but Chingis must still serve, and be recognized by, the non-witch community. She does this by freeing Safa from his confinement, and then by feeding outlaws in the forest. To achieve the latter, she uses her drum and the power of music (the third magic her 'grandmother' has taught her) to summon the spirit of an ageing bear which agrees to give its body in an easy death to feed the starving people. Chingis neither masters spirits, nor is possessed by them: she negotiates with them.

A sense of community, negotiation and shared creativity could be claimed to be characteristics of feminist writing (see Chapter 10 of this volume); these values are not just shown to the reader through Chingis's behaviour but are also enacted in the self-consciousness of the narrative, with its cadences of oral storytelling. As Roberta Trites observes: 'Feminist metafiction often asks the reader to think about the creation of narrative as something that occurs within a community, for the subject manipulating language to create a story usually does so for an audience (i.e., within a dialogue)' (Trites, 1997: 123). The turning point in Chingis's maturation as an individual subject and as an agent in the community occurs, extraordinarily, after her death. The psychic experience of shamanic initiatory death, dismemberment and reconstitution is actualized for Chingis. Kuzma murders her, cuts her up and stakes her down. She finds herself 'already on the other side of the [Ghost World] gate. It was closed and locked behind her. No words would open it. So Chingis knew that she was dead' (Price, 1987: 130). However, her spirit allies with those of three other dead women to return to earth and possess Kuzma. The significance of this is spelt out in Stewig's study of the witch motif in contemporary children's fantasy: 'Thus the four women working together are able to overcome Kuzma's solitary evil' (Stewig, 1995: 123; and see Uses of Magic 5).

Kuzma could be regarded, in a Jungian reading, as Chingis's shadow: such an interpretation is encouraged by Susan Price (personal correspondence, 2002) when she reveals: 'In the earliest versions [of *The Ghost Drum*] Chingis was both heroine and villain, but that gradually changed, and Kuzma became the villain.' Chingis achieves integration with her shadow, by transferring her spirit to Kuzma through a kiss on the mouth. Good and evil are fused, presenting the adolescent reader with moral complexity and doubt, again a characteristic use of magic in young adult fiction.

In *The Ghost Drum*, becoming a shaman is subversive. In the first instance, it is a way of liberating women who are poor. When the old witch first appears, she declares, 'I know all the magics, and am a Woman of Power, yet I was born a slave too' (Price, 1987: 5). As a shaman, Chingis, born in provincial poverty and powerlessness, can challenge the central political authority. The shaman's ability to predict and control her own death, as the old witch does when she has finished training Chingis, defies the claims to godlike power over life and death of the absolute ruler. Safa's choice of death is also a political act. He thereby renounces Czardom, and becomes something greater: 'now he is a shaman and not a Czarevich, I think there are no doors closed against Safa that he cannot open' (164). He dies to be with Chingis: love triumphs over earthly power, and over death itself.

Millicent Lenz (2001) argues that protagonists in contemporary fantasy, such as Pullman's Lyra and Will, mix and exchange traditional patterns of 'male' heroic quest and 'female' initiation. This is also true of *The Ghost Drum*: it is Chingis who goes on the heroic quest, and conversely Safa who emerges from confinement; Chingis's rescue of prince Safa from the tower is a clear reversal of fairy tale gender roles. Chingis is humbly born, and effectively orphaned when the old witch takes her away to give her a name and train her in magic. However, Chingis differs from the 'male' heroic pattern in significant ways: though she overcomes an evil adversary, she also merges with him as her Jungian shadow; though she restores justice and harmony, she does not return home, but finds a new community with her kindred spirits in the Ghost World.

Whereas shamanism is presented as being empowering in *The Ghost Drum*, its successors in the Ghost World series interrogate disempowering aspects of shamanism. In *Ghost Song*, Kuzma seems to resent having no choice about becoming a shaman, about losing his childhood, and about being alone. Malyuta says of his child Ambrosi, 'More treasure I have here than lies in all the Czar's storehouses!' (Price, 1992: 45), and will not allow him to become Kuzma's apprentice. Haunted by Kuzma, Ambrosi makes his own ghost drum, and becomes a hypnotic storyteller and singer. Finally, Kuzma gives Ambrosi the ultimatum of becoming a shaman or being constantly tormented by spirits. Ambrosi resists becoming a shaman to the end, choosing a third way – death.

Shingebiss, in *Ghost Dance* (1994), at first chooses not to become a shaman, because a shaman cannot change the despoliation of the Northlands (Price, 1994: 23). Only when she fails to influence the Czar as she would wish does she change her mind. She enters the Ghost World independently, without tuition: 'Strength and power rushed through her' (149). This stirring triumph for the ideal of young adult agency might be seen as coming at the expense of verisimilitude, though, as it breaks out of the cultural context of a shamanic apprenticeship paradigm.

In all, applying the Uses of Magic to *The Ghost Drum* and its sequels has enabled us to see that Susan Price's Ghost World trilogy succeeds in creating nuanced portrayals of a shamanic culture and adolescent personal development, but the cultural clash between the two means that the texts are pervaded by instabilities. Such instabilities would seem to be inherent to fantasy, since fantasy's modus operandi is the yoking together through metaphor of two different things: an alternative world and the reader's world. Far from being a flaw, this is a strength of the fantasy genre, as it liberates the reader by opening up space for interpretation.

Wolf Brother and *Outcast*: World-view and personal development

Michelle Paver's best-selling Chronicles of Ancient Darkness series is set in the Stone Age, with an imaginary geography based on north-western Europe. As in *The Ghost Drum*, shamans feature prominently: Clan Mages are capable of soul journeying and soul retrieval, foresight and farsight, while the hero Torak is exceptional in his world in discovering he can spirit-walk into animals. Of the six volumes in Paver's series, I have chosen to focus my analysis on the first, *Wolf Brother* (2004), and the fourth, *Outcast* (2007). I shall discuss the world-view expressed in *Wolf Brother* (Uses of Magic 6) and the protagonist's maturation (Uses of Magic 1). *Outcast* is remarkable for its portrayal of adolescent disassociation and depression.

Wolf Brother serves as an excellent example of magic in fantasy fiction being integrated with a world-view, because the shamanic practices of Clan Mages and Torak's ability to spirit-walk into animals only make sense in relation to an animistic cosmology. According to the prehistoric beliefs that Michelle Paver imagines or reconstructs in *Wolf Brother*, every individual partakes of three souls: the name-soul, the clan-soul and the world-soul Nanuak. The world-soul 'link[s] to all other living things: tree and bird, hunter and prey, river and rock' (Paver, 2004: 12). The hunter-gatherers of the story address the world-soul before taking anything, and there is a prevailing ecological ethic of 'not wasting a thing. That was the age-old pact between the hunters and the World Spirit. Hunters must treat prey with respect, and in return the Spirit would send more prey' (42). Constructing a prehistoric world-view in this way doubtless also reflects our current environmentalist concerns and yearnings. More subtly, something of Paver's scientific background may come through when she describes the world-soul as being 'like a great river that never ends. Every living thing has a part of it inside them. ... Sometimes a special part of it forms, like foam on the river. When it does, it's incredibly powerful' (102). This comparison is highly redolent of the river image the physicist David Bohm (1980) uses for his theory that matter (life and non-life) and consciousness are aspects of a holomovement of limitless dimensions.

As fascinating as its cosmology may be, *Wolf Brother* is not an anthropological treatise but a novel, in which the world-view is bound up with a thrilling plot and engaging characters. In a quest narrative typical of the fantasy genre, Torak must solve a riddle and go on a dangerous journey to acquire three artefacts and save his clan. He travels through mixed terrain – forest, river, cave, glacier – in a story packed with incident and cliffhangers. Sometimes the style is the staccato of a thriller, for example: 'Torak had to make a fire. It was a race between him and the fever. The prize was his life' (Paver, 2004: 25). Here short, simple sentences, the first with high modality, the other two existential, convey the urgency. Yet in the midst of the quest, Torak becomes more reflective about his people's beliefs. By implication, the child or adolescent reader may be constructed as similarly curious and questioning about spirituality. Furthermore, a society in the distant past is idealized as having a coherent belief system that our current society may seem to lack.

Torak's character develops through the quest (Uses of Magic 1). He acts heroically, but as circumstances dictate he has to use guile rather than force. Torak's companion Renn learns Magecraft from her Clan Mage, but is resistant to a shamanic calling, preferring to hunt, using her skill as an archer. The same age as Torak ('twelve winters'), she propels him on the quest. Rather like Hermione Grainger in the Harry Potter books, Renn proves more knowledgeable than the ostensible hero at crucial moments in the plot. Torak also has a mentor figure rather like Dumbledore (and so, ultimately, like Dr Arnold in *Tom's Brown's Schooldays* [Hughes, 1857]): Fin-Kedinn, leader of the Raven Clan, who spells out the lessons at the end of the book. Torak's moral growth hinges climactically on a terrible choice between going after Renn or preserving himself; as Fin-Kedinn makes clear, the test is not 'whether you could find the third piece of the Nanuak. But whether you could risk it for a friend' (Paver, 2004: 188). Such overt didacticism may provoke resistance from some readers, who might prefer to be left to deduce – and evaluate – the moral of the tale for themselves. The Western cult of individualism is cast back into prehistory, for Torak's agency is paramount: he has to act when no longer hearing the voice of his dead father, and 'The World Spirit would only help him if he tried to help himself' (215). Such liberal humanist certainty about human nature and personal development being constant whatever the context can be criticized as an 'ahistorical essentialising of adolescence across time and culture' (Waller, 2009: 71).

In the fourth volume of the series, *Outcast* (Paver, 2007), Torak and Renn are clearly adolescents, physically and psychologically. Physical signifiers of their pubescence are prominent: 'Torak thought she looked older than her thirteen summers, and beautiful' (31), and Renn notices Torak's muscular body and breaking voice. Renn's Clan Mage refuses to help her interpret signs, on the grounds that 'Your first moon bleed has brought a fearsome increase in your power – but it is raw, untried!' (111), circumscribing Renn's emerging womanhood with taboo. Renn is torn between childhood and adulthood; when Fin-Kedinn tells her, 'You're no longer a child, Renn. You're old enough to make your own choices', she thinks, 'No I'm not! ... I need you to help me! Tell me what to do!' (116).

Torak is cast out of the clan because in defeating his foes, the Soul Eaters, in the previous adventure, he became too much like them. As an outcast, he is 'as one dead. Cut off from everyone. Hunted like prey' (20). Initially, Torak copes well. The Forest, which Torak honours, helps him to survive; willows whisper, '*You belong here. In the Forest*' (44, original italics). Torak's animistic world-view makes this more than literary personification: in accordance with Todorov's (1970) definition of the fantastic, the reader hesitates between interpretations; or, as Waller puts it, 'alternative beliefs and practices can provide the basis for readings of the fantastic that are not purely metaphorical' (Waller, 2009: 73).

Torak slides inexorably into depression, realizing that 'There is something inside me I can't control' (Paver, 2007: 65). He forgets how to hunt, how to speak with Wolf, how to listen to the Forest. He is driven east to Lake Axehead in an episode that is, in Nicolette Jones's words, 'dark and hallucinatory' (Jones, 2007). Swirling mists, shifting walkways and sinister totems disorient Torak: 'in this nebulous half-world which was neither land nor lake, he was losing his very self' (Paver, 2007: 100). The liminal setting impinges on and reflects Torak's psyche, and represents the adolescent's uncertainty about individual identity and a role in society.

Cast out and clanless, Torak is not friendless: Renn takes great risks to help him. She is impelled to employ the gift for Magecraft that she has previously resisted and denied. Using locks of Torak's hair and howling a charm in the face of a storm, she invokes 'the power of the guardian of all Ravens' (145) and sends it after Torak. As with Chingis and Safa in *The Ghost Drum*, a reversal of traditionally gendered fantasy roles takes place, with Renn being the active hero and Torak being enclosed in a rite of passage. Thanks to Renn's magical actions from afar, Torak adopts a pair of fledgling ravens, thereby distracting him from his self-absorption and taking him out of himself. He starts to recall offerings, words for things, tracking skills. The Forest forgives him, as 'trees live longer than people, and are slower to anger' (Paver, 2007: 159). Reconciled with Wolf and the pack, Torak's mood swings to a manic high: 'a thrill of pure happiness. … For a moment he felt his world-soul reaching out to the world-soul of every living creature, like threads of golden gossamer floating on the wind' (169).

Torak's breakdown and recovery are described in terms of his people's beliefs, but the reader is given every encouragement to draw parallels with the challenges of adolescence in current society, of coping with depressive feelings of incapacity, alienation and loss of identity. As ever, Fin-Kedinn explains things: 'Growing up can be a kind of soul-sickness, Torak. The name-soul wants to be strongest, so it fights the clan-soul telling it what to do' (252) – that is to say, growing up involves coming to some accommodation between what the individual wants and what society expects. So *Outcast* presents depression as a phase from which the adolescent recovers – not as the life-long debilitating illness that it can be for some people – and offers clear explanations and solutions, again idealizing a past society that has an enviably coherent, magical outlook on the world. While one might see this as too neat and comforting, it is still radical for a fantasy novel to create such a sustained and sympathetic portrayal of mental illness.

Conclusion

In this chapter, I have attempted to show that a classification of six Uses of Magic provides a single coherent methodology for analysing the diverse characteristics of children's fantasy fiction. I have also chosen to concentrate on one use of magic in particular – magic as a metaphor for maturation (Uses of Magic 1) – in order to identify and interrogate the ideologies of child and adolescent development embodied in the texts. What has become especially apparent is that there are tensions inherent in fantasy's metaphorical mode, an uneasy balancing act between evoking an alien culture and relating to the implied reader.

The three texts I have considered all feature shamanic figures and abilities, and are part of a wider trend of representing shamanism in children's fiction (Bramwell, 2009: chapter 3), so it may be worth considering the significance of this trend. In part, it could be symptomatic of a post-secular yearning for authentic spirituality. However, the cultural specificity and otherness of shamanism imply that it is largely elusive in the reader's own modern, Western context. Still, there is an appeal to current ecological sensibilities in the romanticized picture of shamans wasting nothing and walking lightly on the earth, though they are also portrayed as fatalistically impotent in the face of environmental exploitation and devastation (as in Susan Price's *Ghost Dance*).

It is possible to see the roles of writers and readers as shamanic. Mongush Kenin-Lopsan (1997: 110) detects a narrative syntax to shamanic performances: 'we see that the seance is a complex and well-structured event, where one can discern a prologue, exposition, plot, author's digression, culmination, denouement, and epilogue'. Furthermore, Kenin-Lopsan's overview is that 'shamans told their listeners of their impressions and actions. It might be said that shamans created worlds through words.' Creating 'worlds through words' is just what writers and their readers do, so that shamanism may be seen as a metaphor for the creative acts of writing and reading. Maria Nikolajeva (1988: 35) observes that 'Secondary worlds in fantasy are projections of ... particular authors' models of the world. They are also products of creative imagination and as such a matter of belief.' Each reading experience, whether of a realist or fantasy or hybrid magic realist text, generates a unique virtual world from the dialogue between the reader's outlook and the author's. Readers accept, reject or negotiate with the ideas they encounter.

In my negotiation with *The Ghost Drum*, *Wolf Brother* and *Outcast*, I have found a developmental construction of childhood predominant, though the outcomes are not entirely conventional. The adolescents in these novels are inducted into a culture, but it is a culture of resistance to the powerful and the power-hungry – the Czar and the Soul Eaters – and, by extension, any kind of political and religious hegemony. The appearance of magic in literature can be argued to be inherently subversive: 'Not just for characters within fictions, but for authors and audiences as well, it is possible that any kind of magic will be problematic because of what it might symbolize: the subversion of religion, rationality, patriarchy, sanity, and science' (Stephens, 2003: 200). Furthermore, the more realistic the fictional evocation of historical, counter-historical or prehistoric cultures, the more obvious it becomes that personal development (whether Jungian, liberal humanist or otherwise) is an incongruous imposition, a culturally specific construction and not an eternal verity of human nature.

WORKS CITED AND FURTHER READING

Children's Books

Hughes, Thomas. *Tom Brown's Schooldays*. Barcelona: Fabbri, 1992; first published 1857.
Paver, Michelle. *Wolf Brother*. London: Orion, 2004.
Paver, Michelle. *Outcast*. London: Orion, 2007.
Price, Susan. *The Ghost Drum*. London: Faber and Faber, 1987.
Price, Susan. *Ghost Song*. London: Faber, 1992.
Price, Susan. *Ghost Dance: The Czar's Black Angel*. London: Faber, 1994.
Pullman, Philip. *The Amber Spyglass*. London: Scholastic, 2001; first published 2000.

Critical Texts

Appleyard, Josep. *Becoming a Reader*. Cambridge: Cambridge University Press, 1994; first published 1991.
Atkinson, Jane. 'Shamanisms Today'. *Annual Review of Anthropology*, 21 (1992), 307–30.
Bohm, David. *Wholeness and the Implicate Order*. London: Routledge, 1994; first published 1980.
Bramwell, Peter. *Pagan Themes in Modern Children's Fiction*. Basingstoke: Palgrave Macmillan, 2009.
Fowles, John. *The Tree*. London: Random House, 2000.
Hollindale, Peter. *Signs of Childness in Children's Books*. Stroud: Thimble, 1997.
Jamal, Michele. *Shape Shifters: Shaman Women in Contemporary Society*. Harmondsworth: Penguin, 1987.
Johnston, Rosemary Ross. 'The Special Magic of the Eighties: Shaping Words and Shape-Shifting Words'. *Children's Literature in Education*, 26.4 (1995), 211–17.
Jones, Nicolette. 'Review of *Outcast* by Michelle Paver'. *The Sunday Times*, 16 September 2007.
Jung, C. G. *The Archetypes and the Collective Unconscious*, trans. R. F. C. Hull. Princeton, NJ: Princeton University Press, 1980; first pub. 1968.
Kenin-Lopsan, Mongush. 'Tuvan Shamanic Folklore'. In Marjorie Balzer (ed.), *Shamanic Worlds: Rituals and Lore of Siberia and Central Asia* (pp. 110–52). New York: M. E. Sharpe, 1997.
Le Guin, Ursula. 'The Child and the Shadow' (1974). *The Language of the Night: Essays on Fantasy and Science Fiction* (pp. 49–60) London: The Women's Press, 1989.
Lenz, Millicent. 'Philip Pullman'. In Peter Hunt and Millicent Lenz, *Alternative Worlds in Fantasy Fiction* (pp. 122–69). London: Continuum, 2001.
Magnusson, Magnus (ed.). *Chambers Biographical Dictionary*, 5th edn. Edinburgh: Chambers Harrap, 1990.
Nikolajeva, Maria. *The Magic Code: The Use of Magical Patterns in Fantasy for Children*. Stockholm: Almqvist & Wiksell, 1988.
Rowland, Susan. *C. G. Jung and Literary Theory: The Challenge from Fiction*. Basingstoke: Palgrave Macmillan, 1999.
Stephens, John. *Language and Ideology in Children's Fiction*. London: Longman, 1992.
Stephens, John. 'Witch-Figures in Recent Children's Fiction: The Subaltern and the Subversive'. In Ann Lawson Lucas (ed.), *The Presence of the Past in Children's Literature* (pp. 195–202). Westport, CT: Greenwood, 2003.
Stewig, John. 'The Witch Woman: A Recurring Motif in Recent Fantasy Writing for Young Readers'. *Children's Literature in Education*, 26.2 (1995), 119–33.
Stonehill, Brian. *The Self-Conscious Novel: Artifice in Fiction from Joyce to Pynchon*. Philadelphia: University of Pennsylvania Press, 1988.

Todorov, Tzvetan. *The Fantastic: A Structural Approach to a Literary Genre*, trans. Richard Howard. New York: Cornell University Press, 1995; first published 1970.

Trites, Roberta Seelinger. *Waking Sleeping Beauty: Feminist Voices in Children's Novels*. Iowa City: University of Iowa Press, 1997.

Waller, Alison. *Constructing Adolescence in Fantastic Realism*. New York and London: Routledge, 2009.

Supermen, Cyborgs, Avatars and Geeks: Technology and the Human in Contemporary Young Adult Fiction

Richard Shakeshaft

15

KEY TEXTS

M. T. Anderson, *Feed* (2002)
B. R. Collins, *Gamerunner* (2011)
Cory Doctorow, *Little Brother* (2008)
Marissa Meyer, *Cinder* (2012)
Robin Wasserman, *Skinned* (2009)

We only have to look at the technology surrounding us to know that the future is already here, but as we still talk and read to acquire knowledge, rather than downloading information directly to our brains, and human bodies still age and succumb to mortal illnesses, we might remain confident that the future is still around the corner. Such blurred distinctions are central to technology's representation in Young Adult (YA) fiction and, as technology moves forward, yesterday's science fiction becomes today's science fact. In 1991 cyborg theorist Donna Haraway wrote that the 'boundary between science fiction and social reality is an optical illusion' (149) and reading contemporary YA novels alongside a magazine such as *Wired*, reporting on how technological innovation is shaping the world, shows this remains true.

The 'always on' members of Generation Y, or the Millennials, seem to accept the reality of the virtual world created by their use of the Internet and social media as the norm; they have known little else. Toddlers lose the right to 'screen time', or playing games on tablets and watching cartoons, for misdemeanours, and adults are increasingly seeing Internet access as a utility on a par with water and electricity. Social psychologists, including Sherry Turkle (1995, 2005, 2011) and Aleks Krotoski (2013), have been examining the change in the relationship between humans and the technology surrounding them for some years, and Nicholas Carr's *The Shallows* (2010) looks at the effect of Internet use on the human brain. But there is much to be learnt about the human/technology relationship through YA speculative fiction, as it holds a mirror up to society and offers glimpses of possible futures.

Writing in 2005, Noga Applebaum discussed the new millennium's adult anxieties about information technology. Adults acknowledge that while it 'contributes to their children's education', they also 'fear that online activities might expose them to harmful influences and even put them in physical danger' (251ff.). She noted the 'technological gap existing between parents and their children' (252), which has resulted in contemporary YA literature reflecting an adult ambivalence towards young people's use of technology. In contrast to this, publishers realized technology's marketing potential and titles and cover designs alluded to technology even when novels included only a limited use of it. Applebaum suggested the books featuring technology often portrayed the dangers of using it, giving the reader a didactic message about their online behaviour.

While these remain concerning issues for parents and teachers, as technology has become increasingly prevalent in society and the early millennium's teenage users have become adults, there has been a massive shift towards its acceptance. Societies have started to respond with new laws as technology-based test cases have emerged, and international security agencies have become focused on cyberthreats as monolithic governmental institutions attempt to catch up with technological developments. Individuals around the world continue to embrace technology: Facebook had 1.28 billion active users in March 2014 (Facebook, 2014), and '44.9m Brits surfed the web' on their PCs with over 34.4 million users accessing the Internet via mobile devices in January 2014 (Azevedo, 2014). Beyond statistics, the English language also reflects technology's influence as brands like Google and Skype become verbs. Despite technology's wider acceptance, contemporary novels have not stopped warning readers about its dangers. However, the situations presented have, generally, moved on from the novelty of using contemporary technology; technology's scope is extended speculatively to create dystopian worlds that force readers to reconsider their unquestioning acceptance of the technology, and possible technologies, surrounding them.

Describing a world as dystopian can only be done from a contemporary perspective, and the use of technology to create such worlds in today's YA novels is often built on underlying fears about technology, usually brought into relief only when issues such as cyberbullying, child pornography, online suicide pacts and cyberterrorism make the news. However, beyond these headlines, there are more mundane recurring features in fictional dystopian worlds which can be seen in the real world. Common fears about technology's infiltration involve consumerism, as in Google's personalized advertisements based on recent searches, or Amazon's algorithmically generated recommendations after similar purchases. There is also the fear of the attenuation of humankind's relationship with the natural world, as naturally grown food is replaced by manufactured products, an issue reflected in debates around genetically modified foodstuffs. In fiction, the environment is often severely damaged by irresponsible human behaviour and technology, and this issue has been discussed openly in reality for decades but, in fiction and reality, technology is also looked to for solutions. In novels there is frequently the sense of society's, or at least its technology's, need to borrow from human culture in such ways as taking names from classical mythology, alluding to religious ideas or quoting literature, possibly in an attempt to make technology appear less threatening or to imbue it with greater respectability.

Just as technology and people's fear of it can be seen at the root of dystopian worlds, technology also offers ways to improve society, but it is often in the quest for such utopias that technology is prioritized and the vicious circle returns to the dystopian world. However, if technology can be understood, it can empower those who grasp its potential. Applebaum discusses the Internet's political might and power to enable 'marginalised groups, which were formerly oppressed by either state or culture, to network globally and make their voices heard' (2005: 259); as a group which has no political voice in society, children and teenagers who understand the Internet's potential are offered a free public platform, which can respond more quickly than traditional powerful institutions to developing events, to make themselves heard.[1]

It is the bringing together of human and technology which I use to explore this continually evolving field, since one area of technological development less prominent in modern society's consciousness is the use of technology within, or as part of, the human body. While prostheses – whether compensating for physical limitations with artificial limbs or extending a human's connectedness through a smartphone – are readily accepted, embedding such technologies or thinking about the human brain as computer-readable bits and bytes, rather than biological neurons and synapses, is shied away from. However, this union of humanity and technology, and the blurring and transgression of boundaries between them, has a long literary history and can be seen in contemporary YA novels through the posthuman (see Box 15.1).

BOX 15.1   A BRIEF HISTORY OF THE POSTHUMAN

Despite 'posthuman' being used adjectivally since 1916, the cyberpunk author Bruce Sterling first used 'posthuman' as a noun and a concept in his 1985 novel *Schismatrix*, labelling two competing posthuman species using technology and biology, respectively, to enhance themselves; the posthuman has been developed as both a concept and a term by writers and theorists since. The familiar 'post-' prefix has come to suggest enhancement and progress in that which will come after the human but, like today's technology meaning we are living in the future while also waiting for it, the notion of the posthuman has existed for three millennia and ongoing technological developments mean we are still waiting for the upgrade to Human v2.0.

Arguably, the earliest posthuman can be seen in the Judeo-Christian idea of the golem in Psalm 139, and the Greco-Roman stories of Pygmalion's statue and the bronze giant Talos. However, it was in the nineteenth century, as the novel became established and the Industrial Revolution's technology shaped thinking, that more familiar literary posthumans were first seen. In particular, E.T.A. Hoffmann's automaton in *The Sandman* (1816) and the animation of the monster in Mary Shelley's *Frankenstein* (1818) emphasize the fusion of technical prowess and the human, blurring the distinction between fictional creations and what the age's developments made possible.

J. P. Telotte suggests that the inter-war period (1918 to 1939), when technology was 'constantly reshaping our world, reworking our culture, even modifying our humanity' (1999: 1), influenced literary posthuman creations. Isaac Asimov's 1940s robot stories subsequently demonstrate a concerned response to technology's rise as he refutes the threat posed by stronger, more intelligent artificial life forms through his original three (but later expanded) Laws of Robotics in his 1942 short story, 'Runaround'. The rise of the robot can be seen in the real-world era of space travel in Manfred Clynes and Nathan Kline's 1960 concept of the 'cyborg'. The name blends the technology of the automatic communication and control systems of 'cybernetics' with nature's 'organism', and was coined to describe the benefits of 'altering man's bodily functions to meet the requirements of extraterrestrial environments' (26). As such alterations push the human's boundaries, the cyborg's purpose is to push the limits of humanity, but the process is seen as going beyond the Darwinian idea of the body adapting to its environment, since Clynes and Kline argued it would be 'possible to achieve this to some degree *without alteration of heredity* by suitable biochemical, physiological, and electronic modifications of man's existing modus vivendi' (26). Thus, in the twentieth-century cyborg, what could be seen as the nineteenth-century technology-based posthuman is inverted by making the biological the starting point, and the human is enhanced without changing that which makes them human. Questions of identity – a common trope in children's literature – and where a human/technological hybrid might fit into society are found throughout contemporary novels, but this is an established idea: in 1818 Frankenstein's monster showed its awareness of its otherness and yearning to be human.

Posthuman bodies

When the variety of posthumans in literature and reality is considered, it is clear that posthumans can be classified according to the way they were created, manufactured or born, and the extent of the humans' acceptance of the technology, or the technology's desire to become human. Mischa Peters (2003) provides a helpful foundation for exploring different types of posthuman, as she considers whether the technology is internalized or externalized and whether the human or technology is prioritized. Her posthuman body types include:

- the *enhanced body*, in which human abilities are extended through internalized technology such as an implant;

- the *modified body*, in which the human is dependent on external technologies, as in a cyborg;
- and the *cyberbody*, in which the human is prioritized but exists in a digital form outside their organic body.

I have extended these ideas and suggest an additional type of posthuman:

- the *geek*, in whom humanity and technology have equal importance, with their technology having moved from being external to becoming internalized through their understanding, and not mere use, of it.

While Peters uses real-world and adult fiction examples to demonstrate her posthumans, I use contemporary YA novels to exemplify the different types and consider the character of the geek. Although these definitions provide a helpful theoretical framework to approach the posthuman, there is a necessary fluidity in the definitions brought about by the acceptance and/or fear of technology's use.

Seeing the posthuman as an entity emphasizes that, as with Hoffman and Shelley's proto-posthumans, Peters's posthumans are created or manufactured, not born. In YA fiction it is regularly the adults' decision, both individually and as representatives of otherwise faceless societies, to enhance their children. This act delineates traditional power boundaries seen within much of children's literature, reflecting real-world hierarchies where adults have economic, political and social power. While there are instances of children taking responsibility for their own modification, these are infrequent and the children's actions challenge societal norms and are made for selfish reasons. The fictional worlds of posthuman stories are dystopian and it becomes the teenage protagonists' quest to save themselves and their loved ones. In contrast to the manufactured posthumans, the geek is likely to be a natural creation, and the absence of authority exerted through technology gives geeks a powerful social and political position, as they neither fear technology nor are subservient to it. However, such posthumans generally accept this responsibility, choosing to act in the interests of saving society, rather than acting egotistically; they appear to understand technology's dangers and attempt to save the world from dystopian fates otherwise awaiting it.

The enhanced body

Science fiction readers will be familiar with characters whose human abilities are extended by technology and in whom technology is prioritized and internalized through an implant to create an enhanced body. In M. T. Anderson's *Feed* (2002), the feed is an Internet-like network through which its users communicate, shop and research but which is accessed by thought. Some 50 years before the feed was available, the teenage narrator Titus explains, people 'had to use their hands and their eyes [because] computers were all outside the body'; he uses a simile to describe such an antiquated system as being 'like if you carried your lungs in a briefcase and opened it to breathe' (47).

Although the comparison of feed access to breathing might seem extreme, it is not dissimilar to society's perception of the Internet as a key utility and the compulsiveness with which people check in on their social media. Technology's internalization might reflect a biological enhancement, as 'the feed is tied in to everything. Your body control, your emotions, your memory' (170). However, the way it is used demonstrates a move away from the human towards a reliance on technology, as the feed's users compensate for their lack of school-learnt vocabulary by checking words in their 'English-to-English wordbook' (23); notably, 'dictionary' is replaced by a compound noun of simpler words. As the characters lose the need to use their brain, they become objects – the generic term for a boy is 'unit' and a girl, 'unette' – and, as in a panopticon, they are viewed by the unseen, but all-seeing, corporations managing society to generate revenue. Indeed, after a hacker attack, the first thing Titus feels is 'no credit' (43), turning money into an abstract sensation or emotion, and at the novel's conclusion he feels his placed orders 'in circulation all around me like blood in my veins' and the products 'winging their way toward me' (294), showing consumerism keeping him alive.

Despite feed users being objects within the consumerist process, there are displays of more human challenges to the system, such as Coca-Cola's promotion whereby 'if you talked about the great taste of Coca-Cola to your friends like a thousand times, you got a free six-pack of it'. By 'being like, *Coke, Coke, Coke, Coke* for about three hours' the teenage characters get a year's supply and 'rip off the corporations' which they find 'a funny idea' (172). While this is a subversive act, it is only within the restrictive constraints of their corporately controlled materialistic world and, after discussing Coke's merits, they succumb to the advertising and buy Coke to assuage their thirst. Another indication of the characters' humanity is the word 'diad' (12) describing a unit and unette in a relationship, but in a technologically rich society the word, through its homophony with 'diode', connotes electronics and being part of a system.

Titus's conventional, technology-accepting family had his feed installed early in life, empowering him by giving him access to information that his society believes he needs. However, his girlfriend, Violet, had the feed installed later in life and is home-schooled away from corporate sponsorship by her father, who only uses the feed through outdated externalized technology. Her parents' choice for her not to have the feed installed is an act of rebellion against society but, as a teenager, Violet wants to fit in and has the feed installed. Nevertheless, she subsequently rebels by trying to confuse it about her interests to make it impossible to predict her consumer choices. Her parents' decision, and her refusal to embrace it, makes her hold on what it means to be human, or her human-ness, more strongly; and, by sending Titus a 'full feed-sim' (245) of her sensations when her hacked feed malfunctions and she nears death, she tries to make him understand her human suffering, which would – if he understands – implicitly make him more human. Although Maria Nikolajeva argues that he remains 'unchanged and reduced to the half-robot he was before he met Violet' (2010: 88), there is a sense of his character maturing, albeit only within the restrictions of the novel's dystopia in which even emotions are commodified. While Violet could be criticized for resorting to technology, rather than describing the effects of her malfunctioning verbally, by using it as a means of communication with which Titus identifies she uses the technology to her benefit, to demonstrate her human credibility rather than accepting or relying on it as other users do. Sharing sensations and experiences in a virtual world is more frequently seen in the cyberbody, but Violet's use of technology raises the question of whether an individual's experiences and identity can be preserved when transferred, or uploaded, from a biological to an electronic medium.

In the real world, scientists, product designers and programmers strive to make technology more human and accessible, but through their embracing of technology humans seem to be becoming more like machines, as can be seen in Violet and Titus. While she is trying to increase the feed-using Titus's humanness by sharing her real physical experiences, the human Violet is reduced to percentages as each chapter title in the novel's final section charts her physical deterioration in a measurable way. Likewise, when she tries to think of 'living to the full' she realizes her ideas are all from the 'opening credits of sitcoms' and asks 'What am I, without the feed?' (217). However, her acknowledgement that her identity has been created by the feed indicates that her humanity is still dominant since, unlike Titus, her technology is neither wholly nor successfully internalized or prioritized, and she questions its influence in the same way as a reader is challenged by technology's influence on society.

The modified body

Peters describes a modified body as a cyborg in which technology is prioritized, but seen as a commodity to the human and therefore external. The eponymous protagonist of Marissa Meyer's *Cinder* (2012), based loosely on the Cinderella story, is a female teenage mechanic who was made into a cyborg after being saved from a fire as a baby. A chance meeting with the Commonwealth's Prince lays the foundations for her to discover her true identity and why she was saved.

The novel's opening indicates both her human and mechanical elements: 'The screw through Cinder's ankle had rusted, the engraved marks worn to a mangled circle. Her knuckles ached from forcing the screwdriver into the joint as she struggled to loose the screw one gritting turn after another' (3). While the human aching and struggling suggest physical weakness, she is removing the foot as she has outgrown it and wants to fit a larger replacement. The technology is therefore dominant and forcing her actions, and it is the subservient human aspect of her character wanting the comfort of the correctly sized foot. As she disconnects the wires they spark and 'her retina display helpfully informed her with blinking red text that she was losing connection to the limb' (6). Despite technology's dominance reporting on her body's condition, the message is unnecessary and the description of it as 'helpful' is sarcastic, a trait allied with humans, not technology. Sarcasm is also used to demonstrate technology's aspirations to become increasingly human when Cinder helps her android friend to use it in conversation, leaving another human confused, as technology is not expected to present ambiguities.

Although considering different body types is helpful in starting to explore varieties of posthumans, the categorizations are not always clearly defined, and aspects of Cinder's technology are internalized, such as when an 'orange light flicker[s] in the corner of her vision' (10) when someone lies. This ability extends her human capabilities, but she is not in control of it, rather 'her optobionics had picked up on something, though she didn't know what' (10). Although many of the natural body's functions are carried out unconsciously, they are the processes used to keep the body alive, rather than extending its abilities. Being 'used to the little orange light [because] it came up all the time' (11) demonstrates a human cynicism and acceptance of human fallibility. Her technology's dominance can also be seen when her 'netlink took over, as it did in moments when she couldn't think for herself. Searching, connecting, feeding information to her she didn't want' (50): rather than simply being a commodity, the technology does not tire, and the active verbs emphasize this in contrast to tiredness as a human weakness. However, her ever-present technology also serves her human side: when she is attacked and collapses, 'red warnings flashed across her vision until, in an act of cyborg self-preservation, her brain forced her to shut down' (68). In this there is a sense of the first of Asimov's Laws of Robotics (a robot cannot, through inaction, allow a human to come to harm), as retaliating would result in greater injuries and the calculated option is to stop fighting. While the technology could simply be protecting itself, the description of the process demonstrates a biological/technological blurring and a wholly entwined relationship in her self, as it is her brain, the biological control, which causes her body to 'shut down', an action associated with computers.

Despite this relationship, it is Cinder's human nature that is inescapable, through which the reader is encouraged to consider technology's status critically. While Cinder's society's humans view cyborgs suspiciously, the cyborgs are encouraged to believe their existence is a gift from the scientists who have given them a second chance at life. However, Cinder's human side does not accept this and her sarcasm can be seen again when she fakes a gasp while discussing opposition to cybernetics and brain–machine interfaces, interrupting, 'No. Who would be opposed to *that*?' (176). While the reader may see the implant in *Feed* as damaging a human brain, the life-saving process of creating the cyborg is destructive to the body and Cinder's feelings towards cybernetics might be understood through a narrative comment: 'If Cinder's body had ever been predisposed to femininity, it had been ruined by whatever the surgeons had done to her, leaving her with a stick-straight figure. Too angular. Too boyish. Too awkward with her heavy artificial leg' (34).

Through her body, her identity is irrecoverably altered by the choices made by scientists to save her life and she has to accept this. As Titus's society expects people to have the feed installed, so she had no say in being made posthuman. However, in a full body scan, a doctor reveals that Cinder is lucky, as her 'reproductive system is almost untouched', when 'lots of female cyborgs are left infertile because of the invasive procedures' (116). Despite technology's importance in her existence, an important aspect of being human – her ability to procreate – remains, and through this, technology is left in the service of the human. Nevertheless, the scientists' decisions are based on creating a particular type of cyborg: first, they have decided not to give her tear ducts so she cannot cry – something her wicked stepmother believes prevents her from being human because, as she announces, 'Humans cry' (279); and second, they prevent her from blushing by having her brain monitor her body temperature and regulate it more closely than a human's (117). Having scientists make these decisions for her suggests a god-like role with the concomitant negative connotations of the fictional creation of Frankenstein's monster, and the real-world decisions made by doctors and parents about intersex babies' gender assignment.

Peters sees the modified body's technology as 'offering something to the user, but at a certain price' (53), and Cinder exemplifies the emotional cost through her rejection by her human stepmother and society's expectation that cyborgs should sacrifice themselves as test subjects in a search for an antidote to the plague which is killing humans. Although not offering their lives for its use, in the real world early adopters of Google Glass – those choosing to modify their bodies with technology – could be viewed as sacrificing their privacy and face criticism from human rights campaigners, with the use of Glass already banned or criminalized in some situations and the label 'glassholes' being coined and perpetuated by Twitter users since 2012 and subsequently taken up by the technology press and in online discussions,[2] to describe its users and separate them from the more human non-users.

Cyberbodies

While enhanced and modified bodies are seen in both fiction and reality, the cyberbody currently remains in the domain of fiction. In Peters's cyberbody, the human is prioritized as 'the technology has become invisible, internalised, or repressed' (56). By this she means a posthuman in which the physical body is immaterial as an individual's consciousness exists in an avatar created in cyberspace, or is transferred to a computer-like storage medium where it lives independently or to another, either organic or synthetic, body.

B. R. Collins's *Gamerunner* (2011) is set in a near future when people rarely venture outside because of corrosive acid rain and feral gangs. Its protagonist, Rick, lives in the headquarters of Crater where his father is the designer of the virtual world computer game, the Maze. Running the Maze involves the player entering an enclosed tank and donning a cap to allow the virtual world's sensations to be transmitted to the player's brain while their actions control their avatar's actions. Rick has little life outside the Maze and gets bored when locked out of it in 'the long hours between 2100 and 0500' (11). Despite the hours he spends playing, he has an ambivalent attitude towards the real and virtual worlds:

> It was a relief to get out of the tank into the liquid grey of real daylight. He paused for a moment, taking in the wide-screen windows, the huge panorama of the real world, the way he did every time; and thought – the way he did every time – how depressing it looked, compared to the Maze. (9)

Regardless of his dissatisfaction with the real world (viewed through windows described as computer displays), there is a sense of being trapped in the physically limiting tank necessary to visit the virtual world. His apparent need to escape to reality shows a division between his mind and body which, although a common feature of the posthuman, is most clearly exemplified in the cyberbody: his consciousness is happier in the virtual world, but his physical body limits him as it cannot stay in the tank indefinitely. Unlike Titus, Violet or Cinder, Rick appears to be in control of his choice to submerse himself in the virtual world, but the reality of his world gives him scant options for passing his time; however, his posthuman existence in a virtual world is only ever temporary, and finishes when he chooses.

When Rick is given the task of completing a mission in the Maze for his father, he is given a female avatar, Athene, as a disguise and has to take time to acquaint himself with his new character. Online worlds have previously been seen as places to experiment with alternative identities, and although Rick is initially troubled by having to put up with the 'stupid way [Athene] moves' (28), he rapidly aligns himself with the new role as he 'brushes imaginary hair away from his face' and 'wiggles his hips' (28). As a result of Rick's bemusement, he watches Athene shake her head and crack up, and he comforts himself with the thought that 'we share a sense of humour' (28). His avatar is controlled by his own actions, so in this passage Rick both accepts a new identity and unifies himself with Athene as he accepts his feminine form, but simultaneously – through the plural pronoun 'we' – sees the avatar as another person detached from his physical self. Again, the mind/body division is clear, but here it is reversed as he accepts what is portrayed as an authentic body in the virtual world with his consciousness in the real world.

In a clear acknowledgement of Daedalus as Icarus's father and creator of the mythological Cretan labyrinth containing the Minotaur, Daed is Rick's father and designer of the Maze; however, he does not use it, choosing to remain firmly in the real world. He is terminally ill and believes that he cannot die leaving Rick to fend for himself because of the protection that living in, and never having to leave, the Crater headquarters gives him from the world outside (111). In this, the boundary between the real and virtual worlds is remoulded as life outside Crater becomes the real world, making life inside Crater a form of alternative reality in itself. Nevertheless, Rick still wants to escape his reality of Crater by entering the Maze's virtual world. The fear of the real outside world is shown in Daed's concern for Rick, as he believes 'I *can't* die … I need to be immortal' (111). Echoes of the Daedalus and Icarus myth resonate as Daed uses his Asterion software to achieve immortality by transferring his consciousness into a new version of the Maze unbeknownst to anyone. When Rick find Daed's dead body in a malfunctioning tank he dismisses the idea that he committed suicide, choosing to believe his death was caused by a technical problem; however, when he eventually enters the Maze, Daed appears to him in a private area of the game, through which there is a sense of the Christian resurrection story and Jesus' appearances to those closest to him after his death. As the Asterion software transgressed the technological/biological division, so

Rick's perception of Daed in the Maze demonstrates an uncertainty about who, or even what, he is:

> It's Daed.
>
> Or … *almost* Daed. There's something wrong with him; he's hard to look at, as if Rick's eyes don't match up with what he's seeing. The image is there, steady and solid, but there's still something flickery about him, something blurry. As if Rick's idea of Daed and the computer's aren't the same. (230)

In Daed's appearance he is neither of the real world nor does he match the high quality graphics Rick is used to in the Maze. It is difficult not to see his flickery blurriness as being caused by the absence of some essential human soul-like element which, despite his 'data' being preserved, leaves what remains of him in a virtual limbo, wholly recognizable to neither human nor machine.

Such tension between human and machine is a key idea in Robin Wasserman's *Skinned* (2009). Lia Kahn has been so badly injured in a car accident that her body is destroyed, but her brain is downloaded to a computer from which it can be uploaded into one, or many, replacement synthetic bodies. The novel follows Lia as she tries to reconcile herself with her posthuman identity, and the first chapter's opening a priori argument shows her trying to make sense of being in limbo between human and machine and life and death:

> Lia Kahn is dead.
>
> I am Lia Kahn.
>
> Therefore – because this is a logic problem even a dim-witted child could solve – I am dead.
>
> Except here's the thing: I'm not. (1)

While Daed chooses to give up his physical body to allow his consciousness to live, Lia's body had been destroyed in a car accident, but technology allows her consciousness to be saved at her parents' behest, making her both dead and not dead. Unlike *Gamerunner*, which only briefly sees Rick trying to accept Daed's decision, *Skinned* is concerned with Lia's attempt to rediscover her own identity as a skinner, or 'computer that [wears] a human mask, hiding wiring and circuitry underneath a costume of synthetic flesh' (33). Lia has to learn how to control her new body, and initially has to have the computer speak for her through a neural link. As is often the case in books where technology is given a literal voice, her computerized words are presented in a monospaced terminal font redolent of the command-line driven computers of the 1970s and 1980s, but the pleas are plaintively human as she begs to be put back 'the way I was', as she does not 'care about the injuries' (34). The subsequent first-person narration of her thoughts develops this further as she repeats that she would not care about her appearance, 'as long as I was human. As long as I was *me*' (34). In only thinking of herself as a human with her own identity, rather than letting the computer voice her thoughts as she does when first trying to make sense of her new self, she is trying to protect what she feels makes her human by separating her mind from her body. However, it is only when she is willing to accept the biological and technological combination that she will be able – depending on the perspective taken – to continue her old life, or start her new one.

Learning that her damaged body has been burnt as 'medical waste' (41) (exemplifying the cyberpunk view of the physical body as meat) forces Lia to attempt to reconcile her mind with her new physical identity. She tries to do this through her zone on the network – a Facebook-like system – where she has lived since she was three. While these virtual existences can be seen as a means of escaping reality, Lia acknowledges that sometimes the 'network seemed more real' (50). In this, she echoes Mark Zuckerberg's implicit hopes that Facebook is a place where people are truthfully represented[3] as, in her case, 'every fight and every make up was reflected in the zone', and it was where her first boyfriend first kissed her. Indeed, she describes the zone as being 'how I knew who I was, how I knew *that* I was' (50). Technology's importance in creating her identity is shown as this claim inverts the opening idea of her body being necessary to define her. This description stretches the boundaries of the cyberbody as, unlike the Cartesian *cogito ergo sum*, she prioritizes the technology to provide her human identity: rather than needing to think, it is through her creation of an online persona she is able to exist in reality; the virtual and real worlds are exchanged, as she reflects that 'Now my av is me, the virtual Lia, the better Lia, the Lia that would exist in a world without limits' (52). While virtual worlds were seen as a place to experiment with identity, Lia's virtual world is shaping her reality in line with more recent research exploring the concept of the 'idealised "me"' (Krotoski, 2011) being developed on today's social media as people manage the online information about themselves to present the best possible image, thereby shaping their reality through their technology.

Despite Lia's hopes for a positive outcome from reconnecting to the zone, it does not reconcile her mind and body, and she chooses to challenge the technology that allows her to remain immortal by refusing to back herself up. This is intended to be a daily procedure 'against the finality of death' as she has 'every experience stored, every memory preserved', so what she calls 'I – the essential *I*, the mysterious sum of seventeen years ... would remain intact' in the event of another accident (193). While showing the inherent difficulty in understanding what makes a person human, this description seems to be partially parroting a pitch from the company responsible for her upload, showing the hope that technology may be more capable than biology. Ironically, however, uploading is reliant on the human choice to back up the data. In refusing to back up her data, Lia could be seen to be trying to protect her humanity as future instances of her will start from the last backup, when the majority of her memories are still from her human life rather than being a mix of human and posthuman. However, as she is still trying to accept her new identity, she is potentially causing her future self suffering, as any new instances will start living from a moment when her mental and physical existences were in conflict.

Lia learns about illicit programs from other skinners which can be installed within themselves to alter their programming. After she acknowledges that, as a computer, she can be reprogrammed, she is convinced to try one and her descriptions as she feels pain and extremes of temperature, experiences the sensations of flying and drowning, and hallucinates (273) are redolent of descriptions of human drug-taking experiences. As drug use is often seen as an act of rebellion or escape, Lia's choice is also an escape from her posthuman reality and a rebellious action. However, rather than rebelling against society's expectations or authority, she is rebelling against the part of her created by others which she refuses to recognize as herself, but which she cannot escape: the technology. As the program provides a way for its users to lose control of what they are, another challenge to the technology is the skinners' practice of leaping into a waterfall. In doing so they experience 'intense feelings – intense *pain* – it's the only kind that feels real' (239). As the cyborg was designed to push the human's boundaries, so the cyberbody's human elements push the boundaries of technology. When Lia jumps, she reflects that 'I had never felt more free. I had never felt less human' (242). Through the human pushing technology's bounds she has achieved mental freedom but, in an uncomfortable paradox, it is only made possible by her technology. However, in this activity the technology can also be seen to be serving the human as, safe in the knowledge that her backup makes her immortal, she is told that the jump becomes about 'facing the fear – and conquering it' and 'mastering all those sordid animal instincts and rising above them' (239). Through this, the cyberbody's human component can be seen to be either teaching itself to be more confident by confronting its fears and thereby creating an 'improved' human, or else using the technology irresponsibly and quashing the posthuman's human fear of danger, much as Cinder's creators prevented her from demonstrating human weakness through crying or blushing to make her a more efficient piece of technology.

Ultimately, Lia demonstrates the most powerful features of the posthuman, as she is able to reconcile her organic and synthetic components. Although it happens as a realization that she can neither continue to deny what she is, nor to be angered or upset by her parents' decision, she ultimately chooses to accept the 'new reality of nonlife after nondeath. *My* new reality' (361). While the implicit contradictions of 'nonlife' and 'nondeath' do not indicate a positive acceptance, acknowledging her new reality suggests Lia is in the process of discovering her identity and is in a position to effect change for herself and others as she recapitulates the opening argument:

Lia Kahn is dead.

I am Lia Kahn.

Except, I finally realized, here's the thing.

Maybe I'm not.   (361)

The final line of the novel's opening quotation makes a mockery of the argument with its certainty, but having learnt about and accepted her technology

Lia now understands there is more to her than being human: not only are her human abilities extended by her technology, but her technology's ability is extended by her humanity. This reconciliation puts her in a powerful position over the humans who created her and the posthumans who rely on their technology.

The geek

I have previously suggested that the contemporary figure of the geek, as a technologically able individual in a world filled with digital insiders, is a form of posthuman in whom humanity and technology are equally important and their technology has moved from being external to being internalized through their understanding of it. Cory Doctorow's *Little Brother* (2008) presents a vision of an America where a well-funded national security service uses surveillance technology in an Orwellian manner, but its teenage protagonist, Marcus, is able to use freely available technology to challenge the totalitarian state machine.

From the outset Marcus is portrayed as being beyond the society's conventions as he 'cracks' his school-issue laptop's 'snitchy' technology (6) and can get 'through the school firewalls like Kleenex, spoof the gait-recognition software and nuke the snitch chips they track [students] with' (2). Although he might initially appear to be positioning himself as the stereotypical anti-social nerd through his screen name 'w1n5t0n' (1), a clear allusion to *Nineteen Eighty-Four* written in leet,[4] it is apparent that his hacking activities are carried out with like-minded friends who are also playing an international alternative reality game with a story based in the real world. In the game, it is the human participants' choices that control the game's direction, and technology is one medium to deliver the game's narrative. In Marcus's life even programming becomes a social task: he watches over his friend's shoulder because '[t]wo people are much better at spotting bugs than one' (147). As an advanced user of technology, Marcus does not display the self-absorption that might be expected from both a teenager and an apparent geek, as he works collaboratively with his friends.

When Marcus is arrested and suspected of being involved in a terrorist bomb attack, he is politicized to defend the right of individuals to live in a society without being subject to authoritarian surveillance. He duly enlists the help of existing friends, but also uses the Internet to recruit a network of supporters, known as the Xnet. However, the Xnet's virtual society contains spies and he resorts to the human to establish a 'web of trust' in which everyone has to meet in person and be vouched for by another individual, thereby making it 'foolproof' (141). Although it could be argued that as the members of the web are all reflections of Marcus through their common interest in technology and motivations for supporting him, thereby fulfilling Elkind's idea of adolescent egocentrism (1981), he also understands the importance of sharing his discoveries with a journalist friend of his parents. Marcus describes the pleasure he takes from his role in society to the journalist, telling her that '[t]eaching people how to use technology is always exciting. It's so cool to watch people figure out how the technology around them can be used to make their lives better' (259). The way he speaks suggests this is not new to him and therefore he is not just reaching the final stage in the process of moving out of adolescence. Indeed, at the novel's conclusion, Marcus's selflessness is shown as he sacrifices himself, thinking of 'everything I had accomplished, that we had accomplished' (334), and placing himself firmly within the society he has united against the government's control.

In Marcus, external technologies have become internalized in his capacity to use them to his advantage and through his understanding of them. However, it is the balance of his immersion in technology with his human beliefs that empowers him and allows an economically powerless teenager to succeed against the government's wealth, might and access to wholly externalized technologies.

Conclusion

The negative outcomes of technology's use in dystopian worlds can be traced to two sources. First, technology is blending with the biological to create the posthuman, which challenges the way people are able to define themselves as human and make sense of their experiences. Second, from the security of the present, humankind is worried by its dependence on technology and the threat of the technological singularity, or time, when it is overtaken in terms of intelligence, power and authority by artificial intelligence. If the past is seen through rose-tinted spectacles, our bleak view of the future through augmented reality glasses reflects a concern about the rise of the machines to a position of ultimate control and their challenging of human creativity and existence, especially when (in a satisfying inversion of posthuman notions) the machines exemplify human characteristics.

However, as awareness of technology and what it means to be technically proficient increases, I see the rise of the geek exhibiting and celebrating the skills valued by today's society in both fiction and reality as a step forward for humanity. Although the stereotype of the nerdy, pallid, sports-hating, computer-literate individual still exists, real-world technological developments have shown this to be less tenable as Google, Facebook and Twitter become household names and their geeky creators are recognized by society and financially rewarded for their work.

By their very nature, technological developments make this a fluid area of study and its representation in novels will continue to be affected by real-world advances presenting humanity and human thought with a range of challenges. Existing and future fictional representations must therefore be continually examined, and the posthuman provides a means of questioning people's relationships with technology as the divisions between speculative fiction and social reality become increasingly blurred and the digital natives and geeks grow up to take positions of power and responsibility in the real world.

WORKS CITED AND FURTHER READING

Children's Books

Anderson, M. T. *Feed*. Cambridge, MA: Candlewick Press, 2002.
Asimov, Isaac. 'Runaround'. *Robot Visions*. London: Gollancz, 2001; first pub. 1942.
Collins, B. R. *Gamerunner*. London: Bloomsbury, 2011.
Doctorow, Cory. *Little Brother*. London: HarperCollins, 2008.
Hoffman, E. T. A. 'The Sandman'. *Tales from the German*, trans. John Oxenford and C. A. Feiling. London: Chapman and Hall, 1844; orig. 1816. Available at http://www.gutenberg. org/files/32046/32046-h/32046-h.htm#sandman (accessed 17 October 2013).
Meyer, Marissa. *Cinder*. London: Puffin Books, 2012.
Shelley, Mary. *Frankenstein*. London: Penguin, 2003; first published 1818.
Sterling, Bruce. *Schismatrix Plus*. New York: Ace Books, 1996; first published 1985.
Wasserman, Robin. *Skinned*. London: Simon & Schuster, 2009.

Critical Texts

Applebaum, Noga. 'Electronic Texts and Adolescent Agency: Computers and the Internet in Contemporary Children's Fiction'. In Kimberley Reynolds (ed.), *Modern Children's Literature: An Introduction*, 1st edn. Basingstoke: Palgrave Macmillan, 2005.
Azevedo, Hélène. 'UK Digital Market Overview March 2014'. *UK Online Measurement Company*. http://www.comscore.com/Insights/Presentations_and_Whitepapers/2014/ UK_Digital_Market_Overview_March_2014 (accessed 26 April 2014).
Carr, Nicholas. *The Shallows*. London: Atlantic Books, 2010.
Clynes, Manfred E., and Nathan S. Kline. 'Cyborgs and Space'. *Astronautics* (September 1960), 26–7, 74–6.
Elkind, David. 'Egocentrism in Children and Adolescents'. In David Elkind (ed.), *Children and Adolescents: Interpretive Essays on Jean Piaget*, 3rd edn (pp. 74–95). Oxford: Oxford University Press, 1981.
Facebook. 'Facebook First Quarter 2014 Results'. *Facebook Investor Relations* (2014). http:// investor.fb.com/releasedetail.cfm?ReleaseID=842071 (accessed 26 April 2014).
Haraway, Donna. *Simians, Cyborgs and Women: The Reinvention of Nature*. London: Routledge, 1991.
Kirkpatrick, David. *The Facebook Effect*. New York: Simon & Schuster, 2010.
Krotoski, Aleks. 'Online Identity: Can We Really Be Whoever We Want to Be?' *The Observer*, 19 June 2011. http://www.guardian.co.uk/technology/2011/jun/19/aleks-krotos- ki-online-identity-turkle (accessed 23 October 2013).
Krotoski, Aleks. *Untangling the Web: What the Internet Is Doing to You*. London: Faber and Faber, 2013.
Nikolajeva, Maria. *Power, Voice and Subjectivity in Literature for Young Readers*. London: Rout- ledge, 2010.
Peters, Mischa. 'exit meat: digital bodies in a virtual world'. In Anna Everett and John T. Caldwell (eds.), *new media – theories and practices of digitextuality* (pp. 47–59). London: Routledge, 2003.
Shakeshaft, Richard. 'Young Adult Fiction: Technology Reading List'. 2013. http://richardshake- shaft.blogspot.co.uk/2013/07/young-adult-fiction-technology-reading.html (accessed 20 July 2013).
Telotte, J. P. *A Distant Technology*. Hanover, NH: Wesleyan University Press, 1999.
Turkle, Sherry. *Alone Together: Why We Expect More from Technology and Less from Each Other*. Philadelphia: Basic Books, 2011.

Turkle, Sherry. *Life on the Screen: Identity in the Age of the Internet*. New York: Simon & Schuster, 1995.

Turkle, Sherry. *The Second Self: Computers and the Human Spirit* (Twentieth Anniversary Edition). Cambridge: MIT Press, 2005.

NOTES

1. A recent UK example has been the primary school pupil Martha Payne, who set up the daily blog NeverSeconds in April 2012 (http://neverseconds.blogspot.co.uk/) in which she photographed her school meals and reviewed them. After receiving wider national media interest, her local council tried to stop her photographing her food, but an online outcry meant the ban was lifted the following day. NeverSeconds now displays students' photographs of their meals from around the world and the revenue generated from advertising is donated to a charity helping to feed pupils in some of the world's poorest communities.

2. The earliest definition appeared on 28 June 2012 as 'Glasshole (noun): One who struts around behaving obnoxiously while wearing Google Glass headsets in public places' (https://twitter.com/savage). The term was later examined by TechCrunch.com in January 2013 (http://techcrunch.com/2013/01/28/glassholes/) and in April 2013 by TheWire. com (http://www.thewire.com/technology/2013/04/rise-term-glasshole-explained-linguists/64363/).

3. Facebook's founder, Mark Zuckerberg, is quoted as saying that '[h]aving two identities for yourself is an example of a lack of integrity' as 'the level of transparency the world has now won't support having two identities for a person' (Kirkpatrick, 2010: 199).

4. Leet is a variant of written English used online since the 1980s in which letters are replaced by numbers or symbols, such as 3 for E or alternating slashes, \/\/, for W. Originally recognized as being used by those who were knowledgeable about computer use, or 'elite', it has lost such currency as it is used by people trying to intimate their technical prowess.

Voicing Identity: the Dilemma of Narrative Perspective in Twenty-first Century Young Adult Fiction

16

Maria Nikolajeva

> **KEY TEXTS**
>
> Malorie Blackman, *Noughts and Crosses* (2001)
> Lucy Christopher, *Stolen* (2009)
> John Green, *The Fault in Our Stars* (2012)
> Geraldine McCaughrean, *The White Darkness* (2006)
> Patrick Ness, *The Knife of Never Letting Go* (2008)
> Ransom Riggs, *Miss Peregrine's Home for Peculiar Children* (2011)
> Meg Rosoff, *How I Live Now* (2004)
> Tabitha Suzuma, *Forbidden* (2010)
> Teri Terry, *Slated* (2012)

Contemporary Young Adult (YA) fiction recurrently demonstrates three prominent narrative features: first-person perspective, present narrative tense, and visual emphasis, such as italics and other variable fonts, used to demarcate narrative levels. Although these devices are not new, and nor are they employed exclusively in YA fiction, it is enticing to explore what aspects of young people's perception of the world, of other people and of themselves, these narrative forms represent.

The ubiquitous theme of YA fiction is identity formation. Self-knowledge is central for our existence, and adolescence is a dynamic and turbulent phase of human life. YA fiction has a strong potential to offer readers accurate portrayals of selfhood. Recently, neuroscience has provided literary scholars with hard facts about the profound changes in the adolescent body and mind. During adolescence our brain develops the ability to recognize and attribute mental states to ourselves as well as other people, a process starting at the age of four, but accelerated after twelve. Adolescents' deviant behaviour is the consequence of the social brain's development. Strong emotions override adolescents' ability to take other people's perspective. Actions such as planning, decision making and synthesis of information are still underdeveloped in the adolescent brain. All these processes take more effort in adolescence than in adulthood. Fiction has always attempted to reflect this laborious development that brain research has confirmed through experiments (see suggestions for further reading on brain research and cognition at the end of this chapter).

Yet this endeavour of YA fiction is a mission impossible. If adolescents have insufficient understanding of their own, as well as other people's, thoughts and feelings, the adolescent perspective in fiction should logically impede the artistic project. If an adolescent mind cannot assess its own reactions, if it defies reason, if it is a pandemonium of random impressions, how can a purportedly adolescent narrative voice convey an authentic, but comprehensible, portrayal of this chaotic consciousness? If lack of coherence is the very token of a young person's state of mind, how can its narrative be sufficiently coherent to be understood by an outsider, that is, the reader? And yet, YA fiction conveys exactly an adolescent's inability to understand the world and other people; the confusion and anxiety of emergent selfhood; the discomfort about the fluidity of mind and body. It takes on the challenge of representing a physiological and psychological condition through the only means fiction has, language; a means highly inadequate to convey sub-verbal mental states.

Recent studies in cognitive criticism (see Box 16.1) have provided literary scholars with stimulating approaches to fiction. What have so far been largely neglected are the implications of cognitive criticism for the study of fiction

---

BOX 16.1   EMPATHY AND THEORY OF MIND

Cognitive criticism is a direction of inquiry that borrows achievements in cognitive science to investigate how readers engage with fiction cognitively and emotionally, and what texts afford in terms of narrative structures. Cognitive criticism explains how our brains, through mirror neurons, can respond to fictional events and characters as if they were real. Studies in cognitive criticism (Zunshine, 2006; Keen, 2008; Vermeule, 2010; Hogan, 2011) demonstrate why we are interested in fictional characters' fictional thoughts and emotions, and how we receive vicarious experience through reading fiction. Two central concepts of cognitive criticism come from cognitive psychology. *Theory of mind* is the capacity to understand other people's thoughts, opinions, beliefs and intentions independently of our own. *Empathy* refers more specifically to the capacity to understand other people's emotions. Neither of these skills is innate, but they develop gradually and can be trained, not least through reading fiction.

targeting young readers, who not only lack real-life experience of a full range of emotions, but who have not yet fully mastered the ability to empathize. This additional dimension leads to a number of issues. First, how is a fictional adolescent's mind represented by authors whose cognitive and affective skills are ostensibly superior? Second, how do texts instruct adolescent readers to employ empathy and theory of mind in order to assess both the protagonist's emotions and their understanding of other characters' emotions? Third, how can fiction affect adolescents' development of empathy?

First-person perspective is a device used to emulate self-knowledge and self-reflection. The reason YA writers use personal narration to an increasing extent is an attempt to create a more intimate, and therefore presumably more authentic, voice. Although first-person perspective was employed in early novels of adolescence, such as *The Adventures of Huckleberry Finn* (1884) and *The Catcher in the Rye* (1951), it was and still is more common to use retrospective self-narration, in which an adult narrator looks back at their adolescence, not only with the knowledge of the completed story, but with the experience, vocabulary and cognitive skills of mature age. *Treasure Island* (1883) is a good example. The separation of the narrating and the experiencing self stimulates readers to enter the gap between narration and experience. However, it also provides guidance for the reader. An older self is presumably wiser and can evaluate their actions and thoughts when young. Retrospective self-narration combines adult capacity for self-reflection with an adolescent experience. For the sake of suspense, narrators may omit information; for the sake of postmodern playfulness, they may emphasize the discrepancy of knowledge.

In contrast, simultaneous or nearly simultaneous self-narration in YA fiction is a challenge for writers and an exacting task for readers. Implied readers can cognitively align with young protagonists/narrators, while the implied author, ostensibly an adult agency, needs to get ideas across to the reader, circumventing the protagonist. While all personal narrators are unreliable, the discrepancy between the adolescent narrative voice and the eclipsed ideological subtext of the implied author – the 'hidden adult' (Nodelman, 2008) – makes YA fiction extremely ambiguous. The text wants to engage readers through the intimate voice and a representation of an adolescent consciousness that young readers find recognizable. At the same time, the text needs to alert readers to the protagonist/narrator's shortcomings, misunderstandings, delusions, and cognitive and affective insufficiencies; in other words, to detach the reader from the protagonist's subject position. The difference between immersive and empathic identification is crucial for successful reader engagement.

In interaction with fiction, we are encouraged to empathize with characters even if we dislike them, find them strange or simply do not share their emotions, beliefs and assumptions. Such detachment is deliberately created through shifting the characters' subject position away from readers. Since empathy is an essential social skill, YA fiction offers a unique opportunity for readers to train their empathetic ability in a safe mode, which can be transferred to real life. Such a text-to-life reading strategy is valuable; yet another reason we read fiction is that we are curious about cognitive and emotional experiences that we – perhaps fortunately – will not encounter in real life.

The opposite, life-to-text strategy implies projecting previous experience, whether real-life or mediated through reading, onto literary characters. There is nothing fundamentally wrong with life-to-text projection; we would not be able to engage with fiction if we didn't have similar life experience stored in our memory. Because of the intimate tone of the first-person YA novels, readers are likely to identify with the protagonist immersively, sharing their literal and transferred point of view, their thoughts and actions, as if they were their own. However, the uncritical 'just-like-me' approach is limited to the readers' scope of experience and does not endorse empathy. In real life, empathy is essential for interpersonal communication. Immersive identification precludes or at least substantially impedes practising empathy and theory of mind, since readers know, or believe they know, exactly what the protagonist thinks and feels by projecting their own real-life experience onto characters.

YA authors have a range of narrative devices to subvert immersive identification while at the same time engaging readers cognitively and affectively. As cognitive criticism claims, literary texts are only truly engaging when they offer experience we lack; when they contain surprises and ambiguity, and therefore demand constant attention and imagination, the foremost engines for brain activity. This cognitive and emotional novelty can be achieved through various means, such as defamiliarization, heteroglossia and metafiction (see Box 16.2).

BOX 16.2 MULTIPLE VOICES, MULTIPLE PERCEPTIONS, PERSPECTIVE SHIFTS AND POSSIBLE WORLDS

Heteroglossia, or multitude of voices, is a feature described by the Russian philosopher Mikhail Bakhtin (1895–1975) as inherent in the contemporary novel, as opposed to the single, frequently omniscient narrative voice of epic prose (1981). It can be achieved by multiple narrative agencies as well as by splitting a fictional consciousness into the experiencing and the narrating parts and separating them in time. *Heteroscopia* is a concept coined by analogy, to emphasize diverse points of view, or multiple focalization, when events are presented through the eyes (external focalization) or the mind (internal focalization) of several characters. The difference between the narrative voice and the point of view is of particular interest in YA fiction since there may be a discrepancy between the cognitive and emotional level of the adolescent protagonist and the purportedly adult (or at least more experienced and informed) narrator. The French narratologist Gérard Genette (1980) claims that the conventional distinction between impersonal, or third-person, and personal, or first-person, narration is of less significance than the distance between the narrating and the experiencing agency, since it is in this gap that readers can enter with their own interpretation.

Defamiliarization, that is, describing familiar events, settings and characters as if they were unfamiliar, is a powerful device for stimulating readers' engagement, since at every given moment they need to orientate themselves to the contingency of possible fictional worlds. A possible world is a concept from philosophy and linguistics, used in literary theory to describe constructed fictional worlds that deviate from the perceptible world in one or more respects. The further a possible world is from the real world as we know it, the more attention and imagination is required from us as readers, since we are not familiar with the rules; in most cases, we are less familiar with them than the protagonists. *Metafiction* is used as an umbrella concept for a set of devices that deliberately draw readers' attention to a text's existence as fiction, for instance, through breaking frames between various levels of narration or through implausible narrative situations.

Defamiliarization

The YA novel emerged in the late 1960s/early 1970s as a hyperrealistic form, anchored in contemporary, predominantly urban settings, and focused on everyday issues that adolescents struggle with, including romantic love and emerging sexuality, alcohol and drugs, risk taking, violence, revolt against parental authority, and social pressure. These are inevitably present in today's YA novels since they are seen as central for adolescent identity formation. Two pervasive themes of YA fiction are death and sexuality, both equally identity-bound. However, it has become increasingly common to employ non-mimetic modes, including thriller, fantasy, paranormal romance, magical realism, science fiction, counterfact and dystopia. These modes allow an exploration of emotions, memory and empathy in situations impossible or unlikely in realist fiction. Alienated possible worlds and defamiliarized minds become fields for thought experiments.

Thus it takes time to realize that the world of *Noughts and Crosses* (2001), by Malorie Blackman, is counterfactual, representing reversed racial positions. Accepting this as the fictional world's contingency, we need to adjust our expectations to be able to assess the characters' actions, feelings and beliefs. By contrast, the opening of *The Hunger Games* (2008), by Suzanne Collins, immediately places the narrative in a possible world of the distant future which nevertheless bears enough resemblance to the actual world to feel relevant. *The Knife of Never Letting Go* (2008), by Patrick Ness, blends science fiction with brutal medievalism. *How I Live Now* (2004), by Meg Rosoff, starts in a realistic mode, as a perennial story of a young girl sent away by a jealous stepmother to stay with relatives. However, the modality shifts abruptly when a war breaks out, and the fictional world is changed beyond recognition. We cannot anticipate the development of the story since we are not familiar with the premises. The title prompts the thought that there is a gap between narrative and narration. Since the novel is narrated in the past tense, the 'now' points at the narrative situation detached from the story. It eventually transpires that the first-person narrator is looking back from a distance of six years. Similarly, in Geraldine McCaughrean's *The White Darkness* (2006), the story starts as a plausible, albeit exotic adventure, but totally subverts our expectations by turning into a mix of thriller and science fiction. *Miss Peregrine's Home for Peculiar Children* (2011), by Ransom Riggs, changes modality several times, playing with readers' expectations and offering a new turn just as they have decided that the narrative is a tall tale, adventure, time-shift fantasy or magical realism. The eclecticism, ambiguity and lack of orientation in the possible worlds we encounter demand uninterrupted attention since we cannot take anything for granted. To engage with the characters, we need to accept that, given their specific possible worlds, they may think and feel differently from us.

However, defamiliarization is not necessarily achieved through distant possible worlds. YA fiction frequently utilizes alienation of narrator/protagonists by making them radically different from anything in an average young reader's experience. As already suggested, we must be able to engage with protagonists empathically, without sharing their point of view; to be curious about unpleasant, ugly, sick, criminal, morally depraved or even inhuman characters. The technologically or neurobiologically augmented protagonists of contemporary dystopias are sufficiently alien to preclude immersive identification, instead encouraging readers to use empathy, attention and imagination. Endowing protagonists with supernatural powers, as in *Miss Peregrine*, is a similar device. Jacob the character does not know until late in the novel that he too is 'peculiar' and still less what exactly his peculiar ability is. Jacob the narrator may know it, but withholds information to keep the reader in suspense. In the end, Jacob the character is trapped in the past, and although the immediate enemy is eliminated, evil forces are still a threat. The choice of remaining in the past is not Jacob's, and throughout the novel he is forced to consider where he belongs. This quest for identity, prompted by what he initially believes are his grandfather's tall tales, involves the acceptance of being peculiar and thus excluded from the normality which he, as narrator, claims in the opening sentence of the novel. Yet it is not obvious whether Jacob the narrator is detached from his experiencing self. Although the narration is in the past tense, there is no indication of narrative distance. Identity formation is still incomplete.

Making a protagonist cognitively impaired is an effective way to invite readers' empathy, as in *The Curious Incident of the Dog in the Night-time* (2003), by Mark Haddon (see Kümmerling-Meibauer, 2012). It is certainly not a coincidence that the protagonist/narrator of *The White Darkness* has a hearing impairment, suggesting that disability contributes to her social isolation and thus a tendency for self-reflection. The protagonist/narrator's terminal cancer in John Green's *The Fault in Our Stars* (2012) alienates her from most young readers. The social stigma of the protagonists of *Forbidden* (2010), by Tabitha Suzuma, potentially contributes to the distance between them and the reader. In all these texts, the delicate balance between immersive and empathic identification is decisive for reader engagement.

Temporality

It might seem that a true exploration of young selfhood is best achieved by the total merging of the narrator and the protagonist, discursively marked by present narrative tense. It is conceivable that authors employ present tense on the assumption that young people live in the here and now and that their perception of time is distorted (which cognitive science confirms). However, the use of present tense sets a limitation on the temporal possibilities offered by fiction. Unlike real life, fiction is an organized and structured narrative, in which events are not necessarily rendered chronologically; in which one event may be narrated in great detail while others are summarized in a sentence; in which the same event can be narrated several times; in which one narrated event may refer to something occurring repeatedly. Fiction also features considerably stronger causality than can be observed in real everyday life.

Temporal shifts are an efficient way to separate textual agencies, the narrating and the experiencing self. The most common devices are to embed the main narrative in a narrative frame as a flashback or shift between 'then' and 'now', which allows the narrator to comment on the story (the way the events happened) and on the discourse (their own narration). A temporal variety is beneficial since it leaves cognitive gaps for readers to explore.

However, retrospection brings in the issues of memory and thus the narrator's authority and reliability. In conventional retrospective self-narration, the assumption is that adult narrators are unequivocally in a position to recall their adolescent experiences. Modernist fiction attempts to approximate the unreliability of memory through devices such as lack of coherence, broken syntax, dashes and ellipses, blank lines and visual images. According to recent memory studies, episodic memory, which preserves our real-life experience, is subjective, incoherent, fragmentary, random and imprecise. In the light of this scientific foundation, the fictitious narrator's memories, whether idyllic or traumatic, are confabulations. The concept of confabulation implies that the narrator honestly believes that the memory is accurate. Fiction deliberately plays on the ambiguity of narration in which the accuracy of memories cannot be verified. We seldom contemplate metaphysical issues while reading, accepting implausible narrative situations. Yet the questions of reliability and the first-person narrator's access to information help to unravel the intricate structures that invite readers' exploration of the narrator's self-reflections. The narrative device of false and alternative memories has been employed in several contemporary YA novels.

Stolen (2009), by Lucy Christopher, is a memory monologue, a form of narrative structured as a deliberate attempt to recollect a set of events, usually for a particular purpose, such as therapy or evidence in court. In addition, *Stolen* employs an unusual second-person narration in which one of the characters is referred to as 'you'. The novel's subtitle, 'A letter to my captor', suggests that the 'you' is also the narratee, the receiver of the narrative within the text. However, subtitle notwithstanding, it is not explicit whether the written letter is supposed to reach its addressee or is simply self-reflections, encouraged by a psychiatrist.

The novel accounts for recent events in story time, yet it is told in the past tense, allowing the narrator to reflect on what has happened. The one-month gap between experience and narration is indicated in the beginning through short comments in the present tense. The past tense, amplified by these flashforwards, suggests that at the time of narration the narrator knows the outcome, but the act of narration helps her in understanding her own behaviour, especially her changing attitude towards her abductor. The 16-year-old Gemma is drugged and kidnapped at Bangkok airport, waking to find herself in the Australian desert. After weeks of terror and anxiety, suicide and escape attempts, Gemma not only reconciles herself to her fate, but develops a strong affection for the abductor.

Stockholm syndrome, or capture-bonding, is a common phenomenon in which captives gradually begin to empathize with their captors and may even take their side in court proceedings. Gemma's narrative reflects this change without referring to it explicitly until the later parts of the novel. The reader is in a position to understand not merely more than the protagonist, but also more than the narrator. The situation is ambiguous and highly demanding. We are expected to have no doubt that abduction is criminal; yet we may be seduced, together with Gemma, into believing that the captor has acted rightly, that he is offering Gemma an exciting and healthy life, that they have a lot in common and will be happy together. Abduction of women has a convincing evolutionary explanation and has been practised throughout human history. The image scheme of women kidnapped by strong, powerful men and living happily ever after is prominent in Western culture, from Homer and the Bible to contemporary popular movies. Readers may decide that ultimately the captor's actions are acceptable, developing a vicarious Stockholm syndrome.

To prevent this, the text must circumvent the narrator and get across the message that Gemma is deluding herself, not only as a character, but also as a narrator. Memory plays a decisive role in this strategy. Moreover, since the whole narrative is a memory, the reader is presented with multilayered, embedded memories, marked by italics, each of which can be imprecise and distorted, by the lapse of time as well as by the traumatized state of mind. Gemma's memories can be suppressed or even supplanted by confabulation, something that has not happened, but that she sincerely believes has. Moreover, her captor provides her with an alternative set of memories in which she is a neglected child while he is her guardian angel. At the climax of the narrative, when Gemma gets bitten by a poisonous snake and the abductor takes her to hospital, thus effectively turning himself in, readers may erroneously infer that this noble action cancels his earlier crime. At the moment of narration, Gemma is recollecting her own earlier recollections, and she may or may not be adjusting them to suit her added perception. When the various story levels are synchronized discursively through present tense, readers are invited to make their own inferences about the narrator's reliability.

Synchronization is a powerful narrative device. Most of Geraldine McCaughrean's *The White Darkness* is narrated in the past tense, and there are initially no indications of any peculiar narrative situation – no flashforwards, no temporal zigzags, and just a few flashbacks evoked by various events. The 14-year-old Sym is telling a story similar to *Stolen*: she is, effectively, kidnapped by her uncle, and a peaceful weekend in Paris evolves into a nightmarish journey to Antarctica in pursuit of a mad scientist's project. Against reason, Sym has full trust in uncle Victor, since he has been supportive to her and her mother after the father's death. Readers have no reason to question the reliability of the narrator, as much fused with the protagonist as past tense allows, even though the nature of events goes beyond the ordinary. It is only when the scope of coincidences becomes too obvious that readers may start to get suspicious, wondering whether Sym the narrator is deliberately withholding her own understanding of the events or whether she is genuinely deluded. Sym's dialogues with her imaginary friend, the Polar explorer Titus Oates, marked by italics, provide readers with some guidance, creating a heteroglot effect with an additional adult voice. In one revelation after another, it finally transpires that Victor has robbed the family, murdered Sym's father and performed illegal pharmacological experiments on Sym that made her deaf – all for his obsessive cause. During the Antarctic expedition, he steals satellite phones, poisons tourists and staff, burns the aircraft and destroys everything and everyone obstructing his goal. At some point between leaving the camp in a stolen vehicle and Victor's voluntary fall into an ice shaft, the narration switches from past to present tense, to multiple effect. First, it makes Sym's unendurable suffering in the Antarctic wilderness more poignant, narrated in minute detail as if in real time. Second, it renders the narrative situation ambiguous since it is no longer clear that the protagonist has survived to tell the story. Narration gradually becomes less coherent, resembling feverish glimpses of failing consciousness. We may even wonder whether the miraculous rescue is a mirage, reminiscent of shiny palaces at the Antarctic horizon. Since the novel no longer presupposes credibility, rather adhering explicitly and implicitly to the tradition of Jules Verne's or Conan Doyle's science fiction stories of undiscovered worlds, it is possible to read the final passages of the book as Sym's death agony, without questioning our access to her first-hand experience.

Tense and memory

Temporality is decisive for our cognitive and emotional engagement with fiction. We only exist in the present, moving irreversibly in one direction. Fiction allows us to oscillate between parallel narratives, to go back in story time, to re-live, re-play and perhaps re-vision memories. The temporal variations contribute to heteroglossia through the narrator/protagonist tension. A consistent present-tense first-person narration is the closest approximation of an explicit 'here and now' experience that does not allow reflection on the past nor anticipation of the future. It constructs the fictional self as static and stable, which is not only contrary to what we know about selfhood, but also counter-productive in terms of reader engagement. A consistent present-tense first-person narration loses the spatio-temporal trajectory, focusing on one singular point of time-space. It loses the depth and dynamism essential for the formation of identity. It confines the reader's vicarious experience to a single consciousness in a temporal singularity. Memory is the greatest narrative engine in fiction. Not only does it mould the fictional characters' identities, making them fluid and more resemblant of a real human being, it also evokes readers' memories and thus affects their identities in interaction with fiction. Some YA novels utilize present narrative tense exactly for the purpose of emphasizing the decisive role of memory in identity formation.

Slated (2012), by Teri Terry, features a 16-year-old protagonist/narrator who has been surgically stripped of memory, her mind becoming a blank slate – 'slated'. The present tense of Kyla's narrative is thus not a trivial convention. Kyla does live in the present. She has no memory beyond the moment she woke up after her surgery. She knows that she used to be someone else, but she has no way of knowing anything about her past. The text, set in a dystopian future, offers readers a big challenge. Few of us have the experience of living without a memory, yet readers are expected to empathize with Kyla, connecting with her empty consciousness. Readers have privilege over the protagonist since they know what Kyla lacks. This is an exacting exercise, but rewarding in the long run. The theme of suppressed traumatic memory is frequent in YA literature, often connected with the death of a relative or friend. However, when it appears in realist fiction we can relate to the characters' emotions even though we have no direct experience of them. We know that bereavement causes denial, anger and grief. Yet we do not know how it feels not to be able to feel grief. Kyla's plight is not focused on her loss, since she does not know much about it. Without memory, she cannot predict any future for herself, nor make decisions. She is a strange, impossible singularity without a trajectory. Her identity is blank because identity is built through memory.

Confronted with the literal single-mindedness of the protagonist, readers need to activate their empathy to come to grips with Kyla's experience. But how can it be possible if her emotion discourse cannot utilize the familiar words and metaphors, and if what Kyla really feels has no adequate correlative in our language? The protagonist/narrator does not have a vocabulary to describe her emotional state that would make sense to us. Therefore, the narrative must circumvent the unreliable narrator and communicate with the reader over her head. It is tempting to identify with Kyla, not least because of the present-tense first-person perspective: we are positioned too close to the protagonist. However, falling for the temptation, we would be as helpless as Kyla in understanding her social network, still less her own interiority. It is also tempting to transpose Kyla's predicament onto more familiar situations, and the text encourages it by introducing motifs such as school bullying, parent/child conflicts, sibling rivalry and budding romance. Perhaps part of the text's intention is to afford readers a metaphorical interpretation: Kyla's mental handicap is a metaphor for other physical, mental and social impairments that abound in YA fiction. However, such interpretation is reductive, since Kyla's deleted memory makes her radically different from victims of bullying and abuse in YA novels. We cannot employ life-to-text strategy because we have no experience of not being able to empathize. Moreover, we seemingly have no use for text-to-life strategy since we are unlikely to experience anything like Kyla's situation. The text effectively resists our empathy, which becomes a particular challenge. We are curious about Kyla, although she is different from anyone we are likely to meet.

Remnants of memory appear in Kyla's incoherent dreams, marked by italics. Representing self-reflection as dreams, revealing self-knowledge suppressed or otherwise unavailable to characters, is a common device in fiction, from the Bible and medieval revelations to the modernist novel. Recent dream research shows that dreaming is not, as earlier believed, a reflection of the individual's subconscious fears or desires, but the brain's way to sort, restructure and store away information acquired while we are awake. Thus dreaming has a significant cognitive function, and dreams in fiction may be used to illuminate the protagonist's understanding of selfhood. With this background, the employment of italics and other hybrid forms to convey dreams and memories in YA fiction is not accidental.

Patrick Ness's *The Knife of Never Letting Go* (2008) is built on premises directly opposite from those of *Slated*. Not only does the protagonist/narrator, the 13-year-old Todd, retain his memory, but he retains all memories he has ever had, visual as well as verbal, in a never-ending buzz in his head. Moreover, he is receptive to the thoughts and memories of other people around him. Todd is a mind reader in a more literal sense than simply possessing theory of mind. So is every male in the possible world of the novel, which is set on another planet but the concerns of which evoke both the European colonization of the New World and the present-day situations of local and regional wars. The novel has a typical adventure plot with pursuit and repeated last-minute escapes, kidnapping and rescue, helpers and traitors, a wide range of dangers, survival and mutual dependence, and a good deal of horrible, explicit violence. It can certainly be read and appreciated on this superficial level; however, it is the narration that makes it compelling.

Like *Slated*, *The Knife of Never Letting Go* is narrated in the first person, present tense, and has italicized passages as well as a wide range of other graphic devices. However, the consequences are different from *Slated*. Todd does have a memory, substantially more than he would like. The present-tense narration creates an illusion of immediacy, but more importantly it emphasizes the simultaneous existence of all directly and vicariously experienced memories in Todd's mind – a situation that the reader cannot possibly be familiar with. If Kyla has no past because it has been severed from her mind, Todd has no past because it is crammed into one singularity, once again, without a trajectory. If *Slated* asks the reader to imagine living without memory, *Knife* depicts the nightmare of not being able to forget.

In this device, *The Knife of Never Letting Go* is reminiscent of one of the early YA dystopias, *The Giver* (1993), by Lois Lowry, in which one child is chosen to preserve all memories of humankind, pleasant as well as painful. *The Knife of Never Letting Go*, however, goes further in its demands on the reader. The italics, bold, various font types and other graphic devices, most often fragments interspersed within narrative sentences, are used to emphasize the chaos of the protagonist's mind. There is some pattern in the chaos, since certain people's thoughts are always conveyed in the same font, but it takes a while for the reader to figure it out. To begin with, the mix of graphics is a way to verbally reflect what is going on in the protagonist/narrator's mind while he is trying to tell his story.

The first-person narration in *The Knife of Never Letting Go* allows the reader a glimpse of this nightmare; yet since Todd does not know any alternative, as a narrator he does not make much of it. The narrative utilizes defamiliarization as well as omission. The narrator simply refers to his condition as Noise, something entirely commonplace. Eventually we get access to the collective memory that explains the phenomenon. Todd does not need theory of mind because everybody's minds are transparent to him, just as his mind is transparent to everybody else. This is where the first-person perspective is crucial, because readers cannot know more than the character. Since the natural laws of Todd's world are unfamiliar to us, we cannot even guess anything that Todd does not know. Finally, unlike Todd, we are not literal mind readers. We only know what Todd decides to tell us. This implies that as a narrator, Todd is totally unreliable; he actually knows more than the reader, but has an option not to share his knowledge. Yet, to tease the reader, every now and then the narrator mentions that he possesses a memory or receives new information that he does not share. Since readers cannot make inferences about the possible world from their own life experience – and not even their previous reading experience, since the world is alien – we can only speculate. Thus the novel demands a keen and attentive reader, able to take a huge leap of imagination and use intricate and contradictory paths of empathy.

Heteroglossia

The two sequels to *The Knife of Never Letting Go*, *The Ask and the Answer* (2009) and *Monsters of Men* (2010), feature two additional first-person narrators who account for their versions of the story. Multiple personal narration is another powerful way of subverting immersive identification, while inviting empathy, since it makes readers aware of the discrepancy between subjective perceptions. Multiple narration makes literal the heteroglossia and heteroscopia that singular narration achieves by other means. The challenge is making the voices, and thus the consciousnesses, sufficiently heterogeneous to be complementary not only on the content level, but also discursively. The narrative failure of Melvin Burgess's *Junk* (1996) lies in the stylistic, cognitive and emotional homogeneity of the narrative voices. The narrative success of Malorie Blackman's *Boys Don't Cry* (2010) is created by the imbalance between the two narrators' agency, where one is preoccupied with external events while the other is focused on self-reflection; one is coherent, the other fragmentary. Introducing two social issues, homophobia and teenage parenthood, the novel plays them against each other in a way that tones down one by emphasizing the other, depending on whose story we hear. The narrative success of Blackman's *Noughts and Crosses* can be attributed to the dissonance between the two narrators, in which neither is ascribed a higher degree of reliability. The multiple perspective amplifies the individual and social conflict of the novel. Similarly, the multiple narration in Tabitha Suzuma's *Forbidden* (2010) invites the reader to make independent inferences about the two protagonists, 16-year-old Maya and her 17-year-old brother Lochan, involved in an incestuous relationship. Incest is one of the strictest social taboos and is considered a severe crime in most jurisdictions.

However, although the threat of societal disapproval and legal punishment is hovering over the characters, their sense of guilt is the pivotal point of the narrative. Through multiple personal narration, the text attempts to maintain the balance between promoting readers' empathy with the protagonists and encouraging the ability to assess their moral flaws. The realization that two young people are in love, a crucial point in myriad works of world literature, is initially connected with happiness. If Lochan and Maya had been lovers divided by external circumstances, like Callum and Sephy in *Noughts and Crosses*, we would be wholly on their side. But Lochan and Maya are not simply secret lovers. The text needs to make readers understand that incest is both a legal crime and a morally unacceptable behaviour. Readers may recognize the situation in which desire is stronger than moral obligations or fear of discovery. In Western culture, the idea that romantic love and sexual attraction stand above legal and moral laws has been strongly perpetuated through literature and popular culture. Morally dubious actions are justified by the irresistibility of desire. The image scheme of star-crossed lovers is firmly imprinted on the minds of today's young readers, who may, therefore, fail to acknowledge the siblings' behaviour as morally deplorable, and may be ignorant of the legal implications until these are eventually spelt out. Further, readers may take the lovers' side in their conflict with societal norms, since society with its legislation is represented by the adults (parents, teachers, social workers, police officers), and child/adult tension is central to all YA literature. Literary conventions may make readers supportive of the siblings, against what may be perceived as societal prejudice and oppression.

Sexuality is a central issue in adolescent identity formation, and few YA novels can neglect it. In *Noughts and Crosses* and *Forbidden*, young people are punished for illicit sexual activity, which is a frequent theme in YA novels, reflecting adult authors' subconscious fear of adolescent sexuality (see Kokkola, 2013). Since both novels employ personal narration, the didactic message must be delivered to the reader over the protagonists' heads. Readers may choose to empathize with one of the two protagonists and view one as a perpetrator and the other a victim. However, multiple, antiphonic structure, in which alternating chapters are narrated in first person by one of the two characters, subverts a fixed subject position and a one-target empathy. Thus readers are effectively prevented from aligning with either of the two since both think and act in ways that readers are supposed to view as inadequate. Yet the implied (adult) author hiding behind the young protagonists' voices must find a way to get the message across, just in case readers' engagement with the characters leads to immersive identification and thus understanding and forgiving. The dilemma of *Forbidden* is especially tangible in comparison with *Noughts and Crosses*. We are more likely to approve of Callum and Sephy's relationship since it interrogates social injustice, making us forget that Callum is after all a terrorist and abductor, and that neither his love for Sephy nor his devotion to his political cause justify his crimes. This makes us perceive Callum's execution as an act of injustice, that, in addition, leads to Sephy's profound grief. In *Forbidden*, Lochan is guilty legally and ethically, and Maya, although under-age, is complacent. Although a young person's death is always a tragedy, Lochan's suicide glorifies his protest against societal norms, making him a martyr dying for love. In both novels, readers are left with ambiguity.

Futurity and metafiction

Alongside sexuality, death is the most pervasive theme in YA fiction (see Trites, 2000; James, 2011). Narrating an adolescent's experience of bereavement, imminent death or realization of their own mortality is a subtle task, and employing temporality and heteroglossia can contribute to its success. John Green's *The Fault in Our Stars* (2012) is the opposite of *Slated* in its temporal premises. While the protagonist of *Slated* has no memory and thus no past, Hazel, the protagonist and narrator of *The Fault in Our Stars*, has no future since she has terminal cancer. Yet, although one would assume that a character in this situation would indeed live in the present, cherishing every moment still available, the narrative utilizes the past tense, with flashbacks and other complex narrative temporalities. The fact that Hazel is telling her story in the past tense has several consequences that ostensibly affect the narration. First, she is obviously alive to tell it, unless we allow the poetic licence that she is telling it from beyond the grave (plausible in *The White Darkness*, but unlikely in *The Fault in Our Stars*). This fact is a promise, albeit tiny, of hope for the reader, in the totally hopeless plot of the novel, in which the overwhelming majority of teenage characters are dead, dying or mourning their dead friends.

Second, telling the story in retrospect Hazel knows the outcome, which gives her privilege over readers, whose engagement with the character is fuelled by awareness of the gaps in their knowledge. The distance between the events and the narration is not specified, but given Hazel's incurable illness, it cannot be great. Yet this distance gives Hazel the narrator a chance to recapitulate the weeks between her first meeting with Augustus and his unexpectedly rapid death. This possibly accounts for the matter-of-fact tone of the narrative, supported by Hazel's forced reconciliation with her own imminent death. It is as if Hazel the narrator deliberately transfers Hazel the protagonist's despair and grief onto the reader. Few young readers are likely to share Hazel's experience of grief or death anxiety, and the text says, in a sarcastic meta-comment, that 'cancer books suck' (48). Hazel's extraordinary life situation defamiliarizes her story, precluding direct identification and inviting empathy. Readers must both empathize with Hazel and understand her understanding of Augustus's thoughts and feelings. Within Hazel's first-person perspective Augustus's mind is opaque to the reader, and instead we are encouraged, together with Hazel, to guess the motivations behind his actions. With the privileged knowledge the narrator possesses (that Augustus is about to die), his selfless gift of the trip to Amsterdam becomes understandable, but without it readers are kept in suspense. We are even lured to forget that both young people are terminally ill and therefore their budding romance has no prospect. Without futurity, Hazel does not invest in identity formation. Her vision of herself in a few years is restricted to a list of condolences on a web page. This heart-breaking story avoids gliding into painful sentimentalism because of Hazel's sober voice, which allows empathy but not pity.

Finally, the fictitious novel which Hazel rereads constantly and which leads to her decisive journey to Amsterdam to meet the writer, is described as ending in the middle of a sentence, which Hazel and Augustus interpret as the narrator dying or being too exhausted to continue writing. This incompleteness of the metafictional text anticipates the ending of *The Fault in Our Stars* and projects Hazel's story beyond the narrative, bound to be similarly interrupted. While Hazel seeks to find answers to her existential questions in the novel, the fictitious writer's replies reveal the futility of her hopes. Here, heteroglossia is provided through the clash of the adolescent narrator's resilience and the adult's cynicism, and although we empathize with Hazel rather than the drunken writer, his comments highlight cracks in Hazel's narrative that further contribute to our engagement.

At the crossroads of fiction and science

Let us reiterate. Adolescents' life experience, and thus the scope of their memories, is restricted, and their perception of time is different from adults'. Adolescents are still in the process of developing a sense of self; therefore the use of personal narration can be confusing rather than encouraging. Adolescents' ability to synthesize information provided by different sources, to project and anticipate future events and evaluate consequences of past and present is limited. Adolescents' capacity for self-reflection is also limited. How then can YA novels employ the richness of narrative possibilities afforded by fiction? Isn't this limitation exactly what adversaries of YA fiction point out as constituting its inevitable inferiority? And yet YA fiction demonstrates a vast range of options to circumvent the inevitable dilemma, the cognitive imbalance between the sender and the receiver. While simultaneous or near-simultaneous self-narration is doubtless over-used in contemporary YA novels, with variable success and not always justifiably, it is still the most effective way of conveying interiority and emerging identity.

Obviously, YA authors are acutely aware of the adolescent condition, in which unstable identity is central, and attempts to understand one's place in a larger human context consequently become compulsive. Individual and collective memories play a significant role in such attempts. To amplify the dilemma, characters are placed in extreme situations in which identity formation is accelerated. The emergence of this trend is hardly a coincidence. We know very much more about how our brains work than we did ten years ago. We know how memory works, and we know that empathy is an indispensable social skill, evolutionarily conditioned. This knowledge is apparently tempting for YA fiction to explore.

WORKS CITED AND FURTHER READING

Children's Books

Blackman, Malorie. *Boys Don't Cry*. London: Doubleday, 2010.
Blackman, Malorie. *Noughts and Crosses*. London: Doubleday, 2001.
Burgess, Melvin. *Junk*. London: Andersen, 1996.
Christopher, Lucy. *Stolen*. London: Chicken House, 2009.
Collins, Suzanne. *The Hunger Games*. New York: Scholastic, 2008.
Green, John. *The Fault in Our Stars*. New York: Penguin, 2012.
Haddon, Mark. *The Curious Incident of the Dog in the Night-time*. London: Jonathan Cape, 2003.
Lowry, Lois. *The Giver*. New York: Doubleday, 1993.
McCaughrean, Geraldine. *The White Darkness*. Oxford: Oxford University Press: 2006.
Ness, Patrick. *The Ask and the Answer*. London: Walker Books, 2009.
Ness, Patrick. *The Knife of Never Letting Go*. London: Walker Books, 2008.
Ness, Patrick. *Monsters of Men*. London: Walker Books, 2010.
Riggs, Ransom. *Miss Peregrine's Home for Peculiar Children*. New York: Random House, 2011.
Rosoff, Meg. *How I Live Now*. London: Penguin, 2004.
Salinger, Jerome D. *The Catcher in the Rye*. Philadelphia: Chelsea House, 2000; first published 1951.
Stevenson, Robert Louis. *Treasure Island*. New York: Signet, 1998; first published 1883.
Suzuma, Tabitha. *Forbidden*. London: Random House, 2010.
Terry, Teri. *Slated*. London: Orchard Books, 2012.
Twain, Mark. *The Adventures of Huckleberry Finn*. New York: Penguin, 1995; first published 1884.

Critical Texts

Baddeley, Alan. *Essentials of Human Memory*. New York: Psychology Press, 1999.
Bakhtin, Mikhail. *The Dialogic Imagination*. Austin: University of Texas Press, 1981.
Baron-Cohen, Simon, Helen Tager-Flusberg and David Cohen (eds). *Understanding Other Minds: Perspectives from Developmental Cognitive Neuroscience*. Oxford: Oxford University Press, 2000.
Blakemore, Sarah-Jayne, and Uta Frith. *The Learning Brain: Lessons for Education*. London: Wiley-Blackwell, 2005.
Doherty, Martin J. *Theory of Mind: How Children Understand Others' Thoughts and Feelings*. Hove: Psychology Press, 2009.
Genette, Gérard. *Narrative Discourse: An Essay in Method*. Ithaca, NY: Cornell University Press, 1980.
Goswami, Usha. *Cognitive Development: The Learning Brain*. New York: Psychology Press, 2007.
Hilton, Mary, and Maria Nikolajeva (eds). *Contemporary Adolescent Literature and Culture: The Emergent Adult*. New York: Ashgate, 2012.
Hogan, Patrick Colm. *What Literature Teaches Us about Emotions*. Cambridge: Cambridge University Press, 2011.
James, Kathryn. *Death, Gender and Sexuality in Contemporary Adolescent Literature*. New York: Routledge, 2011.
Keen, Suzanne. *Empathy and the Novel*. Oxford: Oxford University Press, 2008.
Kokkola, Lydia. *Fictions of Adolescent Carnality: Sexy Sinners and Delinquent Deviants*. Amsterdam: Benjamins, 2013.

Kümmerling-Meibauer, Bettina. 'Emotional Connection: Representation of Emotions in Young Adult Literature'. In Mary Hilton and Maria Nikolajeva (eds), *Contemporary Adolescent Literature and Culture: The Emergent Adult* (pp. 127–38). New York: Ashgate, 2012.

McCallum, Robyn. *Ideologies of Identity in Adolescent Fiction: The Dialogic Construction of Subjectivity*. New York: Garland, 1999.

Morgan, Nicola. *Blame My Brain: The Amazing Teenage Brain Revealed*. London: Walker Books, 2013.

Nalbantian, Suzanne. *Memory in Literature from Rousseau to Neuroscience*. Basingstoke: Palgrave Macmillan, 2003.

Nodelman, Perry. *The Hidden Adult: Defining Children's Literature*. Baltimore, MD: Johns Hopkins University Press, 2008.

Trites, Roberta Seelinger. *Disturbing the Universe: Power and Repression in Adolescent Literature*. Iowa City: University of Iowa Press, 2000.

Vermeule, Blakey. *Why Do We Care about Literary Characters?* Baltimore, MD: Johns Hopkins University Press, 2010.

Waller, Alison. *Constructing Adolescence in Fantastic Realism*. New York: Routledge, 2011.

Zunshine, Lisa. *Why We Read Fiction: Theory of Mind and the Novel*. Columbus, OH: Ohio State University Press, 2006.

Further Reading

This list is intended to guide further reading in the critical debates around children's literature. While there are many fine studies devoted to individual authors and texts, for reasons of space such works are included here only where they have had a significant influence beyond their immediate subjects. See also the suggestions for further reading at the end of each chapter.

Almost all the items listed here are books, but remember that a good deal of children's literature research is published in academic journals. Important articles in this area have appeared in a diverse range of journals, devoted to aesthetics, education and philosophy, and to other forms of literature such as the nineteenth-century novel. However, there are also several journals devoted specifically to children's literature. Among the most important of these are:

Bookbird
Children's Literature
Children's Literature Association Quarterly
Children's Literature in Education
Horn Book Magazine
International Research in Children's Literature
Jeunesse: Young People, Texts, Cultures
The Journal of Children's Literature
The Lion and the Unicorn
New Review of Children's Literature and Librarianship
Papers: Explorations into Children's Literature

Agnew, Kate, and Geoff Fox. *Children at War: From the First World War to the Gulf.* London: Continuum, 2001.
Alston, Ann. *The Family in English Children's Literature.* London: Routledge, 2008.
Appleyard, J. A. *Becoming a Reader: The Experience of Fiction from Childhood to Adulthood.* Cambridge: Cambridge University Press, 1991.
Ariès, Philippe. *Centuries of Childhood.* Harmondsworth: Penguin, 1962.
Arizpe, Evelyn, and Morag Styles. *Children Reading Pictures.* London: RoutledgeFalmer, 2003.
Attebery, Brian. *Strategies of Fantasy.* Bloomington and Indianapolis: Indiana University Press, 1992.
Auchmuty, Rosemary. *A World of Girls: The Appeal of the Girls' School Story.* London: The Women's Press, 1992.
Beckett, Sandra L. (ed.). *Reflections of Change: Children's Literature Since 1945.* Westport, CT: Greenwood, 1997.
Beckett, Sandra L., and Maria Nikolajeva (eds). *Beyond Babar: The European Tradition in Children's Literature.* Lanham, MD: Scarecrow/ChLA, 2006.
Bettelheim, Bruno. *The Uses of Enchantment.* London: Thames and Hudson, 1976.
Bradford, Clare. *Unsettling Narratives: Postcolonial Readings of Children's Literature.* Waterloo, ON: Wilfrid Laurier University Press, 2007.

Bradford, Clare, Kelly Mallan, John Stephens and Robyn McCallum. *New World Orders in Contemporary Children's Literature: Utopian Transformations*. Basingstoke: Palgrave Macmillan, 2008.

Bramwell, Peter. *Pagan Themes in Modern Children's Fiction*. Basingstoke: Palgrave Macmillan, 2009.

Briggs, Julia, et al. (eds). *Popular Children's Literature in Britain*. Aldershot: Ashgate, 2008.

Butler, Catherine, and Hallie O'Donovan. *Reading History in Children's Books*. Basingstoke: Palgrave Macmillan, 2012.

Butler, Charles. *Four British Fantasists: Place and Culture in the Children's Fantasies of Penelope Lively, Alan Garner, Diana Wynne Jones, and Susan Cooper*. Lanham, MD: Scarecrow/ChLA, 2006.

Butler, Charles (ed.). *Teaching Children's Fiction*. Basingstoke: Palgrave Macmillan, 2006.

Cadogan, Mary, and Patricia Craig. *You're a Brick, Angela: The Girls' Story 1839–1985*, 2nd edn. London: Gollancz, 1986.

Carpenter, Humphrey. *The Inklings*. London: HarperCollins, 1978.

Carpenter, Humphrey. *Secret Gardens: A Study of the Golden Age of Children's Literature*. London: George Allen and Unwin, 1985.

Carpenter, Humphrey, and Mari Prichard. *The Oxford Companion to Children's Literature*, 2nd edn. Oxford and New York: Oxford University Press, 1999.

Cart, Michael, and Christine Jenkins. *The Heart Has Its Reasons: Young Adult Literature with Gay/Lesbian/Queer Content 1969–2000*. Lanham, MD: Scarecrow, 2006.

Carter, James. *Talking Books: Children's Authors Talk about the Craft, Creativity and Process of Writing*. London: Routledge, 1999.

Chambers, Nancy (ed.). *The Signal Approach to Children's Books*. Metuchen, NJ: Scarecrow, 1980.

Chapleau, Sebastien. *New Voices in Children's Literature Criticism*. Lichfield: Pied Piper, 2004.

Clark, Beverly Lyon. *Kiddie Lit: The Cultural Construction of Children's Literature*. Baltimore, MD and London: Johns Hopkins University Press, 2003.

Clark, Beverly Lyon, and Margaret Higonnet (eds). *Girls, Boys, Books, Toys: Gender in Children's Literature and Culture*. Baltimore, MD and London: Johns Hopkins University Press, 1999.

Cleverley, John, and D. C. Phillips. *Visions of Childhood: Influential Models from Locke to Spock*. New York and London: Teachers College Press, 1986.

Coats, Karen. *Looking Glasses and Neverlands: Lacan, Desire, and Subjectivity in Children's Literature*. Iowa City: University of Iowa Press, 2004.

Collins, Fiona M., and Judith Graham (eds). *Historical Fiction for Children: Capturing the Past*. London: Fulton, 2001.

Cosslett, Tess. *Talking Animals in British Children's Fiction 1786–1914* Aldershot: Ashgate, 2006.

Coveney, Peter. *The Image of Childhood: the Individual and Society: A Study of the Theme in English Literature*, rev. edn. Harmondsworth: Penguin, 1967.

Cunningham, Hugh. *Children and Childhood in Western Society since 1500*. London and New York: Longman, 1996.

Daniel, Carolyn. *Voracious Children: Who Eats Whom in Children's Literature*. New York: Routledge, 2006.

Dobrin, Sidney I., and Kenneth Kidd (eds). *Wild Things: Children's Culture and Ecocriticism*. Detroit, MI: Wayne State University Press, 2004.

Donaldson, Margaret. *Children's Minds*. Glasgow: Fontana, 1978.

Doonan, Jane. *Looking at Pictures in Picture Books*. Stroud: Thimble Press, 1993.

Dusinberre, Juliet. *Alice to the Lighthouse: Children's Books and Radical Experiments in Art*. Basingstoke: Macmillan, 1987.

Edwards, Owen Dudley. *British Children's Fiction in the Second World War*. Edinburgh: Edinburgh University Press, 2007.

Egoff, Sheila, G. T. Stubbs and L. F. Ashley (eds). *Only Connect: Readings on Children's Literature*, 2nd edn. Toronto: Oxford University Press, 1980.

Evans, Janet (ed.). *What's in the Picture? Responding to Illustrations in Picture-books*. London: Paul Chapman, 1998.

Falconer, Racher. *The Crossover Novel: Contemporary Children's Fiction and Its Adult Readership*. New York: Routledge, 2009.

Flanagan, Victoria. *Into the Closet: Cross-Dressing and the Gendered Body in Children's Literature and Film*. New York: Routledge, 2008.

Foster, Shirley, and Judy Simons. *What Katy Read: Feminist Re-Readings of 'Classic' Stories for Girls: Feminist Re-readings of Classic Stories for Girls, 1850–1920*. Basingstoke: Palgrave Macmillan, 1995.

Fry, Donald. *Children Talk about Books: Seeing Themselves as Readers*. Milton Keynes: Open University Press, 1985.

Gavin, Adrienne E. (ed.). *The Child in British Literature*. Basingstoke: Palgrave Macmillan, 2012.

Gavin, Adrienne E., and Christopher Routledge (eds). *Mystery in Children's Literature: From the Rational to the Supernatural*. Basingstoke: Palgrave Macmillan, 2001.

Gillis, John R. *Youth and History*. New York and London: Academic Press, 1974.

Goswami, Supriya. *Colonia India in Children's Literature*. New York and London: Routledge, 2012.

Grenby, M. O. *Children's Literature*. Edinburgh: Edinburgh University Press, 2008.

Grenby, M. O. *The Child Reader 1700–1840*. Cambridge: Cambridge University Press, 2011.

Grenby, M. O., and Andrea Immel. *The Cambridge Companion to Children's Literature*. Cambridge: Cambridge University Press, 2009.

Grenby, M. O., and Kimberley Reynolds (eds). *Children's Literature Studies: A Handbook for Research*. Basingstoke: Palgrave Macmillan, 2011.

Griswold, Jerry. *Feeling Like a Kid: Childhood and Children's Literature*. Baltimore, MD: Johns Hopkins University Press, 2006.

Gubar, Marah. *Artful Dodgers: Reconceiving the Golden Age of Children's Literature*. Oxford: Oxford University Press, 2010.

Hollindale, Peter. *The Hidden Teacher: Ideology and Children's Reading*. Stroud: Thimble Press, 2011.

Hollindale, Peter. *Ideology and the Children's Book*. Stroud: Thimble Press, 1994/1988.

Hollindale, Peter. *Signs of Childness in Children's Books*. Stroud: Thimble Press, 1997.

Hume, Kathryn. *Fantasy and Mimesis: Responses to Reality in Western Literature*. London: Routledge, 1984.

Hunt, Peter (ed.). *Children's Literature: The Development of Criticism*. London: Routledge, 1990.

Hunt, Peter. *An Introduction to Children's Literature*. Oxford: Oxford University Press, 1994.

Hunt, Peter (ed.). *Literature for Children: Contemporary Criticism*. London: Routledge, 1992.

Hunt, Peter (ed.). *International Companion Encyclopedia of Children's Literature.* London: Routledge, 1996.

Hunt, Peter, and Millicent Lenz. *Alternative Worlds in Fantasy Fiction.* London and New York: Continuum, 2001.

Inglis, Fred. *The Promise of Happiness: Value and Meaning in Children's Literature.* Cambridge: Cambridge University Press, 1981.

Jackson, Rosemary. *Fantasy: The Literature of Subversion.* London and New York: Routledge, 1995/1981.

Johansen, K. V. *Quests and Kingdoms: A Grown-Up's Guide to Children's Fantasy Literature.* Sackville, NB: Sybertooth, 2005.

Keenan, Celia, and Mary Shine Thompson (eds). *Studies in Children's Literature, 1500–2000.* Dublin: Four Courts Press, 2004.

Keith, Lois. *Take Up Thy Bed and Walk: Death, Disability and Cure in Classic Fiction for Girls.* London: Women's Press, 2001.

Kidd, Kenneth B. *Freud in Oz: At the Intersections of Psychoanalysis and Children's Literature.* Minneapolis: University of Minnesota, 2011.

Kincaid, James. *Child-Loving: the Erotic Child and Victorian Culture.* New York and London: Routledge, 1992.

Kirkpatrick, Robert J. *The Encyclopaedia of Boy's School Stories.* Aldershot: Ashgate, 2000.

Knoepflmacher, U. C. *Ventures into Childland: Victorians, Fairy Tales, and Femininity.* Chicago: University of Chicago Press, 1998.

Knowles, Murray, and Kirsten Malmkjaer. *Language and Control in Children's Literature.* London and New York: Routledge, 1996.

Kohl, Herbert. *Should We Burn Babar? Essays on Children's Literature and the Power of Stories.* New York: New Press, 1995.

Krips, Valerie. *The Presence of the Past: Memory, Heritage and Childhood in Postwar Britain.* London and New York: Garland, 2000.

Kutzer, Daphne. *Empire's Children: Empire and Imperialism in Classic British Children's Books.* New York and London: Garland, 2000.

Kuznets, Lois. *When Toys Come Alive: Narratives of Animation, Metamorphosis, and Development.* New Haven, CT: Yale University Press, 1994.

Lathey, Gillian. *The Impossible Legacy: Identity and Purpose in Autobiographical Children's Literature Set in the Third Reich and the Second World War.* Bern: Peter Lang, 1999.

Lathey, Gillian. *The Role of Translators in Children's Literature: Invisible Storytellers.* London: Routledge, 2012.

Lawson Lucas, Ann (ed.). *The Presence of the Past in Children's Literature.* Westport, CT and London: Praeger, 2003.

Leeson, Robert. *Reading and Righting.* London: Collins, 1985.

Lehr, Susan. *Beauty, Brains, and Brawn: The Construction of Gender in Children's Literature.* Portsmouth, NH: Heinemann, 2001.

Lerer, Seth. *Children's Literature: A Reader's History from Aesop to Harry Potter.* Chicago: University of Chicago Press, 2008.

Lesnik-Oberstein, Karin. *Children's Literature: Criticism and the Fictional Child.* Oxford: Clarendon Press, 1994.

Lesnik-Oberstein, Karin (ed.). *Children's Literature: New Approaches.* Basingstoke: Macmillan Press, 2004.

Lewis, David. *Reading Contemporary Picture Books.* London: RoutledgeFalmer, 2001.

Lundin, Anne H. *Constructing the Canon of Children's Literature: Beyond Library Walls and Ivory Towers.* New York and London: Routledge, 2004.

Lurie, Alison. *Don't Tell the Grown-Ups: Subversive Children's Literature*. London: Bloomsbury, 1990.

Mackey, Margaret. *Literacies Across Media: Playing the Text*. London and New York: Routledge, 2002.

Mackey, Margaret. 'Playing in the Phase Space: Contemporary Forms of Fictional Pleasure'. *Signal*, 88 (1999), 16–33.

Mallan, Kerry. *Gender Dilemmas in Children's Fiction*. Basingstoke: Palgrave Macmillan, 2009.

Mallan, Kerry, and Clare Bradford (eds). *Contemporary Children's Literature and Film: Engaging with Theory*. Basingstoke: Palgrave Macmillan, 2011.

Mallan, Kerry, and Sharyn Pearce (eds). *Youth Cultures: Texts, Images, Identities*. Westport, CT: Praeger, 2003.

Manlove, C. N. *From Alice to Harry Potter: Children's Fantasy in England*. Christchurch, NZ: Cybereditions, 2003.

Marcus, Leonard S. (ed.). 2006. *The Wand in the Word: Conversations with Writers of Fantasy*. Cambridge, MA: Candlewick Press.

McCallum, Robyn. *Ideologies of Identity in Adolescent Fiction: The Dialogic Construction of Subjectivity*. New York and London: Garland, 1999.

McCloud, Scott. *Understanding Comics*. New York: HarperCollins, 1994.

McCulloch, Fiona. *Children's Literature in Context*. London: Continuum, 2011.

McGillis, Roderick. *The Nimble Reader: Literary Theory and Children's Literature*. New York: Twayne, 1997.

McGillis, Roderick (ed.). *Voices of the Other: Children's Literature and the Postcolonial Context*. New York and London: Garland Publishing, 2000.

Meek, Margaret. *How Texts Teach what Readers Learn*. Stroud: Thimble Press, 1988.

Meek, Margaret, and Victor Watson. *Coming of Age in Children's Literature*. London: Continuum, 2003.

Melrose, Andrew. *Here Comes the Bogeyman: Exploring Contemporary Issues in Writing for Children*. London: Routledge, 2011.

Mendlesohn, Farah. *The Inter-galactic Playground: A Critical Study of Children's and Teens' Science Fiction*. Jefferson, NC: McFarland, 2009.

Mendlesohn, Farah. *Rhetorics of Fantasy*. Middletown, CT: Wesleyan University Press, 2008.

Mitchell, Juliet. *Psychoanalysis and Feminism: A Radical Reassessment of Freudian Psychoanalysis*. Harmondsworth: Penguin, 2000/1974.

Montgomery, Heather. *Children's Literature: Classic Texts and Contemporary Trends*. Basingstoke: Palgrave Macmillan, 2009.

Moody, Nickianne, and Clare Horrocks (eds). *Children's Fantasy Fiction: Debates for the Twenty-First Century*. Liverpool: Association for Research in Popular Fictions, 2005.

Nikolajeva, Maria. *Aesthetic Approaches to Children's Literature: An Introduction*. Lanham, MD: Scarecrow, 2005.

Nikolajeva, Maria. *Children's Literature Comes of Age: Toward a New Aesthetic*. New York and London: Garland, 1996.

Nikolajeva, Maria. *The Magic Code: The Use of Magical Patterns in Fantasy for Children*. Stockholm: Almqvist & Wiksell, 1988.

Nikolajeva, Maria. *Power, Voice and Subjectivity in Literature for Young Readers*. London: Routledge, 2012.

Nikolajeva, Maria, and Carole Scott. *How Picturebooks Work*. New York: Garland, 2001.

Nodelman, Perry (ed.). *The Hidden Adult: Defining Children's Literature*. Baltimore, MD: Johns Hopkins University Press, 2008.

Nodelman, Perry. *Words about Pictures: The Narrative Art of Children's Picture Book*. Athens, GA and London: University of Georgia Press, 1988.

Nodelman, Perry, and Mavis Reimer. *The Pleasures of Children's Literature*, rev. edn. Boston, MA: Allyn & Bacon, 2003/1996.

O'Sullivan, Emer. *Comparative Children's Literature*. London: Routledge, 2005.

Pearson, Lucy. *The Making of Modern Children's Literature in Britain (Ashgate Studies in Childhood, 1700 to the Present)*. Aldershot: Ashgate, 2013.

Piaget, Jean. *The Origin of Intelligence in the Child*, trans. Margaret Cook. London: Routledge, 1953.

Pinsent, Pat. *Children's Literature and the Politics of Equality*. London: David Fulton, 1997.

Rahn, Suzanne. *Rediscoveries in Children's Literature*. New York: Garland, 1995.

Reynolds, Kimberley (ed.). *Childhood Remembered*. London: NCRCL, 1998; republished by Pied Piper Publishing.

Reynolds, Kimberley. *Children's Literature in the 1890s and 1990s*. Plymouth: Northcote House, 1994.

Reynolds, Kimberley (ed.). *Radical Children's Literature: Future Visions and Aesthetic Transformations in Juvenile Fiction*. New York: Palgrave Macmillan, 2007.

Reynolds, Kimberley, Kevin McCarron and Geraldine Brennan (eds). *Frightening Fiction*. London: Continuum, 2001.

Reynolds, Kimberley, and Nicholas Tucker (eds). *Children's Book Publishing in Britain since 1945*. Aldershot: Scolar/Ashgate, 1998.

Richards, Jeffrey. *Happiest Days: The Public Schools in English Fiction*. Manchester: Manchester University Press, 1988.

Rose, Jacqueline. *The Case of Peter Pan, or, The Impossibility of Children's Literature*, 2nd edn. Basingstoke: Palgrave Macmillan, 1992.

Rudd, David. *Enid Blyton and the Mystery of Children's Literature*. Basingstoke: Palgrave Macmillan, 2000.

Rudd, David. *Reading the Child in Children's Literature: An Heretical Approach*. Basingstoke: Palgrave Macmillan, 2013.

Rudd, David. *The Routledge Companion to Children's Literature*. Abingdon: Routledge, 2010.

Rustin, Margaret, and Michael Rustin. 2001. *Narratives of Love and Loss: Studies in Modern Children's Fiction*. London: Verso, 1987; rev. edn, London and New York: Karnac, 2001.

Sainsbury, Lisa. *Ethics in British Children's Literature: Unexamined Life*. London and New York: Bloomsbury, 2013.

Salisbury, Martin, and Morag Styles. *Children's Picturebooks: The Art of Visual Storytelling*. London: Laurence King, 2012.

Shavit, Zohar. *The Poetics of Children's Literature*. Athens, GA: University of Georgia Press, 1986.

Sims, Susan, and Clare, Hilary. *The Encyclopaedia of Girls' School Stories*. Aldershot: Ashgate, 2000.

Sipe, Lawrence, and Sylvia Pantaleo (eds). *Postmodern Picturebooks: Play, Parody, and Self-referentiality*. New York and London: Routledge, 2008.

Spufford, Francis. *The Child that Books Built*. London: Faber and Faber, 2002.

Stephens, John. *Language and Ideology in Children's Fiction* Harlow: Longman, 1992.

Stephens, John. *Ways of Being Male: Representing Masculinities in Children's Literature*. New York and London: Routledge, 2002.

Stephens, John, and Robyn McCallum. *Retelling Stories, Framing Culture: Traditional Stories and Metanarratives in Children's Literature*. New York and London: Garland, 1998.

Stratyner, Leslie, and James R. Keller. *Fantasy Fiction into Film: Essays*. Jefferson, NC: McFarland, 2007.

Styles, Morag, and Eve Bearne (eds). *Art, Narrative, Childhood*. Stoke-on-Trent: Trentham Books, 2003.

Sumpter, Caroline. *The Victorian Press and the Fairy Tale*. London: Palgrave Macmillan, 2008.

Swinfen, Ann. *In Defence of Fantasy: A Study of the Genre in English and American Literature Since 1945*. London: Routledge, 1984.

Tatar, Maria. *Enchanted Hunters: The Power of Stories in Childhood*. New York: W. W. Norton, 2009.

Thacker, Deborah Cogan, and Jean Webb. *Introducing Children's Literature: from Romanticism to Postmodernism*. London: Routledge, 2002.

Tolkien, J. R. R. 'On Fairy-Stories'. In Christopher Tolkien (ed.), *The Monsters and the Critics and Other Essays* (pp. 109–61). London: George Allen & Unwin, 1983; originally the Andrew Lang Lecture, given at the University of St Andrew's, 8 March 1939.

Townsend, John Rowe. *Written for Children*, 6th edn. London: Bodley Head, 1995.

Trites, Roberta Seelinger. *Waking Sleeping Beauty: Feminist Voices in Children's Novels*. Iowa City: University of Iowa Press, 1997.

Trites, Roberta Seelinger. *Disturbing the Universe: Power and Repression in Adolescent Literature*. Iowa City: University of Iowa Press, 2000.

Tucker, Nicholas. *The Child and the Book: A Psychological and Literary Exploration*. Cambridge: Cambridge University Press, 1981.

Tucker, Nicholas, and Nikki Gamble. *Family Fictions*. London and New York: Continuum, 2001.

von Franz, Marie-Louise. *The Interpretation of Fairy Tales*. Boston, MA: Shambhala Publications, 1996/1970.

Wall, Barbara. *The Narrator's Voice: the Dilemma of Children's Fiction*. London: Macmillan, 1991.

Waller, Alison. *Constructing Adolescence in Fantastic Realism*. London: Routledge, 2008.

Wannamaker, Annette. *Boys in Children's Literature and Popular Culture: Masculinity, Abjection, and the Fictional Child*. New York: Taylor & Francis, 2009.

Warner, Marina. *From The Beast To The Blonde: On Fairy Tales and Their Tellers*. London: Vintage, 1995.

Watson, Victor (ed.). *The Cambridge Guide to Children's Books in English*. Cambridge: Cambridge University Press, 2001.

Watson, Victor, and Morag Styles (eds). *Talking Pictures*. London: Hodder & Stoughton, 1996.

Wilkie-Stibbs, Christine. *The Feminine Subject in Children's Literature*. New York and London: Routledge, 2002.

Zipes, Jack. *The Irresistible Fairy Tale: The Cultural and Social History of a Genre*. Princeton, NJ: Princeton University Press, 2012.

Zipes, Jack (ed.). *Oxford Encyclopedia of Children's Literature*. Oxford and New York: Oxford University Press, 2006.

Zipes, Jack. *Sticks and Stones: The Troublesome Success of Children's Literature from Slovenly Peter to Harry Potter.* London: Routledge, 2001.

Zornado, Joseph L. *Inventing the Child: Culture, Ideology and the Story of Childhood.* New York and London: Routledge, 2006.

Index

Page numbers in **bold** denote a boxed reference; page numbers in *italics* denote an illustration.